ONE WEEK LOAN

This book is due for return on or before the last date shown below.

PROBATION:
WORKING FOR JUSTICE

edited by

David Ward, John Scott
and Malcolm Lacey

*This book has been printed digitally and produced in a standard specification
in order to ensure its continuing availability*

OXFORD
UNIVERSITY PRESS

Great Clarendon Street, Oxford OX2 6DP

Oxford University Press is a department of the University of Oxford.
It furthers the University's objective of excellence in research, scholarship,
and education by publishing worldwide in

Oxford   New York

Auckland   Cape Town   Dar es Salaam   Hong Kong   Karachi
Kuala Lumpur   Madrid   Melbourne   Mexico City   Nairobi
New Delhi   Shanghai   Taipei   Toronto
With offices in
Argentina   Austria   Brazil   Chile   Czech Republic   France   Greece
Guatemala   Hungary   Italy   Japan   South Korea   Poland   Portugal
Singapore   Switzerland   Thailand   Turkey   Ukraine   Vietnam

Oxford is a registered trade mark of Oxford University Press
in the UK and in certain other countries

Published in the United States
by Oxford University Press Inc., New York

A Blackstone Press Book

© David Ward, 2002

The moral rights of the author have been asserted

Database right Oxford University Press (maker)

Reprinted 2010

ISBN 978-1-84174-190-1

Printed and bound in Great Britain by CPI Antony Rowe,
Chippenham and Eastbourne

Contents

Foreword

Eithne Wallis

I am writing, at a time of transformation in the probation service, to welcome this book. Its arrival is timely, since the most significant reforms of probation for a century are now having a profound impact on the service's practice with offenders and victims and its relationship with the communities we serve.

The Criminal Justice and Court Services Act 2000 established the National Probation Service for England and Wales. As the first National Director, I have been involved throughout in the design of the changes and led the transition programme, which introduced new Probation Boards, new orders and new methods of work. I have been well placed therefore to observe the commitment and energy of probation leaders, at area level and at the centre, as they have worked to implement the changes. Equally, as a former probation officer, I have been impressed by the way practitioners have risen to the challenge of new practice to deliver accredited programmes aimed at reducing reconviction rates, combined with more effective enforcement of community sentences. In the National Probation Service we have an able, committed work force. The diversity of this staff group across England and Wales is one of the service's greatest strengths. This diversity is more than gender or race, age or background; it is in the new configuration of skills and experience now being brought together in our probation boards, probation areas and national directorate, teamwork at every level is the key to success.

Change, to be effective, requires organisations to retain the best of their traditional strengths and roles. Solid foundations are a prerequisite for radical and new developments. Probation staff are renowned for their ability to engage at an intellectual and emotional level as they work with offenders and victims. This book will provoke thought and feelings because it brings together a collection of contributors, who can reflect on the achievements of the past, analyse the challenges of the present and inspire us about the potential and shape of the new service.

It is opportune that academics and practitioners, policymakers and managers, have contributed chapters. The interplay between their different perspectives will stimulate wide debate and, I trust, greater understanding of the new National Probation Service's contribution to the Criminal Justice System.

Service policy and practice needs to be strongly based on evidence and research. I want the unified probation service to be a learning organisation, which is characterised by a willingness to pose questions and to find answers. The complexity of the world in which probation staff operate, and the size of the challenges which we face in winning public confidence for community sentences, cannot be overestimated. The joint endeavour, whether you are a new recruit or an experienced member of staff, whether you are working in local areas or at the centre, is to understand the context for probation policy and practice and to apply that understanding in the workplace. I hope this book, and others, which will follow, will enable us, with integrity and renewed energy, to 'work for justice'.

Eithne Wallis
Director
National Probation Service

List of Contributors

Gwyneth Boswell is Principal Lecturer in the Community and Criminal Justice Studies Unit at De Montfort University and has previously worked at the University of East Anglia and the Merseyside Probation Service. She is co-author, with Davies and Wright, of 'Contemporary Probation Practice' (Avebury 1993) and editor of 'Violent Children and Adolescents: Asking the Question Why' (Whurr Publishers 2000).

Rob Canton is now a Senior Lecturer in Community and Criminal Justice at De Montfort University, after working for the probation service for many years. He has extensive experience, as practitioner, manager and trainer, of work with mentally disturbed offenders.

Karen Chouhan is Director of the 1990 Trust, an NGO and national charity to network and capacity build in Black communities. She is also Chair of the Belgrave Baheno Women's Centre and the 'Peepul Centre', Leicester.

David Faulkner is a Senior Research Associate at the University of Oxford Centre for Criminological Research and was Deputy Secretary in charge of the Criminal Research and Statistics Department of the Home Office from 1982 to 1990. He is the author of 'Crime, State and Citizen: A Field Full of Folk' (Waterside Press 2001.)

Norman Flynn works at the London School of Economics and Political Science where he specialises in management in the public sector and directs the Public Services Management Programme.

Cedric Fulwood has been a founding member of the Youth Justice Board since 1998 and is Chair of the Penal Affairs Consortium. He joined the Manchester Probation Service in 1963 and worked for the Scottish Office as Deputy Chief Social Work Adviser from 1978–82.

Jane Furniss was seconded to HM Inspectorate of Probation in 1995, having worked in various probation service roles since 1975. In 1997 she was promoted to HM Assistant Chief Inspector and was again promoted to HM Deputy Chief Inspector from 1999. She was responsible for managing HMIP's staff and for its strategic developments, including its *What Works* project. In the summer of 2001 she left HMIP to become Head of the Home Office Justice and Victims Unit.

Liz Hill is Chief Officer at Essex Probation Area. During her career as a probation officer she has worked in Northumbria, Middlesex, Inner London and HM Inspectorate. She has had Chief Officer responsibility for Crown Courts in London (including the Old Bailey) and led the thematic inspection into work in the criminal courts, published in 1997.

Paul Holt has recently worked as a Research Fellow in the Community and Criminal Justice Studies Unit at De Montfort University. He has been involved on a consultancy basis in the implementation and evaluation of case management in the Merseyside area, leaving De Montfort at the end of 2001 to take up a Senior Probation Officer post in the same area.

Keir Hopley is Head of Policy, National Probation Service at the Home Office.

Chris Johnson is an Assistant Chief Officer with the National Probation Service, West Yorkshire. He is currently seconded to the National Probation Directorate as Head of Community Reintegration Projects, in which role he has overall responsibility for the community punishment pathfinder projects.

Hazel Kemshall is Professor of Community and Criminal Justice Studies at De Montfort University. Her research interests are in risk assessment and risk management of offenders, and the evaluation of multi-agency public protection panels.

Charlotte Knight is Principal Lecturer in Community and Criminal Justice at De Montfort University and Programme Leader of the BA (Hons) Community and Criminal Justice/Diploma in Probation Studies.

Malcolm Lacey trained at the LSE and became a probation officer in Hertfordshire in 1963. In 1976 he became Head of Social Work at Lanchester Polytechnic (now Coventry University) before being appointed as Chief Probation Officer in Dorset in 1982.

Mike Nellis is Senior Lecturer in Criminal Justice Studies at the University of Birmingham. He has written widely on aspects of community justice and penal practice. His current interests are restorative justice and electronic monitoring.

John Raine is Professor of Management in Criminal Justice at University of Birmingham's School of Public Policy. He has undertaken numerous research projects for the Home Office, Lord Chancellor's Department and local criminal justice agencies and has published widely on the impacts of managerial agendas on the justice process.

Peter Raynor, a former probation officer, holds a chair at the University of Wales, Swansea. Over the past twenty-five years he has published a wide range of research, particularly on the impact and effectiveness of the work of the probation service.

Sue Rex currently holds a fellowship with the Economic and Social Research Council to conduct a research programme to develop community penalties in theory and practice. Her main research interests are in sentencing practice and the supervision of offenders in the community.

John Scott has been Chief Officer of Bedfordshire Probation Area since 1994. He is a member of the Home Office Advisory Board on Restricted Patients and the Conférence Permanente Européenne de la Probation as the United Kingdom representative. He is also a Chief Officer member of the National Probation Directorate's working group on human rights.

Paul Thurston is Assistant Chief Officer in West Yorkshire and a former Chair of the Association of Chief Officers of Probation's Hostel and Housing Group.

Ira Unell is Lecturer in Substance Misuse at Leicester University and Leicestershire NHS Drug and Alcohol Service. He teaches alcohol and drug counselling and has special interest in dual diagnosis, children of substance misusing parents, the criminal justice system and homelessness.

David Ward is Professor of Social and Community Studies and Head of the School of Health and Applied Social Sciences at De Montfort University. Having trained and worked as a probation officer, he has maintained a special interest in probation matters throughout his career in higher education.

Brian Williams is Reader in Criminal Justice at De Montfort University, Leicester. His recent books include 'Working with Victims of Crime' (Jessica Kingsley, 1999) and 'Victim-focused Social Work' (as editor: Jessica Kingsley, 2001.)

Anne Worrall is Reader in Criminology at Keele University. A former probation officer, she has also been a Lecturer in Social Work at Manchester University. She has published widely in the area of women and crime, and is currently coediting a book on girls and violence with Christine Alder from the University of Melbourne.

Proceeds

The editors and contributors to this book have agreed that proceeds will be donated in equal measure to:

The Prison Reform Trust, which aims to create a just, humane and effective penal system by inquiring into the workings of the system; informing prisoners, staff and the wider public; and by influencing Parliament, Government and officials towards reform.

The Edridge Fund, which provides help to probation service employees, retired staff or bereaved partners, who are in need or distress.

Introduction

John Scott and David Ward

In Roman mythology, Janus, the god of doorways and passageways, was the patron of the beginning of the day, the month and year, after whom January is named. He is depicted as having two faces, looking both forward and back. This book arrives at the beginning of a new probation era, and has involved its writers in the demanding task of understanding the dynamics of changes happening to the probation world contemporaneously. The contributors have produced their chapters either on the cusp of the implementation of the Criminal Justice and Court Services Act 2000 on 1 April 2001 or shortly after, so inevitably, the book explores the 'doorways and passageways' of probation with many a glance backwards and the odd strained neck trying to obtain a clear forward view.

The purpose of the book is to place probation policy and practice in the mainstream of thinking about justice and human rights in the United Kingdom. Political understanding of probation and commitment to its contribution to the criminal justice system have wavered over the past decade. Our commitment to the centrality of the probation role has remained constant, so an important aim of the book has been to harness the insights of academics and the experience of senior managers and policymakers to demonstrate the strengths of past probation work and to challenge future developments.

In her lecture, given as the third Bill McWilliams Memorial Lecture at the Institute of Criminology at the University of Cambridge on 28

June 2000, Barbara Hudson called for a 'Positive Rights Agenda' as a way of squaring the circle between due process and crime control (Hudson 2001a). This book is in part an answer to that call and shares her view that probation's involvement in the criminal justice process and in community safety partnerships should be on the basis of three fundamental principles, that:

(a)   offenders remain part of the community;
(b)   justice embraces principles of fair punishment as well as principles of risk control; and
(c)   community justice means commitment to principles of equal freedom and equal respect (Hudson 2001a, p. 112).

In each chapter, the writer has sought to explore the outworking of these principles in different aspects of the probation task. We believe there is both inspiration and common sense in the resulting book for a wide criminal justice audience. Transferability is a key part of any learning, so we have not restricted the scope to probation practice alone, and there will be relevance for other criminal justice agencies — Youth Offending Teams, prisons, police and partner organisations. We are also conscious of the impending increase in trainee probation officers and the planned increase in other types of staff, and hope that this book will help to shape their understanding of justice and rights at the same time as stimulating their more experienced colleagues to think afresh about their work.

As an editorial team, comprising a former Chief Probation Officer, an academic involved in training new probation officers and a Chief Officer in the new National Probation Service, we have lived through the reforms and were keen to commission chapters from a wide range of writers, so that a breadth of experience and analysis of the unfolding arrangements for probation could be captured. We have been grateful to the contributors, of whom many were caught up in the throes of implementing the changes or in new jobs themselves, for the positive way in which they have responded to the demands of deadlines and of amending scripts. We hope the reader will appreciate the balance between the academic and the practitioner, the manager and the policymaker, the current and the former employee, and that the interplay of ideas and perceptions will promote clarity in understanding the role of probation at a time of radical change in practice and structures.

Two major legislative reforms dominate this book: the Human Rights Act 1998 and the Criminal Justice and Court Services Act 2000. There is a chapter dedicated to the Human Rights Act and, since its implementation on 2 October 2000, there has been opportunity for contributors to this collection to reflect upon the impact of the incorporation into United Kingdom law of the European Convention on Human Rights. We will not duplicate those considerations here. However, there has been less time for commentators to assess the impact of the Criminal Justice and Court Services Act, so we intend to outline the scope and intent of the legislation to set the scene for the book.

The Criminal Justice and Court Services Act 2000, which was given Royal Assent on 30 November 2000, restructured the probation service and created a unified service to be known as the National Probation Service for England and Wales. Forty-two local areas, based on the boundaries of police services, each with an area probation board, replaced the 54 Probation Committees. Accountability for the National Probation Service was, from the commencement date of 1 April 2001, directly to the Home Secretary; and the funding of the new service became 100 per cent the responsibility of the Home Office, departing from the previous 80:20 split between the Home Office and local authorities. The Act established the Children and Family Court Advisory and Support Service, to which family court work staff and their responsibilities were transferred from the probation service on the same vesting day of 1 April 2001, creating a probation service which was solely dedicated to work with offenders.

Section 1 of the 2000 Act defines the purpose of the service as 'assisting courts in sentencing decisions and providing for the supervision and rehabilitation of persons charged with, or convicted of offences' (Probation Circular 25/2001, p. 2). Section 2 sets out the following aims:

(a) to protect the public;
(b) to reduce reoffending;
(c) to provide for the proper punishment of offenders;
(d) to ensure that offenders are aware of the effects of their crimes on their victims and on the public; and
(e) to rehabilitate offenders.

Clear functional responsibility for the National Probation Service now lies with the Secretary of State, but local probation boards were established under s. 4 to administer the 42 services and to 'allow national priorities to be interpreted in the light of local circumstances and local needs' (Probation Circular 52/2001, p. 2). Section 4(6) enables the Secretary of State to alter probation areas at a later date.

Section 5 details the functions of local probation boards, to include:

(a)   employment of all staff;

(b)   contracting for the provision of services with partner organisations, such as other boards, private companies, voluntary organisations and individuals;

(c)   ensuring the quality of the service provided by a contractor;

(d)   providing hostel accommodation; and

(e)   contributing to the development and implementation of the local crime reduction strategy.

Sections 6 and 7 address the role and functions of the inspectorate, changing the titles, but not the arrangements, under which the inspectorate operates. The Secretary of State will determine the criteria against which services are to be inspected, and is enabled to give the Chief Inspector powers to inspect partner organisations and to call for reports, when there are concerns about the performance of a service.

Section 8 gives the Home Secretary power to contract out work undertaken by local probation boards, such as support services. This provision is designed to achieve greater efficiency or value for money and is particularly relevant to common services, for example, information and communication technology or payroll services, where national or regional contracts could be cost-effective. Section 9 gives authority to the Secretary of State to approve premises for bail and supervision cases.

Default powers are addressed in section 10. The Secretary of State can now make a management order as a last resort, which can alter a local board's
composition by:

(a)   removing one or all of the chair, or the chief officer or other board members;

(b)   replacing them with an alternative contracted organisation.

Chapters II and III of Part I of the 2000 Act dealt with the formation of the Children and Family Court Advisory and Support Service, and the transfer of staff under the same codes and conditions. Section 22 gives effect to the transfer of chief probation officers, from being employees of probation committees to the employ of the National Probation Directorate as chief officers.

Part II of the legislation is concerned with the protection of children and covers disqualification orders, indecent conduct towards children and the increase of maximum penalties in child pornography cases.

Part III is entitled 'Dealing with Offenders', with Chapter I covering community sentences. Sections 43, 44 and 45, renamed orders as follows:

- probation orders   became   community rehabilitation orders
- community service   became   community punishment orders
  orders
- combination orders   became   community punishment and
                                     rehabilitation orders

Two new community orders have been introduced in sections 46 and 47: exclusion orders and drug abstinence orders. Exclusion orders prohibit an offender entering a specified place for up to two years; different periods and different places can be specified and the order can be linked to electronic monitoring. Drug abstinence orders relate to offenders over the age of 18 years, who are required to abstain from class A drugs for a specific period and provide samples when required. Section 49 provides for pre-sentence drug testing.

Sections 49 to 52 enabled drug abstinence, curfew, exclusion and electronic requirements to be added as conditions of community rehabilitation orders.

Section 53 prescribes the circumstances in which an offender must be given a warning for failure to comply with a community sentence and be taken to court, where the magistrates 'shall impose a sentence of imprisonment' for the original offence, unless the court is of the opinion:

(a)   that the offender is likely to comply with the requirements of the order during the period for which it remains in force; or

(b)   that the exceptional circumstances of the case justify not imposing a sentence of imprisonment.

Section 54 provides the Crown Court with new powers to issue a summons and warrant in respect of failure to answer a summons for an alleged breach of a community order.

Section 55 allows for the regulation of community orders, so that the Secretary of State is empowered to set standards for the delivery of all community orders.

Sections 56 to 61 are miscellaneous provisions covering reprimands and warnings for young offenders, powers to test people for drugs in police detention, and the relevance of drug misuse to the right to bail and detention. Section 61 brings about the abolition of sentences of detention in a young offender institution of custody for life for offenders under the age of 17.

Sections 62 to 65 concern the release of prisoners on licence. Electronic monitoring of licence conditions become allowable under sections 62 and 63 for adults and young offenders. Section 64 gives powers to probation staff to require a drug test 'for the purpose of determining whether the person is complying with any of the conditions' of a licence; the person must be over 18 and imprisonment must have been imposed for a 'trigger' offence that is drug related.

Sections 66 to 68 dealt with sexual and violent offenders, with section 66 amending the Sex Offenders Act 1997 by increasing penalties, altering requirements, enabling courts to make restraining orders and improving the information held about sex offenders. Sections 67 and 68 create new requirements for the 'responsible authorities', the chief officers of police and probation for each area, to establish arrangements for the purpose of assessing and managing the risks posed by sexual and violent offenders. The chief officers are now required to report annually upon the arrangements and to monitor their effectiveness.

Section 69 creates a duty for probation boards to take 'all reasonable steps' to ascertain whether a victim of a sexual or violent offence wishes to:

(a)   make representations about whether the offender should be subject to any conditions or requirements on his release and, if so, what conditions or requirements; or

(b)   receive information about any conditions or requirements to which the offender is to be subject on his release.

The remaining sections of the 2000 Act contain general provisions and supplementary sections about subordinate legislation and schedules. Of significance to the probation service is Schedule 3, which makes provision for the transfer of property to the Lord Chancellor's

Department and to the Home Office away from the former probation committees.

The significance and breadth of these reforms for probation cannot be overstated. It is this legislation which has laid the template for governance and the direction of probation for the foreseeable future, and which 'modernises' the probation service. Early opinion about the Act has been divided. Andrew Rutherford (Rutherford 2001, p. 150) stated: 'The Act is now one aspect of an increasingly bleak penal landscape.' He forecasts an increase in the prison population, because: 'The Act borrows from the recent American experience of technical violations, virtually to ensure that a higher proportion of the prison system's intake will have resulted from breach proceedings.'

Mary Anne McFarlane (McFarlane 2001, p. 143) takes a more pragmatic and incrementalist view of the reforms: 'The Act probably represents the most fundamental change to the service for nearly a century but it can also be said to reflect shifts in practice that have been taking place over the past ten years.' She welcomes the fact that the service's work on public protection has been recognised and placed on a statutory footing, and identifies the assumptions behind the legislation as being (McFarlane 2001, p. 144):

(a)   that the service is capable of dealing with offenders in the community to a high standard of research-based practice;

(b)   that its role centres on public protection and enforcement of court orders; and

(c)   that it is part of a much wider system under the Strategy Board for Correctional Services which now oversees the prison and probation services and, even more widely, as part of a more joined-up criminal justice system.

The probation landscape is changed by the Act, which provides the setting for this book.

Two other aspects of the context need to be drawn into this introduction: criminology and politics. There is no doubt that crime and criminals are now big news and big politics. Keeping cool when the political heat is intense will be one of the challenges faced by the new leadership of the probation service in the National Probation Directorate. Facts and comparative criminology will help. Thus we would seek to place this book in the context of international crime trends, and turn to the Home Office's authoritative *Statistical Bulletin* (Barclay *et al*, 2001) for an overview of trends as they impact upon crime in the United Kingdom.

The information is for the period 1995–1999 inclusive, and comes with standard statistical health warnings about absolute comparisons possibly being misleading because of differences in legal systems and methods of recording. However, there is value in comparing trends over a period of time and in referring to percentage changes, rather than absolute changes, on the assumption that other internal factors will have remained constant. The main points from the Bulletin are:

- Total recorded crime in the period 1995–1999 fell by 1 per cent in the European Member States and by 10 per cent in England and Wales.
- England and Wales had one of the lowest homicide rates in Western Europe.
- Violent crime rose by 11 per cent on average in the European Union, but rose by 20 per cent in England and Wales.
- Domestic burglaries fell on average by 14 per cent in the European union and by 31 per cent in England and Wales, the highest recorded fall.
- Thefts of motor vehicles rose on average by 7 per cent in the European Union, but fell by 27 per cent in England and Wales, although Germany recorded the highest fall of 46 per cent.
- Drug trafficking offences rose on average by 31 per cent in the European Union, but fell by 6 per cent in England and Wales.
- England and Wales (at 125 prisoners per 100,000 general population in 1999) had the second highest *per capita* imprisonment rates in Western Europe (compared to the average of 87 prisoners per 100,000 and Portugal's rate of 131).

These recent trends mask the high starting point of crime levels in England and Wales, which were experienced as ineluctable rises in crime during the 1980s and early 1990s and led to a public and media perception that crime and fear of crime were reaching epidemic proportions. Clearly, violent crime is increasing in Europe, but at a greater rate in Italy (37 per cent), The Netherlands (34 per cent) and in France (31 per cent) than in England and Wales. The wider international picture is mixed, with the United States recording a 20 per cent fall in violent crime, and Cyprus and Switzerland recording rises of 65 per cent and 41 per cent respectively.

Other categories of crime, primarily property offences, are decreasing across Europe, with the exception of theft of motor vehicles, where German and British success in significantly reducing vehicle crime failed to offset rises elsewhere.

Perhaps the best estimate of absolute levels of crime can be obtained from the *International Crime Victims Survey* (van Kesteren *et al*, 2001). This relates to victims' experience of crimes in 1999 in 17 industrialised countries. Of the countries examined, England and Wales had the second highest recorded rate, at 26 per cent, of respondents reporting that they had been a victim of crime once or more often in 1999. Australia had the highest rate at 30 per cent, and there were several countries with very similar rates to England and Wales, such as The Netherlands and Sweden (each with 25 per cent), Canada (24 per cent) and Denmark, Poland and Scotland (each with 23 per cent).

It is in the context of relatively high international levels of crime victimisation, albeit with a downward trend, that the use of custody in England and Wales needs to be seen. The result of the combination of Michael Howard's Prison Works strategy and New Labour's tolerance of a growth in the use of custody is best seen by contrasting countries with similar victimisation rates with the imprisonment rate of England and Wales (see Table 1 below). It is clear that England and Wales' incarceration rate aligns with North American and Eastern European patterns, rather than European Union or Scandinavian.

	Victimisation Rate	*Imprisonment Rate per 100,000 population in 1999*
England and Wales	26	125
Netherlands	25	84
Sweden	25	59
Canada	24	123
Denmark	23	66
Poland	23	142
Scotland	23	118

Table 1   Selected countries — victimisation rates related to imprisonment rates 1999

Source: Home Office Statistical Bulletin, Issue 6/01, May 2001 (Barclay *et al.*, 2001)

Different contributors to this book address the challenge faced by the new National Probation Service in winning public and sentencer confidence for community sentences to reverse the trend towards increased custody. Our population's experience of crime remains high, so the stakes are high for the Government's strategy to reduce crime and the fear of crime, which leads us to the political context.

The Labour Government, elected in 1997 and returned for a second term in 2001, has embarked on a fundamental reform of the public services. This reform has two aspects. In addressing the way public services operate, reform is presented as 'modernisation', a concept examined by John Raine in Chapter 20. However, no less significant is the Government's intent to change the perception of the public services on the part of their recipients. In some cases, such as health and education, the tone is stridently consumerist, stressing 'rights' and service expectations. In others, however, where dependency or compulsion, rather than choice, is involved, the approach is significantly different. Here the Government's preoccupation is more about disengagement and social fragmentation, and the corresponding need to reintegrate and resocialise people who have put themselves — or, indeed, have found themselves through no fault of their own — on the margins. The Government has transposed the notion of the 'safety net' to that of the 'trampoline', there to bounce citizens back into active engagement (Jordan 2000). It is a regime of 'tough love', of 'welfare to work', 'hand-ups not hand-outs', of being 'tough on crime, tough on the causes of crime'. It makes demands. In certain circumstances, obligations take precedence over rights and, for those who fail to respond to apparently benign forms of support, the consequence may be more coercive interventions (Langan 2000, p. xi). It is a restatement of the social contract between the individual citizen and the state.

The new National Probation Service finds itself at the cusp of these different threads of reform. As Faulkner, Flynn, Raine and others identify in this book, the organisation and management of the service are responding to the rigours of 'modernisation'. Long recognised but unresolved questions about the Service's loyalty, about who are its primary recipients or clients, have now been clearly specified. The Service's responsibilities are to the public, to the courts and to victims. Offenders will merit community sentences only so long as they participate, collaborate and respond appropriately in the processes and programmes of rehabilitation and reintegration provided for them.

To back up these policies, the Government has provided a massive injection of resources. In the case of criminal justice, these have come both directly to the probation service and partner agencies, as described throughout this book, and also, indirectly, through schemes to improve the worst social and environmental conditions. Examples of the latter include: New Deal, Sure Start, Education Action Zones and Health Improvement Plans.

This preoccupation with policies and resources has diverted attention from the skills and methods needed by the agents of the new agenda. Moreover, the coercive aspects of the renewed social contract, perhaps reinforced by the authoritarian traits to be found in modernisation and its 'new managerialist' implementation, have seeped into the structuring and delivery of direct work. Research (Boeck 2000) is revealing how deeply the market-driven and managerially authoritarian policies of the past 20 years have penetrated professional practice on the ground. Indeed, a recent Joseph Rowntree Report (JRF 1999) highlights the risk of the service recipient becoming lost within social inclusion policies, because many professionals are unaware of key aspects of engaging their participation and commitment. As Ruth Lister notes, in relation to work with families, in the face of the demands of statutory obligations, all too frequently social services label and manage families, rather than engage with them to address their problems (Lister 1998, p. 16).

There is no implied questioning of the efficacy of What Works, which has taken such a dominant position in probation practice in recent years. Indeed, almost all our contributors are positive about this approach to effective and accountable practice with offenders. The principles of effective implementation of What Works demand a real matching of needs to intervention and empathetic engagement with the motivation of participating offenders. The question is whether the reality of mass and managed implementation meets the requirements of these principles.

Without attention to these issues, the danger is that offenders will not engage. Indeed, preoccupation with enforcement may be fatally diverting attention from 'drop-out' and understanding and remedying this. A few years hence, who will carry the responsibility for the 'failure' of policies and be the butt of accusations of wasted resources? The fear is that it will not be the policy makers, who have always revealed the capacity to reinvent themselves to fit new fashions. Rather it will be the intended recipients, again blamed as incapable, unwilling, unmotivated and undeserving, and practitioners, who will be identified as being ill-trained and incompetent.

This opens up the prospect of a nightmare scenario, one that is fast developing in the United States. There, the social commentator Charles Murray (1999) says that the public has run out of patience. Crime has been reduced, but at the cost of a prison population that will reach 2 million. Murray calls what is being created 'custodial democracy'. In this, the affluent and successful maintain the excluded through programmes and handouts. They also wall them off, not just in prisons but in ever-deteriorating inner cities. Here the boundaries can be defined and patrolled, with the population holed up in public housing and welfare shelters. Elsewhere, life goes on pleasantly and ever more prosperously for the respectable majority. In effect, Murray argues, custodial democracy takes as its premise that a substantial portion of the population cannot be expected to function as contributing citizens. Could it happen here?

It need not be the case. The positive commitment of the Government to human rights and justice, within which the contributions to this book are framed, asserts a more hopeful future. The space for manoeuvre may well be limited, but it is in this space that the National Probation Service, drawing from its deep well of experience together with the latest knowledge of What Works, is well qualified to work effectively. Its traditions, values and skills are entirely consistent with the core of the Government's agenda and should be confidently asserted. At the heart of current Government policy, the search for regeneration through *The Third Way* (Giddens 1998), is the view that people are shaped by the world around them, but they are also creative beings with a capacity to innovate and change. They have their own biographies, through which the social world is reproduced and, at the same time, can be transformed (Giddens 1984). Although constrained by their inheritance and the conditions in which they live, people do have choices and some control over what happens to them.

Undoubtedly, it is crucial that the right volume and quality of concrete resources are invested, that they are targeted to the right places and that their deployment is managed efficiently. But this is not enough. Following Giddens' perspective, it is clear that investment will not automatically open up people's capacities to find new and better solutions. Resources and recipients need to connect. Many of our contributors excavate the rhetoric of What Works to show what this might mean in practice, refocusing on the importance of sensitive, responsive and anti-discriminatory practice for all offenders.

In conclusion, we would wish to thank the authors of the following chapters. The editorial role has been refreshing, rather than a burden; it has had the flavour of a crash course in contemporary probation thinking, and we hope that what has stimulated us will be of intellectual and practical use to a wide readership. Probation was once anonymously mocked for being the 'too intelligent service'. There are worse insults, but the implication is that when action is required, probation is weak. That is not our experience — the service has responded to a wide range of initiatives over its history with an energy and commitment which is rooted in service to communities all over the country, where the damage caused by crime is real and the intervention needed by offenders is urgent and demanding. It is now embarked upon major reforms and, like every other public service, is under pressure to deliver. We hope this book will enable broad reflection on the task ahead and, as we work for justice, the rediscovery of the force of Disraeli's dictum that: 'Justice is truth in action.'

PART ONE
Justice in Focus

1 Human Rights: a Challenge to Culture and Practice

John Scott

The Human Rights Act means learning to understand and accept responsibilities and the rights of others in the community.

(Straw 1999)

INTRODUCTION

In his speech at the Annual Constitution Unit Lecture, the Home Secretary outlined the act of faith upon which his modernising Government had embarked. Bringing human rights home (Council of Europe 1999) was the aim, and the Human Rights Act 1998 became the vehicle for embedding the European Convention on Human Rights into United Kingdom law — as radical a step for the Home Office as surrendering power over interest rates had been for the Treasury.

From 2 October 2000, courts at every level gained the power to adjudicate on the human rights dimension in cases before them, and public authorities became accountable for their decisions. If a public authority failed to comply with the Articles of the European Convention on Human Rights, a court could rule that it had acted unlawfully and grant the injured person any remedy that was within its normal powers to grant and was considered appropriate and just in the circumstances, balancing the interests of the individual and of the community. The 'balancing act' which was required to weigh the responsibilities of public authorities against the rights of the community and individuals, was anticipated by the Home Secretary's reference to learning. He berated 'selfish, dutiless rights' and clearly sought a cultural shift across society, which should understand rights only in the context of responsibilities.

This chapter examines the implications of the Human Rights Act 1998 for probation. It argues that the debate about offenders' rights and responsibilities should take place within the framework provided by the 1998 Act. Probation's responsibilities to protect the public and to address the needs of victims need to be seen as part of a wider cultural change in Britain — for people to be perceived as and to act as citizens, not subjects. Offenders' rights and responsibilities lie at the heart of probation practice. Other chapters in this book demonstrate the importance of offenders facing responsibility for their behaviour and taking responsibility for personal change. This is essentially a learning and understanding process, an exercise in citizenship.

There is a deep symbolism in the deprivation of the right to vote for prisoners. The state has determined that a basic right of a citizen is removed for certain categories of offenders. When this was recently challenged before the Queen's Bench Divisional Court (reported in *The Times*, 17 April 2001), Lord Justice Kennedy dismissed an application for judicial review of the refusals of electoral officers to enter prisoners' names on the electoral register. He also dismissed an application for a declaration of incompatibility under s. 4 of the Human Rights Act 1998. The ruling stated that 'Prisoners were by definition being treated differently from other citizens,' and that 'Parliament had taken the view that convicted prisoners in custody had forfeited their right to have a say in the way the country was governed'.

Because probation is integrally involved at each stage of an offender's career, it is incumbent upon practitioners to see their interventions as critical to the human rights and to the responsibilities of offenders as citizens. Rehabilitation and resettlement of prisoners need to include the construct that offenders are on a journey to win back their citizenship and their rights. The 'living instrument' of the

European Convention on Human Rights creates a dynamic and responsive framework for probation supervision, an appropriate post-Modernist replacement for static social work values.

This chapter:

- outlines the background to human rights and the European Convention on Human Rights
- describes how the Human Rights Act 1998 operates
- considers the impact upon organisational culture
- proposes a model for assessing human rights implications for practice and operational decisions
- draws conclusions about the importance of human rights for the modernised probation service.

BACKGROUND TO HUMAN RIGHTS AND THE EUROPEAN CONVENTION

The Universal Declaration of Human Rights was adopted and proclaimed by the General Assembly of the United Nations on 10 December 1948. Thirty Articles of rights and fundamental freedoms set out the common standards of achievement for every country. The aim was to secure 'their universal and effective recognition and observance' in member states. The Universal Declaration became the template for a series of treaties from the United Nations covering rights, for example, of women and children, the prevention of discrimination, slavery and injustice, freedom of information and association, and conventions covering employment, marriage, family and youth and social welfare. Further declarations establish rights about culture, nationality (statelessness, asylum and refugees), war crimes and crimes against humanity, including genocide.

The treaties and conventions have the status of international law. The Universal Declaration has the status of a pledge. It is in this context that the Council of Europe took the first steps on 4 November 1950 for the collective enforcement of certain of the rights stated in the Universal Declaration. By signing the Convention for Protection of Human Rights and Fundamental Freedoms, governments undertook to honour its Articles and to recognise the authority of the European Court of Human Rights, which was established to ensure the observance of the Convention and the Protocols.

The political and cultural significance of the European Convention cannot be overstated. It was adopted by the democratic governments of Western Europe only five years after the end of the Second World War, which had been waged against the fascist regimes of Hitler and Mussolini. The recent horrors of torture, slavery and the Holocaust were uppermost in the minds of the drafting lawyers, most of whom were British. However, it would be a mistake to overlook the other realities of post-war Europe — Stalin dominated a Soviet Russian empire and fascist regimes remained in Portugal and Spain. Addison and Taylor (1999, p. 17) highlight the infamous legal system of Stalin's communist rule, which was based on the principles of the Soviet Chief Prosecutor, Andrei Vyshinsky, who declared: 'The concept of innocence before trial is a Bourgeois fallacy.' In this context, it was crucial for the development of democracy across a geopolitical area emerging from the devastation of war for governments to 'commit themselves to a formal set of binding principles, which rejected totalitarianism and which embraced the concepts of the rule of law and affirmed the rights of the individual' (*ibid.*).

The success of the Convention, widely regarded as embodying the fundamental principles of the English common law, is evidenced by the expansion of signatories to include members of the former Eastern Bloc and the new democracies of southern Europe. Perhaps the most effective component was the establishment of the European Court of Human Rights, which could hold governments to account, create a new body of case law and develop a monitoring system.

Although the United Kingdom ratified the Convention in 1953, the Articles were not specifically incorporated into domestic law. The British Government had no power to overturn any of the Articles since becoming a signatory, but British citizens only had the right to seek redress for a breach of the Convention from the European Court of Human Rights at Strasbourg. For nearly 50 years, human rights issues in the United Kingdom were a secondary consideration in legal terms after statute and common law (precedent). Redress involved the cumbersome and supra-national process of application to the European Court, rather than recourse to domestic courts. During this period, legislators sought to 'Strasbourg proof' Acts of Parliament, keeping a defensive eye on the Convention and the possibility of unfavourable rulings by the European Court, rather than positively seeking to embed human rights in the proceedings of domestic courts.

DESCRIPTION OF THE EUROPEAN CONVENTION OF HUMAN RIGHTS

The European Convention on Human Rights is a lengthy document, the vast weight of which is concerned with procedures for the operation of the European Commission and Court of Human Rights. Until November 1998, the Commission reviewed cases at first instance, publishing advisory opinions prior to referral onwards to the European Court, reflecting the European 'inquisitorial' approach to dealing with legal matters. Since November 1998, all cases have been considered directly by a chamber of the Court. If an application is found admissible, it is referred to the Court for adjudication. At the Court, hearings may be contested before a chamber of international judges, leading to judgments which are binding on all signatory parties. The Commission remains in existence to deal only with outstanding cases that were in the system before November 1998.

The substance of the Convention is to be found in its first 18 Articles and additional protocols, subsequently added to the 1950 original. The Convention is a product of the Council of Europe, which should not be confused with the European Union. The Council of Europe has a wider membership, including Norway, Turkey and Switzerland, as well as former communist states from Eastern Europe. The Council of Europe exercises moral, but not legal, authority over its members; for example, it is possible for any country to give formal notice of derogation to opt out of a particular aspect of the Convention — an illustration of this would be the United Kingdom's anti-terrorist legislation in Northern Ireland.

In an article 'Human Rights and the Probation Service' (Scott and Ward 1999), the rights were grouped in the following categories:

(a) *Fundamental rights* — the right to life (Article 2), with a subsequent protocol abolishing the death penalty; freedom from torture, inhuman or degrading treatment (Article 3).

(b) *Judicial rights* — the right to liberty (Article 5); right to a fair trial (Article 6); freedom from arbitrary punishment (Article 7).

(c) *Social rights* — no forced labour (Article 4); freedom of expression (Article 10); freedom of assembly and association (Article 11); right to personal possessions (Protocol 1); right to education (Protocol 1); right to freedom of movement (Protocol 4).

(d)   *Personal rights* — the right to respect for private and family life (Article 8); freedom of thought, conscience and religion (Article 9), the right to marry (Article 12), with equal legal rights for spouses added in Protocol 7; prohibition of discrimination (Article 14).

Legal writers tend to cut the cake differently, distinguishing *absolute rights* (Articles 2, 3, 4 and 7) from *strong rights* (Articles 5, 6 and 14) and then *qualified rights* (Articles 8, 9, 10 and 11). This is to differentiate the rights on the basis of their legal strength, whereas Scott and Ward chose to categorise by social content. The dangers of attempting to categorise complex rights, which are part of a 'living instrument', are perhaps best illustrated by considering the 'absolute' right in Article 2, which states: 'Everyone's right to life shall be protected by law.' As Fox (2000) pointed out, the poignant case of the conjoined twins, 'Mary and Jodie', had to balance the right to life of one twin against the inevitable death of the other, if an operation to separate them proceeded. The dynamic of this situation has led to a redefinition of the right to life as being a strong, rather than an absolute, right. Inevitably, the use of categories is an arbitrary construction, but they can help in understanding the scope of the Convention.

For much of the European Convention, there is an overriding exemption regarding the rights and freedoms in the case of war and emergency. Of greater relevance to practitioners in the criminal justice sector are the exceptions limiting the rights in Articles 8, 9, 10 and 11 — the rights to respect for private and family life, freedom of thought, conscience and religion, freedom of expression and freedom of assembly and association. The wording of the exceptions varies, but Article 8(2) provides the basic construction of the Convention's approach to exceptions:

> 2.   There shall be no interference by a public authority with the exercise of this right except such as is in accordance with the law and is necessary in a democratic society in the interests of national security, public safety or the economic well-being of the country, for the prevention of disorder or crime, for the protection of health or morals, or for the protection of the rights and freedoms of others.

To these exceptions are added:

(a)   such limitations as are neessary for the protection of public order (Article 9);

(b)   such formalities, conditions, restrictions or penalties as are prescribed by law and are necessary:

(i)   in the interests of territorial integrity or public safety,

(ii)   for the protection of the reputation of others,

(iii)   for preventing the disclosure of information received in confidence,

(iv)   for maintaining the authority and impartiality of the judiciary (Article 10);

(c)   lawful restrictions on the exercise of the rights of freedom of assembly and of association by members of the armed forces, of the police or of the administration of the state (Article 11).

It is in balancing the basic human rights with these exceptions that the exercise of discretion by practitioners and the decisions of public authorities will be tested in the courts.

Beyond the general rights are two provisions specifically directed at 'aliens' or non-nationals. The Convention (Article 16) specifically exempts aliens from the protection afforded in relation to Articles 10 (freedom of expression) and 11 (freedom of assembly), although the subsequently added Protocol 7 provides for legal rights regarding expulsion for 'lawfully resident' aliens.

As is the case with so many attempts at reform through legal and transparent means, the European Convention is a 'curate's egg', reflecting the compromises that have to be made when widely differing traditions and systems are brought together. Alongside its progressive potential, some significant omissions and limitations have to be acknowledged.

Overall, the Convention is limited in scope, when compared with the United Nations Declaration of Human Rights. Unlike the UN Declaration, there are no stated rights to employment, to social security and to the means for achieving an adequate standard of living, such as housing, medical care and social services. The British Government has, in the past, been subject to serious criticism for not meeting the standards set by the UN in the United Nations Convention on the Rights of the Child. However, it might be argued that, with its more circumscribed focus and legally binding status, the European Convention has more chance of being honoured than the global exhortations of the UN Declarations.

It has been noted particularly that the European Convention has no generic anti-discrimination clause. Article 14 prohibiting discrimination applies only to the specific rights set out in the Convention, so can be pursued only in conjunction with an alleged breach of another Article. Article 14 itself does not include disability or sexual orientation in the categories stated. Linked with this, there are indications that the Convention is set within a narrowly defined, arguably northern European cultural discourse, emphasising the individual rather than the family or 'clan'. Remedial action can be initiated only by individuals. Third party or group actions are not allowed. In this way, the Convention specifies the rights of individuals and not the duties and obligations of and to others, which would receive stronger emphasis in other cultures well represented in Europe and the United Kingdom.

Within the Articles of the Convention there are contradictions which will give enhanced attention to controversial matters, some of which are very familiar to the probation service. For instance, what is the right to privacy (Article 8) and to freedom of expression (Article 10) in the case of sex offenders? Inter-agency protocols, which have been established through tough experience, will receive renewed attention in the courts with human rights considerations in view. The European Convention will take us into an arena that will be operating to new and different precepts. As the legal process moves beyond national institutions, there will be different modes of operation, procedures and traditions coming to bear upon decisions. While this may have been the case ultimately (and somewhat theoretically up to now) if recourse was taken to Strasbourg, the implementation of the Human Rights Act 1998 has brought the Convention to the forefront of day-to-day decision-making in the United Kingdom.

THE HUMAN RIGHTS ACT 1998

The Human Rights Act 1998 incorporates the European Convention for the Protection of Human Rights and Fundamental Freedoms into United Kingdom law and applies to all public authorities. Since 2 October 2000, all common law and statute has been interpreted in the light of the Convention, and judges are in a position to develop British law using the instrument of common law rulings. Equally, rulings in British courts will feed into the development of human rights in Europe with the positive potential of a reciprocal judicial relationship.

The incoming Labour Government gave a high priority to enacting this landmark law early in its administration and clearly hoped to gain political capital from improving access to human rights justice, while reducing the costs and damaging fallout of regular antipathetic rulings from Strasbourg. The full impact of the Human Rights Act 1998 will take several years to assess and represents a jurisprudential act of faith and a political risk. The political imperative was articulated by the Home Secretary:

> It seemed to us that we were having the worst of both worlds because we were subject to the Convention but we couldn't gain what the Convention jurisprudence calls a margin of appreciation of having it interpreted by our own judges. (Straw 1999)

The 1998 Act works by making all decisions of public authorities open to challenge. Challenges can be brought in both criminal and civil courts, but a breach of the Act is a civil matter and carries no criminal liability. Remedies could include quashing an unlawful decision, acquitting a defendant or quashing a conviction, ordering a public authority not to take a proposed action or awarding damages.

Under the terms of the 1998 Act, a public authority includes:

(a) a court or tribunal; and
(b) any person certain of whose functions are functions of a public nature (s. 6(3)).

The Act therefore applies to the National Probation Service, area probation boards and probation contractors or partners. It would also encompass Crime and Disorder Partnerships and other multi-agency organisations and agencies, with which probation is engaged. It is unlawful for a public authority to act in a way which is incompatible with a Convention right, so any breach by a probation employee, contractor or partner could lead to the imposition of a remedy.

The Act states that 'So far as it is possible to do so, primary and subordinate legislation must be read and given effect in a way which is compatible with the Convention rights' (s. 3(1)). When a court finds that it is not possible to interpret legislation in a way that is compatible, it may, according to Probation Circular 59/2000:

(a)   quash or disapply subordinate legislation; or

(b)   if it is a higher court, make a declaration of incompatibility for primary legislation (this will trigger a new power, allowing a Minister to make a remedial order to amend the legislation to bring it in line with the Convention rights); or

(c)   be required to take account of Strasbourg case law and be bound to develop common law so as to make it compatible with the Convention rights.

Courts cannot strike down legislation; but by issuing a certificate of incompatibility, Parliament will be required by a higher court to reconsider the legislation, and Ministers have access to a fast track method of amendment for the first time.

Only individuals (in law this could include a corporation) who are considered a victim or who are directly affected by the action of a public body can engage the Act by taking the authority to court for a breach of Convention rights, or by relying on the Convention as a defence in any other proceedings. The matter must be taken to court within a year, but a court can allow extra time, if considered 'equitable having regard to all the circumstances' (s. 7(5)(b)). This means that pressure groups are unable to bring a case, unless they are themselves a victim, but they could provide support and resources to assist an individual claimant.

In summary, the following Articles from the European Convention on Human Rights have been incorporated into the Human Rights Act 1998:

- Article 2 (right to life)
- Article 3 (prohibition of torture)
- Article 4 (prohibition of slavery and forced labour)
- Article 5 (right to liberty and security)
- Article 6 (right to a fair trial)
- Article 7 (no punishment without law)
- Article 8 (right to respect for private and family life)
- Article 9 (freedom of thought, conscience and religion)
- Article 10 (freedom of expression)

- Article 11 (freedom of assembly and association)
- Article 12 (right to marry)
- Article 14 (prohibition of discrimination)

- Protocol 1, Article 1 (protection of property)
- Protocol 1, Article 2 (right to education)
- Protocol 1, Article 3 (right to free elections)
- Protocol 6, Article 1 (abolition of the death penalty)
- Protocol 6, Article 2 (death penalty in time of war).

IMPACT UPON THE ORGANISATIONAL CULTURE OF PROBATION

During 1998, the Human Rights Unit in the Home Office undertook a review of probation legislation, policies and approved practice, and concluded that they were compatible with the Human Rights Act 1998 and that no changes were necessary to ensure compliance. To date, there have been no sustained court actions against the probation service, although it is too soon to comment on specific issues which have been raised as potential challenges. The impact on probation has been muted by an organisational priority upon the Criminal Justice and Court Services Act 2000, which became the focus of the Home Office's Probation Unit and of probation areas' concerns to implement the Government's modernisation agenda. Whereas other criminal justice agencies invested heavily and early in training their staff and sentencers, probation implemented a cascade training programme only in September 2000, shortly before the coming into force of the 1998 Act. The Home Office, in conjunction with the Association of Chief Officers of Probation, ran a national workshop, followed by regional events and an event for trainers. The understandable priority of preparing for the National Probation Service, amalgamations of areas and new orders has meant that the impact upon managers and staff of the probation service has started from a low base.

However, an important circular was issued in September 2000 (Probation Circular 59/2000), which gave detailed written guidance on how the Human Rights Act 1998 applied to probation areas as public authorities and how to respond to any human rights claims that might be made in the context of probation work (Home Office 2000h). Of particular usefulness was Annex C, which identified nine examples of likely challenges, each followed by counter-arguments drafted by lawyers and probation practitioners with human rights expertise. These counter-arguments set a style of response based on confidence in previous European rulings, for example, in citing the 1930 International Labour Office Convention on Forced Labour to be read in conjunction with Article 4 to demonstrate that community punishment orders (formerly community service orders) are exempted from the Article 4 prohibition. The Circular equipped managers and practitioners to handle barrack room lawyers and doubting colleagues, and provided a starting point for challenges in court — although the advice was, and remains, to seek legal expertise if a case throws up a Human Rights Act challenge, or if proceedings are initiated against the probation board as a public authority.

It is likely that the impact of Human Rights Act 1998 implementation upon probation practice will be slow and linked to case findings. Practice will be influenced not just by probation-specific cases, but also by transferable findings from:

(a)   other statutory criminal justice agencies — police, prison, courts, Crown Prosecution Service;

(b)   partner organisations — voluntary or commercial contractors;

(c)   allied statutory agencies — housing, mental health, social services, education.

The new concept of legislation as a 'living instrument' has meant that predicting impact has been an inexact science. Before implementation of the 1998 Act, there were fears about a litigation culture developing, which have not materialised. In an earlier article, Scott and Ward (2000) identified six most likely categories for challenge:

(a)   *Failure to protect* the public from known and avoidable dangers by not enforcing court orders.

(b)   *Failure to inform* individual offenders about their past records, or denying the public information essential for the well-being of their families.

(c)   *Failure to provide* a service because of resource allocation and the effects of imposing priorities on service provision.

(d)   *Right to life* — victims and relatives of victims challenging the actions and judgements of professionals and public authorities.

(e)   *Degrading treatment* in care, in prisons, in hostels, in police stations, in probation offices.

(f)   *Discrimination* — secondary actions arising from racial prejudice or unfair discrimination.

Probation could be subject to an action under each of these categories. Sex offenders, exchange of information, changes in services, an offender committing a murder whilst on supervision, bullying in a hostel or a racist incident — it is not difficult to extrapolate from general human rights concerns to specific actions against a probation service. Practitioners need to know the 1998 Act and be kept abreast of relevant case law. The advent of the National Probation Service, with a strong centre coordinating training and information about Human Rights Act developments, will help develop a human rights culture at practice level. The Circular on Guidance (59/2000) establishes a mechanism and method for collating probation-relevant findings, which the National Probation Directorate will adopt. A group convened by the Directorate continues to plan for future training and for the need to update circulars.

A major impact upon probation culture will be the reinforcement of the role of National Standards. It is a requirement of the Human Rights Act 1998 that courts interpret Convention rights from the United Kingdom perspective. In a probation challenge, it is anticipated that a court would use National Standards as the embodiment of national policy on supervising offenders in the community and as a yardstick to help interpret the domestic margin of appreciation. The margin of appreciation is an international legal doctrine, which recognises that domestic courts and institutions are in the best position to assess local and national factors. As the political, cultural and social aspects of a challenge are considered, compliance with National Standards — for example, in timeliness of reports or reviews — will help a probation area demonstrate that its actions and decisions about a case were neither arbitrary nor unfair.

The main organisational culture change required of probation is to develop structured decision-making in relation to Human Rights Act 1998 issues. Some commentators, for example Afzal and Schuller (2000, p. 4) interpret section 6 of the Act as creating a legal obligation for public authorities to act compatibly with the Convention:

A negative obligation only requires the authority to refrain from interference with particular rights. However, the Act imposes a positive obligation, which requires that a public authority also takes positive steps to ensure that individual rights are protected from the actions of another individual in a horizontal relationship to themselves.

Probation supervision cases and the operational decisions entailed in, for example, breach, or protecting the public or a specific victim, expose the public authority to challenge. An audit trail, with written records of actions and reasons for decisions, becomes a necessity to demonstrate defensible decisions and to meet the requirement of the Act to act in line with the principle of proportionality and balance. The Convention introduces proportionality to the law, because most of the rights are qualified and interference with a right is allowed under the exceptions discussed earlier. Afzal and Schuller (2000, p. 4) summarise proportionality 'as not using a sledgehammer to crack a nut'. The stronger the human right, the 'tougher the test will be for the need for the interference'.

Fox (2000) urged probation practitioners to mark and follow the way in which courts have been trained to think about human rights challenges, by asking four questions:

(a)   Is there an interference with a Convention right?
(b)   Is the interference prescribed by law?
(c)   Does the interference serve a legitimate purpose?
(d)   Is the interference necessary in a democratic society?

Fox went on to suggest that a simple process would aid practitioners — Stop, Think, Act, Record.

For policymakers or strategic managers, Afzal and Schuller (2000, pp. 6, 7) propose the following decision-making process, which is also based on posing the correct questions in a structured way:

1.   In cases where a decision by the authority may be considered incompatible with or to interfere with a right:
   •   Identify whether the decision is incompatible with or interfering with a specific right or rights.
   •   Ensure that, if it is, this is a deliberate decision rather than accidental — begin by assessing if the infringement can be avoided by an alternative decision or action.

2. If the infringement cannot be avoided:
   - Identify if the decision is required by statutory legislation.
   - If it is, is the action proportionate?
3. Decide if the Article is absolute, strong or qualified:
   - Is the interference permitted by law?
   - If so, is there good reason for it? (Refer to stated exceptions.)
   - Is it proportionate to the problem being solved? (Any infringement should occur because there is a major problem to be solved.)
   - Is this the best course of action that can be taken (in the light of localised restrictions such as resourcing, lack of viable alternatives)?
   - Is the decision discriminatory?
4. Record your decisions and the factors taken into account.
5. Offer independent adjudication and representation to the challenger.

This process may require some adaption for probation purposes, but used systematically would create the necessary audit trail.

At board level, the new accountability structure of local boards and a National Probation Directorate will require clarity about Human Rights Act responsibilities. A strong challenger may well decide to act against both a local board and the National Probation Directorate — both are public authorities and have as yet untested roles and responsibilities in the development of policy and the delivery of services. Just as statutory obligations require statements and processes to honour health and safety and equality of opportunity legislation, so too the new boards and Directorate should have in place a compliance statement and a process for ensuring that human rights issues are monitored and honoured. Human rights must not be another hygiene factor for an organisational checklist; it must represent a fundamental commitment by probation to develop a new culture.

A MODEL FOR ASSESSING HUMAN RIGHTS IMPLICATIONS FOR PRACTICE

Scott and Ward (2000) have proposed that one way of assessing the implications of the European Convention for the probation service could be to consider it as operating at three levels: primary, secondary, and tertiary. These levels can apply to the service or, for that matter, to any other organisation in or outside the criminal justice system.

- *Primary level* — where human rights relate to day-to-day practice as a service provider; for example, the provision of a community punishment order work placement, in which the service is relating directly with both offenders and members of the community.
- *Secondary level* — where unwittingly the actions of a third party for whom the service has responsibility could lead to a human rights issue for the service; for example, an offender under supervision harms someone, thereby transgressing their human rights. Equally, there is the contentious potential of actions against partner organisations, which are not public authorities but are contracted to perform public duties.
- *Tertiary level* — where the service is working in an arena where another agency, which is not accountable to it, may be transgressing human rights; for example, where probation staff are seconded into other criminal justice settings — prisons, Youth Offending Teams or courts. They may identify human rights concerns about procedures or practice. The service could be called to give witness evidence.

At the primary level, the Human Rights Act 1998 clearly opens up a new avenue for actions against probation services, where individuals will go to court for redress. It remains to be seen what might happen at the secondary and tertiary levels as the courts begin to deliver rulings. Within the criminal justice system, the anticipated early rush of actions in Autumn 2000, with lobby groups sponsoring and advising individuals in test cases, did not occur following implementation of the Act. Police, prisons and Crown Prosecutors remain most likely to be in the first phase of actions, but probation services are public authorities operating in the sensitive domain of criminal justice and must prepare for cases. Service users and employees will be able to utilise the legislation for issues currently handled through formal complaints or grievance procedures.

In the course of carrying out their duties, probation staff experience the dark side of the criminal justice system and, as a result of the Human Rights Act 1998, all judgments, professional decisions and moral issues can be placed in the court arena. Practitioners and policymakers alike need to build this new dimension to the legal system into the way they approach their work, whether at the primary, the secondary or the tertiary level.

The framework set out in Table 1.1 is designed to enable Human Rights Act issues to be assessed. Specific examples are cited to demonstrate how the framework could be used. It is envisaged that a service delivery unit, such as a hostel, could use the framework as part of a training or risk assessment exercise.

Table 1.1 Probation and human rights: a framework to identify risks

Category of Action	Article/Protocol	Primary Example	Secondary Example	Tertiary Example
1. *Failure to protect* — the public from known and avoidable dangers by not enforcing court orders.	Article 2 — 'Everyone's right to life shall be protected by law.'	An offender dies whilst undertaking a community punishment order placement.	An offender, under the supervision of the probation service on a community order, commits a murder. The service's incident report identifies a catalogue of failures in the supervision, leading the victim's family to take legal action.	A Parole Board decision is challenged by a person whose life has been threatened by a parolee.
2. *Failure to inform* — individuals about their past or denying them information essential for the well-being of their families.	Article 8 — 'Everyone has the right to respect for his private and family life, his home and correspondence.'	Access to records by offenders.	People living near a hostel wanting information about risks posed by residents.	Probation staff in a Youth Offending Team witness inappropriate use of information during a parenting order.
3. *Failure to provide* — a service because of resource allocation and the effects of imposing priorities on service provision.	Articles 2, 5, 8, 14 — a range of Articles could be breached if a service is withdrawn or one category of offender is preferentially treated.	Cuts in resettlement lead to offenders sentenced to less than 12 months being refused a service.	An unescorted bailee commits a serious offence because no staff were avaiable for escort.	Not applicable.
4. *Right to life* — victims and their relatives will challenge the actions and judgments of professionals and public authorities.	Article 2 — 'Everyone's right to life shall be protected by law.'	A death in a hostel.	A footbridge built by offenders on community punishment orders collapses and a member of the public dies.	A mental health patient diverted from court proceedings commits suicide in hospital.
5. *Degrading treatment* — offenders will challenge the way they are treated in prisons, hostels, police stations and in probation premises.	Article 3 — 'No one shall be subjected to torture or to inhuman or degrading treatment or punishment.'	Menial work projects on community punishment orders or in hostels are challenged as degrading.	A recalled licensee challenges the basis of the decision to recommend revocation and a return to prison.	Prison based staff observe degrading treatment of a prisoner by a contractor.
6. *Discrimination* — service users will take action against public authorities arising from racial prejudice or unfair discrimination.	Article 14 — 'The enjoyment of the rights and freedoms set forth in this Convention shall be secured without discrimination on any ground such as sex, race, colour, language, religion, political or other opinion, national or social origin, association with a national minority, property, birth or other status.'	A person is required to report to a probation officer on a religious holiday.	A black offender breaches a community punishment order, he claims out of fear resulting from racial abuse by other offenders on the team.	A member of staff in a voluntary hostel ignores a woman resident's plea for protection against sexual harassment by male members of staff.

THE IMPORTANCE OF HUMAN RIGHTS TO THE MODERNISED PROBATION SERVICE

Peter Riddell (1999) writes:

The post-war notion of people as passive recipients of welfare and public services fitted well with a paternalistic view of citizenship. Both are now invalid. People are now both more demanding about standards of public services and about relations with the State.

The Government's programme of modernisation through constitutional reforms and improvements in public services is a systematic attempt to satisfy the demands for higher standards of performance and accountability. The Human Rights Act 1998 is a modernising measure for justice. A third 'living instrument' has been added to statute and the common law, so that all decisions in courts will be affected by a new jurisprudence linked to European traditions of purposive interpretation. The 'living instrument' is defined usefully in Probation Circular 59/2000 as meaning:

that the rights are given a broad and fluid interpretation rather than a strict legalistic one that relies on a rigid interpretation of what the actual words mean. This is to ensure that the Convention Rights are practical and effective within an evolving society, so their scope may change over time as values in society change. (Home Office 2000h)

The importance of human rights to probation is that a new dynamic has been introduced into the relationship between society, courts and offenders — the interface where probation works. The 'living instrument' is essentially European in its operation and may presage a shift towards embracing European understandings of community sanctions and punishments.

The modernisation of the probation service through the Criminal Justice and Court Services Act 2000 is emblematic of the raft of reforms which have introduced new accountability, performance management, standards and methodologies across the public sector. Human rights concepts reinforce these reforms. Proportionality, balance, reasonableness and openness are characteristics which probation would wish to claim as its heritage, but the modernised service needs to build these concepts into new systems and procedures as the National Probation Service and area boards are established, if a human rights culture is to predominate in the unified service. One of the Government's specific aims in introducing the Human Rights Act 1998 was to ensure that, in balancing rights and responsibilities, when difficult service dilemmas are determined, public services could be seen to be acting in the interests of the general public, as the Home Secretary stated about the Act (Straw 1999):

> It means a greater confidence in the fairness of our political institutions. It means a shared moral language for resolving clashes of rights. It means involving citizens in democratic decision making in their communities.

The challenge to the modernising probation service (modernisation processes began on 1 April 2001; they did not conclude) over the coming decade is to identify the key components which are required to develop and sustain a human rights culture. Barbara Hudson captured the essence of the challenge (Hudson 2001a, p. 112): 'The culture of rights is a culture of social inclusion, where no one is outside the constituency of justice.'

This chapter concludes with an outline of the priorities which should shape the human rights and social inclusion agenda for probation:

(a)   *Openness and community involvement.* Greater confidence in probation will require greater consultation at local and national levels to ensure that probation is acting in the interests of the public. 'Shared moral language' implies the development of a dialogue between probation areas and the communities they serve. Opening board meetings to the public is a symbolic first step on a journey which will involve effective community consultation on priorities, strategies and plans, and feedback on performance.

(b)   *Citizenship.* Offenders are citizens, for whom a combination of punishment and rehabilitation is necessary to restore their place in their communities. When they supervise court orders, probation staff are at the centre of a mediation process between the state, the court, the victim and the offender. Probation programmes, therefore, consciously need to identify their role in restoring to offenders their respect for rights and responsibilities. Pro-social modelling best illustrates the potential of practical citizenship in orders. Every accredited programme needs to carry a culture of human rights into face-to-face work with offenders. A probation human rights culture has to be taken into service delivery, not merely discussed in courts, board meetings or tearooms.

(c) *Partnerships and protocols.* Contracts, service level agreements and protocols all need revision to ensure that statutory and voluntary agency partnerships add to the human rights culture in the criminal justice system and beyond. The Multi Agency Public Protection Panels are a prime example of a development which will benefit from being located in a Human Rights Act 1998 framework, within which the dilemmas and community tensions can be assessed and rationally accounted. It would be a mistake for probation to attempt to put its own human rights house in order and to ignore the reality that 'resolving clashes of rights' entails the whole system in dialogue.

(d) *Investment in staff.* Cultures can take years to change. Although human rights developments may go with the grain of probation, training and staff development need to be sustained and go beyond basic introductory courses to ensure that managers and practitioners integrate the concepts into their decisions. As Human Rights Act 1998 case law evolves, there will be an onus upon the National Probation Service to explain the implications to staff. At national and local area levels, there will be a need to utilise legal expertise so that transferable rulings in allied fields can be applied to probation issues and decisions. A culture of communication will be a key to changing probation staff across the country.

(e) *International dimension.* Just as probation cannot be isolated within the criminal justice system, so too the United Kingdom needs to be inclusive in ensuring that international developments and Strasbourg rulings are monitored and incorporated into transferable learning.

The unified probation service needs to adopt this agenda to ensure that the full dynamic of the Human Rights Act 1998 is incorporated into practice. In a fast changing society, the Act will prove to be a lever to institutional change — as the armed forces have found in relation to Strasbourg rulings about acceptability of homosexuals in the ranks, and as the Scottish legal system found in the unacceptability of Temporary Sheriffs. The development of consistent rules, procedures and standards by a strengthened centre must incorporate human rights principles and compliance to build an acceptable consistency to probation practice and programmes. Equally, as probation staff exercise discretion within the framework of National Standards, they must incorporate the same principles. From the National Probation Directorate to the individual practitioner, we will be as strong as the weakest human rights link — pro-human rights modelling begins with the very first contact with every offender.

2 Justice, Humanity and Mercy

Malcolm Lacey

Humanity means not just everybody, but also kindness (Zeldin 1999, p. 32)

INTRODUCTION

On 27 January 2001, there was a fascinating episode on the 'Today' programme. Lord Woolf, the Lord Chief Justice, said he thought that too many offenders were being jailed. Many people in prison do not need to be there; a situation which is only adding to overcrowding. Attempts had to be made to find punishments within the community that were more acceptable to the public and to convince them that such alternative punishments could actually provide better safeguards for the public. In a striking analogy, Lord Woolf commented:

> On the whole, politicians are very good about race, they don't approve of playing what is called the race card. I wish they also took the same view with regard to the prison card. I'm afraid they don't. They do see prison as something which the public feels is an important safeguard, and so they will be in favour in the rhetoric that they use of more and more prison, but that actually is not necessarily in the interests of the public.

He said that this was hindering attempts to rehabilitate the UK's more serious offenders.

Some 20 minutes later, the then Conservative leader, William Hague, called for more offenders to be locked up, and said that a rising prison population would be the inevitable consequence of a tougher approach to law and order which, he said, a Conservative Government would bring:

> I think that it may be necessary to have more people in prison, in order to deal with the law and order situation in this country.... I don't think it is being dealt with at the moment. Crime is rising, the number of police is falling and everybody around the country knows that it is an increasing problem and it must be dealt with.

What is instructive is the way in which Mr Hague responded. It was extraordinarily quick; so quick that he could not have reflected upon what Lord Woolf — who had, after all, completed ten years earlier the most searching review of our prison system since the Gladstone review in 1895 — was suggesting (Woolf 1990). Neither did he make any pretence that he was going to. (taken verbatim from www.bbc.co.uk archive.)

Just over a month later, the same argument was played out with the Labour Home Secretary. On 31 January 2001, Mr Jack Straw, in a lecture to the Social Market Foundation, declared that community penalties did nothing for 80 per cent of the 100,000 hard-core of most persistent offenders:

> Almost without exception, every persistent offender has been through the mill of community sentences and has re-offended. If we are to get on top of this problem of persistent criminality and are to process more through the prison system, numbers may well have to rise. We have factored that into our spending plans ... It was time to make the sentence fit the offender, rather than the offence.

A few hours later, in his Prison Reform Trust Lecture, Lord Woolf reiterated his view that the best way of cutting crime was a higher detection rate rather than an increase in the prison population of 62,000, which is already forecast to rise to more than 78,000 by 2007:

What has to be realised here, and I include the Government here, is that a short custodial sentence is a very poor alternative to a sentence to be served in the community. It is far more expensive. It will do nothing to tackle the offender's behavioural problems. It should be regarded as no more than a necessary evil.

(Both lectures reported in *The Guardian*, 1 February 2001, p. 3.)

The divide is no longer, except in emphasis, between the political parties but between the politicians and those who have to operate the criminal justice system. As Martin Narey, Director General of the Prison Service, put it in a speech to the Prison Service Annual Conference, politicians make common assumptions about the primacy of victims and public protection, and few people are concerned with 'the very immorality of our treatment of some prisoners and the degradation of some establishments' (Narey 2001, p. 3). This has been deftly caught in the crossword puzzle clue 'Thatcher's choice as home secretary', to which the answer is, of course, 'straw'.

This is the context in which the new National Probation Service was created on 1 April 2001, an event unremarked by the national media, yet one welcomed across all grades by most people in the service, including many members of the probation committees, which were abolished. It put an end to a decade of uncertainty, during which, at times, there was a real possibility of probation being disbanded and an entirely new body formed, as the community arm of the prison service. It seems to offer the opportunity to play a leading role in criminal policy. There is certainly a welcome for a strong sense of direction to overcome the inconsistencies that were generated by 54 areas. Substantial new funding is being made available, which indicates that the Government, too, wants this opportunity to be grasped. It has brought an influx of probation staff into the Home Office, with a former chief probation officer as the National Director, who has direct accountability and access to the Minister. There is widespread relief that the new director, Eithne Wallis, comes from the probation service, and enthusiasm for her vision for the future. A greatly increased number of new entrants are being trained to degree level. There is also a belief that the Government means better than it says, prepared to do good, if only by stealth. Offenders will be helped to take on the responsibilities of being good citizens, though if they fail to take advantage of the facilities offered to them, they will face increasing periods of imprisonment.

In this chapter, we seek to explore some of the tensions that the new service will experience. It is argued that these tensions are the result of new social and economic conditions, to which politicians respond, and that the probation service, as a government agency, is bound to reflect these political realities. The agenda is being set for the twenty-first century, and it is different from the one that dominated the twentieth.

HISTORICAL BACKGROUND

So far as penal policy was concerned, the criminal justice system in the twentieth century was framed by the Gladstone Report on prisons in 1895 and, at the end, by the Criminal Justice Act 1991. The Gladstone Report, for the first time, suggested that rehabilitation should be afforded equal weight with deterrence and retribution in the prison regimes. It profoundly influenced official thinking. The 1991 Act made imprisonment the punishment of the last resort, to be imposed only when the crime was 'so serious' that no other punishment could be considered; community penalties were to be the norm for the majority of 'mid-range' offences. During the century, there was other landmark legislation. The Asquith administration established juvenile courts and the Borstal system, and passed the Probation of Offenders Act 1907. The Criminal Justice Act 1948 abolished flogging, and the Criminal Justice Act 1967 introduced community service and parole. Just as in other areas of social policy, such as childcare and mental health, where the drive was towards treatment in the community, so in penal policy there was the trend towards parole and alternatives to prison, such as community service and the use of hostels and day centres. Probation was a child of the twentieth century. This is not to say that it was not a struggle to achieve these reforms. There was always an undertow crystallised in the comments about forgetting the victims and pampering the offender; and in the last quarter of the century, the 'nothing works' research sapped the earlier confidence. Nevertheless, there was a sense of working with the grain of received opinion.

The 1991 Act was undermined almost immediately. The proportionate system of unit fines was abolished and the constraints on considering previous criminal character were loosened by an early judgment in the Court of Appeal. And before long, Michael Howard, when he was Home Secretary, contradicted the philosophy with his dictum that 'prison works'. Looking back, this can be seen as the turning point, when the century-old assumptions about the criminal justice system were being abandoned. The first edition of this book was published in 1995. In the chapter entitled 'Fairness' (Lacey 1995), this author wrote that the amendments to the 1991 Act in the Criminal Justice Act 1993 came as a morale-shattering blow, yet felt there were still strong reasons for claiming that the service could remain at the heart of the criminal justice process. Now we have to ask: 'What will "probation" mean in the twenty-first century?'

PROBATION IN THE TWENTY-FIRST CENTURY

This is a more fundamental question than recognising that there will in future be a National Probation Service with a new and far more interventionist and controlling structure than the traditional, highly-devolved service. Paid chairs will report to the Home Secretary through the National Director. The Home Office employs the chief officers. The philosophy and purpose of the service is to be set from the centre. It is emphatically no longer the case that Government is accepting the ideas and practice of voluntary bodies and philanthropists, as was largely the case with the birth of the probation service; rather, it is a case of Government using the service to implement a politically-driven programme. Such transparency is to be welcomed.

These changes have happened because politicians have responded to an undoubtedly serious problem of crime, one that their constituency surgeries and focus groups have told them they cannot ignore. This is the genesis of Mr Straw's ten-year plan, which includes breaking 'the cycle of re-offending' of the 100,000 persistent offenders said to commit over half of all recorded crime (though we should be clear that it is a constantly changing core as young offenders grow out of crime and are replaced by others). There is a great deal of sense in this strategy. Of these persistent offenders, over half are under 21, around two-thirds use drugs, more than a third were in care, and four-fifths are unemployed. Not usually mentioned by the Home Office or the Press, substantial numbers have also experienced physical and mental health problems and/or have attempted suicide, and many have suffered bereavements at an early age. These characteristics are well known (Cox and Pritchard 1995; Smith 1993). They are *descriptive* of the caseloads of probation officers as well as of the prison population. However, as West and Farrington (1973) showed, they are also *predictive*. We can identify, at a very early age, which young boys are likely to become the young persistent offenders, as well as the neighbourhoods and schools where they live and learn; yet we wait until they have become very damaged and damaging people before we address the issue.

The issue is, at bottom, one of social policy. To its credit, the Labour Government has committed itself to eliminating child poverty and has an agenda of social inclusiveness. But it seems politically impossible to acknowledge that these persistent offenders are the 'end point' of failures of parenting and of under-resourced social and educational intervention. One only has to read a series of pre-sentence reports to learn how chaotic are these offenders' backgrounds and how often they have been affected by events, such as the death of key figures in their childhood; to recognise that these are people driven by anger deriving from a sense of unmet need. One psychiatrist, working in a young offenders' institution, took a random sample of 12 inmates and, with their permission, gave them a relaxant drug. It enabled them to talk about their childhood in a way that normally they could not. All of them, these brash and frightening young men, told their stories in tears (personal communication).

None of this is recognised in the press releases from the Home Office. In press reports, any work that is done in the community by probation officers on the problems of offenders is often coupled with a mention of 'custody plus', or the return to prison of anyone, who does not cooperate. The word 'probation' is hardly mentioned. It is part of that 'liberal' legacy, whose name cannot be spoken. So the fight to prevent the name of the service being changed and to keep it separate from the prison service has, in effect, been bypassed. Offenders will, *de facto*, be dealt with in a seamless way by the penal services, partly in custody, partly in the community. The political ends, of presentation and of emphasising punishment, have been gained. This has to be set alongside the new optimism referred to earlier.

It is remarkable, given the resources which are now being allocated to the service, that the creation of the National Probation Service in April 2001 went entirely unremarked in the national media. This need not have been the case. Had Ministers wanted the public to know about their aspirations for the new service, they would have ensured a high-profile launch. Yet it seems that they have made a calculation that dealing with offenders in the community is a strategy that will harm them electorally. Does this silence matter so long as they continue to support the service in its work, however quietly; so long as they continue to resource the evaluation and accreditation of What Works programmes and fund the recruitment and training of probation officers? Yes, it does matter. We live in an age when 'branding' is of the highest consequence. Commercially, and in the voluntary sector, much attention is given to branding. Companies know that they have to grab attention before they can begin to sell; and once they have sold their product, the brand gives a guarantee of satisfaction, essential if customers are to return. Similarly, voluntary societies need recognition before they can attract donations and sign up long-term supporters. Business experience shows that there is only a fleeting moment to catch the attention of potential customers; if you miss the moment, you cannot begin to persuade. If the new National Probation Service does not establish a high profile then it cannot get into dialogue with members of the public. If there is no dialogue, there is no persuasion and no opportunity to move to giving a guarantee of satisfaction through good practice and addressing people's real worries. A failure to brand can have serious negative for effects, if the 'product' is not championed, do its supporters really believe in it? Is it really trustworthy? In the long term, the National Probation Service has to get public backing to give it legitimacy and support when things go wrong and when the next economic squeeze comes along. If Ministers will not do it, then chairs and chief officers must.

Further, we should try to understand why the service fought so hard to keep the name and to keep a separate service. But first we have to understand why there has been such a shift in penal policy. Richard Sennett's (1998) book, *The Corrosion of Character* is helpful in understanding this. In one passage, he describes a first-generation Italian immigrant into the USA and his son. The father had worked hard at the same job over many years. He had been strict with his children. He was intolerant of blacks and homosexuals. In all areas of his life, he sought to achieve security and stability. His son benefited from this and went to university, and now has a well-paid and responsible job. His very different life experience had led him to become a liberal 'in the generous American sense of caring about the poor and behaving well to minorities like blacks and homosexuals' (pp. 15–31). He had become ashamed of his father's intolerance.

At work, unlike his father, the son had had to become used to taking risks, to face uncertainty, to move and forgo the benefits of a rooted social life. He did not want to return to those circumscribed and strict values, yet he was afraid that his children would become involved in anti-social behaviour because they were not so closely supervised and were claiming for themselves the freedom that comes with the modern pattern of life: 'Like most of his peers, he loathes social parasites, embodied for him in the figure of the welfare mother who spends her checks on booze and drugs. He has also become a believer in fixed, Draconian standards of community behaviour, as opposed to those values of "liberal parenting", which parallel the open-ended meeting at work.'

The son had become a 'cultural conservative', which is a way of capturing 'an idealised symbolic community' that might restore some coherence to a life that has been fractured by the risk taking, geographical mobility and competitiveness demanded by the new global economy. This cultural conservatism is fueled by both economic insecurity and by the fear of failure. It is not the case

> that if we have enough evidence of material achievement we won't be haunted by feelings of insufficiency or inadequacy . . . One of the reasons it is hard to assuage feelings of failure with dollars is that failure can be of a deeper kind — failure to make one's life cohere, failure to realise something precious in oneself, failure to live rather than merely exist. (Sennett 1998, *ibid.*)

Our British experience is not the same as this. Nevertheless, the mass redundancies, the foreclosures on mortgages, the repeated advice to look for transferable skills not a job for life — all so familiar over the last 20 years and affecting the middle classes, whose lives had been built upon achieving solid respectability — have brought about a similar acknowledgement of the precarious nature of modern life. It is accompanied by the same quest for coherence, the same cultural conservatism, most cogently articulated by the *Daily Mail*.

Offenders are a demonstration of failure. There is little sense of 'There but for the grace of God, go I'. Rather, a clear boundary has to be established between success and failure, between participation in the system and apparent rejection of it. The boundary asserts the gulf between a belief in that 'idealised symbolic community', with its comforting sense of coherence, and those people who seem to have rejected it and forged an alternative lifestyle of their own. We are driven to such speculation because the political and media response to the problem of crime goes beyond rationality to the extent that rehabilitative solutions are rejected, even if they can be shown to have some effect. Even restorative justice is difficult to get into the public debate. The views of the Lord Chief Justice, mentioned at the beginning of this chapter, are repudiated.

Another, very different, modern development is the effect of living in what we might call the digital age. The power of computers is pervasive. All information can be captured and communicated through a series of on/off pulses, whether it be a letter, a telephone conversation or a symphony. Further, this digital approach applies to the *program*, i.e., the set of rules and commands, that orders the information. To put it another way, both the vocabulary and the grammar of this new language are expressed in digital form. Such a powerful technique is bound to affect our ways of thinking very profoundly. It is surely not simply a coincidence that university degrees are now frequently based on a modular rather than a strictly sequential and cumulative curriculum; Nor that NVQs, job descriptions and job appraisals focus on discrete competences, which apparently can be measured.

Neither, within criminal justice, can it be coincidental that the What Works programmes are built up of a series of modules, each of which has to be taught in a consistent, replicable fashion regardless of the personality of the educator. One of the attractions of the method is that it does not necessarily have to be delivered by a probation officer — a probation service officer or a prison officer can do it just as well, so little room is there for responsiveness or discretion. Similarly, the Pre-Sentence Report in future will be very largely concerned with the OASys prediction of future offending. Even HM Chief Inspector of Probation (Smith 2000) has indicated that OASys may become the subject of attack on human rights grounds, presumably infringing Article 7 of the European Convention forbidding arbitrary punishment, in that it could be used as a prediction against which other factors would have no standing. (It is, of course, only an indicator, the implications of which have to be addressed both by the offender and by the probation officer.) And, in accordance with these developments, probation records no longer present a strong narrative account of what has been happening, but a standardised, brief and, at worst, a 'tick box' codification of the offender's performance.

A recent example, told to the author by a member of a mental health tribunal (personal communication), was of a man under supervision who committed a murder. He was attending regularly at his What Works programme, but little notice was taken of his alcoholism. Yet the receptionists at the office had seen that he was often as 'high as a kite', as well as being distressed at his own inability to control himself. This was not picked up until it was too late. The tribunal noted that not only had there been a failure of communication but, more importantly, the whole man had not been seen, and his treatment had been as fragmented as his personality.

This is not to imply that there has been no progress. As a former chief probation officer, who led a re-fashioning of practice so that the majority of people on probation went through a What Works programme, this author is committed to this approach. Neither would a return to diffuse, often vague and sometimes purely imaginative recording based on a threadbare psychodynamic approach be welcome. Nevertheless, a note of caution should be sounded. We should not expect achievement of some of the more optimistic forecasts — of a big decrease in the rate of offending of those who go through the programmes — unless the programmes are also accompanied by an equal concentration on offenders' social needs, especially of education, housing and health. Probation officers, too, need time to work with offenders as persons who have a need to understand the narrative of their life. A narrative is a way of achieving coherence and understanding. The need of offenders for a coherent rationale to understand and control what has happened to them is just as great as for the rest of us.

The forces of cultural conservatism and those of the digital revolution are very different and sometimes contradictory. Yet the tendency of the former to stereotype offenders and the dangers of fragmentation in the latter can both lead to, and perhaps reinforce each other in, a de-personalisation of the offender. To these must added a third factor.

The new service is tasked to focus on the punishment of the offender and the protection of the public. The welfare of the offender comes into the picture only in so far as his rehabilitation will contribute to public safety. Generally speaking, any organisation which has been set up to serve the interests of an abstract 'public', rather than being at least equally concerned with the well-being and dignity of its charges, has ended with public scandals. The continuing failure of so many prisons is the prime cautionary example. The scandals which have beset so many public welfare institutions, such as psychiatric hospitals, children's and old people's homes, underline the danger. Ostensibly, such institutions have had a duty of care for the ill, the abandoned and the vulnerable; yet even so, the human rights of the patients or the residents have been overridden. That stems from their being perceived as troublesome rather than troubled, or as being in some sense 'undeserving', or from the view that the public needed to be protected from them. The ethical rule of 'respect for persons' is, in the end, the only bulwark against such oppressive practices. It is one the new probation service must maintain.

For three decades, probation officers have been seconded to work in prisons. Occasionally, probation officers have brought injustices or bad treatment to light. But we do have to face the profoundly worrying issue that the service has been working in institutions which have been found by HM Chief Inspector of Prisons to be places which do not come anywhere near the minimum standards of care, or even cleanliness, laid down by the rules. As a chief probation officer, this author had regular meetings with a succession of governors in Portland young offender institution; I seconded astute and dedicated senior probation officers over a period of 15 years; with one of them I held a series of meetings with young offenders in Portland to find out how their aftercare could be improved. Yet at no time did we suspect (nor would the governors have tolerated such abuses had they evidence of them) the kind of behaviour which led to one of the most damning of the HM Chief Inspector of Prisons' reports (2000) and to a police investigation of violence against inmates (Dodd 2000). This is not an isolated example. If the probation service is to become, *de facto*, a branch of the prison service within the community, where will it stand on these issues? Will it be able to act as a whistleblower more effectively than this author was able to? If offenders are consumed with anger at the way they are treated, as the HM Chief Inspector of Prisons suggests in his latest report on Winson Green (1999), they will see no reason to modify their own behaviour. For as the chilling last line of *The Corrosion Of Character* observes, a regime 'which provides human beings no deep reasons to care about one another cannot long preserve its legitimacy' (Sennett 1998, p. 148).

It is ironic that a service with its roots in advising, assisting and befriending the offender, is, from July 2001, subject to the scrutiny of the Ombudsman for Prisons to ensure that the power exercised by probation staff is not abused.

The traditional probation service grew out of a voluntary movement, which was committed to a belief that even the most hardened criminal ought to be treated as a human being worthy of respect, despite acts which might rightly put him beyond the pale of living in the community. This is an uncomfortable stance to maintain, especially when there is so much fear of crime, but unless it is maintained, the fight to retain the name of probation will have been pointless. Indeed, the fight to maintain the name was indicative of that deep-rooted belief.

This belief is the main bulwark against the real danger of a coarsening in its attitudes and practice, becoming less sensitive to the often horrendous childhood experiences of offenders, less conscious of their rights, less willing to be open to their pain, which is, in the end, the only way to help them find a way out of the impasse into which they have fallen. This has to be demonstrated in the ways in which staff actually treat offenders. Traditionally, this has been through 'the relationship'. Often this has been put forward, to the despair of practice teachers, as though it is an end in itself. Of course, it is not. It is the means through which offenders are enabled to learn new skills, both in practical matters and in the way they handle their own relationships. It aims to make sense of their experiences so that they can begin to understand and control them, rather than reacting impulsively and angrily to the pain and distress they bring. The What Works programmes can bring real benefits to most offenders because they focus on controlling immediate impulses - 'Count to ten before you say anything' — and modulating responses to others. Offenders begin to have some empathy with what other people expect.

The danger will be that this learning will not stick unless there is someone alongside offenders who will encourage them through the difficult patches, support them when they fail and congratulate them on their successes. This does not have to be a probation officer, though, since probation caseloads consist of the most damaged and damaging people in society, this is a very demanding role, requiring insight and resilience. Probation officers have found it hard to adapt to the role of a case manager, as though it in some way diminished their casework skills rather than enhancing them. It will certainly, in the future, be the key role, along with assessment, in maximising the effectiveness of the service.

Recently, this author took part in some of the interviews for Continuing Members of the new probation boards. The way in which a number of people wanted to continue because they had developed 'an affection' for the service was striking. This is a very remarkable term to use in relation to a statutory service. It reflects admiration for the dogged *care* which probation officers showed for their *clients*. These 'forbidden' words are used because they contain a sense of the person for whom they felt themselves responsible and whose interests they had to take into account — nuances which are quite absent from the terms now recommended to describe people under supervision. Nor were probation officers seen as sentimental in this, or as betraying the real need to protect the public. Rather they were at one with the comment of a senior judge: 'We need the probation service to express the enlightened and compassionate part of the criminal justice system' (Smith 2000). And, to take another example, Lord Allen (1995), a former Permanent Secretary at the Home Office, referred to 'safeguarding the probation service' (p. 4). All these statements point to something *precious* — a word with the dominant meaning of great value, but a subsidiary one of being affected and over-fastidious, rather like the probation service itself, often betrayed by an over-zealous defence of values and an insufficient recognition of the need for effectiveness. But the large truth is that it was the only organisation in the criminal justice system that was explicitly set up to advise, assist and befriend the offender. And it is these qualities which elicit affection, the recognition of something unique and the importance of safeguarding it.

In 1995, Jerome Miller, who did so much to reform juvenile justice in Massachusetts, addressed a conference on punishment:

What might be of greatest interest about California for people here in Great Britain, which has still maintained some decency and integrity in its probation service, is that in California, of the 130,000 persons incarcerated, approximately 40,000–50,000 are there because they have technically violated the conditions of their probation or parole. They are not there because they have committed a new offence sufficient to warrant a court hearing or a conviction, but they have kicked off (*sic*) the probation officer. They have had a dirty urn (*sic*) or they've moved without permission, or married without permission, or haven't kept appointments, or haven't gone to their Alcoholics Anonymous meetings. Consider events like those and you have some measure of how the fine traditions of probation have been totally degraded. (Miller 1995, p. 11).

The ever-stricter conditions now being applied to probation in England and Wales, risk the same outcome. They are part of a penal policy increasingly moulded by the fear of crime and the need to punish the offender. These are not the roots out of which the probation service grew. But those roots run deep. Enlightenment and compassion will flower because judges and magistrates will continue to expect probation officers to keep those elements alive within the criminal justice system. They will flower because we all need to see, within our public services, a respect for our common humanity, despite all the modern pressures towards fragmentation and depersonalisation. And so, justice may be tempered with mercy.

3 Probation, Citizenship and Public Service

David Faulkner

INTRODUCTION

This chapter examines the political and social context in which the National Probation Service became established under the Criminal Justice and Court Services Act 2000; the influences which shaped the Act and are likely to shape the service's development in the future; and the professional values and relationships which will help the service to respond to those influences, or, if necessary, to resist them.

Writing in the first edition of *Probation — Working for Justice* (Ward and Lacey, 1995), David Ward and others described the transition from a period of relative optimism about the probation service's prospects, influence and status in the early 1990s, to the Conservative Government's apparent contempt for the service and what it stood for by the time the book was published in 1995 (Ward 1995). The change of Government in 1997 led to another period of relative optimism, reflected, for example, in the proceedings of the colloquium in *New Politics, New Probation* held in Oxford at the end of that year (Faulkner and Gibbs 1995), although it quickly became apparent that Ministerial criticism of the service's failure in its duty to protect the public was to continue unabated. This time, however, the service's experience was not one of Ministerial indifference and a willingness to see it relegated to the margins of the criminal justice process, but of a strong political determination to transform the service into something different. The difference was to be seen in organisation — a national service under central direction; in its aims and purpose — punishment and public protection rather than rehabilitation or support for offenders; and professional culture — much less tolerance of variations in performance, whether by offenders or by members of staff. How the difference would come to be expressed, in working methods, professional relationships and styles of management, was still unclear at the time of writing. These are matters which are still to be decided, either as questions of policy or more probably by a process of practice, experience and adjustment. How they are decided is likely to have a greater impact on the service, and on the service's work for its stakeholders and for the country and its citizens more generally, than the detail of the statutory provisions contained in the Criminal and Court Services Act 2000. The influences on that process, and the service's response to them, are therefore supremely important.

NEO-LIBERALISM AND NEW MANAGERIALISM

Two influences over the last ten or 15 years have dominated criminal justice in Great Britain, in the English-speaking developed world, and to a lesser extent in continental Europe. They are what academics call neo-liberalism and the new public management, or managerialism. Both are part of 'late modernity' (Garland 2001; Stenson and Sullivan 2001). Neo-liberalism is about the decline of representative institutions and traditional forms of authority; about markets, not just as a medium of exchange but also as a source of authority; about individualism and consumerism; about single-issue politics and the changing character of political parties and political allegiances. 'New managerialism' is about targets, performance indicators, competition, downsizing, contracts and privatisation. Both emphasise safety and the avoidance of risk, personal and public protection, personal responsibility and social control. Both claim to be pragmatic, evidence-based, quantified and free from dogma, but they also effectively impose their own political, professional or moral values. They take a utilitarian and instrumental view of criminal justice. They are inclined to favour the 'rights' of the majority, as against those of suspects, defendants or offenders. They set great store by the use of new technology. They are linked with the 'new criminology' and 'actuarial justice' (Feeley and Simon 1992; Walton and Young 1998). Their exponents try to give a sense of progress and modernisation, but they also convey a sometimes frightening sense of inevitability, of impatience with any suggestion of criticism, and of powerlessness in the face of public opinion and globalisation.

MODERNISING CRIMINAL JUSTICE

This set of influences has resulted in the politicisation of crime and criminal justice; in a need for governments to 'modernise' the system and demonstrate its 'effectiveness' in reducing crime and protecting the public; in governments' readiness to accept that criminal justice is 'failing', while they claim to have the means to put it right; in what may nevertheless be an unrealistic view that the criminal justice system can and should be expected to achieve results in controlling crime and changing behaviour; and, more generally, in an 'exclusionary', rather than 'inclusive', view of society and citizenship. Robert Sullivan (2001) argues that for 300 years 'liberal' states have practised a schizophrenic form of criminal justice — one for the privileged, another for the underclasses. Although a government may claim to be committed to 'evidence-based policy', David Garland's judgement of the situation in Great Britain and the United States is that

> Crime strategies and criminological ideas are not adopted because they are known to solve problems. The evidence runs out well before the effects can be known with any certainty. They are adopted and they succeed because they characterise problems and identify solutions in ways that fit with dominant culture and the power structure upon which it rests. (2001, p. 26)

Subtle, but often significant, changes have taken place in the use of language. 'Liberal' has become a term of abuse. Clichés and 'sound-bite' are used to give an appearance of activity, while concealing gaps in thought. Protecting the public, and efficiency and effectiveness in providing that protection, takes precedence over freedom and justice. The word 'freedom' is hardly used. 'Justice' is used more often in its secondary sense, as the process of law or the exercise of legal vengeance, rather than in its primary and substantive or normative sense, as the quality or principle of justice or fairness in relation to all the elements in the situation and all the persons involved in it. In the secondary sense, justice can be seen as an instrument of the state, even of the Government; in its primary sense, justice stands in its own right.

David Garland has described how attempts to control crime have historically focused either on criminal acts or events, or on criminals as people. The emphasis has been different at different times. Crime has to be prevented, victims deserve to be supported, and those who commit crime have to be dealt with and sometimes (but not always) punished. The first is mainly the business of wider social policies and specific programmes of prevention and support; the second is the business of criminal justice. The distinction is not absolute; and it cannot be rigidly sustained in professional and operational practice. Just as a country misdirects itself if it supposes that it can resolve the problems of crime by programmes of social and economic reform, so it is misguided if it tries to resolve them by concentrating on the criminal justice process and focusing all its attention on individual so-called criminals. It must consider the nature of society as a whole, and of the relationships and responsibilities within it. No service should be restricted to one role to the exclusion of the other, and the great strength, and value, of the probation service is that it can perform both.

Tony Bottoms (2001) has identified the four types of influence or mechanism which he sees as underpinning law-abiding behaviour: those which are instrumental or prudential (incentives or deterrence); constraints, which may be physical or socio-structural (for example, most forms of situational crime prevention); normative influences based on belief, attachments or relationships, or legitimacy; and those which are based on habit or routine. He argues that all four are interconnected; each will need to be supported by any or all of the others; and normative influences are pivotal.

Even if the criminal law and the criminal justice process are not the principal, or most effective, instruments for preventing crime and supporting victims, they are still a uniquely important part of the apparatus of the state. They set and enforce the framework within which the state controls its citizens and regulates their behaviour. Criminal justice is not only about pursuing, convicting and punishing offenders, it is also about the exercise of the state's powers of interference, intrusion, control and ultimately of coercion, and the limits which should be placed upon those powers. In a liberal democracy, the state's possession of those powers, the Government's policies for using them and their actual use in practice, must be proportionate, democratic, accountable and above all legitimate. Criminal justice, or what David Garland calls the criminal justice state, must not become Leviathan (Garland 2001; Hobbes 1651). The primary purpose of criminal justice is not to prevent crime, nor even to protect the public, unless protection is understood as the defence of freedom in a sense which includes, but which is wider than, freedom from crime and fear of crime. Its purpose is to achieve justice.

There are now signs of a reaction against the harsher forms of neo-liberalism and managerialism — of an attempt to identify some larger principles, a sense of social and political values, a vision which is more inspirational and capable of giving a more coherent sense of national direction. The Blair Administration in this country and the Clinton Administration in the United States tried to do that with 'The Third Way'. They do not seem to have been very successful. The Third Way has been described as 'ideological cross-dressing', and it has seemed more often to be a justification for ambiguity and compromise than a political philosophy in its own right. But two themes are emerging from the present debate, which may offer a more promising sense of progress. They are citizenship and public service. Both have important implications for criminal justice, and especially for probation.

CITIZENSHIP

Until the mid-1990s, the idea of citizenship seemed rather old-fashioned. It was used in the Citizen's Charter to depict the citizen as consumer or customer of services, consistent with the market-orientated, neo-liberal politics of the time. Before that it had been associated with the social and economic rights of the welfare state (Marshall 1977), and earlier still it had been associated with the Enlightenment and the social contract. It was to be found in Aristotle and the Greek city-state.

Citizenship was rediscovered in the mid-1990s, when it came to be linked with other ideas such as community, social inclusion, social capital, civil society, human rights and responsibility. These ideas, and the writers who promoted them (for example, Giddens 1998), informed the thinking of the Labour Party during its later years in opposition, and a version of them is still prominent in the Labour Government's policies and thinking today. A central feature is the balance between rights and responsibilities.

On the view of citizenship which is now emerging, citizens are entitled to personal safety, respect for their private lives and to freedom of expression. All these are human rights protected by the European Convention on Human Rights and by the Human Rights Act 1998. Citizens should also be able to expect decent public services; social support when it is needed; a safe and unpolluted environment; and protection from crime, from improper discrimination, and from corruption, oppression or abuse of power by the state. In return, citizens have a duty to obey the law and pay taxes, and a responsibility to show consideration and respect for others, to support themselves and their families, and to care for their children.

Citizenship is also about taking an active part in society. The Government is urging citizens to 'do their bit' for society through various forms of voluntary or charitable work. Lay justice — both lay magistrates and juries — will be an important feature of the debate following Lord Justice Auld's review of the criminal courts. 'Community justice', or the involvement of ordinary citizens in measures to deal with crime and people who commit it, is one of the ideas associated with the various forms of restorative justice. It is an important part of citizenship, in the sense that citizens should themselves take some responsibility for dealing with the problems of crime in their communities, and for the reintegration of those who commit it. They should not see that responsibility as someone else's business — a matter for the state, or for the police, courts, and the prison and probation services — or as a commodity for which people should pay, if they can afford it. It is interesting that this wider view of citizenship was expressed in connection with the death of Damiola Taylor in South London, but tragic that it needed an event of that kind for it to be taken seriously.

The commercial sector has similar responsibilities. It is useful, but not enough, to support good causes with cheques or sponsorship. Companies should also conduct their businesses in ways which are socially responsible — in methods of production, marketing and employment, including the employment of ex-offenders. Banks and insurance companies have responsibilities to provide affordable services in run-down areas and to disadvantaged individuals. Pharmaceutical and oil companies have those responsibilities on a global scale.

A more active view of citizenship would also emphasise citizens' rights to a voice in the governance of their country and their local communities; and to opportunities to influence the nature and quality of the public services which are provided on their behalf, or important decisions which will affect them. In some services there is a sense of 'democratic deficit' (Hutton 2000), but the Government is encouraging greater consultation, involvement and participation, for example, through the provisions of the Local Government Act 2000 and the guidance issued under the Act; and the Public Administration Committee of the House of Commons issued an important report on *Innovations in Citizen Participation in Government* (House of Commons 2001a).

This account of citizenship might lead to dispute about its practical applications, but it is not particularly controversial. There are, however, within it two contrasting views, which might be called the 'open' and 'closed', or 'inclusive' and 'exclusionary' interpretations of citizenship. The 'open' view values ideas, such as equality, empowerment, tolerance, trust, reciprocity, respect for diversity, reintegration and restorative justice. Citizenship and the rights and responsibilities which go with it, are part of a person's status and identity as a human being; they are not conferred by the state and they are not to be qualified or taken away. The role of the state is to secure those rights and to facilitate the performance of those responsibilities. The state, civil society and individual citizens have responsibilities of care and support towards people, who are vulnerable, disadvantaged, or at risk.

The 'closed' view is more conditional and authoritarian. It emphasises security, protection and the avoidance of risk. It is more ready to blame, stigmatise, disqualify and punish. It implies that there are outsiders, even an enemy, who do not belong. The role of the state is not so much to facilitate the exercise of rights as to enforce the performance of responsibilities. Those who fail in their performance no longer deserve to be full citizens and can be disqualified from exercising the rights of citizenship or enjoying its benefits — social security benefits, driving licences, passports, the right to vote, even their own property if they cannot prove that it has been lawfully acquired. Protection is for those who deserve it, against the danger of or nuisance from those who do not.

These are all current or recent issues in England and Wales. Both views can be seen in the language of politics and in the policies of the present Government. For the probation service, the challenge is to apply the active and inclusive view of citizenship in all its work with offenders, and to promote it in their communities.

PUBLIC SERVICE

Public service and public services are what give citizenship reality and content. They are also the link between the citizen and the state. But public service can mean different things. It can be a career, like nursing or teaching and (still perhaps) probation; an activity, like jury service; or an organisation or institution, such as the probation service.

Public service organisations take different forms and have different definitions. Definitions are important in law in deciding whether the organisation is liable to judicial review, and they may become important in deciding an organisation's position under the Human Rights Act 1998. Public services include publicly-owned services, such as the probation service; privately-owned companies providing public services, such as the security industry, privatised utilities and railway companies; and voluntary organisations providing services on their own account, or under contract from government or a public authority. They all have different relationships with citizens, with the state and with the Government of the day. One characteristic is that public services matter not only to those people who may be using them at any one time, but also to society, the country and communities as a whole. A judgement of their success depends on more than the bottom line in their balance sheet. They are part of the apparatus of the state, but they are not simply at the disposal of the Government, still less an instrument for maintaining a form of social order which the Government finds acceptable. They belong to the citizens, whom they exist to serve.

Public services have been much influenced by neo-liberalism and new public managerialism, including the performance culture of targets, indicators, 'best value', and 'evidence-based' practice. That culture has some admirable features, but it can also undermine integrity and generate a culture of blame and lack of trust, resembling the closed view of citizenship. There are some signs of a reaction against the new public management, as there has been against some of the other ideas which became prominent in the 1980s. They are so far to be seen more in individual expressions of dissatisfaction with the police and prison services than in any new Government policies or new developments in managerial practice (Neyroud and Beckley 2001; Bryans 2001). Voluntary organisations may be less reticent (or less intimidated) than statutory services if they find their role in partnerships and as providers of public services frustrated by an overbearing, top-down bureaucracy of competition, benchmarking and performance indicators.

These indicators have brought changes in the culture, dynamics and sometimes the role of public services, perhaps nowhere more than in the probation service. The situation is complex, and there is no consistent pattern. In the police, there is still a strong emphasis on local accountability and on devolution to basic command units, while the National Probation Service has been unified under Ministerial direction and central control. The police are becoming more of a social service, while the probation service is becoming more an agency of law enforcement.

This is a difficult and confusing time for public services of all kinds. Their work is increasingly a matter for public and political attention and often criticism, and their identities and values are being merged into a common, grey culture of performance, management and quantitative measurement. But difficult questions are now being asked by the Public Administration Committee of the House of Commons among others (House of Commons 2001b). Those questions are about leadership — about the relationship between professional leadership and political authority, and between leadership and management; about accountability — to central or local government, or to appointed boards or authorities; and about legitimacy. Legitimacy is that quality which gives services like the probation service, police and the prison service their authority and their right to public respect, and which causes people to obey the law and to comply with rules and instructions, even when it may be inconvenient or against their immediate interests to do so (Tyler 1990; Beetham 1991; Bottoms and Hay 1996). It is what enables them to operate by consent, as they must do in any democracy. A necessary condition for legitimacy is a relationship of mutual trust, confidence and respect between the service and the citizens whom it serves. Citizens often feel that sense in respect of their schools and hospitals, less often for their courts or for their police, and hardly ever for probation or prisons. Legitimacy is closely linked to justice, and neither can be sustained without the other.

IMPLICATIONS FOR CRIMINAL JUSTICE

An important conclusion to be drawn from this analysis is that although the probation service is part of the criminal justice system and its work needs to be integrated with that of other services in the system, its work should not be confined to administering the criminal justice process. Like the police, it should be an agency, as much of social intervention and support as it is of law enforcement. If it is to be successful in its function of preventing crime, including re-offending, its work has to include both types of activity. And it has to work not only with offenders, but also with communities and civil society.

These ideas of citizenship and public service show the need for criminal justice to focus on:

(a)   people as citizens, on their rights and responsibilities and their involvement and participation in their communities;

(b)   offenders and their families as people in the same spirit;

(c)   public institutions and services, not as agents of government but as citizens' servants and representatives;

(d)   the role of the state to facilitate, encourage, protect and, when necessary, to regulate but not to manage;

(e)   the role and capacity of civil society to support citizens and communities independently of any intervention by the state.

Services have to acknowledge the utilitarian or democratic dilemma that the wishes and interests of the comfortable majority must not prejudice the position of a less fortunate minority (Rawls 1973). There is a similar dilemma in services and institutions (especially prisons) over the balance between the needs of the individual and those of the institution as a whole. Both are more acute if they become politicised, or there is a shortage of resources.

APPLICATION TO PROBATION

Some of the implications for probation practice may seem obvious, perhaps even old-fashioned, but they are still worth repeating.

Arrangements for offenders need to be individualised, varied and related to local conditions and circumstances. They should be closely integrated with services in the community, and especially with those for health, education, social services and housing. They should have regard to the whole person, including the person's relationships with their family and communities, and, where relevant, their schools or employers; and they should take account of the legitimate interests of victims. Staffing arrangements should be flexible, allow for greater movement between services, and accommodate a wide range of professional experience and disciplines. Consistency of treatment should be maintained within a national legal framework, national standards and a consistent approach to sentencing, but there should be scope for local initiative, innovation and development. A proper emphasis on 'what works' and on monitoring and evaluation should not result in a 'single track' approach to supervision, especially while the empirical base for What Works still needs more assessment, development and research. An emphasis on accreditation should not discourage probation officers from exploring new ideas or developing new schemes, or prevent them from introducing relevant programmes — for example, to deal with racist behaviour and attitudes — because they do not match the criteria. An emphasis on record-keeping and the bureaucracy of performance measurement should not drive probation officers into offices and away from the homes, the streets and the places of work or entertainment of those for whom they have responsibility. Programmes should provide opportunities for recognition and rewards for success, as well as punishment for breaches of conditions.

Looking beyond its work with individual offenders, the service should have a more general influence in its various communities, helping to generate and support a sense of citizenship and of civil and social responsibility, and to promote the projects, programmes and activities that can give it practical effect. It should help its communities to invest in social capital and to mobilise the resources of civil society. Like other public services, it must be fully accountable, and its lines of accountability must run in several directions vertically, connecting the services' managers and practitioners with government departments, Ministers and Parliament; and horizontally, with other organisations and interests and the citizens whom they serve. Ministers' concern that the service should be accountable to central government and responsive to the national responsibilities which they wish the service to undertake, must be matched by the local understanding, support and commitment which are needed if Parliament's legislation and the Government's own policies are successfully to be put into effect.

The service should also accept some responsibility, and some accountability, towards those whom it supervises. In particular, there should be formal duties of care and support and standards to which

should conform. The Children (Leaving Care) Act 2000
a possible model. To give those duties and standards statutory
force would give formal expression to offenders' continuing status as
citizens.

A modern probation service needs the outward-looking problem-
solving orientation, the skills of listening and consultation, and the
ability to manage conflicts, tensions and ambiguities, which have been
discussed in the previous chapters. It needs to exercise skills not only in
relation to offenders under its supervision or about whom it is writing
reports, but also in relation to its stakeholders and partners (other
services, voluntary or community organisations), communities and
victims of crime. The service must establish a sense of identification and
understanding between itself and local communities, and also a sense
of ownership and responsibility on the part of those communities
themselves. It is needed not only because it is the means of generating
the sense of public confidence which is so important both for the
Government and for probation itself; but also because it helps to
mobilise the resources of civil society and the sense of civic responsibility which are, or should be, important elements in the Government's
own thinking.

Racial equality is the subject of Chapter 8. The probation service, like
all public services, must acknowledge the inadequacy of the 'colour
blind' approach, which at one time dominated race relations: it must
recognise that more is needed than to prevent discrimination; it must
work actively to promote racial equality, as it is required to do under the
Race Relations (Amendment) Act 2000; and it must positively value
cultural diversity (Commission on the Future of Multi-Ethnic Britain
2000). It must do all these things, not because they benefit a group of
people who have in the past been thought of as 'ethnic minorities', but
because they are part of the service's responsibility to the country as a
whole and all citizens, whatever their characteristics or background,
deserve equal respect.

A sense of local ownership and responsibility will be especially
important if restorative justice is to be developed, as many people now
hope. John Harding (2000) and Barbara Hudson (2001a) have described
the role which a modern, reorganised and revitalised probation service
might play in community (and especially restorative) justice, and the
conditions which would have to be satisfied for it to do so. David Smith
and John Stewart (1997) have examined the effects of social exclusion

on young people supervised by the probation service; they have suggested strategies for more inclusionary and integrative practice, and have considered what local structures might be needed to put them into effect. As well as the changes in attitude, understanding and behaviour, for which the proponents for restorative justice are hoping among offenders, victims and communities, one of the greatest benefits may be in the culture of the criminal justice services themselves.

PROBATION, LEGITIMACY AND JUSTICE

Neither the service nor the Government will realise their ambitions for the new structures for probation unless two requirements are satisfied. These are for legitimacy and justice. The two are closely connected, and neither can be sustained without the other. Necessary conditions for both include the following:

(a) The powers available to the state and its institutions and agencies must be exercised on behalf of its citizens as a whole, and not for the benefit of any particular sector or interest.

(b) Those powers, and the use which is made of them, must be proportionate to the purpose they are intended to serve. If the state or its agents wish to prevent people from doing what they want to do, it is for the state, and not for the citizen, to justify itself.

(c) Proposals for extending those powers, and policies for their use, must be based on a rigorous and honest examination and analysis, and on well-informed consultation and debate. They must have the consent, the support and the engagement of those who will be affected by them and who will have to exercise them.

(d) Policy and practice must observe the principles of equity, consistency and proportionality, and of equality of consideration and respect for all citizens, including especially members of minority groups.

(e) Decision-making authorities must be properly constituted and competent for their purpose and the functions they have to perform. They must be accountable to the citizens whom they exist to serve, through mechanisms which are appropriate and effective, which include mechanisms located at the most local practicable level. Citizens have not only the right, but also the responsibility to hold those authorities to account.

(f) Decision-making processes must be open, accessible and similarly accountable. They must be operated scrupulously and with integrity.

(g) All citizens are entitled to dignity, decency and respect in all their dealing with agents of the state, and to protection from injury, loss or abuse of power or process.

(h) Any interference with citizens' liberty, lives or privacy must be within a framework of legality, established by domestic and international law, including especially the European Convention on Human Rights, with safeguards and effective opportunities for redress.

These conditions will be set by a combination of statutes, organisational structure and administrative directions. Within that framework, probation officers will have to resolve conflicts and reconcile priorities. Some conflicts will be ethical — for example, between public protection and respect for the individual, or between equality and diversity; some will be professional, perhaps between speed or economy and consultation or accountability; some will be managerial to meet different targets or satisfy different budgeting requirements. Risks must be managed and not simply avoided. How the conflicts are resolved will largely depend on probation officers' own ethics, integrity and culture, their professional wisdom and culture, their sense of confidence and trust, and the extent to which they have discretion to apply their own professional wisdom and judgement.

This chapter draws on material assembled for the author's Kenneth Younger Memorial Lecture, given in Edinburgh on 12 February 2001. The arguments are developed more fully in his book, *Crime, State and Citizen: A Field Full of Folk*, Winchester: Waterside Press, 2001.

4 The Social and Criminal Policy Context

Cedric Fullwood

INTRODUCTION

Over the past hundred years, the lifetime of the probation service, the astute observer would need to see legislative and policy developments determining the direction and development of the probation service in a wider context, encompassing social policies as well as penal, criminal and civil justice. Overall the service has been weak at observing this principle, leading at certain times to an insular quality in its standing and contribution to these wider developments.

The last decade has witnessed great improvements in this regard. During this period, senior representatives of the service have been members of all the major reviews and consultative bodies set up by government and independent foundations to consider improvements and changes to how crime and breakdown in our communities are tackled. Senior probation managers were members of, and made substantial contributions to, the Carlisle Review of Parole, the Morgan Report of the Standing Conference on Crime Prevention, the Criminal Justice Consultative Council, the Trial Issues Group, the Task Force on Youth Justice, the Sentencing Advisory Panel, and a variety of national, independent sector initiatives. In addition, senior staff have been seconded to head up women's prisons policy in the Prison Service

Headquarters, into the Social Exclusion Unit at the Cabinet Office, as well as the modernisation programme for the future of the probation service based at the Home Office. The contribution of previous chief probation officers in other spheres is evidenced by their becoming (the first) Chief Inspector of Prisons, Chief Social Services Inspector, Chair of the Commission for Racial Equality, Chief Executive of the National Society for the Protection of Children, Vice-Chair of the National Association for the Care and Rehabilitation of Offenders, and special advisers/experts to criminological committees of the Council of Europe.

Developments in the probation service have frequently been difficult to set in traditional policy contexts, and consequently to communicate clearly to the wider criminal justice community of interests, never mind the general public and the media. At its very inception, a tussle between rehabilitation and punishment was in evidence. When the Probation of Offenders Act 1907 was being implemented, a nervous correspondent wrote the following year to the *Justice of the Peace* with the request for the following clarification: 'will you kindly say if, in your opinion, a court may order a child to be whipped and also put him on probation for a term?' (*Justice of the Peace* 1908, p. 165). The reply came back: 'the point is not free from doubt; but in our opinion, they cannot do so.' The last decade of the same century was marked, some would say irretrievably, by a debate about 'Punishment in the Community' and the role of the service.

At the beginning of the twentieth century, the fledgling probation service grappled with the operational implications of its first real legislative base and its rallying call 'to advise, assist and befriend'. The voluntary workers from the various Christian and temperance movements struggled with the tension between professional paid workers and their vocational calling. However, the policy context, even in those days, was much wider. The Gladstone Report of 1895 on the state of prisons led to a new form of institutional penal training, which eventually took its name from the village in Kent, Borstal, where the experiment started. The issue was: should young offenders stay longer inside (than the offence or their circumstances would merit) in order to allow 'training'? A hundred years later, the proposition is: should offenders stay inside longer for the 'protection of the public'? Senior civil servants visited the United States to bring back ideas to reform and rehabilitate in the community. There were other, more sinister policy contexts, which Professor David Garland has detailed in his book

Punishment and Welfare — in particular, his chapter on social security and eugenics (Garland 1985). Anyone interested in the history of penal strategies in the late nineteenth century should read Garland's book; and that history, especially as far as young offenders is concerned, is followed through in Victor Bailey's book *Delinquency and Citizenship: reclaiming the young offender 1914–1948* (Bailey 1987). Treatment and training were the focus rather than 'working for justice'.

At the start of the twenty-first century, the new and first Director of the National Probation Service for England and Wales, Eithne Wallis, entitles her strategic vision for the new national service as 'A New Choreography' (Wallis 2001). The context of this statement is clear early on in the document, where it states that the National Probation Service operates within the Government's Correctional Policy Framework, contributing primarily to two Home Office aims:

(a)   delivery of justice through effective and efficient investigating, prosecution, trial and sentencing, and through support of victims;

(b)   the effective execution of the sentences of the courts so as to reduce re-offending and protect the public.

The National Director's vision is set within an ethical framework, and emphasis is given to fewer victims, better protected and given real information and access to the process of justice. The work of the service is set in the context of community safety strategies, and high priority is given to fair and equal responses to all sections of our communities. Apart from the expected references to criminal justice legislation, there is equal stress given to the reform of the Mental Health Act, public safety, dangerous offenders and the joint review by Home Office and Department of Health of the severe personality disordered offender. Drug policies and their overlap with the work of the service also receive prominence.

The structural changes affecting the new National Probation Service are partly fashioned by the wider context of the realignment of criminal justice boundaries (bringing co-terminosity to police, probation, Crown Prosecution and magistrates areas), together with a lighter regional framework linked to the regional Government Offices. The redesigned Area Criminal Justice Strategy Groups, most now with local authority representation, deliberately match these 42 criminal justice areas. Newly appointed Crime Reduction Directors, based at regional Government Offices, complete an embryonic framework for more coordinated policies and their implementation. The new National Probation Service is clearly set in this broader criminal justice and community safety structure.

Although the prison service still continues to sit uneasily with these other structures, it is expected to align itself with them and there are attempts so to do. The new Youth Justice Board, which has strong links with all the agencies referred to, is nevertheless bound to local authority boundaries (normally education and social services). Despite the interrelationship between aspects of the work of the probation service (as well as police, courts, and youth offending teams) with the Health Service, there is still an uneasy fit with their structures — regional, area and Trust. To complete the picture, certainly from an operational perspective, we need to include the private sector.

The 1990s saw the significant development of the private sector in the operation of prisons, secure training centres (for young offenders), escort and security services in the criminal justice system, as well as electronic monitoring for curfews and home detention conditions of early released prisoners. The independent sector has a long tradition, under its earlier nomenclature of the voluntary sector, of providing services to and for offenders — this stretches back to the nineteenth century, but has really blossomed over the past 20 years. The most recent development has been the private sector, in the form of consultants, being awarded big contracts to advise on, monitor and, in some areas, coordinate service developments, e.g., PA Consulting and Ernst and Young working with the Youth Justice Board. This is of quite a different order to the work of Information Technology specialists helping (*sic*) the probation service with the introduction of IT Systems.

Returning briefly to the prison service: whilst it struggles with conflicting Government messages in a highly-charged political atmosphere, and a prison population (both in numbers, dangerousness and disadvantage) confined within, in the main, outdated and inadequately staffed/resourced buildings, there are examples of good practice which should be nurtured. The Government of 1997, whilst reviewing the possibility of merging the prison and probation services, was wise to step back from what would have been a very damaging development, especially for the smaller of those two services. Although Lord Woolf's recommendation (after the prison disturbances of 1991) for 'community prisons' is still on the agenda by the skin of its teeth, there needs to be a continuing emphasis on links between 'local' prisons and their communities. Ideas from Canada and Western Europe, which have more boldly tackled this area, should be tried out within the context of the closer working relationships between the prison and probation services. The sharp end of working for justice can be seen when these two services attempt the resettlement of sex and dangerous offenders in local communities.

A major feature of the new National Probation Service is that it came into operation (1 April 2001) after two to three years' intensive planning for an evidence-based strategy to inform practice developments on an unprecedented scale. The What Works conferences, promoted by Greater Manchester and Hereford and Worcester Probation Services, over ten years tapped a rich vein of international research and practitioner interest — an interest which was sustained during the low point of 'prison works' policies in the mid-1990s. Preoccupied, rightly at one level, with the implementation of its own version of this evidence-based strategy (HMIP 1998a), supported by an eminent accreditation panel, the service should be wary of two things. First, it should be ever conscious of the wider evidence-based strategies in other parts not only of the criminal justice system, but also of the wider public sector (e.g., in education and health). These criminal justice strategies are to be seen in intelligence-based policing, the seminal 'Heathrow' report, 'Reducing Offending: an assessment of research evidence on ways of dealing with offending behaviour' (Home Office 1998d); and in health, with the National Institute for Clinical Excellence (NICE). Secondly, it should be wary of the unplanned vicissitudes of a national application of local effectiveness — an application which can attract the dross of sterile managerialism, unimaginative and routinised application, almost by unthinking rote, and a disconnection from the offenders, their families and communities the evidence is intended to serve.

With the introduction of the Human Rights Act 1998 and its incorporation of elements of the European Convention on Human Rights into domestic law, the courts recently have been responding to a variety of applications and challenges — some from a penal basis (prisoners' rights, appeals against administrative and executive actions), others from wider rights perspectives (Fullwood 1999). This author's McClintock public lecture, given in Edinburgh in 1998, addressed the issue of civil liberties and social control in the community, and called for a review and consultation on human rights and community penalties (Fullwood 1998). This has not been forthcoming. A chief probation officer and an academic, writing in *Vista*, expressed concern on similar issues (Scott and Ward 1999); but a senior High Court judge speaking at the AGM of the Central Probation Council, of which he was President, took the authors to task and basically stated that the probation service would not be troubled by the new Human Rights Act (Garland 2000). It should be noted, however, that the Director of the National Probation Service, in 'A New Choreography', states that the introduction of the European Convention on Human Rights into domestic law in October 2000 will continue to act as a potent reminder that offenders too have inalienable rights of citizenship, which include fair and humane treatment (Wallis 2001). She also refers to the need for probation staff not to superimpose any degrading treatment on offenders, for the degree and nature of incapacitation to be determined by the court, and for the level of incursion into the lives of offenders to be curtailed by certain factors. After the first waves of appeals in these early days of the Human Rights Act, it may not be long before some offender and his or her representative takes action in respect of a particular form of imposed treatment, incapacitation, or incursion.

Lord Justice Rose, Vice-President, Court of Appeal, speaking in the mid-1990s, reflected on earlier decades, when there was often one Criminal Justice Act every ten years, whereas during the 1980s and 1990s it had felt as if there had been an Act every year (Rose 1996). Certainly, with secondary legislation and regulations, the welter of national instruction and guidance seemed unmanageable. Since 1997 and the Labour Government's new emphasis on cross-cutting reviews and initiatives, in particular as part of its Comprehensive Spending Reviews, the interweaving of social and criminal justice policies has taken on a more interesting and, some would say, complex aspect. The probation service should be attentive to the broad thrust of these departmental policies and initiatives.

Nationally, in the new service structure there should be some identified role for coordinating and communicating the relevant aspects of them. Similarly at local area level, there should be a focal point for active coordination. The relevant multi-agency teams are Youth Offending Teams and Drug Action Teams (which now share common boundaries); the Youth Support Service, now renamed Connexions; Health Action Zones; Community Safety (Crime and Disorder) partnerships; and employment and education/training initiatives. During

2000–2001, probation representatives were appointed to and based in Regional Government Offices, where not only Crime and Disorder, but also wider social and economic regeneration teams are working. Sadly, the time and commitment to develop these partnerships is never recognised and is always an add-on to other, more probation-specific demands. As the current Government (and no doubt future ones of whatever political persuasion) targets disadvantaged geographical areas where crime and breakdown abound, the contribution of the probation service, supervising as it does some of the most prolific and/or dangerous offenders in those communities, will be more and more crucial.

As if this was not enough, a number of current reviews will have a significant impact on the service. The Review of the Sentencing Framework, announced in May 2000 by the Home Secretary (Straw 2000a), is partly a return to some of the underlying principles of the radical Criminal Justice Act 1991, in particular the issue of courts being able to take account of an offender's previous convictions, but partly an assessment of semi-custodial options like 'custody plus' and weekend imprisonment. Rather similar to the build-up to the 1991 Act, this review is tackling the underlying principles of sentencing, as well as operational options and the management framework for their implementation.

Two interesting themes will appear in the Review. First, whether there is a community-based mix of semi-custodial options (probation hostels, probation centres, attendance centres, etc.), which, if reconfigured, could provide courts and the criminal justice system with a viable alternative to place between straight community orders and imprisonment. This exercised not only the authors of the 1991 Act, but also, two decades earlier, the Advisory Council on the Treatment of Offenders, especially Baroness Wootton and Lord Younger and their reports on non-custodial and semi-custodial alternatives to imprisonment (Advisory Council on the Penal System 1970, 1974). The current Review will attempt to enunciate the principles which should inform sentencing.

The second theme of the Review of the Sentencing Framework is how to extricate ourselves and our country from the assumption that the only 'real' punishment has to be some form of penal incarceration. The Review was cherry-picked for ideas in the run-up to the Spring 2001 election, rather than allowing the integrity of the Review's Report as a whole to be carefully assessed. The subsidiary theme, but no less radical for that, of enhancing the present Sentencing Advisory Panel into more of a Sentencing Council, or Commission, is likely to receive an outing, and the role of a probation perspective on such a Council/Commission would be significant.

Lord Justice Auld's Review of the Criminal Courts process (Home Office 2001b), excluding sentencing, sits alongside the Sentencing Framework Review. The organisational arrangements for the greater integration of the structures for criminal courts, both Crown and magistrates', which draw on Professor Rod Morgan's work on lay/ stipendiary magistrates (Lord Chancellor's Department, forthcoming), are an important aspect of this and will have implications for the probation service. This review of the criminal courts follows the overhaul of civil justice procedures conducted by Lord Justice Woolf (Lord Chancellor's Department 1998). The singular lesson from that review, when considering the practical application of the civil justice changes, is how difficult it is to achieve radical and effective change in court processes on the ground, which deliver real services.

There are a number of other policy developments which are relevant to the probation service. The Lewis Report (Department of Health 1999b), commissioned by Ministers at the Department of Health, on the future of social work services in the three high security hospitals in the light of the Fallon Report on Ashworth Hospital (Fallon et al. 1999), makes a number of specific recommendations for the probation service, building on its experience with mentally disordered offenders. The continuing joint review of offenders and others characterised with severe personality disorders will draw on the service's experience of working jointly with police, forensic psychiatrists and voluntary agency specialists (such as the NSPCC). The joint initiatives with the Department for Education and Employment on training and skills developments linked into employer-based schemes have relevance for the service's work in prisons, resettlement programmes (especially the Social Exclusion Unit's latest project on this theme, due to report in 2001) and effective community-based programmes stemming from court orders.

One particular policy development requires a section on its own, partly because of the complexity of what has been achieved and partly because of the implications for future developments in the wider criminal justice system. This is the Government's Youth Justice reforms. Many of the elements have been present in previous attempts by successive Governments to tackle, often in innovative ways, the complexities of offending by young people. What has distinguished the period 1997–2001 is the presence of almost all the elements of any major strategy: detailed preliminary work by senior advisers to the incoming Home Secretary; a business-like approach from an effective task force; a well thought through legislative base; additional resources linked to specific aspects of the strategy; and, for the first time ever, a national focus for driving the reforms in the shape of the Youth Justice Board, chaired by someone with an extremely close working relationship with the Home Secretary. This national focus, harnessing over 150 local steering groups, development funds and related training, support and research/monitoring facilities, has included some excellent contributions from the private/ consulting sectors. There are other elements and much more detail, but the implications for the new National Probation Service are to ensure that these elements of a strategy are in place during the first years of its endeavours.

Lastly, the other distinguishing and unique feature of the local Youth Offending Teams is the bringing together of all the main agencies that practitioners and decades of research stress should be playing a full part in tackling the prevention of youth crime, supporting families from an early stage and imaginatively responding to the more prolific young offenders. Symbolically, the way the Youth Justice Board is promoting the concepts and the practice of restorative justice spells out that this really is a new agenda and not a repackaging of the old. Rightly, some commentators (e.g., Goldson 2000) are still critical, but at this relatively early stage on the scale of such a step change, practices are clearly making a difference that is valued by many in the system.

In concluding this inevitably broad sweep of the policy context for the new National Probation Service, it is worth listing three other developments, which the service would be wise to keep an eye on:

(a)   The future of public services generally is going through a period of substantial change (Faulkner *et al.* 1999), not just in the context of new arrangements for local, regional and national governance, and not only in response to such initiatives as the pursuit of the European Model of Excellence, but also as regards the public's own expectations of what 'services to the public' and our communities should deliver.

(b)   The renewal of policy and practical interest from multi-faith communities in wanting to make their contribution to the vexed problems of community breakdown, alienation and moves to social inclusion (Newell 2000).

(c)   Creative initiatives to tackle the criminal justice system's and the public's perception of community penalties, in particular their demands and effectiveness compared with imprisonment. The service is part of the work of Payback and, it is hoped, will be associated with the million pounds initiative by the Esme Fairburn Foundation on this theme. The Lord Chancellor's Department is in the lead on similar interdepartmental work.

The probation service has been subject to much criticism over the years, but it has the opportunity for launching itself at the start of the twenty-first century in a way of which our forebears would have been proud. The international interest in the probation service in England and Wales has never been higher. We are a net exporter of ideas, presently being received in countries from the Caribbean to China, as well as by East European countries planning penal and criminal justice strategies associated with their wish to be members of the European Union. The probation service has a remarkable track record over the past 20 to 30 years, a record that has weathered some harsh political climates. If it continues to pursue its objectives and, as importantly, its values with courage and conviction in equal measure, it will no doubt make a substantial contribution not just to the criminal justice system, but to the social policy challenges of this country.

> No fundamental change in the status quo will take place unless the approach is freed from short-term considerations and distortions prompted by political expediency. No progress will be forthcoming unless influential and sturdy bipartisan support is secured to make it a matter of 'important national concern'.

So said Sir Leon Radzinowicz, writing on the theme of 'Penal Regressions' in 1991 (p. 444) and quoting John Howard from 1777.

In the first decade of the twenty-first century, what would an 'influential and sturdy bipartisan approach' from the National Probation Service focus on? Six themes suggest themselves from the above analysis:

(a) The probation service should work with the Youth Justice Board on guidelines for effective practice across the range of interventions necessary to reduce offending by young people.

(b) The service should engage with the other departments in the Home Office and outside (e.g., the Department for Education and Employment) on emerging policy developments such as drugs, prisons and resettlement, education and training, so that these initiatives are an integral part of the service's work.

(c) As the Youth Justice Board has purchased and commissioned the juvenile secure estate, the service should, with an open mind, participate in purchasing and commissioning for the 18–25–year–olds, both in institutional and community-based services.

(d) The service should embrace the role of the private sector, not from an ideological perspective but from an added value and effectiveness perspective.

(e) As Lord Justice Auld's report (Home Office 2001b) points the way to a more radical restructuring of an integrated criminal justice system, with the overarching role of something like a Criminal Justice Board, the service should help shape developments from the perspective of its hundred years' history.

(f) Over that century much has been said about education and training in the response to offending and breakdown. The service (as well as other agencies) should place this requirement more centrally in its services and programmes.

Some would argue that the prison reform lobby has 'failed' in its overall purpose, because its endeavours have coincided with a trebling of the prison population. The service should be a major voice in initiatives to change the climate in this country, so that the public expects more of prevention and community rehabilitation and less of imprisonment.

PART TWO
Justice in Practice

5   Justice for Victims of Crime

Brian Williams

CRIMINAL JUSTICE AGENCIES AND VICTIMS OF CRIME

Introduction

The great majority of crime victims coming into contact with criminal justice agencies have suffered offences of theft or burglary. While these offences can involve victims in considerable inconvenience and annoyance, they rarely cause lasting trauma. However, the probation service also works with victims of serious, violent and sexual crime, and the effects of these types of offence can be profound and lasting. It is impossible to predict how a particular individual will react to criminal victimisation, and this makes it necessary to provide at least a basic level of services to all victims, including those who have suffered the more common types of victimisation.

Information from and for victims

The research has clearly established that one of the needs most often expressed by victims of crime is to be kept informed. They want to know what decisions are being made about 'their' offender at each stage of the criminal justice process, and what the implications are for them. The provision of this information is an important symbol of respect for their wishes and needs (Zedner 1997). The criminal justice system in England and Wales has not historically found this an easy need to meet. Information has, at best, been provided haphazardly, or only due to the particular efforts of dedicated individual staff members within the criminal justice agencies (see Williams 1999, pp. 93 and 100–14). What is required is a two-way process, with the information provided by victims being used in work with offenders, and information about the offender being fed back to the victims. This is an extremely sensitive process, and there is a need for care and selectivity in terms of the information exchanged and obtaining the explicit permission of the parties about doing so. Not only the rights, but also sometimes the safety, both of victims and offenders, may be at stake.

There has been some policy confusion in England and Wales about which agency should be involved in this process of information exchange. The police clearly have a part to play at the pre-court stage, as do the probation service and Youth Offending Teams, if a pre-sentence report is requested. The prosecution and probation services have a role at court, and all the agencies may be involved subsequently. This has caused conflict about where the responsibility lies in any particular case, and consequent failures to communicate important information to victims. In the case of offenders with mental health problems, clinical confidentiality has prevented information being passed to victims (although this is currently under review). Some information has been routinely withheld from victims for fear that it might contaminate their evidence; even the treatment they may need for post-traumatic stress has sometimes been denied for this reason (but these arrangements have recently been changed and they are to be further clarified (see Crown Prosecution Service, 2001; Home Office 2000l; Williams, forthcoming).

The probation service struggled with implementing its responsibilities under the original Victim's Charter, not least because this had to be done within existing (and at that time diminishing) resources, but probation practice has improved considerably in the ensuing decade (Williams 1999). The Inspectorate report on probation work with victims of crime bears this out, but it also points to a need for substantial improvements in a number of areas (HMIP 2000e). The thematic inspection reported wide disparities between the level and type of service given to victims between areas, and a lack of central policy direction. The report also pointedly observed that 'effective practice principles are now established as the basis for work with offenders. A similar initiative for victim contact work is now required' (HMIP 2000e, p. 107).

The revised Victim's Charter is likely to require more consistent consultation with greater numbers of victims, and this will involve not only the probation service, but also Youth Offending Teams and the police, prosecution and prison services. The advent of the National Probation Service in April 2001 has already led to central policy replacing some of the local inconsistencies. Further improving practice will necessitate consultation with victim agencies, and the establishment of liaison arrangements with Rape Crisis centres, Victim Support schemes, Women's Aid refuges, racial equality councils and other victim support services, where these are not already in place. The probation service is now required to make contact with the victims of all offenders who are sentenced to 12 months imprisonment or longer (a large and growing group), to offer them ongoing contact. This allows victims' views to be obtained before imprisoned offenders are considered for release.

Obtaining information from victims is also an issue for a number of criminal justice agencies at various stages of the criminal process. Relatively minor young offenders have been involved in various types of reparation schemes, since the introduction of Youth Offending Teams in 2000. In some cases, there is direct reparation to individual victims, although this normally tends to be reserved for more serious cases. Both Youth Offending Team staff and probation officers are increasingly encouraged to include assessments of the effect of offences on victims, when preparing court reports on offenders. Although this rarely involves direct contact with victims, it clearly has implications for them.

The introduction of Victim Personal Statements in October 2001 involves victims in the sentencing process in new ways. The experience of the pilot projects, and of victim impact statements in other countries (Justice 1998; Erez 1999), suggests that most victims welcomed the opportunity to make a statement about the impact that the crime had on them, but a significant minority expressed dissatisfaction about the process. This seems to have arisen largely because the introduction of the procedure raised unrealistic expectations about the extent to which victims' views would influence statutory agencies' decisions (Hoyle *et al.* 1998). Similarly, the One Stop Shop experiment, whereby the police attempted to provide all victim services under one roof, made most victims feel more in control of the criminal justice process and helped to reduce some people's levels of anxiety. Many felt, however, that they received information too late and that some information excluded from the scheme should have been included (such as notifying victims of decisions about granting defendants bail, and the reasons for such decisions).

The new Victim Personal Statements involve collecting information from victims at an early stage, and it is made clear to them that the impact of the crime will be taken into account, rather than their personal opinions about sentencing (Clarke 2000). The statements are made available to all the criminal justice agencies, including prisons, and it is important that victims are routinely made aware of the limitations this imposes on the possibility of protecting the confidentiality of any information they supply. It is crucial to ensure that victims understand that their involvement in the preparation of these statements is voluntary. For many years, victims' organisations opposed the introduction of victim impact statements on the grounds that victims did not welcome greater involvement in decision-making about offenders (see, for example, Reeves and Wright 1995). Many individual victims still want to avoid such involvement. Where they do take part, their consent needs to be well informed. The experience with other forms of information exchange (such as probation contact with victims of offenders who are sent to prison) suggests that no guarantees can in honesty be given about protecting the sources of information used in making decisions about offenders.

The fact that the victims giving information for Victim Personal Statements are self-selected raises some questions about fairness in relation to sentencing. It remains to be seen whether courts will find ways to avoid being unduly influenced by such statements — for example, in cases where victims were particularly vulnerable but this fact was unknown to the offender.

The role of criminal justice agencies in liaising with victims is an ambiguous one. It is often unclear why information is being exchanged. In some cases, victims are clearly being notified of official decisions, but at other times it is unclear whether the exchange constitutes notification or consultation. The probation service has a particular role in ensuring that victims and offenders are clear about the purpose and implications of such discussions. There is unambiguous evidence, however, that victims and offenders can benefit from the exchange of information about their cases, and there are also possible benefits in terms of improved decision-making. Here again, the probation experience of victim contact in the case of serious sexual and violent crime provides an example (Crawford and Enterkin 1999; Williams 1999). Victims' expectations should not be raised unrealistically, and greater consistency between geographical areas is required.

If these problems can be overcome, there are undoubted benefits for victims and for the administration of justice in providing victims with information about 'their' offenders. Greater knowledge about the victim can also assist in the preparation of court reports and in rehabilitative work with offenders. Its routine availability has done a good deal to change the occupational culture of the probation service, increasing sensitivity to victims' needs and wishes. A similar shift could be achieved in other agencies by involving their staff in keeping victims informed.

There have been difficulties in implementing the requirement to include victim information in pre-sentence reports. Poor communication between the Crown Prosecution Service and those required to produce court reports has meant that such information is often not available. Pre-sentence reports have been intended, since 1995, to assess the impact of the offence upon the victim and adult offenders' attitude towards their victims; similar requirements were introduced in respect of the youth courts in 2000. In practice, however, only half of all court reports contained information about victim impact in 1999 (HMIP 2000e; Dominey, forthcoming). Where it is included, it helps probation officers make more accurate assessment of risk and patterns of offending, and provides them with information on which to base effective future work with the offender (Dominey, forthcoming).

THE POLITICS OF VICTIMISATION IN ENGLAND AND WALES

Politics and victim policy

It has frequently been observed that becoming a victim of serious crime can challenge people's belief in a just world to such an extent that their sense of security is completely destroyed, at least for the time being (Lerner 1980; Rock 1998). Sadly, politicians' attempts to make political capital out of the suffering of crime victims can have a parallel effect, challenging victims' belief in the legitimacy and compassion of the criminal justice system. Once law and order became a political battleground in the UK in the 1980s (Downes and Morgan 1997), it was only a matter of time until issues relating to victims became part of the struggle. The emergence of a diverse and increasingly confident victims' movement doubtless inadvertently accelerated this tendency (Williams 1999). Not so many years ago, criminal justice policy was made without any explicit reference to victims of crime. It is noticeable that this would no longer be possible today (Zedner 1997), but the consequences for victims have not all been unambiguously positive.

For example, victims are increasingly encouraged to play a part in official decision-making about offenders. Recent years have seen the introduction of Reparation Orders, Victim Personal Statements and other initiatives, which, although supported by sections of the victims' movement, do not seem very popular with individual victims, if take-up rates are anything to go by. By and large, victims want to be kept informed of what is happening to those who offended against them, but they would prefer to avoid undue direct involvement in criminal justice decision-making (Reeves and Wright 1995). The purpose of involving victims in decision-making needs to be clarified before such experiments are extended (Edwards 2001).

Politicians have also been increasingly insensitive in their attempts to gain political support by using arguments about victims, even involving named individuals in many cases. The thinly coded racism of William Hague's attack on the alleged effects of the Stephen Lawrence Inquiry Report (Watt and Travis 2000) was only a single, particularly blatant, example of this trend. He argued that the Report of the inquiry into police handling of the murder of a young black man, which condemned police racism and incompetence, was an example of 'political correctness' which had 'contributed directly to a collapse of police morale and recruitment and has led to a crisis on our streets'. Similarly, as Home Secretary, Jack Straw introduced 'Sarah's law', mimicking 'Megan's law' in the USA and invoking a child victim's name to justify new legislation aimed at controlling sexual offenders.

Such political interventions are in danger of repeating the North American experience, chronicled by Robert Elias (1993): victims' issues are co-opted as part of political campaigns for stronger law and order, and offenders are duly treated more harshly, and their rights curtailed, without substantial corresponding benefits for victims. Part of the problem here is the rigid and simplistic conceptual separation of offenders and victims, as if the two groups were discrete and completely distinct. In fact, we know that many offenders have themselves been victims of crime, and vice versa (Boswell 1996; Peelo *et al.* 1992; Miers 2000). If this were more widely known and accepted, policy debate in this area might be more rational. As it is, victims are called in aid of many emotive arguments against the just and humane treatment of offenders.

Sadly, one aspect of the political debate about victims of crime has been a tendency to make largely symbolic, cosmetic changes to the criminal justice system in victims' name (Williams 1999). Lip service can thus be paid to victims' rights without actually conferring any. The obvious example is the original version of the Victim's Charter, which contained largely aspirational statements about how victims should be treated, in some cases creating false expectations (as in the statement that courts will always consider ordering offenders to pay compensation; although required by law, this does not always happen in practice). The Charter also says that pre-sentence reports contain an assessment of the effect the crime had on the victim; yet in practice, report writers often have no information on which to base such an assessment. A survey by HM Inspectorate of Probation found that in some areas no such assessment was provided in 50 per cent of cases (HMIP 2000e, p. 66).

However, the pace of change in criminal justice since the new Labour Government came to office in 1997 has been rapid, and it seems likely that a new Victim's Charter, which reflects the recommendations of the Stephen Lawrence inquiry report and of the working parties on vulnerable and intimidated witnesses, will lead to substantial improvements in this area (Macpherson 1999; Home Office 1998e; Scottish Office 1998; Home Office 2001a). The provisions of the Youth Justice and Criminal Evidence Act 1999 relating to witnesses have already come into force, extending the use of evidence given by video or in private and the use of protective screens and aids to communication between witnesses and the court. The Act also provides additional safeguards for witnesses and victims of sexual offences, and for people with disabilities. The review of the Victim's Charter envisages the creation of a victims' ombudsman and the introduction of new statutory rights for victims, as well as a strengthened and better-publicised charter. The new provisions are likely to include a right to immediate payment of compensation from a fund, which would then recover the money from offenders (Home Office 2001a).

The guidance issued to probation areas soon after the establishment of the National Probation Service in 2001 made it clear that work with victims was seen as one of the Home Office's key priorities for the service (NPS 2001). It drew attention to the coming into force of the Criminal Justice and Court Services Act 2000, whose provisions included for the first time a statutory duty to consult the victims of people imprisoned for sexual and violent offences. The guidance also included much clearer and more categorical instructions on precisely how to implement the new statutory arrangements, and was followed up by a number of detailed Home Office circulars. In this author's view, it would be a mistake to read this merely as a change of style: priorities have clearly changed at the centre, and victims are likely to become much more central to probation policy and practice in future.

The Human Rights Act 1998 and victims' rights

The passage of the Human Rights Act 1998 might have been expected to lead to increased activity in the field of victims' rights. To date, however, there has been little sign of this. The Act reflected the preoccupations of the 1950s, when the European Convention for the Protection of Human Rights and Fundamental Freedoms was drafted and promoted by the Council of Europe. At that time, legislators were relatively unaware of victims of crime and their rights. Such issues were barely touched upon in the Convention, and the same applies to the Human Rights Act, which incorporated its contents into UK law. It has also been argued that a process of 'Strasbourg proofing' preceded the passage of the Act; other legislation was scrutinised, not to ensure that it complied with human rights, but in a defensive way, to avoid triggering challenges (Scott and Ward 1999). This grudging compliance is also a feature of the Home Office circular which introduced the Human Rights Act to the probation service (Home Office 2000h). The circular gives a number of examples of challenges which might be made to probation practice under the Human Rights Act, but none of these involves victims.

Some criminologists have argued that considering victims in terms of human rights has considerable radical potential, in that it would bring to light questions about the role of the state in producing victims, and highlight gender, age and racial discrimination (Mawby and Walklate 1994). Recent United Nations and Council of Europe activity in relation to victims has certainly tended to link criminal victimisation with wider issues of oppression and abuse of power. It is this later phase of international activity which has influenced recent and proposed changes in England and Wales, rather than human rights legislation. The recent review of the Victim's Charter, for example, responds to a 1999 United Nations initiative and a decision of the EU in 2000, and the Human Rights Act is not mentioned in the Consultation Paper. Similarly, the Scottish Strategy for Victims acknowledges the influence of the UN Declaration of Basic Principles of Justice for Victims of Crime and Abuse of Power, but not the Human Rights Act (Scottish Executive 2000). There were no challenges on 'probation related issues' under the Human Rights Act in its first 18 months of implementation in Scotland, where it came into force earlier than in England and Wales (Home Office 2000h, p. 9).

It is possible, nevertheless, that the Human Rights Act 1998 will be used to defend and strengthen victims' rights in particular cases. The Act makes it unlawful for any public authority to act in a way which is incompatible with any of the rights set out in the European Convention. The European Court judgment in the Thompson and Venables case led to substantial changes in court procedures throughout the UK (NACRO 2000).

In particular, one can envisage the possibility of cases being brought under Articles 3 (the prohibition of inhuman and degrading treatment), 6 (the right to a fair trial), 8 (the right to respect for private and family life) and 14 (the prohibition of discrimination) of the Convention, and under Article 1 of the Protocol 1 (the right to peaceful enjoyment of possessions). For example, Liberty has agreed in principle to take a case under Articles 3 and 8, challenging any failure to investigate and act properly in relation to 'domestic' violence (Liberty 2001). It is conceivable that a similar case might be taken in respect of probation service failure to provide appropriate services to victims (see Scott and Ward 1999). The right to respect for private life might also be invoked in relation to agencies exchanging information about victims of crime without their knowledge or consent. Court procedures are likely to be affected by challenges under Articles 3 and 8; the respect already accorded to defendants' rights will have to be extended to cover those of victims and witnesses. Victims' anonymity has been protected in one Strasbourg case. Victims' rights to take civil actions claiming negligence by state authorities, when offences are detected but not prosecuted, have also been extended by the Strasbourg Court (Wadham and Arkinstall 2000).

However, there were only 15 successful cases brought under the Human Rights Act 1998 during its first six months in force (Dyer 2001). Of these, only one directly affected victims of crime, and the effect of the ruling seems likely to reduce, rather than increase, victims' rights. The case challenged legislation protecting rape complainants against being questioned about their previous sexual conduct. It is not yet clear whether a 'declaration of incompatibility' will be made in this case (Dyer 2001). The effects of the Act in relation to victims' rights remain largely the subject of speculation, until such time as there is a more substantial body of case law on which to base firmer conclusions.

The Victim Movement and Victim Support

The charity Victim Support has successfully positioned itself as the main organisation representing victims of crime in the UK. Both Conservative and Labour Administrations have seen it as 'the body with which they would do business' (Rock 1998, p. 258). There are many reasons for this. Until the mid-1990s, Victim Support studiously avoided political comment; and when this position slowly changed, care was taken to avoid becoming involved in controversy about general criminal justice issues including sentencing, and to restrict any comment about victim policy to fit in with its charitable status. Political influence grew from this neutrality. Its innovations have always been preceded by careful research, ensuring steady growth with corresponding increases in Government financial support (the process of 'domain expansion' described in the sociology of voluntary sector organisations: see Williams 1999, p. 129).

Victim Support does not publicly compete with rival victim organisations, but it is clearly in direct competition with a number of other groups; and one way in which this has been managed has been to take over part of their work. For example, Victim Support volunteers are increasingly involved in longer-term work with the survivors of rape and 'domestic' violence, racial harassment and violence and the family members of murder victims, although official relationships with organisations such as Rape Crisis, Women's Aid and SAMM (Support After Murder and Manslaughter) remain cordial. Indeed, in the case of SAMM, Victim Support has become the conduit through which official financial support is channelled, and it provides the group with an office (Rock 1998).

To a large extent, the probation service has replicated the unequal power relations created by Home Office funding of Victim Support and the comparative official neglect of the remaining victims' organisations. Probation partnerships with local Victim Support schemes have emerged in some areas (such as Northumbria and Derbyshire), but few similar relationships with Rape Crisis, Women's Aid or the other self-help victims' groups have been developed. Indeed, as probation staff become busier (and qualified staff thinner on the ground), the voluntary work which was done by many in previous years serving on the committees of victims' groups and assisting with staff supervision, has become more difficult to sustain.

However, the growth of the victims' movement and the increasing understanding of hate-motivated crime (discussed below) make it increasingly important that the probation service builds up its relationships with the relevant victims' organisations, and it may also have a role once again in building and sustaining capacity in the voluntary sector. It is noticeable that policy in Scotland is much more inclusive: partnerships with Women's Aid, Rape Crisis and the Commission for Racial Equality are explicitly endorsed by the Scottish Strategy for Victims (Scottish Executive 2000).

THE CRIMINAL JUSTICE SYSTEM AND VICTIMS OF CRIME IN ENGLAND AND WALES

Hate crimes and professional practice

Official agencies have been slow to accept that a considerable amount of crime is motivated by racial hatred, homophobia, disability discrimination or ageism. However, racial aggravation has long been accepted as an influence on sentencing, and this is now specifically covered in the Crime and Disorder Act 1998. Some victims and their advocates clearly welcome the introduction of harsher sentences for such offences, as a symbol of social disapproval of hate crimes (Iganski 1999; Knight and

Chouhan, forthcoming), although others have argued that longer sentences offer no solution (Hudson 1998). Rather, they suggest, offenders need to be provided with opportunities to reflect and to change. Local community crime prevention work, encouraged by central government since the 1998 Act, has highlighted the extent of homophobic violence, and the Government has encouraged official agencies to include both black and gay and lesbian organisations in crime prevention policies and consultation (Home Office 1998a). However, racially motivated crime is the only category of hate crime so far covered by legislation in England and Wales (Iganski 1999).

It is clearly important that criminal justice agencies respond appropriately to hate crime, broadly defined. The police response to racially motivated crime still leaves a good deal to be desired in many cases (Iganski 1999; Knight and Chouhan, forthcoming). There is a failure to recognise the cumulative effects of a series of incidents, each of which may be minor in itself, but which add up into a frightening and stressful experience (Bowling 1998). The police definition of racially motivated crime has been clarified by the Stephen Lawrence Inquiry Report (Macpherson 1998) and by s. 28 of the 1998 Act. Reporting (at least in London) has substantially increased. This is probably a direct result of these changes and of the introduction of a specialist squad in London, which works with housing departments and other agencies to secure prosecutions and evictions, but also to warn racist offenders of police and local authority powers in this area. Police practice in the provinces lags some way behind this initiative.

With reference to 'domestic' violence, the police have begun to adopt more proactive strategies in a number of areas, notably London, West Yorkshire and Lothian and Borders (see Morran et al., forthcoming). These sprang from 'zero tolerance' campaigns by local authorities and women's organisations. At their most basic, they involve a police policy of interviewing women, who report violence in the home, separately from the alleged perpetrator. In some areas, they also include specialist 'domestic' violence units and pro-arrest policies, which mean that the offender is at least temporarily removed from the scene.

The probation service has begun to run a number of programmes targeted at hate crime perpetrators. These include 'domestic' violence projects based upon Scottish group work programmes, aimed at changing the behaviour of violent men, and racial violence pro-grammes. Such arrangements go some way towards answering Hudson's (1998) objections to the criminalisation strategy reflected in the Crime and Disorder Act, by making victim perspectives central to one criminal justice agency's response to certain types of offending, albeit in few areas as yet. Offenders are shown society's disapproval for their behaviour, but supported in the community through a change programme, while victims are offered some protection.

Probation group work programmes with 'domestic' violence perpetrators are currently at their most sophisticated in Scotland. In Edinburgh, for example, the Domestic Violence Probation Project has been running since 1990. It involves abused women in the assessment of the perpetrator, and maintains contact with them by treating them as consultants on individual cases. Offenders have to attend a group as a condition of a probation order, where they are required to discuss the details of their offences and encouraged to develop strategies to reduce or eliminate their violent behaviour. This project has been going long enough to be rigorously evaluated over a substantial period, and the results are very encouraging (Dobash *et al.* 1996). Similar programmes have since been established in other parts of the UK, some influenced by American rather than Scottish models. In West Yorkshire, for example, specialist domestic violence courts sentence perpetrators to educational programmes as a condition of probation, and a voluntary agency supporting victims of violence starts work with the family members, as soon as sentence is passed (Walsh 2001).

Probation work with groups of racially motivated offenders usually arises out of multi-agency initiatives aimed at improving reporting rates and the treatment of victims by all the agencies, including Victim Support and local racial equality councils. In the case of serious offenders who are imprisoned, the normal victim contact arrangements apply (Tudor, forthcoming). A training pack, 'From Murmur to Murder', provides a structured programme, which probation staff can use to address racially motivated offending behaviour (Kay *et al.* 1998). However, few areas have either developed effective partnerships with local black community agencies, or begun to produce detailed policy guidance to staff on working with racist offenders. Where this has been done, it has invariably arisen from the kind of multi-agency partnership work mentioned above (HMIP 2000f). The Probation Inspectorate has now recommended that local probation areas produce policies and action plans, provide appropriate staff training and develop partnerships to take this work forward. The Government has also invited suggestions on the most appropriate treatment of hate crime victims as part of its consultation on the revised Victim's Charter (Home Office 2001a). There is clearly scope for probation to play a much greater role in this area.

The youth justice system

The youth justice system and its effects upon victims of crime have been described in detail elsewhere (Haines 2000; Williams 2000). Understanding the full effects of the Crime and Disorder Act 1998 in this field will take some time, given the contradictory nature of the legislation and its partial modification by the Youth Justice and Criminal Evidence Act 1999. However, the main thrust of the new law involves earlier intervention with young offenders, greater opportunities for victim involvement in the youth justice system, and a range of new community penalties. The changes affecting victims have not been implemented with the same urgency as other aspects of the legislation in many areas, partly due to ideological resistance to victim contact work on the part of many youth justice workers (Bailey and Williams 2000).

The new court orders reflect the Labour Government's 'rights and duties communitarianism', which has been described as 'prescriptive rather than voluntary' (Driver and Martell 1997, pp. 38–9). The Crime and Disorder Act 1998 contains a number of compulsory orders — in some cases, compulsory on the part of young offenders' parents, as well as on that of the young people themselves. It had its roots in pre-election campaigning in 1996, when new initiatives on youth justice were promised by the Labour Party in opposition. Part of the argument for radical change was the assertion that the youth justice system was in disarray, sentencing took too long and community supervision was 'unconvincing'. The strong emphasis upon compulsion was perhaps thought likely to impress a sceptical electorate with New Labour's seriousness about being 'tough on crime and tough on the causes of crime'.

Sadly, the effects on victims were not properly thought through. Reparation orders, under which young offenders directly or indirectly make good to victims the damage they have caused, are compulsory for the offender. They are not meant to be imposed upon victims against their wishes, but there is some evidence that this has occurred, partly because of courts' concern to process young offenders as quickly as possible (Dignan 2000). Since these problems emerged in the pilot areas, the national Youth Justice Board has imposed National Standards, which make it very clear that victims' consent is a prerequisite. There remains an issue, however, about the extent to which victims wish to participate in decision-making in respect of 'their' offenders. This is also a concern in relation to Victim Personal Statements (which involve the victims of adult as well as young offenders).

It has been argued that the legislation on young offenders is essentially punitive, and that victims' rights and needs are not best served by such changes (Williams 2000). In any event, it seems unlikely that the outcome of the new arrangements will be a significant shift towards restorative, rather than retributive, justice, given the marginality of the new arrangements for victims in the overall scheme of things. Some victims will be asked whether they wish to make their views known via Youth Offender Panels and Youth Offending Teams, and a minority will either receive direct reparation or be told about indirect reparation made by 'their' offenders. The most important aspect of the changes from the victims' point of view seems likely to be the more systematic provision of information about the decisions which are made in relation to young offenders. From the point of view of the probation service, which provides at least one member of staff for each Youth Offending Team, the new arrangements represent another substantial increase in the service's responsibilities for victim work. Probation responsibility for contact with the victims of the most serious young offenders, those sentenced to imprisonment for 'grave crimes', also adds to the workload.

Conclusion

Systematic probation involvement with victims of crime is a recent phenomenon, and it was an unwelcome innovation in the eyes of many probation staff. Some felt that it would change the culture of the probation service, and there is evidence that it has done so. Youth justice now faces similar changes. The probation service has seen an enormous expansion in victim contact work with its introduction in 2001 in relation to all offenders sentenced to 12 months' imprisonment or more. The third version of the Victim's Charter seems unlikely to introduce further specific changes in respect of the probation service, but if it is well publicised, it will increase victims' awareness of their existing entitlements.

The first national inspection of probation work with victims of crime highlighted a need for improved and more consistent service provision, but it generally endorsed the high standard of service delivery. The current climate of political and civil service opinion seems to favour innovation, and there are opportunities for probation, if the new national service is minded to seize them. To give only one example, the area of hate crime is ripe for imaginative approaches at both national and local levels. Probation appears to have put its suspicions about engaging with victims behind it, since tentatively beginning to implement the first Victim's Charter. It remains to be seen whether it will embrace the spirit of the forthcoming third charter.

6 Working in the Courts

Liz Hill

INTRODUCTION

The Criminal Justice and Court Services Act 2000 can be seen to have marked a watershed in the relationship between the probation service and the courts. With roots that go back to Police Court Missionaries, it is unsurprising that for much of the probation service's life, probation officers have seen themselves, and have been seen, as officers of the court. While the reality of that relationship has been changing for many years, the existence of a statutory requirement to have Probation Liaison Committees (PLCs) was, if nothing else, an emblem of a different kind of link between the magistracy and the probation service. The existence of a designated group of magistrates holding responsibility for regular liaison with the probation service suggested a special relationship, in some way different from the court's relationship with other agencies. With the establishment of the National Probation Service through the Criminal Justice and Court Services Act 2000, the statutory framework for Probation Liaison Committees disappeared and the probation service became as other criminal justice agencies in the courts, an organisation with a contribution to make to the overall process of the delivery of justice.

In addition, the employing body for probation services prior to 1 April 2001, the Probation Committee, consisted primarily of magistrates, together with a local judge, an arrangement which sustained the formal link between the probation service and the courts. Area probation boards, as the new employer of local staff, still include magistrates, but also a range of other local representative members, all appointed by the Home Secretary rather than nominated by the local Magistrates' Courts Committees. Links remain, but the special relationship has changed.

Probation Liaison Committees had worked with varying degrees of success in achieving good liaison between the service and the courts. Where they worked well, they provided channels of communication which ensured that benches were well informed about developments in the service and that the service was responsive to the changing needs of the courts. In other places, a small number of committed magistrates worked hard to use PLCs to keep themselves and their colleagues up to date, while the majority of magistrates were unaware of the changes taking place in the probation service. Breaking the statutory link has been viewed as a negative step by many of those who worked hardest to ensure that PLCs worked well. Given their variability, however, it must be right to take the opportunity to take a fresh look at how best to ensure that communication between the service and the courts is productive for both organisations. In order to do so, it is important to know the nature of the task of the probation service in courts.

The quote from Paul Boateng, Minister for Prisons and Probation, that the probation service is 'a law enforcement agency — it's what we are, it's what we do', has been widely used. When he said it in October 1999, many in the service found it too stark to be comfortable, and it clearly can give only a partial view of the complexity of the task which the probation service is in business to deliver. As a statement of principle, it does provide a background to help think about how the nature of the work of the probation service in courts is different. The 'probation service in court' is no longer a probation officer as officer of the court. In exploring the nature of the work of the service in court, the shift of emphasis from a historical focus on social work to a current requirement to enforce the law is critical. One of the major planks of achieving enforcement of the law is through ensuring that what the service does is effective. In this context, the question of how the work of the service in courts is, or should be, different from the past prompts the further question 'What is effective?' in court, and how the work in court contributes to effective work with offenders in the community.

PURPOSE OF THE PROBATION SERVICE

From the court's perspective, the probation service is present in court to provide information about community disposals and about defendants, and to assist in the processes of remand and sentencing. Clarification of the nature of the task needs regular restating. The view that servicing the courts has always to be recognised and accepted as an integral element in the work of the probation service (Samuels 1996) is one which would be widely accepted in the sense of providing the court with a service, i.e. the provision of high quality, timely information and advice. However, the notion that magistrates rightly expect the probation officer to be in the court (Samuels 1996) does not necessarily follow from that acceptance. There have long been differing views among magistrates about the need for a probation presence in the courtroom, and the days of the court duty officer sitting through the proceedings in court, on the off chance of hearing something useful, are (it is hoped) long gone. Her Majesty's Inspectorate of Probation's Thematic Inspection Report, 'The Work of the Probation Service in the Crown and Magistrates' Courts' (HMIP 1997), found that over a quarter of the time court duty officers were in court was spent either collecting results, or 'being available in court' but otherwise not active on court activities. The pressures since then have been to make better use of resource in the court, and such use of time would not now be seen as an efficient way of providing a service to courts.

The activity recording exercise undertaken by that inspection also found that a total of 7 per cent of the time of a court duty officer (CDO) was spent in engagement with offenders, and only 1 per cent engaging with members of the public. There may be those who would regret the passing of a time when the probation officer might be called on to look after a baby or a dog, while the court process occupied the parents or owners. It might have been equally likely that officers would be using significant levels of skill to manage difficult or distressed people, whether defendants, victims, witnesses or simply members of the public. Neither fits easily, however, into the primary professional role, which is defined in terms of providing high quality, timely information to sentencers, although people and liaison skills will continue to be a key requirement of probation staff in courts, who are working to that purpose.

The move to greater involvement of courts in the direct oversight of offenders, signalled by the introduction of drug treatment and testing orders (DTTOs), not only extends the involvement of the courts in their engagement with offenders, it also extends the nature of the service's engagement in the court process. Some magistrates have long wanted an opportunity to seek further information or clarification about the offender in front of them. In 1996, a bench chairman wrote: 'What is needed — but is not available — is the ability to contact the reporting officer should a question arise.' (Sleightholm, 1996, p. 148). DTTO review courts will give some magistrates significantly more involvement than simply an opportunity to question a reporting officer. Review courts will also involve DTTO staff in an engagement with the court about the progress of a particular offender, which has been in decline or absent since the demise of Case Committees, the forerunners of Probation Liaison Committees. This exercise is distinct from everyday court duty and begins to point in the direction of an input to the court process by the probation service, which may be more detailed at times and also more targeted by being focused upon drug-related offending behaviour. It also has the effect of providing a section of the magistracy with the opportunity to become significantly more informed about the nature of the service's work with specific offenders — a model of oversight which sentencers may wish to replicate.

WORK IN THE COURT AND WHAT WORKS

Before discussing the nature of the task in court, it is important to look at the purpose of the engagement from the point of view of the probation service. Work in the courts is an activity at the interface of the two organisations, and the way the task is undertaken must serve the purposes of both the court and the probation service. While there is a straightforward requirement to channel information from court proceedings to the service and to ensure that service information is conveyed accurately and positively to the court, there is also a need to answer the question of how work in the court contributes to the effective work of the service with offenders. Service staff in court are usually the first point of contact between an offender and the service. It therefore behoves court duty staff to ensure that they are modelling the right kind of behaviour, which is consistent with effective practice, and that they are acquainted with the nature of how the service works with offenders and the focus of programmes which offenders may join. This need to begin the work of the service with an offender effectively also dictates that the links between court duty staff and those working with offenders in the field are streamlined and that communication is good in both directions. Pre-sentence report (PSR) appointments and first appointments for community sentences provided to the offender at court save time and sustain momentum in the engagement between the service and the offender. They also help to achieve delivery of the service to the required standard, and assist in the process of securing compliance with the orders of the court by ensuring that offenders remain in contact and aware of their obligations.

Agreements between courts and probation services designed to facilitate cooperative working have been in existence in some areas for many years. Such 'protocols' were identified as good practice in the Inspection Report in 1997 and are widely used as a vehicle for both organisations to ensure, through regular review, that arrangements continue to be productive. Although considerable collaborative work was done between the Home Office, the Lord Chancellor's Department, the Justice's Clerks Society and the Association of Chief Officers of Probation following publication of the Inspection Report, the product of that collaboration was not to produce national standards for probation service court work. It remains a moot point whether such standards would help to improve the quality of work done in the courts, and by what measure staff could be judged to have met such standards. Guidance in relation to the production and management of joint agreements has laid the foundation to encourage good local collaboration, and the universal existence of court users groups offers a forum for local managers to ensure such collaboration is working.

AREA CRIMINAL JUSTICE STRATEGY COMMITTEES

It would be wrong to engage in discussion of the work of the probation service in courts without reference to Area Criminal Justice Strategy Committees. With the move to increasingly common boundaries for agencies within the criminal justice system, collaborative working has been generally encouraged. The boundaries chosen were those of the police areas and, as part of this drive towards collaboration, Area Criminal Justice Strategy Committees were established in 2000, involving all those working in and with the courts within an area.

Designed to take a strategic view and ensure that different parts of the system facilitate rather than obstruct each other's efforts, these Committees involve the most senior people in the six criminal justice agencies in the area — police, prisons, probation, Magistrates' Court Service, Crown Court, Crown Prosecution Service — together with representatives of the legal profession and others involved in the work of the criminal justice system. Their task is wider than simply the business conducted in court, and a number have functioned as catalysts for important pieces of work (for example, on race issues in the criminal justice system). In general, they are reflected in similar groupings at operational level, where the day-to-day business of the court is more the focus.

THE TASK OF THE PROBATION SERVICE IN COURT

Once the purpose of probation service work in court is defined in terms of collecting and channelling information and beginning effective work with offenders, the nature of the task becomes clear. It is no longer the case that probation is in the court to provide a social work service to court users. Effective work with offenders requires that some engagement with offenders in the court takes place, which may be similar to the service's historical experience. For example, it is important that the defendant, who is distressed or overwhelmed by the proceedings, is assisted to understand what has taken place and how the court's decision links with the sentence to be served. There are now others, for example, the Witness Service, whose job it is to assist many of the court users who may have occupied probation staff's time in the past.

BAIL INFORMATION

The initial contact with an offender may be at the point of a bail investigation. A court-based bail information service is a requirement for all probation areas, and the task needs to be included as part of probation service duties in the court. Probation staff make enquiries, often by visiting defendants in police stations before the court sits, to validate information about proposals for bail. Bail information schemes draw upon knowledge of the defendant from previous involvement with the probation service and upon knowledge of options in the local community for accommodation, for example in bail hostels, to provide objective information upon which magistrates can make decisions about bail and relevant conditions. Some services operate 'second chance' bail information schemes. Based in prison probation departments, the aim is to make enquiries in the period immediately following a remand in custody to explore bail arrangements, which could not be assessed in the pressured timescale of the initial court hearing. Effective bail information work requires good liaison with the Crown Prosecution Service (CPS) both at management level and in the court, including, on the day, the ability to acquire the details of previous convictions at court. The provision of useful information to inform the bail decision assists a positive relationship with CPS and the court, and the exercise could be seen to set a pattern for the activities and skills needed by probation staff in court and to establish, at the beginning of the defendant's experience of the court process, that probation interventions will inform decision-making.

SPECIFIC SENTENCE REPORTS

This pattern of good liaison and of collecting and presenting information continues through the court duty process in the collection and delivery of information to inform sentencing. The needs of the court and the service are complementary in this exercise. The information needed by the court to inform sentencing overlaps with information which is needed to ensure that offenders given community sentences are targeted by the probation service at the right programmes. However, there are pressures pushing the service and the courts in apparently different directions. Specific Sentence Reports (SSRs), where the court puts a case back for the probation service to make brief inquiries as to the defendant's suitability for a community punishment order or short community rehabilitation order, have been in existence since the mid-1990s. A survey of probation areas about the use of SSRs in March 2001 (Smith 2001) identified that, of the 41 areas which responded, all were making some use of SSRs and 90 per cent were using them in all courts. However, four areas saw a tension between the extension of SSRs and the move they perceived towards fuller and systematic assessments, which are a key component of the What Works developments.

This is an example of where the work of the probation service in court will need to be more focused in future. Speedier justice is an imperative for all concerned in the court system, although its achievement must not be at the expense of each defendant receiving the appropriate level of attention. The use of the SSR is growing, as courts discover the benefits of receiving the information they need in some cases on the same day, and as probation areas experience the benefit of delivering reports on some straightforward cases without the need for a full scale pre-sentence report (PSR). Speed becomes a benefit for court, defendant and the probation service, when an appropriate outcome results. There is still work to do to ensure that the benefits of SSRs are not at odds with the need for proper assessment to ensure that the right offender ends up with the most appropriate disposal. In this context, the targeting tools available to the service are critical. For as long as OGRS2,[1] or a tool which provides similar information (OASys,[2] when it is available), can deliver the necessary information for appropriate targeting of offenders into programmes, there is no reason why the preparation of SSRs should be at odds with the delivery of What Works. The implication is that staff on court duty will need access to previous convictions in order to calculate the OGRS score and determine whether or not the case is appropriate for an SSR.

In these circumstances, it becomes possible to envisage the kind of focusing of resources referred to above. The court duty officer has a task to do in ensuring that those defendants who can be dealt with quickly through use of an SSR, are properly identified via the targeting tool (OGRS2 at the moment). Those who are more appropriate for a full PSR would then be the focus of the greater attention which is available through that process. The importance of achieving the right assessment will need to be understood by the courts so that recommendations for a full PSR, made on the basis of targeting evidence, are met with a sympathetic response by the court. In the interests of ensuring that this necessary streamlining of resource is effective, there will be a need over time to evaluate the disposals which result from SSRs and PSRs, to determine whether there is a difference in outcome between the two. Such evaluation will help in the communication with the court.

---

[1] Offender Group Reconviction Score.
[2] Offender Assessment System.

PRE-SENTENCE REPORTS

The presentation of PSRs (and of Social Inquiry Reports (SIRs), the predecessor of the PSR), and the collection of information from the remand hearing for their preparation, has long been part of the function of a court duty officer (CDO). The shift from the SIR to the PSR reflected the move away from the social work focus in court to a much clearer view that the purpose of the report should cover the range of issues about the offender which the sentencer needs to consider in passing sentence. A critical difference is the focus on risk presented by the offender, both of re-offending and of causing harm to the public. Recent moves to make the sentence fit the offender, as well as the offence, can be seen to have had a precursor in the PSR's need to alert sentencers to the potential harm a particular offender may present, when considering their sentence.

It is clear from feedback from judges and magistrates that PSRs are more consistent in presentation and content than SIRs were, and that they better meet the sentencer's need for advice about sentence. Service efforts to improve the quality of reports[3] have paid dividends. Gatekeeping, a method of peer review introduced in the 1980s on the initiative of practitioners, began the process with a focus primarily on discriminatory language and bias. After some initial success, by the time the thematic inspection was undertaken by Her Majesty's Inspectorate of Probation (HMIP 1997), there was little evidence that the process was generating any further improvements. It had become a significant use of resource and an obstacle to achieving faster throughput. Monitoring arrangements currently being introduced by the National Probation Directorate and HMIP will require senior probation officers to ensure the quality of reports prepared by their staff.

BREACH

As a law enforcement agency, a key part of the task of the service in court is to prosecute breaches against those who fail to comply with the requirements of their community sentences. The fact that, in a number of services, this activity is undertaken by specialist breach officers

---

[3] ACOP/HMIP PSR Quality Improvement Programme.

reflects the particular nature of the task. In practice, however, the opportunity to use such staffing distinctions is sometimes more a reflection of the size of a particular area than the needs of the task. As part of the service in court, the prosecution of breaches conveys important information to offenders and to the courts about the probation service's reliability in supervising offenders effectively by being seen to enforce the law. It is therefore a critically important part of the engagement between the service and the court.

THE COURT DUTY OFFICER

The task for the service representative in court is one which involves a level of skill in collecting information, a degree of skill in assessment, including risk assessment, and concise presentation of the results of those processes both for bail information and in relation to SSRs and PSRs. It is also the case that there is a more mundane side to the job. The Inspection Report (HMIP 1997) identified that in addition to spending over a quarter of their time collecting results or 'being available', CDOs were spending nearly one-fifth of their time on administrative tasks, such as checking court lists and completing paperwork. These findings have, in the intervening period, influenced at least some areas to revise their view about who should be responsible for the task in court. In the Inner London Probation Service, probation service court officers (PSCOs) were introduced in 1998 at probation service officer (PSO) grade. This was a post which combined the responsibility for in-court work with the requirement to complete all associated administration. Its introduction was preceded by significant training for the unqualified staff involved, and the task was overseen by a senior probation officer.

The SSR survey (Smith 2001) showed that, of the 41 areas which responded, the majority were of the view that probation officers should provide SSRs. However, the probation service is in transition, and the question of who should do its work in court may depend on how successful it is in raising the level of skill and training for staff across the board. The concerns of some areas have been about ensuring the right level of skill among those engaged in delivering the service to the court. There have also been concerns among some probation officer staff about the downgrading of the service and the replacement of trained probation officer grade staff with probation service officers (PSOs) who have not received probation training. It will be apparent from discussion of the nature of the task above that there is a level of skill required in delivering what is needed by the court and the service, which does imply training. However, many more staff in the service now than in the past have some degree of engagement with offenders, and all those staff require skills to perform their work. The service is recruiting large numbers of PSOs and providing an unprecedented level of training for them. This is only part of a drive for the service to become a 'learning organisation'; and far from downgrading the service to the courts, use of PSO staff, who are trained increasingly to recognised qualifications, can only enhance the service and, therefore, the status of the probation officer. Both the service and the courts have a need for those delivering the probation service's task in the court to be effective. The use of PSOs in this role depends on having the right tools, the right levels of training and the right levels of supervision.

CONCLUSION

With the coming of the National Probation Service, work in the courts, along with much of the rest of the service's work, is in a process of change. At management level, liaison is being re-thought and re-launched in an environment which is different but not necessarily more difficult. Whatever replaces Probation Liaison Committees, probation and the courts have an opportunity to start afresh, with the hope of building on the drug treatment and testing order experience and achieving a better level of understanding among sentencers about the work of the service than has been possible for decades. As information becomes increasingly available about the effectiveness of the What Works approach, the importance of the channels of communication with the courts will increase. As the service becomes as effective in its work with offenders as it aspires to be, the information about what works and with whom will need to be shared with sentencers, so that their future decisions are as well informed as possible.

For service staff working in the courts, their task is increasingly clarified and focused. Using targeting tools to ensure that the proper attention is paid to the right offenders, probation staff in the courts are in a position not only to help provide high quality and timely information for sentencers, as defined in service targets, but also to make a real contribution to effective work with offenders. Court duty has sometimes been described as the shop window of the probation service, but the image is far too passive for the nature of the task for the future. The CDO must be seen to play a key role in beginning the engagement with offenders. That role carries with it as much responsibility for positive modelling as for any other member of staff involved in delivering What Works.

7 Risk, Public Protection and Justice

Hazel Kemshall

INTRODUCTION

The start of the twenty-first century sees risk occupying a central place in the work of the probation service. Through legislation, national standards and Home Office guidance, the service now has a duty and responsibility both to assess and manage adequately the risk posed by offenders in the community. However, 'risk' has been variably defined and understood in criminal justice policy and in probation practice — from the prediction of reoffending to the regulation of sex offenders and public protection. This chapter considers the growing emphasis upon risk within broader considerations of the 'risk society' (Beck 1992) and what Frank Furedi has disparagingly called the 'climate of fear' (1997). The chapter concludes with a consideration of the implications of the new emphasis upon public protection for justice and human rights.

WHAT IS RISK?

Risk has been defined as the probability that an adverse event will occur (Kemshall 1996), and as such contains key features: probability; adversity, undesirability or negative outcome; and a sense that such outcomes can be calculated (for example, probability-based predictions) and, if predicted, can be avoided by the appropriate risk management. This materialist understanding of risk has stemmed largely from the industrial and engineering sector (Ansell and Wharton 1992; Horlick-Jones 1998), and was given added impetus throughout the twentieth century by concerns with high consequence risks, like nuclear discharge. This actuarial approach to risk is rooted in probability thinking and the rise of mathematics and science in the eighteenth and nineteenth centuries. By the eighteenth century, risk was associated with marine insurance and the calculations of whether ships would return safely to port or not with their cargo (for example, Lloyds of London); and later with life insurance for soldiers in the Napoleonic Wars (for example, Scottish Widows). These risk calculations were still largely rooted in personal knowledge and market forces, rather than formalised statistical calculations (Daston 1987). Personal calculations were gradually replaced by 'prudential insurance' based upon mathematical models of risk assessment and actuarial tables (Hacking 1987). Equitable Life was the first company to apply statistics on death rates to life insurance, and established the first insurance actuaries in 1762.[1] As a consequence, the actuarially based insurance industry as we know it today was born. This was supported by the expansion of numerical information and databases and the mathematical identification of frequencies and averages within the population — the birth of statistics, which was essential to actuarial risk calculations (Hacking 1987, 1990).

The language of probability has contributed much to the field of risk (Bernstein 1996), and it facilitated the twentieth-century framing of risk, within engineering and science, as a statistically calculable hazard. As Hacking has put it, we began to persuade ourselves that we really could calculate the odds, that 'chance could be tamed' (1987). Risk became associated with probability calculated prediction and the identification and avoidance of adverse events. This approach to risk was extended to almost every aspect of social life and public policy in the twentieth century (Rowe 1977). For example, the collective insurance of the welfare state epitomised by National Insurance and the National Health Service.

However, as we enter the twenty-first century this understanding of risk is shifting. The work of both Giddens (1991, 1998) and Beck (1992)

---

[1] This company was sold to avoid bankruptcy in 2001, a situation that arose through its miscalculation of future financial risks and subsequent over-exposure on policies sold.

has been significant in challenging the materialist and probability framing of risk. Central to their theses is the notion that contemporary risks are largely incalculable; for example, the future impact of genetically modified foods, the full extent of bovine spongiform encephalopathy (BSE), or the likely environmental impacts of global warming. They both argue that what they label 'post-modernity' is characterised by global risks, indeterminate and contingent knowledge about the probability of such risks, and uncertainty over future outcomes and impacts (Beck 1992; Giddens 1991, 1998). As Giddens expresses it: 'We cannot know before hand when we are actually "scare mongering" and when we are not' (1998, p. 20). These 'new' risks are seen as internally produced by the activities of social actors and their systems of regulation, manufactured risks rather than existing 'out there' in nature. They are seen as the very products of science and technology. Rather than saving us from risks, science and technology produce them (for example, genetically modified organisms). The 'risk society' is preoccupied with those internally produced risks generated by the very processes of industrialisation, scientific advance and modernisation. Such risks challenge the 'myth of calculability' we have all held for so long (Reddy 1996, p. 237), and have served to fuel a 'climate of fear' (Furedi 1997) in which safety is worshipped and our approach to risk is characterised by the precautionary principle — better safe than sorry.

This has been paralleled by an increasing individualisation of risk. Exposure to risk is increasingly personal, a matter of personal choice and calculation, and of the risk management choices we make (personal insurance, pensions, private health care, personal security). Giddens has argued that this is not only more anxiety provoking, it also requires a high degree of self-monitoring or reflexivity to manage risk choices successfully: 'People have to take a more active and risk-infused orientation to their relationships and involvements' (1998, p. 28). It also means that individuals are more critical of risk policies and seek to avoid risk burdens, especially those they see as inequitable and involuntary. The risk society is peculiarly defensive, and is concerned with the distribution of risks, who produces them and why, and upon whom they fall. For both Giddens and Beck, the result is individuals living in a climate of 'manufactured uncertainty' (Beck 1992, p. 12). Hence the feeling that we encounter risks everywhere.

Such risks are also blameworthy and less forgivable than those arising from nature. If produced by someone, then surely someone is to blame?

This results in a peculiar defensiveness against the subsequent search for the organisational failing or human error that is to blame. As Green puts it: accidents happen, but risks are caused (1997).

A key feature of risk is liability, and hence increased accountability (Douglas 1992), resulting in the pursuit of 'defensible decision making' (Carson 1996) and the creation of audit trails to justify decisions in the light of 'hindsight bias' (Kemshall 1998a). The result is a society defensive about risk, concerned with risk avoidance and prevention of harms, even harms not yet known and incalculable without future knowledge (Beck 1992). Crime risks and penal policy have been no exception.

RISK AND PENAL POLICY

Risk and classification

Risk has long played a role in penal policy, not least in the classification of prisoners in the early panopticon (Foucault 1977). Whilst incarcerating largely petty criminals, Northleach House of Correction (an early panopticon) classified its prisoners in the 1800s thus:

Class 1: The most atrocious males
Class 2: Idle apprentices, servants and less atrocious males
Class 3: All males not on hard labour
Class 4: All females.

(*Source*: 'Prison at the Crossroads: the House of Correction at Northleach' Cotswold District Council, 1994, p. 6.)

The regime reflected a broader concern with the regulation of the working class, particularly apprentices and servants who absconded or were negligent in their duties, deserters, drunkards and prostitutes. Conditions were harsh and hard labour mandatory, with discipline and strict timetabling key features. In 1827, conditions became still harsher with the introduction of a tread wheel — with steps set at eight inches, a prisoner would literally climb between 10,000 and 12,000 feet a day. Northleach epitomises Foucault's panoptical prison concerned with discipline, regulation and normalisation of prisoners.

In addition to sites of risk management and discipline for whole sections of the population, prisons have long concerned themselves with individual risk assessment at time of parole. The Burgess parole assessment tool represents one of the earliest examples of a statistically based approach to offender risk (Burgess 1928, 1936), and still underpins much of the present-day approach to risk prediction. It is a key example of an insurance-based approach to social problems, and is an early example of actuarial risk calculations influencing penal policy. In essence, actuarial risk factors associated with parole violation are generated from a large number of cases. Of the 22 generated by Burgess, the following have been the most replicated:

- Nature of the offence
- Nature and length of sentence
- Age at conviction
- Number of previous convictions
- Personality type
- Social factors such as accommodation, marital status, social background.

(Burgess 1928, 1936; Copas *et al.* 1996; Gottfredson and Gottfredson 1993)

Risk, therefore, has been central to prison practice for some time, both for the internal classification of prisoners and for their early release. The twentieth century saw a growing preoccupation with classification, not only for reasons of safety, but also for reasons of cost. Flynn (1978) has argued that the growing preoccupation with classifying risk in the United States reflected the burgeoning costs of custody and the requirement more accurately to release prisoners early without compromising public safety. Similar issues faced other Anglophone criminal justice systems, as public spending was subject both to heavy challenge and restriction from the late 1970s onwards. As a consequence, the National Crime Prevention Council of Canada, the National Crime Prevention Board in Australia, and the equivalent body in the United States all pursued the design and implementation of risk classification schemes. The tools were all largely concerned with the prediction of the risk of reoffending or parole violation. Central to the development of such tools was research into reconviction predictors (Burgess 1929; Glaser 1955, 1962; Farrington and Tarling 1985; Gottfredson and

Gottfredson 1985, 1986) and the profiling of 'at risk' populations, such as young males.

The quest was also fuelled by increased concern over juvenile delinquency and the desire to predict more accurately who is likely to embark upon a criminal career (Glueck and Glueck 1950 is one of the earliest studies of this type). Such classification was extended to offenders in the community, for the rational allocation of resources such as probation supervision (Andrews *et al.* 1990; Andrews and Bonta 1995), and for 'bifurcated sentencing' (Bottoms 1977). The latter was seen as a response to prison overcrowding and the demise of the rehabilitative ideal, in particular a growing recognition that prison did not reform. One ideal response was to demarcate effectively between the 'really dangerous' and 'the rest' (Bottoms 1980, p. 7). The inherent difficulty in achieving this (identified by Bottoms) has persisted to the present day (Kemshall 1998b). As Bottoms states, the initial classification operated with 'class-loaded conceptions of dangerousness — lower class assaultists were included, but drunken drivers and the keepers of persistently unsafe factories were not' (1980, p. 7). The difficulties in accurate prediction of dangerousness, and the severe ethical issues involved, fuelled a substantial debate over sentencing policy (the 'dangerousness debate') (Floud and Young 1981). Bifurcation enjoyed a rather chequered existence in the years that followed, with some areas, such as young offenders and parole, subject to it (Home Office 1980; Home Office 1988b); with other areas subject to 'prison works' and 'just deserts' (Smith 1996), depending upon political responses to populist winds.

In Britain, the 1980s were characterised by the increasing marginalisation of the probation service from policy matters and the use of the new public sector managerialism to bring it into line with New Right aspirations for the public sector (Raine and Willson 1993). Interestingly in this period, the service saw itself not as tasked with the identification and prediction of reoffending, but with the identification of those 'at risk' of custody. A common tool, the Cambridge Risk of Custody Score, was routinely applied to social inquiry reports, and sentencing recommendations to courts were made accordingly (Bale 1987, 1990). The service positioned itself as an 'alternative to custody', and its framing and use of risk reflected this. Risk of Custody Scores were seen as essential to ensuring non-custodial options at court, especially for young offenders after the 1982 Criminal Justice Act, and involved the service in strategic attempts to influence bifurcated sentencing, particularly in the magistrates' court. This tactical positioning, as McWilliams has characterised it (1987, 1990), also reflected the 'nothing works' era (Martinson 1974) and the demise of both treatment and rehabilitation. The role of the service became one of selecting and managing offenders into alternatives to custody (community service, day centres) rather than treatment (McWilliams 1987; Mair 1996). Risk, in the era of the 'justice model', was used predominantly to rescue offenders from the over-use of custody, and to allocate offenders rationally to intervention programmes.

Re-offence prediction was not essential to such selection, although the Bale score used reconvictions in its calculation of 'at risk'. Re-offence prediction in Britain was given impetus by the 'just deserts' legislation at the beginning of the 1990s (*Blackwell's Guide to the Criminal Justice Act 1991*) and, in particular, the new parole arrangements proposed by the Carlisle Committee and enshrined in the Criminal Justice Act 1991. Risk was to be placed at the centre of parole decision-making, but this would require a more systematic and less anecdotal approach (Glaser 1973). The 1991 Act also differentiated between property offences and serious offences against the person; and, while focused on a 'just deserts' proportionality, it also introduced the notion of disproportionality on the grounds of risk. Both legislative initiatives required a more rational and consistent approach to risk. This was offered by two prediction tools: the Offender Group Reconviction Score (OGRS) for use with pre-sentence reports (Copas *et al.* 1994) and the Parole Reoffending Predictor (Copas *et al.* 1996). Tools originating in Canada and the United States were also considered — for example, the Level of Service Inventory (LSIR) (Andrews and Bonta 1995) — and actuarially researched tools began to produce individual risk factors for use in scoring tools or as structured assessment guides.

Risk, criminogenic needs and protective factors

The 1980s also saw the production of individual risk factors or 'criminogenic needs' (Andrews *et al.* 1990) and attendant 'protective factors'. While superficially the generation of such factors seems little more than the production of actuarially based research into offender risk, recent commentators have linked their rise to the 'death of the social' (Rose 1996) and the separation of the social causes of crime from crime management policies (O'Malley 2001). This New Right approach to crime management separated criminal justice from social justice, and emphasised personal responsibility for risk factors and tied the notion of prediction to prevention. If risks could be predicted, they could be prevented: either by disproportionate sentencing based upon risk (Criminal Justice Act 1991, s. 2(2)(b)), or by early interventions for those predicted to have criminal careers before them. Just deserts sentencing was therefore subject to the caveat of risk, particularly the risk of serious harm to the public, introducing into legislation the notion of preventative sentencing.

Risk was placed at the heart of sentencing and parole decisions (Criminal Justie Act 1991), and hence at the heart of the probation service's assessment work. Interestingly, this did not result in the production of a reliable risk of harm tool, but in the pursuit of various tools to predict reoffending (OGRS) or to structure officer assessments towards 'criminogenic needs' (LSIR). The continued language of need obscured an important transition in the service's approach and relationship to offenders. Offenders were no longer 'at risk' — they were transformed into the site of risk, a repository of 'needs' that inevitably results in criminal behaviour, if appropriate interventions are not provided or protective factors enhanced. In effect, an individualised deficit model of criminal behaviour was adopted, reinforced by official guidance from Her Majesty's Inspectorate of Probation (Chapman and Hough 1998; Underdown 1998). Within this, certain needs were de-legitimated, either those not directly correlated with offending, or those social problems beyond the scope of individual officers (Aubrey and Hough 1997). Needs were not only reframed as those problematic to law and order, but as those most amenable to the emerging new 'treatments' of programmed community correction (for example, STOP).

Recent commentators, such as Rose (2000) and O'Malley (2001), have contended that this development represents a growing trend in both risk regulation and penal policy: the displacement of risk management on to individuals (e.g., for their own security) and, within this, on to individual offenders for their own self-risk management. Rose argues that advanced liberal or 'risk' societies no longer govern 'through society' and its key mechanisms, such as the welfare state, but govern at the 'molecular level' through indirect controls located at the level of individual, family and community networks, and through the promotion of *responsibilisation* (1996). The self is made responsible for his or her risk choices, and only 'good' choices are rewarded by inclusion in society; those who make 'bad' choices, or continue to be a 'bad risk', are excluded (for example, by the use of prison). The prudent citizen will make the right choice, and it is the role of the state and its organs to educate, correct and facilitate the citizen to the right choice. Those who do not make the right choice are recast as the blameworthy agents of their own misfortune. In such a discourse, disadvantage, misfortune and exclusion are re-framed as matters of personal choice and not the outcome of structural processes. As Wright Mills (1970) expresses it: 'Public issues become private troubles.' Imprudent citizens, of whom offenders are a core group, are seen as ripe for re-moralisation and 'ethical reconstruction as active citizens', through 'training, counselling, empowerment, and community action' (Rose 1996, p. 60). In the case of offenders, the moral engineering is provided by risk identification and classification for cognitively based programmes focusing on 'straight thinking', 'rational thinking', 'think first' and 'rational choice'. In essence, the no fault citizen of social engineering (of which the offender-client was sometimes one) has been replaced by the concept of a moralised and entrepreneurial citizen (O'Malley 1996). Citizens (in this case offenders) who fail to show the necessary 'moral fibre' are classed as in need of 'ethical reconstruction' (Rose 2000). This places the probation service and its emphasis upon criminogenic needs in a strategic place in the use of criminal justice policy to regulate conduct through techniques of responsibilisation and risk management. In doing so, it naturally weakens the service's commitment to issues of social justice, and places it in a position where it may inadvertently contribute to a policy of 'incapacitating exclusion' (O'Malley 2001). As offenders fail to comply with programmes and are breached, or fail to self-risk manage effectively as a result of programmes, the incapacitating responses on the grounds of risk are clear. Protective factors are equally problematic. While they may indicate the existence of the 'causes of crime' and underlying social conditions, protective factors are usually re-framed as individual requirements. Thus the loss of employment opportunities becomes 'skills training' and social conditions are transformed into individual failings by the discourse of risk (O'Malley 2001). Individual correction, rather than social justice, is promoted.

THE RISE OF PUBLIC PROTECTION

Exclusion and individualisation have also underpinned the rise of public protection as a key concept in penal policy. In essence, the public is entitled to protection from the 'Monsters in Our Midst' (Channel 4). The emphasis upon public protection reflects a defensive attitude to risk and a growing precautionary principle, especially in relation to specific groups, like sex offenders, paedophiles and the mentally ill. While the attempt to bifurcate sentencing and the subsequent 'dangerousness debate' had focused attention on the identification of dangerous offenders, the notion of public protection did not gain momentum until the late 1980s. By 1988, the Home Office was instructing services to create registers of Potentially Dangerous Offenders (Home Office 1988c). This was followed by legislation in the form of the Criminal Justice Act 1991, the Victims Charter (Home Office 1990b) and National Standards (Home Office 1992b, 1995a), that all emphasised seriousness, risk and protection of the public. The 1990s saw a continued emphasis upon seriousness, risk, protection and preventative sentencing (Home Office 1988a, 1996, 1997b, 1998f). Within the service, there was increased activity around pre-sentence reports to identify serious offenders accurately and to address appropriately the 'risk of harm to the public' (Kemshall 1998b), and to increase the effectiveness of service delivery to key risky groups, such as sex offenders. This activity was also paralleled by increased anxiety, particularly as individual risk management failings came into public view. Sparks (2000, p. 131) sums this situation up thus:

> Their work comes into unwelcome focus when 'mistakes' or 'accidents' occur.
>   This knowledge constrains the range of choices they can feasibly make and directly influences the systems they institute for coping with their work.

In addition to the systems of scrutiny and regulation instituted by individual services as part of their risk management procedures, the probation service has also engaged in the set-up, development and maintenance of multi-agency procedures for risk assessment and management of 'high risk' offenders. While often multi-agency in nature, their development stemmed almost entirely from the legislative requirement placed upon the police for the registration of sex offenders under the Sex Offenders Registration Act 1997. This placed a duty upon the police to 'manage' the risk that each registered offender poses (Power 1999; Plotnikoff and Woolfson 2000). In practice, such offenders, who are often shared by the two agencies, experience registration with the police and supervision by probation; hence the development of systems for speedy information exchange and dual approaches to risk management. This development paralleled legislation towards longer and indeterminate prison sentences for dangerous offenders, and the desire to provide lengthy and sometimes indefinite surveillance and monitoring for those released. While initially the main focus was upon offenders leaving prison, and particular concerns over the release of predatory paedophiles (for example, Sydney Cooke), panels now consider any case referred by the partner agencies, including those offenders and individuals considered dangerous but who have never been convicted, and offenders under supervision for non-dangerous offences but about whom 'concerns' are raised (Kemshall and Maguire, forthcoming; Maguire *et al.* 2000).

The net of panels has continued to widen, encompassing non-sexual offenders considered dangerous, those subject to bail but not convicted, offenders 'suspected' of dangerous activities, and offenders for whom statutory supervision has ceased. The ethical and human rights issues raised by panels, particularly in relation to the disclosure of information, have attracted attention, not least disclosure to concerned third parties and the public. This was significantly fuelled by the murder of Sarah Payne and media coverage in the summer of 2000, events which illustrate rather more than media hype and moral panic over sex offending. The late 1990s saw a worldwide recognition of the prevalence of sexual offending against children (Grubin 1998), with particular emphasis upon paedophile rings and 'stranger danger' (Kitzinger 1999) in sharp contrast to the extent of intra-familial sexual abuse (Wyre 1997). Research also fuelled scepticism about the rehabilitation of sex offenders, portraying them as recidivist offenders resistant to change, actively targeting children and committing high volume offences (Hughes *et al.* 1996; Hebenton and Thomas 1996; Grubin 1998). Treatment was replaced by 'tracking' in the United States, and the notion of surveillance and monitoring took hold in Britain through the public protection panels. Management *in place* has subsequently replaced rehabilitation, and public protection panels have become the key mechanism for providing it.

Increased responsibilisation of citizens has also heightened anxiety and resistance to risks seen as both involuntary and inequitable (exemplified by NIMBY). This results not only in challenge to the expertise of professionals, who are seen as 'offloading' risks on to the community, but also in the active patrolling of community and social boundaries to determine which kinds of people are deemed acceptable for inclusion and those who are not. Such patrolling can extend beyond the boundaries of those known to be dangerous, to those whom the community merely suspects (for example, the civil disturbances at Portsmouth). The result is an essentially pessimistic penality, in which never-ending surveillance replaces the possibility of change (Kemshall and Maguire, forthcoming), and criminal justice experts are subject to constant challenge for the location of the 'dangerous' in the community.

Public protection panels, accountability and the 'logic of risk'

Public protection panels can also be seen as an example of a move from traditional disciplinary practices of rehabilitation and normalisation to an 'informative system', in which the exchange and use of risk knowledge by some groups provides control over others (Pratt 1995). Ericson and Haggerty (1997), in their thesis on contemporary policing practices, label this the 'logic of risk', in which the main task for the police in risk management is one of constant reappraisal, refinement and exchange of information for use by other agencies (for example, probation supervision). This 'logic of risk' can justify almost endless information exchange; the perceived dangers are used to justify and legitimate disclosure across the agencies (Kemshall and Maguire, forthcoming). Gatekeeping this effectively is almost impossible, not least due to the anonymous and distanced nature of computerised data and its access:

> It is impossible to control such knowledge by using institutional border-guards because of the sheer volume of risk communications, the fact that knowledge can be taken but yet remain in its original place, and the fact that once known, knowledge can never be reclaimed. Remote control means that no one is in control. (Ericson and Haggerty 1997, p. 107)

The situation is exacerbated by the dispersed accountability, again a key feature of advanced liberal societies, in which accountability is dispersed away from the governmental centre (Rose 1996), and, of course, the dispersal of responsibility for risk (Leiss and Chociolko 1994). Lack of accountability at the centre for the development of public protection panel work, and the lack of procedural guidance and a national risk assessment tool evidence this.[2] In addition, formal accountability for panel work varies enormously across areas, and accountability and responsibility are diffused within the panels, with police having a statutory duty for surveillance and the register of sex offenders, probation holding statutory responsibility for community orders and licences, and other panel agencies largely free from statutory duties. This is reflected in recent legislation (Criminal Justice and Court Services Act 2000), which places the statutory duty for panels on police and probation jointly.

The major 'product' of public protection panels is information and its exchange, which has implications for individual rights. The Home Office has provided guidance for information exchange between panel agencies and has legally sanctioned limited disclosure to third party individuals and organisations (for example, those wishing to work with children) (Home Office Circular 39/1997). However, the risk assessments at panels, and the information exchange upon which they are based, are often anecdotal and rarely evidential (Kemshall and Holt 2001; Maguire *et al.* 2000). Media coverage and public reaction, in the wake of the murder of Sarah Payne in the summer of 2000, have also led to calls for a Sarah's Law based largely upon the Megan's Law of the United States (Hebenton and Thomas 1997).

While legislation, including that covering sexual offences, must be compatible with human rights legislation on privacy and private life (Article 8), the right to liberty (Article 5), the right to 'a fair and public hearing' (Article 6) and freedom from 'degrading treatment or punishment' (Article 3), such legislation must also preserve the rights of victims and those deemed to be vulnerable, in particular children (Lacey 2001). It is clear that the right to privacy may be infringed on the grounds of preventing criminal actions and that, in general, risk will outweigh privacy (Fennell 1999). However, this should not remove the responsibility on panels and their personnel to provide objective and evidenced assessments of risk, and information exchange rooted in

---

[2] This may shortly be rectified by both legislation (Criminal Justice and Court Services Act 2000) and practice guidance from the Dangerous Offenders Unit, Home Office.

observation and fact, rather than opinion. Challenge to the practice of panels is also lacking; unlike child protection case conferences, where parents may attend, there is no presumption that either the offender or the victim (if known) will be present. Panels are, in essence, a closed professional system with all the dangers that can bring (Reder *et al.* 1993). It is possible that panels may also face challenge if they fail to protect the right to life (Article 2) and known victims are harmed or killed because of identifiable risk management failures. This leaves panels at great pains to make 'defensible decisions' and to ensure the correct balance between offenders and victims (both known and potential).

RISK AND JUSTICE

Justice has been largely redefined in the risk society. It is recast as being 'tough on crime' (O'Malley 2001) and being fair to victims, as reclaiming threatened spaces (Rodger 2000), and 'letting the punishment fit the crime' unless the level of risk 'justifies' otherwise. Fairness and proportionality have been replaced by considerations of risk, even allowing 'first strike' principles of preventative sentencing for those deemed risky enough. Punishment follows the risk, although such punishment is often recast as a risk management strategy; prison is not a punishment, rather it is an incapacitating strategy for those deemed too risky for public safety. As Hudson points out, this may result not only in disproportionate sentencing, but also in discriminatory sentencing (2001b). She sees some women, for example, as likely to attract disproportionate and risk-based sentencing, not because they are as risky as high-risk men, but because risk assessments will show them as more risky than other women. A risk-based penology also has the capacity to re-form and re-enforce excluded groups, for example young males (particularly those who are economically inactive), those excluded from the new 'workfare society' by virtue of capacity, skill or competence (Leonard 1997), those who are deemed 'intransigent' and those who fail to comply with the requirements of moral engineering. It is unlikely that human rights legislation will afford much protection or justice for such groups, particularly as they will be stigmatised by the label 'offender' and, in some instances, the label 'dangerous offender'. Justice in these areas will always be subject to prevailing views of risk and notions of 'balance' — literally a weighing of public and victim safety against the rights of persons who are seen as dangerous, unworthy, imprudent and to a large extent responsible for their own predicament. It is unlikely that legal rights alone can offer resolutions to these larger issues, particularly in the present 'climate of fear' (Furedi 1997).

At heart, the issues are about reintegration and inclusion of risky people, the risk perceptions of communities, and public perceptions about the acceptability and tolerance of community risks. These require a broader debate and engagement with the public about risk, including the negotiation of what levels are acceptable in the community given particular safeguards and effective risk management systems. To date, the probation service has largely avoided this difficult but pressing task, often communicating with the public about risk 'after the fact' and about individual and often notorious cases. Energy has been placed in systems, procedures and assessment, with little attention given to effective communication strategies with local communities, and little attention to defining, providing and evaluating effective community risk management. This would require the service to broaden its remit from individualised risk to community risk management in the broadest sense, in which reconciling communities and offenders, and working in partnership with local people to deliver risk management, would be key features. Enhanced communication, especially in a proactive and planned way about positive risk management outcomes, is likely to build trust, essential to securing support for risk strategies (Wilkinson 1997).

Professionals and experts can no longer expect and secure unquestioning public trust and confidence — it has to be earned. Transparency in decision-making, high engagement with communities about risk, and the obvious sharing of risk burdens would greatly assist. At present, professionals are seen to off-load their risks too readily, often to those communities most exposed to risks and with fewer resources to manage it (e.g., inner city housing estates). One technique used currently in health is citizens' juries (Khan 1998), and such juries could usefully consider the following questions:

- How great are these risks?
- How should they be borne, by whom and in what circumstances?
- What is the appropriate balance between risk avoidance and proactive risk management?

- What kinds of partnerships can risk management agencies and publics form to manage risk effectively? (Kemshall 2000b)

This will require the probation service and central government policymakers to move away from the never-ending pursuit of the perfect risk assessment tool, and to face a more uncertain risk world in the 'risk society', in which not everything can be calculated and not all risk predicted. It also requires the probation service to look out from the internal regulation of risk procedures to the external world of public perceptions of risk — certainly a more demanding world, but probably more necessary. Perhaps it is time that the probation service took a risk with risk?

8 Race Issues in Probation

Karen Chouhan

INTRODUCTION

His crime was theft. He paid with his life, murdered by a rabid racist
. . .

When Zahid Mubarek, 19, was sentenced to 90 days in Feltham
young offenders' institution for shoplifting £6 worth of razor blades
and interfering with a motor vehicle, he and his family were shocked.
Zahid, from east London, was a well-meaning lad, perhaps a touch
naive, who had fallen in with the wrong crowd. He seemed genuinely
sorry, and in letters to his family he speculated about joining the army
full time, having spent time on manoeuvres through the Prince's
Trust.

He never got the chance. Tragically, the short sharp shock turned
out to be a life sentence. Five hours before he was due to be released,
while his family were preparing a welcome home celebration, Zahid
was beaten to death with a wooden table leg by his cell mate, Robert
Stewart, 20, a racist psychopath with a history of violence, who was
on remand for sending malicious communications.

In the early hours of March 21 this year, Stewart took the table leg
and, in the dim glow cast by the toilet light, began to batter the
sleeping Mubarek. He hit him between seven and 11 times. 'It was
mad,' he wrote in a subsequent letter to a friend also charged with

murder. 'His head splattered all over like a tomato fucking every-where.' (Kelso 2000)

Vicious race hate crimes are sickeningly not uncommon. The official *Statistics on Race and the Criminal Justice System* (Home Office 2000n), showed a 107 per cent increase in the number of racially motivated attacks. However, for this race hate murder to have happened in a young offenders institution, where we expect a high degree of surveillance and security, and which we should also, rightly, expect to be free from racism, reflects many contemporary questions about race and the criminal justice system, including the probation service.

In Britain, Black people have suffered from a culture of denial of racism and racial attacks (Chouhan and Jasper 2000). For example, although racism and racial attacks had long been known about and had been the subject of numerous complaints, race hate crime was not a matter of public policy until 1981, following the presentation of a dossier of 11,000 racial attacks put together by the Joint Council Against Racism (Bowling 1998). A Home Affairs Select Committee (Home Office 1981) was called to investigate racial attacks and ran parallel to the Scarman Inquiry. But both of these much needed initiatives and the recommendations that emerged seemed to have been lost to the mists of time (Chouhan and Jasper 2000). Consider these recommendations:

- Collect data on racial attacks.
- Liaison arrangements to be explored.
- Ethnic minorities to assist in training.
- Reporting of racial incidents to be immediate.
- Ways of combating racist activity among young people are needed.

These are not, as we may think, from the latest race policy guidelines, but from the Forward, by William Whitelaw, to the 1981 Home Office report into racial attacks.

In attempts to deliver race equality, there is seemingly a repetitive cycle of recommendation — incident — recommendation. This would not be problematic, if the initial recommendations were taken up and the cycle demonstrated an upward spiral. However, the evidence for this seems to be lacking. Indeed, as far as the probation service is concerned, Her Majesty's Inspectorate of Probation Report (HMIP 2000f) had this to say (at pp. 15 and 22):

In the 1980s and early 1990s, probation services were amongst the first of the criminal justice agencies to develop anti-discriminatory practices and procedures. However, many staff, at all levels and in all services, felt that the attention given to the promotion of equal opportunities had diminished in recent years.... The publication of the Macpherson report following the murder of Stephen Lawrence had acted as a catalyst for action to many services ... It was disappointing that despite the promise of the work undertaken in the 1980s and early 1990s, so little had been achieved.... HMIP strongly believes that the promotion of race equality is synonymous with the development of good practice and contributes to the service fulfilling its core task of protecting the public ...

As an Appendix, some of the key findings and recommendations of this Report are set out alongside some related guidelines on race equality taken from the Race Relations (Amendment) Act 2000; the Commission for Racial Equality's Standards for Local Government 1995 and recommendations from the Lawrence Inquiry 1999. This is to demonstrate that various bodies repeatedly try to address the same or similar issues.

While it may be argued that the Race Relations (Amendment) Act came into force only in 2001, so that the detail was not known, the other two documents mentioned pre-date the HMIP Report. In addition, there has been a multitude of other race policy documentation from which the probation service could have drawn. If there has been little attempt to learn from all of this documentation in the past, will this HMIP Report bring about the required changes?

WHAT ARE THE DIFFICULTIES AND BLOCKS TO DELIVERING RACE EQUALITY?

One, or a combination, of the following is suggested:

- Institutional racism manifest in discriminatory practices and procedures.
- Institutional paralysis brought about by a fear of dealing with race issues, a lack of knowledge of relevant concepts and inter-cultural competency, feeling overwhelmed by different policy guidelines and the new legislation.

- Resistance brought about by individual or political[1] racism.
- Lack of political commitment and leadership.

To pick up one of these points, currently there is a plethora of legislative and policy guidelines on race, for example:

- the Human Rights Act 1998 (came into force October 2000)
- Article 13 of the Amsterdam Treaty (the Race Directive and the Employment Directive)
- the Race Relations Acts 1976 and 2000
- the Crime and Disorder Act 1998 (new offences of racially aggravated crime and the requirement for crime prevention strategies)
- the Stephen Lawrence Inquiry implications
- *Race Equality in the Public Services* (Home Office 2001f)
- modernising Government agenda (particularly Best Value)
- Commission for Racial Equality standards for local authorities, for the youth service and for schools (CRE 1995)
- Social Exclusion Unit documentation
- Multi-ethnic Britain Report.

In addition there are the numerous reports either concerned directly with probation, or which have central relevance. These include *From Murmur to Murder: working with racially motivated and racist offenders* (Kay *et al.* 1998) and the HMIP Report (2000f). The legislative and policy imperatives above sit alongside the economic and moral imperatives spelt out by the Government in their detailed guide to the new Race Relations (Amendment) Act (Stationery Office 2000):

Moral Imperative

The Government believes that race equality is essential in order to build strong, inclusive, communities. There is a moral case for striving for race equality. It is a basic human right to be treated with equality and fairness. This is recognised in the European Convention on Human Rights and reflected in the Human Rights Act 1998.

---

[1] By political racism, the author refers to the argument that to keep black and minority people in underclass or inferior positions suits the needs of the organisation, or ultimately the needs of capital, to have an expedient and malleable labour force.

Economic Imperative

There is an economic case for race equality too, as everyone's potential can be utilised. In a diverse nation such as ours, whose history has seen successive waves of migration both in and out of the country, that is all the more important.

To those who may argue that it is difficult to grasp new language, new paradigms and new policy guidelines, when so much else is happening and being demanded, it is instructive to consider how readily all the new technology and new managerialist language and concepts of the late 1980s and early 1990s were put into place. By this is meant the language of quality standards, quality assurance, Total Quality Management, Human Resources Management, performance indicators, etc. Similarly, the way in which Best Value regimes have been implemented, despite heavy demands on time and resources. A Best Value review can warrant up to 20 days' inspection per review. Despite the fact that Best Value was virtually unheard of until 1997, it has been astonishing to witness the zeal with which this cause, like a mantra, has swept through the public services. If the same number of inspection days were given over to each new race equality strategy, we would be nearer to reaching the level of attention that is required to ensure implementation.[2]

It is therefore not a matter of difficulty of understanding, or resources, but one of leadership, and political and individual commitment. This is an issue which the HMIP Report commented upon and is apparent in the key findings. The text of the Report had more detailed comment, including:

Since its launch the Leadership Challenge (an initiative by the CRE) had succeeded in gaining over 300 signatories, including John Hicks, the then chair of ACOP, who in 1997 committed the association to examine the management of racially motivated and racist offenders. Despite the lead given by John Hicks as chair of ACOP, the number of individual CPOs formally to sign up to the Leadership Challenge was disappointingly low. (HMIP 2000f, p. 154)

---

[2] The Greater London Authority has recently suggested a Best Value Equalities Review, i.e., a thematic review which centres on the delivery of equalities.

The required leadership, however, cannot be based on a simplistic model of strength of voice, as leaders in race equality have to have a depth of understanding of power relations and the management of the transfer of power. They must have a knowledge so detailed and refined that they can drive through institutional barriers and stand up to the fiercest critics. They have to change such norms as:

- Policy without practice;
- Rhetoric without reality;
- Commitment without consultation (or vice versa);
- Service delivery without strategy or system;
- Individualised good practice without institutionalisation.

A framework within which they might do this is suggested below. What follows represents a summary of the broad themes to have emerged from most of the contemporary race legislation and policy guidelines. We also explore one of the most important current discourses that leaders will have to grasp. This is by way of an example of how important it is to keep up with the latest conceptual thinking.

The key issues for the police to emerge from the Lawrence Report concerned accountability, community confidence in the service, representation within the service, and an overall change in culture from one of denial of racism (Chouhan and Jasper 2000) to an acceptance of institutional racism. In the report by the 1990 Trust, *A Culture of Denial* (Chouhan and Jasper 2000), the authors state that, ultimately, wholesale reform of the institution of the police is required to ensure a sustainable response to the Inquiry's recommendations. The same is true of probation services. The model used in *A Culture of Denial* for the police is reproduced and adapted here for the probation service. Note that the bullet points under each heading do not represent exhaustive lists of what is possible; they are offered as examples.

Baselines required for a just probation service: two foundational conditions

- Human Rights and Radical Valuing of Diversity.

- Acceptance, Understanding and Commitment to Implement Legislative, Economic and Moral Imperatives.

Within these conditions there are five prerequisites:

(i)   Accountability
For example:

- Probation committees and Chief Officers should ensure that their plans for achieving race equality are transparent and publicly accessible. They should work in conjunction with local communities.
- Inspections and investigations must be rigorous, transparent and publicly accessible.
- Staff appraisals and supervision to include staff work on developing their anti-racist practice. The HMIP Report stated (at para. 11.56): 'Review the appraisal framework and issue guidance to ensure that it addresses accountability, development needs and support for all staff.'
- Disciplinary procedures must include specific offences concerning racism, equivalent to gross misconduct, based on civil standards of proof (balance of probability) and actioned even where retirement is possible. Retirement should not be allowed, except on proven medical grounds or because of age. If misconduct is found, retirees' pensions should be amended accordingly.

The HMIP Report (2000f) found a lack of consistency in understanding and applying disciplinary, grievance and complaints procedures with regard to racism. It therefore recommended that the Home Office ensure that a separate complaints' procedure is established so that any complaints made by probation service staff are given proper consideration (para. 13.35). It also recommended that probation committees and Chief Officers adopt the definitions of racist behaviour and institutionalised racism given in the Macpherson Report as the basis for disciplinary and complaints procedures, and ensure that the implications of this change are reflected in future policy and practice guidance.

(ii)   Community Involvement
It is necessary as a minimum to:

- replace tokenistic consultation with ethical consultation underpinned by equitable power partnerships

- ensure consultation and access to decision-making forums at the highest levels
- develop a set of clear consultation aims, objectives and protocols
- give recognition and response to the weak position of community organisations and individuals in relation to multi-agency approaches
- engage in proactive work with communities.

(iii)   Representation and Experience of Employment

To achieve acceptable representation of Black probation officers, it is necessary to improve employment of Black probation officers at all levels. It is necessary to:

- have fair and innovative recruitment and selection strategies
- change the occupational culture by accepting and challenging institutional racism
- facilitate the networking of officers through ABPO and NAAPs[3]
- deal vigorously with officers found guilty of racism, including senior officers
- task senior officers to set clear examples — avoiding mixed messages
- review further the model framework for the recruitment and selection of trainee probation officers
- review and issue guidance to all services on the recruitment and selection of all grades of staff
- ensure appropriate minority representation on the new probation boards. (HMIP 2000f, para. 10.46)

(iv)   Improvements in Operational Probation

There needs to be:

- clarity about what is and what is not a racial incident (see Appendix, below)
- clarity about dealing with perpetrators of racial crime (see Appendix, below)
- improved Pre Sentence Reports (see Appendix, below)

---

[3] ABPO: Association of Black Probation Officers; NAAPS: National Association of Asian Probation Officers.

- improved information flows
- improved family liaison and victim and witness support
- linked crime prevention strategies.

(v)   An Anti-racist Probation Service
It is necessary to:

- create a new environment with new cultural symbols
- punish racist officers
- reward anti-racist practice
- demonstrate a strong and unequivocal lead from senior officers.

Having offered the above framework, it is suggested that this must sit alongside a detailed understanding of human rights and the 'politics of difference'.

THE DISCOURSE OF DIVERSITY AND DIFFERENCE

Beginning briefly with human rights, the requirement here is to change the focus. Rather than seeking to create a level playing field by training people to understand equal opportunities, all operations must be predicated on the principle that everyone has the same set of positive human rights. This goes to the heart of the case for truly accepting the 'politics of difference'.

Discussions with staff indicated that some equated equal opportunities with treating everyone alike, whereas others, often because of their own uncertainties, avoided the issue to the detriment of the offender. Other report writers were clearly able to acknowledge difference in a culturally sensitive way and use relevant information about the offender's background and experience to enhance the report. These reports had a credibility and strength that others lacked. (HMIP 2000f, p. 45)

Probation officers are not alone in struggling with a shift from the politics of equal recognition to the politics of difference, and learning about what diversity strategies actually mean. However, it is important to grasp that:

Where the politics of universal dignity fought for forms of non-discrimination that were quite 'blind' to the ways in which citizens differ, the politics of difference often redefines non-discrimination as requiring that we make these distinctions the basis of differential treatment. (Taylor 1992, p. 38)

Treating people differently in order to achieve equality is not particularly new as a concept. However, its acceptance into the discourses around equality in academic settings, and the demands that this is translated into practice in the field, are providing a challenge to the liberal maxims of treating everybody the same, or 'do unto others as you would have them do unto you'. Many professionals are finding it difficult to differentiate between cultural knowledge as perpetuating a stereotype, and cultural knowledge as enhancing the quality of service.

As worrying was the finding of the inspection that a quarter of the reports written on African/Caribbean and Asian offenders contained information that was irrelevant. ... Examples included the depictions, which though factually accurate created racial stereotypes such as describing an Asian offender as working in a local corner shop. (HMIP 2000f, p. 44)

The difficulties of fully internalising the implications of diversity strategies, which work with a politics of difference, arise from the mindset changes required by a new and developing political and social ideology. Over the last 100 years, the British have had to accept that they are no longer 'rulers of the waves', a dominant and superior race with an empire. They have had to accept the notion of a multicultural society and that they must respect 'others'. And because 'others' are by definition different, with Black people the most visibly different, this has caused problems for the internalised racism, which blocks an appreciation of difference as equal. A range of ploys has been developed to deal with this difference, which achieves the result of an appearance of respect but in effect maintains the status quo. By this is meant the maintenance of a dominant white superiority culture in Britain, reflected not just in demographics, but also in terms of power and perceived social and moral superiority. This form of respect for others equates to little more than a power-laden and patronising concept of tolerance, in which difference is diminished and viewed implicitly as inferior — not 'equal', but 'less than'. This is the deficit model of difference.

Tolerance is the exercise of largesse by the powerful, ultimately on behalf of the powerful. It is the generous extension of forbearance toward someone who is intrinsically objectionable or not deserving of the privilege being allowed. (Husband 1994, p. 65)

The politics of difference, as opposed to the politics of equal recognition, requires a shift from tolerance. It implies:

Anti-racism (which) recognises that in order to treat Black people equally you may have to treat them differently. It requires ... officers not just to be passively non-racist, but to be actively anti-racist. It is around these crucial issues that an ideological battle may be taking place between the [perceived] old-style traditionalist hawks and the progressive anti racist doves. (Chouhan and Jasper 2001, p. 86)

The shift is from the implementation of ethnic integration to ethnic pluralism, in which all cultures have equal status and rights.

This does not seem at first to provide any radical challenge. However, when faced with the reality of having to accept that the status quo, the world in which you have been raised, is no longer the accepted norm, there has been a tendency to feel threatened, to feel that it implies a reduction to a 'lesser status'. It is seen as moving to a lower common denominator, rather than seeing the elevation of all to a higher denominator. It is also described as the 'victimisation of the majority'.

There is another radical challenge also embedded in the politics of difference. Previous models of tolerance and respect were based on an implicit understanding that tolerance has a threshold. It would be fine to respect others, as long as it did not challenge your position. Hence, alongside the implementation of the Macpherson Report (1999), the Race Relations (Amendment) Act 2000 and numerous diversity strategies, there is a dominant idea that has been central to the politics of race relations since the late 1950s, that numbers must be curtailed. Consider this quote from Roy Hattersley in 1965:

Any policy towards immigration and race relations must start from where we are today and not from some different position to which some people in the House and country think or wish we could go back. First, we have a community made up of a preponderant indigenous majority and a small, but nevertheless substantial, minority of different ethnic origins with family ties in Africa, Asia and the Caribbean. This part of our community is now developing into a second generation. Secondly, the British people occupy a largely urban, densely populated, industrialised island of limited size, possessed still of great natural and human resources, but also with real economic and social problems and limitations. Our imperial history combined with the maladministration of wealth and prosperity in the world has traditionally produced strong pressures to migrate to this country. These are basic facts. They necessitate both a strict limit on the amount and rate of inward immigration for settlement and an acceptance of certain well-defined obligations to those we have already accepted here and are settled. (cited in Barker 1981, p. 19)

Barker (1981) points out that such speeches are very dangerous, for they conceal myths that are stated as fact. For example, in this one, it is suggested that 'ethnic minorities' immigrating into Britain are exclusively from Africa, Asia and the Caribbean: the majority of immigrants are white and from Australasia and Europe.

The debate on race, racism and race relations was one in which cultural difference could be tolerated only to a limited extent. This was graphically expressed in Margaret Thatcher's now (in)famous speech:

If we went on as we are, then by the end of the century there would be four million people of the New Commonwealth or Pakistan here. Now that is an awful lot and I think it means that people are really rather afraid that this country might be swamped by people with a different culture. And, you know, the British character has done so much for democracy, for law, and done so much throughout the world, that there is a fear that it might be swamped. People are going to react and be rather hostile to those coming in.

This speech, made in 1978, marked the beginning of what has been termed the 'New Racism' (Barker 1981), an ideology which continued to grow during the 1980s and 1990s. The 'New Racism' argument is that it is in our nature to be wary of strangers, and only natural that we would wish to protect those closest to us. It is therefore not racist to dislike strangers or alien cultures, only commonsense. It is natural. It plays on 'genuine fears' and attempts to naturalise bigotry. Therein lies the danger.

In this context, the Draconian measures implemented against asylum seekers and refugees can sit alongside an amended Race Relations Act, which is the most comprehensive yet. Diversity strategies beg us to value difference. If this is really to be the case, it entails giving up on Margaret Thatcher's induced fear of strangers.

The politics of difference (Taylor 1992; Brah 1992), together with the new legislative and policy framework with regard to race, can create a basis for reform of the values, beliefs and operation of many public and state institutions, the probation service included. However, these implications, for giving up existing notions of tolerance and fear of strangers, are not widely understood.

The resource pack, *From Murmur to Murder: working with racially motivated and racist offenders* (Kay *et al.* 1998), states:

> If probation services are to work effectively with racially motivated and racist offenders, then there needs to be a reassessment of the value base that informs practice and the development of values and beliefs, which are not eurocentric and which are relevant for probation work in contemporary Britain.

To challenge and change the value base of the probation service requires an agenda which takes on board the politics of difference. This may be framed by a radical diversity strategy. However, a diversity strategy means different things to different people, and we must therefore ensure the right model.

MANAGING DIVERSITY

Managing diversity has emerged from within the new managerialism that has been adopted by a large number of organisations, public and private, over the last decade. It sits alongside the new managerial paradigms of 'total quality management' and 'human resources management'. All three of these concepts have elements in common — not least, they are driven by the need to make business more efficient. The primary motive, especially in the profit sector, is economic gain. In the public sector, it is about economic efficiency and 'best value'. The business case for managing diversity is that heterogeneous organisations are more creative and encourage lateral and imaginative thinking, giving the organisation a qualitative competitive edge. In addition, the politics of representation requires organisations to demonstrate their commitment to equality in a visible and demonstrable way. Put more simply, it makes sense to reflect the communities served by the organisation, private or public.

Diversity discourses offer an opportunity to create a shift from a British cultural norm of fearing strangers to one in which difference is valued and seen as critical to the development of the nation. If this can be embraced and understood by probation services, it also offers a way forward.

However, while diversity concepts theoretically embrace the need to recognise difference as positive, there are dangers rooted in the way they have come about, and there needs to be awareness of these dangers if they are to be avoided. The difference in quality is dependent on the level of political understanding, and that is what will shape the conceptualisation and implementation process. In summary:

(a)   Features of liberal diversity

- Different ethnic groups are seen as amorphous masses, without internal differences.
- Diversity is seen as a celebration of superficial difference.
- Multicultural events focus on them and us — saris and steel bands.
- Ethnicity is seen as exotic, not political.
- Valuing diversity is a nice way of speaking about 'tolerance'.
- The politics of recognition/difference are too hot to handle.

(b)   Radical diversity

- Challenges the denial of racism and the Thatcherite naturalisation of xenophobia.
- Recognises difference and the politics of difference.
- Mainstreams issues of race and anti-racism.
- Challenges the negative aspects of occupational culture by a critical examination of its symbols, traditions, customs, policies and practices.
- Recognises that racism is a violation of human rights.
- Carries a clear anti-racist message.
- Is implemented with rigour and vigour through education, sanctions and clarity of purpose, and in partnerships with Black communities.

- Involves institutional reform.

(c)   Radical diversity features

- Monitoring of all elements from recruitment to service delivery.
- Consultation which is ethical and non-tokenistic.
- Positive action programmes.
- Integration/mainstreaming of race and ethnicity issues into all elements of policy.
- Quality assurance programmes/inspections.
- Recognition of institutional and indirect racisms.
- Emphatic leadership — it is conceived as a top management priority and as part of corporate strategic planning.
- Accountability.
- Customer evaluation.
- Partnerships.

Put simply, 'managing diversity' is a concept which can be located at the level of multicultural voyeurism rather than as a positive challenge to the negative aspects of occupational culture and a refusal to collude with racism in wider society. That said, if it does translate to anti-racist practice with a strong emphasis on monitoring and sanctions, it can result in challenging the discrimination that is inherent in the deficit model of difference. It can be a radical policy tool to ensure equality in service provision and in the workplace.

CONCLUSION

If Zahid Mubarak had not received a custodial sentence for this petty crime and instead had good probation care . . . If racism was monitored closely . . . If the cellmates were monitored closely . . . If the first sign of racism was dealt with . . . However, this level of attention to detail is not routine or part of the cultural practice of criminal justice agencies, including the probation service. Feedback from probation officers confirms this — that it would be seen as too specific and too political. Typically, a report would say that the offender was vulnerable and, therefore, by implication, needing to be placed, if at all possible, in a non-threatening environment. However, the extent to which the reports would be able to say, for example, that here was a Muslim lad, particularly affected by racism in society, in need of culturally sensitive practice, such as prayer time and counselling and education from an Imam or member of the community, and that he should not be placed with any racists, is far more questionable. It would be dependent on the experience and skill of the probation officer, the culture of the local service, and on National Standards being translated effectively into local practice with respect to racism. The HMIP Report shows how much would be left to chance; and indeed, gives rise to the question of whether, even if the issues had been raised, they would have been ignored.

A few well-informed officers may raise the issues, but are limited in their effectiveness by what is and is not politically acceptable. Pockets of good practice are insufficient in a sea of bad practice; examples of good practice must be institutionalised.

The argument here has been that there are extant and ample legislative and race guidelines, and it is time to take the next step to deliver race equality. This fundamentally requires leadership, which has political commitment, depth of knowledge and strength of will. There is no excuse for race equality initiatives not to be implemented, except the racism of indifference.

Lastly, two fundamental questions arise:

(a)   To what extent is wholesale institutional reform being implemented which should strike at the heart of institutional racism?

(b)   To what extent have the politics of difference been understood and adopted by the probation service?

If it is to move forward, the probation service must conduct an analysis of all contemporary race legislation and policy, to extract strategic objectives to fulfil their requirements and, from these, devise an action plan, which is monitored and inspected in an open, publicly accountable process.

APPENDIX

There follows a comparison of the HMIP (2000f) findings and selected recommendations with selected Lawrence Inquiry recommendations, selected requirements from the Race Relations (Amendment) Act 2000 and from the Commission for Racial Equality's Standards for Local Government 1995 (CRE, 1995). Although the standards were written for local government, they should be read as if applying to probation. In the original document, the outcomes are supported by levels of action that should be taken to achieve them.

HMIP Key findings and recommendations	Lawrence Inquiry 1999, CRE Standards 1995 and the Race Relations (Amendment) Act 2000
A significantly higher quality of reports overall written on white than on minority ethnic offenders Probation committees and CPOs should: 7. Take action to improve the overall quality of PSRs on minority ethnic offenders by: (a) setting an annual target for improvement from 2001; (b) revising policy statements and practice guidance in respect of PSRs to take account of specific issues relating to minority ethnic offenders; (c) collecting and using comprehensive monitoring data, including the race and ethnic background of offenders; (d) ensuring that quality assurance measures address the particular circumstances of minority ethnic offenders. (para 4.49)	*Lawrence Inquiry 1999* The prevailing theme of differential treatment is reflected in the Inquiry's conclusions about Institutional racism. 'Institutional racism consists of the collective failure of an organisation to provide an appropriate and professional service to people because of their colour, culture or ethnic origin. It can be seen or detected in processes, attitudes and behaviour which amount to discrimination through unwitting prejudice, ignorance, thoughtlessness and racist stereotyping which disadvantage minority ethnic people'.
The failure of many services to collect data on race and ethnic origin Probation committees and CPOs should: 16. Ensure monitoring systems are in place and information is collated which is used to inform and improve employment practice and work with minority ethnic offenders. (para 14.24) The Home Office should: 6. Require probation services to meet set targets for the submission of race and ethnic data. (para 14.24)	*CRE standards 1995* AREA 1 — POLICY AND PLANNING The local authority should be able to evaluate progress towards achievement of its racial equality objectives. Members and officers should have more comprehensive information from which to plan and implement the programme, internally and externally. *Race Relations (Amendment) Act 2000* All public employers that are made subject to the general duty to promote race equality have a specific duty to ethnically monitor staff in post and applicants for jobs, promotion and training, and those with 150 or more employees have a specific duty to ethnically monitor and analyse grievances, disciplinary action, performance appraisal (when this results in benefits or sanctions), training and dismissals and other reasons for leaving. All of the public employers made subject to these particular duties should publish annually the results of their ethnic monitoring.
Significant concerns in relation to African/African-Caribbean offenders, regarding risk assessments, the level of contact particularly during the later stages of the order, and enforcement practice.	*Lawrence Inquiry 1999* Differential treatment that is detrimental to a particular racial group goes to the heart of Institutional Racism.

HMIP Key findings and recommendations	Lawrence Inquiry 1999, CRE Standards 1995 and the Race Relations (Amendment) Act 2000
A number of services had submitted their programmes for working with minority ethnic offenders to the Home Office for development as a Pathfinder. Despite the requirement of the national standard that a risk assessment on offenders should be undertaken before a community service placement was arranged, the sample showed that no assessment had taken place in a higher proportion of African/African-Caribbean cases than white and Asian cases. CPOs should: 17. Ensure that in implementing and monitoring the revised national standards and local What Works strategies, they should make specific provision for effective work with minority ethnic offenders. (para 5.50).	*Lawrence Inquiry 1999* Differential treatment that is detrimental to a particular racial group goes to the heart of Institutional Racism.
Although there was a commitment to work with racially motivated offenders, few of the services had, as yet, produced the detailed guidance necessary to translate this into operational reality. CPOs should: 18.(b) Undertake a review of CS policy and practice guidance and ensure that the potential for racist attitudes and behaviour is assessed as part of the CS risk assessment. 17. Ensure that in implementing and monitoring the revised national standards and local What Works strategies, they should make specific provision for effective work with minority ethnic offenders. (para 5.50).	*Race Relations (Amendment) Act 2000* New RRAA — General Duty It requires specified public bodies to have due regard to the need to eliminate unlawful racial discrimination and to promote equality of opportunity and good relations between persons of different racial groups when performing their functions.

HMIP Key findings and recommendations	Lawrence Inquiry 1999, CRE Standards 1995 and the Race Relations (Amendment) Act 2000
It was apparent that all services had considerable work to do to improve their standing and gain the confidence of local minority ethnic communities, both in terms of work with offenders and as a potential employer. Probation committees and CPOs should: 9. Demonstrate that, as part of service strategies to meet the different needs of minority ethnic offenders, the development of formal and informal partnerships has been informed by the advice and expertise of local community groups. (para 8.22)	*Lawrence Inquiry 1999* PUBLIC CONFIDENCE IN THE POLICE 1. That a Ministerial Priority be established for all Police Services: 'To increase trust and confidence in policing amongst minority ethnic communities'. *CRE standards 1995* AREA 2 — SERVICE DELIVERY AND CUSTOMER CARE • The local authority's position on racial equality is clear to all service users and organisations with contracts, or seeking contracts. • Staff in all service delivery directorates are clear on the policy and the action needed to implement it. • The consultation process leads to greater satisfaction with the local authority's services from all sections of the community. • Members of the public are aware that breach of the policy will be met with action from the authority.
[While] 53 services had developed an equal opportunities policy, it was difficult to estimate the effect of either the equal opportunities or the anti-racism policies in the absence, in the majority, of a supporting action plan with agreed outcome measures Probation committees and CPOs should: 10. Ensure that, in order to promote race equality: (a) all existing equal opportunities and anti-racism policies are reviewed, and amended as appropriate, to ensure that they cover the full range of employment practices and work with offenders; (b) action plans are produced which include specific measurable objectives to support the implementation of the policies; (c) equal opportunities policies, anti-racism policies and related action plans are monitored and reviewed annually by the probation committee. (para 9.38).	*CRE standards 1995* All employees, service users, contractors and organisations which come into contact with the local authority are aware of its racial equality action programme. The internal consultation process ensures that all employees are informed of the value of equal opportunity, and are committed to that policy. *Race Relations (Amendment) Act 2000* Prepare and publish a Race Equality Scheme. Assess which of its functions and policies are relevant to the general duty. Set out its arrangements for assessing and consulting on the impact on the promotion of race equality of policies it is proposing for adoption. Set out its arrangements for monitoring for any adverse impact.

HMIP Key findings and recommendations	*Lawrence Inquiry 1999, CRE Standards 1995 and the Race Relations (Amendment) Act 2000*
Minority ethnic staff were under-represented at chief officer level and other management grades. Probation committees and CPOs should: 11. Develop workforce planning strategies from April 2001 to meet set targets for the recruitment of minority ethnic staff and implement positive action measures to address imbalances. (para 10.46).	*Lawrence Inquiry 1999* SELECTION AND PROMOTION 59. That the Home Office reviews and monitors the system and standards of Police Services applied to the selection and promotion of officers of the rank of Inspector and above. Such procedures for selection and promotion to be monitored and assessed regularly. RECRUITMENT AND RETENTION 64. That the Home Secretary and Police Authorities' policing plans should include targets for recruitment, progression and retention of minority ethnic staff. Police Authorities to report progress to the Home Secretary annually. Such reports to be published. 65. That the Home Office and Police Services should facilitate the development of initiatives to increase the number of qualified minority ethnic recruits. 66. That HMIC include in any regular inspection or in a thematic inspection report on the progress made by Police Services in recruitment, progression and retention of minority ethnic staff.
Although staff at all levels emphasised the importance of training on race equality in relation to service delivery, little was available to date. Probation committees and CPOs should: 12. Ensure the inclusion of appropriate mandatory training for all staff to promote race equality in annual training and staff development plans from 2001 giving priority to: (a) probation committee members; (b) white managers supervising minority ethnic staff; (c) minority ethnic managers; (d) race equality training, including raising cultural awareness, and considering implications for specific aspects of service delivery or organisational practice; (e) work with racist and racially motivated offenders. (para 12.30).	*Lawrence Inquiry 1999* TRAINING RECOMMENDATIONS All Police officers, including CID and civilian staff, should be trained in racism awareness and valuing cultural diversity. 48. That there should be an immediate review and revision of racism awareness training within Police Services to ensure:- (a) that there exists a consistent strategy to deliver appropriate training within all Police Services based upon the value of our cultural diversity. (b) that training courses are designed and delivered in order to develop the full understanding that good community relations are essential to good policing and that a racist officer is an incompetent officer. 49. That All Police officers, including CID and civilian staff, should be trained in racism awareness and valuing cultural diversity. 50. That Police training and practical experience in the field of racism awareness and valuing cultural diversity should regularly be conducted at local level. And that it should be recognised that local minority ethnic communities should be involved in such training and experience.

HMIP Key findings and recommendations	Lawrence Inquiry 1999, CRE Standards 1995 and the Race Relations (Amendment) Act 2000
	51. That consideration be given by Police Services to promoting joint training with members of other organisations or professions otherwise than on Police premises.
	52. That the Home Office together with Police Services should publish recognised standards of training aims and objectives in the field of racism awareness and valuing cultural diversity.
	53. That there should be independent and regular monitoring of training within all Police Services to test both implementation and achievement of such training.
	54. That consideration be given to a review of the provision of training in racism awareness and valuing cultural diversity in local Government and other agencies including other sections of the Criminal Justice system.
It was clear, however, that no common understanding existed across individual services about what constituted racist behaviour. It was a matter of serious concern that over half the staff who completed the questionnaire had experienced racist behaviour during the course of their work, 52 per cent from offenders and 57 per cent from colleagues or members of external organisations. Probation committees and CPOs should: 8. Adopt the definition of a racist incident in the Macpherson report and produce revised policy and practice guidance to ensure the effective supervision of racially motivated offenders. (para 7.32). The Home Office should: 5. Ensure that a separate complaints procedure is established so that any complaints made by probation service staff are given proper consideration. (para 13.35).	Lawrence Inquiry 1999 RACIST INCIDENTS 12. That the definition should be: 'A racist incident is any incident which is perceived to be racist by the victim or any other person'. 15. That Codes of Practice be established by the Home Office, in consultation with Police Services, local government and relevant agencies, to create a comprehensive system of reporting and recording of all racist incidents and crimes. POLICE ACCOUNTABILITY, EMPLOYMENT, DISCIPLINE & COMPLAINTS 55. That the changes to Police Disciplinary and Complaints procedures proposed by the Home Secretary should be fully implemented and closely and publicly monitored as to their effectiveness. 56. That in order to eliminate the present provision which prevents disciplinary action after retirement, disciplinary action should be available for at least five years after an officer's retirement. 57. That the Police Services should through the implementation of a Code of Conduct or otherwise ensure that racist words or acts proved to have been spoken or done by police officers should lead to disciplinary proceedings, and that it should be understood that such conduct should usually merit dismissal

HMIP Key findings and recommendations	Lawrence Inquiry 1999, CRE Standards 1995 and the Race Relations (Amendment) Act 2000
Few of the services visited made any significant use of the [monitoring] information collated either with staff or to inform discussions with the probation committee or at senior management level. It was difficult to see how the majority of services could monitor their performance, make any strategic decision on provision for minority ethnic offenders or promote race equality on the basis of the monitoring information currently available. Probation committees and CPOs should: 16. Ensure monitoring systems are in place and information is collated which is used to inform and improve employment practice and work with minority ethnic offenders. (para 14.24).	*Lawrence Inquiry 1999* METROPOLITAN POLICE PROCEDURES 22. That the MPS review their internal inspection and accountability processes to ensure that policy directives are observed. *Race Relations (Amendment) Act 2000* • Monitor its workforce, taking steps to ensure that ethnic minorities are treated fairly • Assess how its policies and programmes could affect ethnic minorities, identify any potential for adverse differential impact, and take remedial action if necessary • Monitor the implementation of its policies and programmes to ensure that they meet the needs of ethnic minorities • Have a publicly stated policy on race equality
The absence of a clear national direction had undoubtedly contributed to the low priority given to race equality by some probation services. The level of attention given to the promotion of race equality by chief probation officers and probation committees varied considerably. The majority of services who had acted on the recommendations of the Macpherson report and the Home Secretary's Action Plan were still in an initial phase of identifying areas of work to be addressed. It was evident from discussions with minority ethnic staff at all services and from feedback from the questionnaire that the Macpherson report and the subsequent response by the Home Secretary had raised expectations of significant change in the culture, management and performance of the service. The Home Office, probation committees and CPOs should: 1. Provide clear direction and guidance to probation services in order to inform their development of equal opportunities and anti-racism policies. (para 15.27)	*Lawrence Inquiry 1999* PUBLIC CONFIDENCE IN THE POLICE 1. That a Ministerial Priority be established for all Police Services: 'To increase trust and confidence in policing amongst minority ethnic communities'. 2. The process of implementing, monitoring and assessing the Ministerial Priority should include Performance Indicators in relation to: i. the existence and application of strategies for the prevention, recording, investigation and prosecution of racist incidents; ii. measures to encourage reporting of racist incidents; iii. the number of recorded racist incidents and related detection levels; iv. the degree of multi-agency co-operation and information exchange; v. achieving equal satisfaction levels across all ethnic groups in public satisfaction surveys; vi. the adequacy of provision and training of family and witness/victim liaison officers; vii. the nature, extent and achievement of racism awareness training; viii. the policy directives governing stop and search procedures and their outcomes; ix. levels of recruitment, retention and progression of minority ethnic recruits; and x. levels of complaint of racist behaviour or attitude and their outcomes. The overall aim being the elimination of racist prejudice and disadvantage and the demonstration of fairness in all aspects of policing.

9   Missed Opportunities? The Probation Service and Women Offenders

Anne Worrall

INTRODUCTION

> To accept that 'justice' and 'equality' are to be achieved by parity of treatment is to collude in the acceptance of the inequalities, which co-exist with such 'equal treatment'. To assume that justice for women means treating women like men is to ignore the very different existences, which distinguish the lives of women from the lives of men of similar social status. (Eaton 1986, p. 11)

> Effective action to prevent discrimination requires significantly more than a willingness to accept all offenders equally or to invest an equal amount of time and effort in different cases. The origin, nature and extent of differences in circumstances and need must be properly understood and actively addressed. (Home Office 1992a, p. 32)

It is a salutary reflection that if men committed the same amount of crime as women, the whole criminal justice system would collapse overnight — and most criminologists would be out of work. The crime prevention industry would be bankrupted; house and car insurance premiums would plummet; tabloid newspaper circulation figures would drop through the floor; 'Crimewatch UK' would be off the air and crime writers would be reclassified as historical novelists. But the world would be a different place in other ways as well. The home would be safer, little girls (and boys) would be safer, old women (and men) would be safer, even multi-national corporations would be safer! Crime would be at a level that any civilised society ought to be able to tolerate.

The inescapable fact is that female crime, as a social phenomenon and despite media hyperbole, is still no threat to society. That is not to argue that female crime is not 'real crime', or that a handful of individual female criminals are not dangerous, or greedy or both. Rather, it is to make the point (see Carlen 1990) that if all women's prisons were closed tomorrow, except for one wing in a closed prison, it is quite possible that no one would notice.

Women constitute only 17 per cent of known offenders (Home Office 2001i), and most of them will be cautioned or conditionally discharged. Only 12 per cent of offenders given community sentences (probation, community service and combination orders) are women, and only 5 per cent of the prison population are women. Women commit fewer crimes than men, their offences tend to be less serious and their criminal careers shorter. But percentages can be falsely reassuring (or falsely alarming, depending on their use). In absolute numbers, we now lock up twice as many women as we did in the early 1990s. The female prison population has increased from 1,500 to over 3,000. Of these, 400 are juveniles (compared with 200 in the early 1990s). The number of girls in local authority secure accommodation has also doubled in that time (Department of Health 2000). These latter figures are of particular concern, since the numbers of known female offenders under the age of 18 years have actually fallen during this period (Home Office 2000d). This fall has been accompanied, however, by a fall in the rate of cautioning and a consequent rise in the numbers being processed through the criminal justice system. One in four of the women in prison is from a minority ethnic group (Home Office 2000p; Prison Reform Trust 2000a). While half of these are foreign nationals, the remaining proportion is still twice that of the population outside prison. When it comes to dispensing justice to women, crime becomes inextricably entwined with race, class and sexuality (Worrall 1995).

In 1995, in the original version of this chapter, it was argued that, although women may commit very little crime we hold them responsible for a great deal of it. As victims of rape and domestic violence, they 'ask for it'. As partners of child sexual abusers, they 'collude' with it (and increasingly aid and abet men, or even act independently — see Matravers 2001). As lone mothers (and working mothers), the media would have us believe that they produce and rear the next generation of its perpetrators. The reality, if not the theory, of parenting orders (introduced by the Crime and Disorder Act 1998) is that they fall disproportionately on mothers (Drakeford and McCarthy 2000, p. 107). The 'responsibilisation' of women in the context of crime takes a number of forms, ranging from the demonising of single, teenage mothers as welfare scroungers and disciplining them for 'poor parenting', to 'discovering' their propensity for violence and sexual offending. Additionally, it is no longer acceptable to view 'experiences such as poverty, abuse and drug addiction' as explanations of women's law-breaking. These things only 'lead some women to believe that their options are limited' (Home Office 2000p, p. 7, emphasis added). According to the Government, 'there are always positive choices open to them that do not involve crime' (*ibid.*), and this is because the Government is already tackling the social exclusion which has hitherto resulted in the 'poor thinking skills' that lead women into crime. The argument is not that there has never been a connection between social injustice and women's crime; rather, it is argued that the Government has now broken that connection through its 'wider programme to tackle social exclusion' (*ibid.*). As with juvenile offending in the late 1990s, there are now 'no more excuses' for women's offending.

In revisiting the argument that justice for women can be achieved only 'through inequality' (Worrall 1995), the purpose of this chapter is to demonstrate the impossibility of separating criminal justice from social justice and human rights, when attempting to understand and deal with women who commit crimes. The achievements of the probation service in relation to many women offenders will be acknowledged, but it will be argued that the service has missed opportunities to remain a major player in the lives of women offenders. As the discourse of rehabilitation turns away from social work and towards cognitive behavioural psychology, the role of the probation officer (no longer a social worker, but not yet a psychologist) in the new National Probation Service may now be less clear than it was even five years ago, and certainly less than it was a decade ago.

THE DILEMMAS OF VISIBILITY — THE RECENT HISTORY
OF WOMEN OFFENDERS AND CRIMINAL JUSTICE

The 1980s might well be viewed in the world of criminology as the decade when female crime was rendered visible. It is no longer possible to introduce a book or article on women and crime by saying that it is a contribution to a neglected area of criminology. Over the past two decades, interest in the subject has increased exponentially and there is now a well-established theoretical literature, which challenges the conventional wisdom that female criminals are peculiar and of only marginal interest. Pioneering work by Carol Smart (1976) caught the imagination of an increasing number of women students on criminology courses and CQSW/ DipSW probation options. Collaboration between women criminologists, probation officers and ex-prisoner campaigning groups ensured that the treatment of women offenders was placed on conference and training course agendas. Research projects burgeoned. Anecdotal evidence matured into respectable data (despite the scepticism of some established criminologists — see, for example, Nigel Walker 1981) and the tide of accusations of sexual discrimination in the criminal justice system became unstoppable. Women offenders, though few in number, were being judged as doubly deviant — as breakers of gender norms as well as of criminal law. They were being sentenced more for the type of women they appeared to be than for the seriousness, or otherwise, of the crimes they had committed. Rendered invisible and mute, they were being written out of the scripts of their own lives by experts in medical and social regulation, who claimed to know more about them than they could ever know about themselves.

For a while in the early 1990s, there was some cause for optimism. The Criminal Justice Act 1991, based on the principle of 'just deserts', should have resulted in a fairer deal for women criminals. If sentencing was to depend predominantly on the seriousness of the current offence, the implication should have been that fewer women would go to prison for relatively minor offences, however frequently committed. It did not automatically follow that women who commit serious offences would be dealt with by community disposals — probation centre programmes and community service orders. Nevertheless, it did enable such sentences to be argued for on the basis of a different logic — namely, that refusal to give such opportunities amounted to discrimination, as defined in s. 95(1)(b) of the 1991 Act. Given that the Government had also tentatively suggested in its preceding White Paper, *Crime, Justice and Protecting the Public* (Home Office 1990a), that it might be possible to abolish custodial detention for young women under the age of 18 years, it was not unreasonable to think that someone, somewhere, at some time, was hoping that courts would send fewer women — and certainly fewer young women — to prison.

Although, as several writers pointed out, Lord Justice Woolf did not consider women's prisons in his Report on the 1990 prison disturbances (1991), the implications of his principles for women's prisons were discussed creatively (NACRO 1991; Player 1994; Hayman 1996). In particular, one interpretation of the concept of 'community prisons' was the proposal for a large number of locally based houses set aside for the purpose, where women would reside (possibly with their children) making use of community facilities and resources to provide their daily regime (NACRO 1991). Examples of such 'transitional' arrangements exist in other countries, such as The Netherlands (see Hayman 1996) and parts of Australia (personal research in Queensland, New South Wales and Victoria), but in this country hostel provision for women offenders remains under-funded and neglected (Howard League 2000).

But the optimism of the early 1990s soon passed. The Criminal Justice Act 1993 restored to courts the right to take previous convictions into account indiscriminately. (As we know, the 1991 Act never removed the right absolutely, it just made courts think twice before doing so.) The so-called 'flexibility' of the Youth Court to treat 16- and 17-year-olds as either juveniles or adults resulted in a steady increase in the numbers of juvenile girls being imprisoned, and the escape attempts at Whitemoor and Parkhurst ensured that any post-Woolf progress in women's prisons had been reversed by the middle of the decade. (For a more detailed account of the politics of women's imprisonment in the 1990s, see Carlen 1998.) Sadly, an uncritical adoption of a misunderstood 'liberal feminism' may have contributed to this. As Smart predicted, crude calls for equality of treatment have resulted in women being sent 'in their droves to dirty, violent and overcrowded prisons for long periods of time' (1990, p. 79). On the other hand, as Carlen has consistently argued, however theoretically brilliant some critiques of penal reform may be, there is a danger that they may simply foster a view that 'nothing works' and that reform is therefore pointless (Carlen 2001).

Neither perspective — calls for equality, or eschewing official reform agenda — has been very helpful in offering guidance to probation officers who, whilst trying to avoid viewing women offenders as merely passive victims of an irredeemably discriminatory system, nevertheless believe that women must be helped to stop offending because it is women themselves who suffer most from their crime.

TRENDS IN WOMEN AND COMMUNITY SENTENCES

As Harris (1992, p. 98) says, 'part of the problem is that it is unclear what the "better treatment of women" actually means'. In the early 1980s, the predominant concern among those probation officers willing to cast a critical eye over their work with women offenders was that too many were being placed on probation. While women represented between 15 and 17 per cent of known offenders, 33 per cent of probation orders were on women. In absolute numbers, that was nearly 12,000 in 1981, compared with 24,000 men (Home Office 1993d). And far too many of those (36 per cent compared with 17 per cent of men) were first offenders. There was some concern about the numbers of women sent to prison (about 1,100), but there was an assumption (informed by theories of labelling and deviancy amplification) that diverting women from probation would automatically reduce the numbers in prison. The theory worked for juvenile crime in the 1980s, but it failed spectacularly for women (although it has to be said that juvenile justice workers demonstrated a much greater commitment to keeping young people out of custody, even at the risk of incurring magistrates' wrath, than probation officers have ever done to keeping women out of prison).

By 1993, the numbers of women on probation had fallen to 7,104 (a mere 16 per cent of all orders) but numbers in prison had risen to 1,500 (Home Office 2001e). From 1994, probation orders for women began to increase too, but only reached 12,000 again in 1999. In comparison, probation orders on men increased to around 44,000 by 1999, so orders on women still represented only 18 per cent of all orders. The picture changes somewhat, though, when trends in community service and combination orders are considered. To quote *Probation Statistics England and Wales 1999* (Home Office 2001e):

There was an average of 18 men with a CS order for each woman with a CS order in 1989. This ratio has fallen to 8 men for each woman with a CS order in 1999. Sentencers have become more ready to give a sentence of CS to a woman over the period 1989–1999.

The ratio is similar in respect of combination orders. But any hope that the increase in community service and combination orders may be keeping more serious female offenders out of prison has to be tempered by the knowledge that over half the women on community service are now first offenders (Home Office 2001e, p. 26), compared with 30 per cent in 1992 and 18 per cent in 1981 (Worrall 1995). If one adds into these calculations the decline in fines on women (Hedderman and Gelsthorpe 1997), there seems to be a trend towards a greater use of community service for women who would previously have been fined or placed on probation, rather than sent to prison. So although the worst excesses of net-widening in relation to minor offending by women appear to have been curbed in the past decade, those who remain within the system are being propelled towards custody as fast as, if not faster than, ever. This is happening despite evidence that women's criminal careers are shorter than those of men and their reconviction rates (following all disposals) are lower (Home Office 2001i, p. 35).

WHO IS TO BLAME?

In 1995 this author argued that the probation service was too introspective, cautious and self-blaming about its apparent failure to keep more women out of prison. Its concern, over the previous decade, had been to exorcise 'irrelevant' information and discriminatory language in social inquiry and pre-sentence reports, which might result in the reinforcement of stereotypical gender and racial expectations. This process was very successful in persuading courts that (white?) women who commit relatively minor crimes are not necessarily doing so as a 'cry for help', neither do they necessarily need someone to talk to about their problems — no more so than any law-abiding woman, that is! But the message that the probation service could offer something to women who, for whatever reason, were deemed to be at risk of losing their liberty, was not being heard. Such an argument now seems rather quaint. It is no longer a question of how the probation service makes its voice heard in relation to women offenders, but of whether it does in fact have anything to offer.

In the early 1990s, over half of all probation services were engaging in group-work with women offenders (Carlen 1990), and in 1995 this author wrote enthusiastically in the first edition of this book about various examples of woman-centred practice in the service. Looking for up-to-date examples of similar work has been difficult, and it was saddening to read that, as late as 1998 (Hay and Stirling 1998), it was still necessary to 'start from scratch' every time a women's group was run in order to convince management that the provision of some 'all-women' programmes did not imply managerial weakness in the face of subversive radical feminism. But perhaps we should not be surprised, since the recent publication, *The Government's Strategy for Women Offenders*, reports that the Association of Chief Officers of Probation identified (only) 19 group-work programmes specifically for women (Home Office 2000p, p. 18). The same document reports only one pilot offending behaviour programme (the South Glamorgan programme mentioned below) and one 'being developed' (by Derbyshire probation service).

Community service fares no better, despite the increase in the number of orders being made on women. None of the six community service pathfinders (funded by the Home Office) is aimed exclusively at women offenders (Home Office 2000p, p. 19). As the Howard League discovered (1999, p. 18):

Across the country, the picture which emerges is of community service units dealing with women sent to them but on a case-by-case basis ... [I]f women continue to be regarded as an anomaly, then it is unlikely to engender sentencer confidence.

The Howard League's call for a national initiative to promote and develop community service for women seems to have fallen on stony ground, though the new Director of the National Probation Service appears to accept the existence of a problem of discrimination against women in relation to community service (Roberts, 2001). The problems surrounding community service for women are well known but by no means unresolvable. What is required is a change in the attitude that regards community service predominantly as a punishment for 'fit, young men' (Worrall 1997, p. 98). Better child-care arrangements, more female supervisors and consideration for the kind of working environments most suitable for women would also result in greater use. Whatever the perceived disadvantages to women of doing community service, they cannot possibly outweigh the disadvantages of imprisoning those same women. Indeed, with the introduction of the Human

Rights Act 1998, it might be possible for women denied community sentences and given short prison sentences to claim violation of their right to respect for their private and family life (under Article 8 of the European Convention), especially if that involves separation from small children and imprisonment at an unreasonable distance from home (Prison Reform Trust 2000b).

WHAT WORKS FOR WOMEN OFFENDERS?

To the question, 'What works for women offenders?', the official response is 'What works for men offenders with a few adjustments', judging by the first report of the Joint Prison/ Probation Accreditation Panel (Home Office 2000t). There are now a number of accredited offending behaviour programmes, which can be used with either men or women, and areas may tailor these to all-women groups, if they wish — and if they have sufficient numbers of women with whom to work. However, programmes designed specifically for women are apparently having greater difficulty in obtaining accreditation. The Hereford and Worcester (Probation Service) Women's Programme, chosen as an original 'pathfinder' and much praised by the Wedderburn Report (Prison Reform Trust 2000a), was considered to lack focus on factors linked to offending (in particular, drug misuse) and on offending behaviour itself (despite the inclusion of a specific module for persistent offenders). It was deemed 'unlikely ever to be an accreditable ... approach' (Home Office 2000e, p. 9). Slightly more hopeful was a programme for women involved in acquisitive crime designed by South Glamorgan Probation Service and described by the panel as 'encouraging' (*op cit.*, p. 14). This has been superseded by developmental work on a programme designed by the Canadian owners of the Reasoning and Rehabilitation programmes due to be piloted in several probation areas from 2002.

The failure of the Hereford and Worcester programme to obtain accreditation throws into sharp relief the conflict between criminal and social justice. In order to be accredited, programmes are required to meet 11 very specific criteria,[1] which demand clarity in respect of

---

[1] These can be found in Annex A of the First Report from the Joint Prison/ Probation Accreditation Panel, available on www.homeoffice.gov.uk.

evidence-based models of change, targeting of risk factors,[2] use of effective (for which read 'cognitive behavioural') methods, programme integrity (consistency of delivery), monitoring and evaluation. Such criteria, proponents argue, 'eliminate subjective, arbitrary decision-making, bias and prejudice', with issues of gender and race being 'added in' without undermining the basic model (Shaw and Hannah-Moffat 2000, p. 164). In line with the new penology (Feeley and Simon 1992), they ensure that offenders are classified objectively, using actuarial tools of risk assessment, and dealt with in the most efficient, effective and economical way. The Hereford and Worcester programme operates on rather different (though, arguably, not incompatible — given a little creative thinking) assumptions about the lives of women who offend: 'The aim is to help women avoid further offending by increasing their abilities to solve complex problems legitimately, by holding in balance the demands made upon them, the external resources and legitimate opportunities available to them, and their own capacities and abilities. (Prison Reform Trust 2000a, p. 70–71). The programme designers would argue that it does, in fact, meet the criteria for accreditation (Roberts, J., forthcoming). For example, evaluation appears to demonstrate that while the reconviction rates of completers and non-completers were similar after six months, differences began to appear between the two groups after a year and were considerable after two years. However, two 'conceptual strands' that guided the development of the programme appear to have proved unacceptable to the Accreditation Panel:

> One of these was 'normalisation', which encouraged an effort to reduce female offenders' isolation from community based networks of support. The second, complementary strand was to reduce the emphasis on the probation service as a focal resource for women who were seen to have social and personal needs in common with many non-offending women. (Rumgay 1999, cited in Prison Reform Trust 2000a, p. 71)

The Wedderburn Report's recommendation for the setting up of a network of Women's Supervision, Rehabilitation and Support Centres (Prison Reform Trust 2000a, p. 70), giving women better access to a range of community agencies under one roof, was based on a probation

---

[2] For more details of Prison Service research on the criminogenic factors associated with female offending, see Stewart 2000 and Home Office 2000b.

service experiment (Roberts, J., forthcoming), but appears to have met with little response from the service as a whole. The idea of women-only provision remains controversial, and the suggestion that probation officers and psychologists might not be the most vital or influential people in the lives of women offenders is apparently difficult to accept, though it is wholly in line with other critical appraisals of the What Works agenda. Hannah-Moffat (1999) warns us about the danger of redefining women offenders' 'needs' as 'predictive risk factors'. When policymakers start talking about 'adapting' programmes and risk assessment tools for use by women, they rightly adopt the language of 'need'. However, rather than analysing and seeking to meet those needs through better access to community resources, 'needs talk' may merely replace 'risk talk'; and 'high need' women become 'high risk' women, who can then be subjected to the same programming as 'high risk' men. The main difference, according to Stewart, is that women are more 'responsive' (which means that they talk more), so 'the overall structure of the courses did not need to be changed; rather the emphasis was on providing additional, more appropriate role-play scenarios' (2000, p. 42). Approached in this way, women present only a minor challenge to the delivery of programmes.

But advocates of such an approach may wish to ask themselves why, despite the evident logic of their case, they are meeting with so much resistance, not just from academics, but also from women, who have spent many years of their lives working with women within the criminal justice system. The small number of women who commit offences are driven to do so not by 'cognitive-behavioural deficit', but by the complexity of the demands placed upon them. They not only believe that they have few positive legitimate options, but, in reality, they have few positive legitimate options. Important as enhanced thinking skills and anger management undoubtedly are, they can only be, at best, a prerequisite to empowering women to make better choices, if the choices genuinely exist. At worst, they become an end in themselves and a means, albeit implicitly, of persuading women to accept the limitations on genuine choice.

LITTLE GIRLS, DRUGS AND SOCRATIC DIALOGUE

It has been argued so far that little has changed in the attitude of the probation service towards women offenders in the past five years and, if anything, provision may have worsened. But this indifference should be set in a socio-political context where at least three things have changed in the representation of women offenders and the work of the service. The first is the increasing desire of the public and the media to believe that girls are getting more violent and require penal incarceration at ever younger ages; the second is the undeniable increase in drugs-related crime among women; and the third is the extent to which psychologists have taken over from probation officers in the delivery of programmes for offenders (both male and female) in prison and, perhaps to a lesser extent, in the community.[3]

The plight of girls in prison was highlighted in 1997 by three events: a thematic review of women in prison by HM Chief Inspector of Prisons; a report by the Howard League on the imprisonment of teenage girls; and a High Court ruling that a teenage girl should not be held in an adult female prison. It has become clear that holding girls under the age of 18 alongside adult prisoners contravenes the UN Convention on the Rights of the Child and fails to protect them from harm under the Children Act 1989. The Howard League called for legislation prohibiting the use of prison custody for all girls aged under 18 years and the placing of 'those girls who genuinely require secure conditions in local authority secure accommodation units' (1997, p. 11). After several U-turns, the Government announced its intention to do just that in relation to 15- and 16-year-olds (Howard League 1999), though probably not for several years.[4] In the meantime, probation officers, who belong to Youth Offending Teams, are party to the detention and training orders (introduced by the Crime and Disorder Act 1998), which have resulted in the doubling of the numbers of juvenile girls in prison since 1993 (Home Office 2000d). Everything we know about the backgrounds of adult women prisoners indicates that these girls will become the 'hard core' of recidivist women offenders destined for the revolving door of prison.

Hedderman and Gelsthorpe (1997) discovered that although many women offenders were, statistically, still being dealt with more leniently than men offenders by magistrates, the two groups for whom this was

---

[3] It would perhaps be fairer to say that the discipline of psychology has replaced the discipline of social work, since the author has no real evidence that the Probation Service (unlike the Prison Service) is rushing to recruit qualified psychologists.

[4] In March 2001, the Youth Justice Board announced its intention to build two new secure units for girls.

no longer true were women, who were first-time violent offenders and women who were recidivist drug offenders. The increase in the number of women charged with drug and drug-related offences is undeniable, though this is also true for men, and women still constitute only 21 per cent of drug offenders (Home Office 2001i). Nevertheless, levels of substance misuse among prisoners are roughly comparable for men and women (ONS 1999, cited in Howard League 2000, p. 5), though women are proportionately more likely than men to be users of opiates and crack cocaine — the drugs most strongly associated with offending. For this reason, the Prison Service Women's Policy Group regards the misuse of drugs as a 'major issue for women in prison' (Stewart 2000, p. 42) and increasing resources are being made available for drugs treatment in women's prisons (e.g., at Holloway and Drake Hall). But there is now a danger that courts will send more women to prison precisely because this is the one place in the criminal justice system where such treatment may be available. A briefing paper from the Howard League (2000) argues that the introduction of drug treatment and testing orders[5] could provide a promising diversion from custody for women, if probation officers are willing to give special attention to the needs of women who misuse drugs. But if from the outset no attention is given to women's practical difficulties (suitable accommodation, pregnancy issues and child care), the orders will become yet one more male-centred provision, which will be only half-heartedly 'adapted' for women.

The Chief Inspector of Prisons' thematic report on women's prisons recommended that every women's prison should have a psychology team to inform and take part in offending behaviour programmes. Almost all women's prisons now run cognitive skills programmes, having adapted Reasoning and Rehabilitation, Enhanced Thinking and Problem Solving Programmes for use by women (Stewart 2000). Probation officers are involved in the delivery and management of these programmes, but psychologists play increasingly significant and leading roles. The ascendancy of psychology in both male and female prisons has been at the expense of the traditional (though always ambivalent) role of the prison probation officer. In one women's prison, psychologists have moved into brand new, centrally located premises, while probation officers have been relegated, literally and symbolically,

---

[5] Introduced by the Crime and Disorder Act 1998, piloted in Croydon, Gloucestershire and Liverpool and operating nationwide from December 2000.

to a temporary building on the periphery of the estate (Worrall 2000). Cognitive behavioural programmes are now viewed as the domain of psychology within the prison, and one wonders how long it will be before this becomes true in the community as well. While psychologists may well have many of the skills required for direct work with women offenders, this author remains unconvinced that what is being done in practice requires the mystification it is currently receiving. Indeed, she despairs when told that the Enhanced Thinking Skills programme is delivered to women in at least one prison through the method of 'Socratic dialogue'. Socratic dialogue is a classical philosophical approach, which involves systematic and lengthy questioning by the 'teacher' of his or her eager and voluntary 'pupils' in order to stimulate their curiosity and thirst for knowledge. The use of this phrase in the context of an offending behaviour programme in a prison leaves the author speechless and probably in need of an Anger Management programme! Kendall's (2000) critique of anger management courses, in what she terms 'coercive environments', makes the point that, while women may benefit in the short term from cognitive behavioural programmes, there is a danger that they are simply learning to cope with oppressive conditions: 'In helping women to tolerate oppression, we may be teaching them to internalise it' (Kendall 2000, p. 39).

But maybe this author is guilty of falling into the trap identified earlier, believing that 'nothing works' and that all attempts at reform are either a conspiracy of management or a construction of the New Penology?

CONCLUSION

In this chapter it has been argued that:

(a)   there is still a need for the probation service to celebrate the low level of women's offending and to avoid collusion with statements and policies that criminalise women's poverty, colour and sexuality, or hold them responsible for the crimes of men;

(b)   now, more than ever, there is a need for the service to take risks with radical non-custodial provision for women offenders and not to collude with the raucous voices claiming that women are more violent, more dangerous and generally more nasty — and at a younger age — than ever;

(c)   justice for women offenders will not be achieved through What Works programmes, or conventional equal opportunities policies, unless there is also a recognition of the particular social injustices with which many still have to contend — disproportionate experience of violence and abuse, disproportionate responsibility for parenting and disproportionately limited access to employment — all of which result in gendered poverty and lack of genuine choices.

In the early 1990s, Eaton (1993) identified the factors that enabled women ex-prisoners to turn their lives around. Women offenders, she argued, will change their lives only when they have access to the structural preconditions of social justice — housing, employment and health facilities. None of these things has changed at the millennium (Gray 2000; Lowthian 2000; Kendall 2001). But structural factors alone are insufficient. Eaton also argued that women offenders need to feel that they are people of worth, who can sustain and be sustained in reciprocal, rather than subordinate or exploitative, relationships. No amount of risk assessment and programme accreditation will disguise that reality, and unless the new National Probation Service recognises this, opportunities for justice for women offenders will continue to be missed.

10   Deconstructing Dangerousness for Safer Practice

Gwyneth Boswell

INTRODUCTION

The dangerous offender, defined as someone likely to cause serious physical or psychological harm to others, is the only person for whom otherwise liberal penal reformers are wont to make an exception, on the grounds of 'public protection'. This latter is an expression which has become very familiar to criminal justice professionals during the 1990s and beyond. For the probation service, public protection is now a primary aim, and in 1999, the Dangerous Offenders Unit was set up as part of the National Probation Directorate. Dangerousness and public protection have moved into an uneasy juxtaposition, where official rhetoric suggests that the former can be predicted and contained, and that the latter is a service which can be provided by probation staff 24 hours a day, seven days a week.

It is, nevertheless, true to say that violent crime, which, for the purposes of this chapter, includes sexual crime, has increased somewhat during the last decade, and that the probation service's official oversight of violent offenders has also risen. At the same time, the effective practice (or What Works) agenda (Chapman and Hough 1998) and the updating of National Standards (Home Office 2000k) have begun to drive the locus of professional activity towards risk assessments, high risk registers of various kinds, early warning mechanisms for the release of potentially dangerous offenders (known as PDOs), serious incident reports and so on, in order to provide some kind of scaffolding around an inherently unsafe construct.

'Dangerous' has replaced 'potentially violent' as a characteristic of a certain type of offender, who has risen to prominence on the political agenda. 'Dangerousness' has become an attributable state, which the probation service and other criminal justice professionals are called upon to assess, manage and minimise. Thus, it is time to afford some serious attention to those offenders around whom this label is hung and with whom, as now in all things, the probation service is expected to practise effectively.

This chapter invites practitioners and managers to reflect on the notion of cause, and ways in which it might be identified and addressed, aside from the frenzy of form-filling activity. It focuses, in particular, on a group frequently singled out for attention by politicians and the media and (perhaps, partly as a consequence) much feared by the public — violent young offenders — and draws out from this wider messages for probation practice in the daunting realms of dangerousness. In so doing, it identifies issues of justice for offenders who themselves experience the inherent violence of social and legal censure, and whose human rights are normally afforded little attention, so heinous are their crimes perceived to be. First, however, it is necessary to examine this phenomenon of dangerousness, as it applies to the caseload of the probation service.

PROBATION AND DANGEROUSNESS

The serious harm which potentially dangerous offenders are deemed to be at risk of posing, is defined in Home Office Guidance to the Police and Probation Services as 'harm which is life threatening or traumatic and from which recovery, whether physical or psychological, can be expected to be difficult or impossible' (Home Office 2000i, p. 7). The same document offers interpretation of s. 67 of the Criminal Justice and Court Services Act 2000 in respect of offenders at risk of behaving in this way. Essentially, these categories are as follows:

(a)   those subject to the notification of Pt. 1 of the Sex Offenders Act 1997;

(b)   those convicted in England and Wales of a sexual or violent act (within the meaning of the Powers of the Criminal Courts (Sentencing) Act 2000), and sentenced to imprisonment, young offender institution, or detention for 12 months or more;

(c)   those convicted as above, or found not guilty by reason of insanity or disability, who are sentenced to or made the subject of a hospital or guardianship order within the meaning of the Mental Health Act 1983.

Although, in probation circles, it is often averred that the service is now supervising more high-risk offenders than ever, the evidence for this assertion is rarely adduced or analysed. An investigation of the most recently published set of *Probation Statistics England and Wales 1999* (Home Office 2001e) shows that the proportion of offenders sentenced to probation for indictable violence doubled from 6 per cent in 1989 to 12 per cent in 1999, and those sentenced to community service from 7 per cent to 13 per cent over the same period. Extended requirements in probation orders for sex offenders increased from 70, at this measure's inception in 1992, to 1,124 in 1999, and from 6 to 109 in respect of combination orders. Post-prison release supervision of sex offenders to end of sentence increased from zero in 1992 to 357 in 1999. Lifers on licence increased from 530 in 1989 to 876 in 1999. Young people released from detention under s. 53 of the Children and Young Person's Act 1933, increased from 60 in 1989 to 104 in 1999. Offenders on psychiatric hospital conditional discharge increased from 160 to 182 (though this figure had remained steady until 1998).

The above are not the only categories of violent/potentially dangerous offender supervised by the probation service. Some adults and young offenders subject to automatic or discretionary conditional release on licence, and a proportion of the very small number of persistent offenders on extended sentence licence, may also be assessed as dangerous, though the total number of offenders in both these last groups has decreased significantly since 1989. It is also the case that the service may be supervising people for non-violent offences who, nevertheless, have a history of violence, or who first behave dangerously during the course of their supervision. This is demonstrated in an analysis of 157 Serious Incident Reports, prepared on offenders starting probation service supervision in 1999, who were convicted of murder (29), other violent offences (63) or 'any offence likely to attract significant media interest or to raise wider issues of national interest' (65) (Home Office 2001e, p. 9). Scrutiny of these reports by the service, the Home Office and HM Inspectorate of Probation showed that 'in many cases there was little or nothing that the service could have done to anticipate or prevent the incident' (*ibid.*). Of these cases, 103 (around two-thirds) of those thus convicted had been serving community sentences, for which their risk would have been assessed as no higher than medium.

The above two paragraphs serve to demonstrate the complexity in determining which offenders are violent, which may become violent, which of these are 'potentially dangerous' and to what extent their prevalence within the probation service domain has actually risen over time. What is most apparent, however, is that the service's responsibility for post-release supervision of those in specialised categories, i.e. sex offenders, lifers, s. 53 offenders detained for 'grave' crimes, and conditionally discharged psychiatric hospital patients, has effectively doubled from a grand total of 750 in 1989 to 1,519 in 1999. Although an even distribution across the 42 police and probation areas cannot be assumed, the average for each area would be 36 PDOs from those four categories — a significant responsibility for boards, senior managers and practitioners alike.

It is important to emphasise, however, that while the presence of offenders in these categories makes them identifiable as normally having committed acts of violence, it is not necessarily this fact that makes them classifiable as dangerous. What really makes them dangerous is the combination of factors which interact to make them violent, which may or may not still be present, or which may conjoin only once in a lifetime — for example, where, as is frequently the case, murder is committed within the confines of a family and is the product of particular interlocking dynamics at that time. Probation staff clearly have to be alert to the presence of factors, including previous violence, which may, to an extent, be predictive of the future behaviour of a particular offender group. However, the unique skill of the professionally trained probation officer is to identify, assess and seek to reduce the reasons for an individual's offending at any given point in time. As John Gunn, in an eloquent discussion of the notion of dangerousness, points out: 'In psychiatry a strange cliché "nothing predicts violence like violence" has sprung up. Where does this notion come from? It is a misunderstanding of statistics' (Gunn 1996, p. 53). Gunn goes on to explain that, while certain statistical findings (e.g., Blomhoff *et al.* 1990) may suggest that recidivists, who have committed previous acts of violence, generate more subsequent violence than those who have not, this is not in itself the predictor of further violence. In other words, violence should not be taken in isolation from other background factors. Further analysis shows that such recidivists were also more likely to have come from violent homes and to have used illegal drugs. These are prime examples of factors which begin to provide the links in the complex chain which leads to violent offending, and the perpetrator, thereby, to the status of 'potentially dangerous offender'. This is not to minimise the importance of assessing and managing risk, but rather to take time out of organisational exigency to ask the fundamental question 'Why?'.

ASKING THE QUESTION 'WHY?'

There have always existed small minorities of people who have committed acts of violence and murder. From time to time, particular cases rise to the forefront of public attention and gain long-lasting notoriety. While particularly dangerous repeat adult sex offenders unsurprisingly come into this category, more perplexingly so do quite young juvenile offenders. In England, in recent times, these have included the 1968 conviction of 11-year-old Mary Bell for the manslaughter of two infant boys, and the 1993 conviction of two 10-year-old boys for the murder of two-year-old James Bulger. Phrases such as 'born evil' and 'the devil incarnate', become easy currency within the condemnatory media and public debate which surrounds such cases. Frequently, such notions appear to pass as explanation, with little attention being afforded to the fact that unsanctioned violence and murder constitute unusual behaviour for people of any age (Boswell 2000).

What is so difficult about asking this question 'Why?'? The quest may, perhaps, most usefully begin with an examination of the cultural legitimacy given to violence across the world. As 'the global village' becomes more accessible, so it becomes increasingly apparent that physical and psychological violences are embedded in prevailing societal cultures. The study of history, in particular, reveals an almost universal culture of physical violence in the shape of militarism.

Likewise, regimes predicated upon political oppression have both portrayed violence as a behavioural norm for individuals and communities and engaged them in it.

The primacy of violence is also demonstrated across the world in military and religious architecture, statues, art, music, press and television coverage of more than 300 wars, since the end of World War II. It is further enshrined in the response of a range of justice systems to criminalised anti-social behaviour, i.e. torture and other forms of physical retribution, and capital punishment, despite wide international ratification of the Universal Declaration of Human Rights (United Nations. 1948). Similarly, mental and physical violence to victims of child prostitution and child labour is to be seen not only in Asia, the Far East, Central and South America, but also in parts of the 'developed' world — Europe, North America and Australia (Bureau of International Labor Affairs 1996,1998). Physical violence between family members is viewed as normal in many societies (Gelles and Straus 1988). Early in this new millennium, for example, the British Government took the decision not to make the disciplining of children by smacking illegal. At national and international levels, then, the cultural legitimacy of violence can be seen as being reinforced to successive generations. This despite the United Nations' exhortation to the media to exercise its social responsibility to minimise the promotion of pornography, violence, drugs, alcohol and abusive power relations generally (United Nations Riyadh Guidelines 1990).

Another increasingly familiar media image is that of the abuse of children by adults, whether this is physical, sexual, emotional or organised in nature. The second half of the twentieth century was the time when 'the battered baby syndrome' was discovered (Kempe *et al.* 1962), and when multiple child abuse cases in Western countries such as Canada, Belgium and the UK erupted in investigations which became known across the world. More recently, the age of the computer has spawned Internet paedophile rings and 'cyber terrorists', and all of whom are potentially dangerous offenders, all of whom are subject to the law, if only they were visible.

Thus it may be seen that legitimised violence forms a backcloth of confusing models and messages for those moving through developmental stages and trying to gain a sense of identity and morality, against a complexity of interacting sociological, cultural, psychological and other influences, to which they may also be vulnerable. However, most people will survive this complexity without becoming violent, and it is to a more detailed examination of background factors in violent young offenders in particular that this discussion will now turn.

SECTION 53 OFFENDERS

Young people between the ages of 10 and 17 years inclusive, who have committed grave crimes (for example, murder, manslaughter, arson, rape and certain other offences involving actual or intended violence) are sentenced to be detained during Her Majesty's Pleasure under ss. 90 and 91 of the Powers of the Criminal Courts (Sentencing) Act 2000. They are known as s. 53 offenders because, until these provisions were subsumed under the 2000 Act, they were detained under s. 53 of the Children and Young Person's Act 1933, on the grounds that no other methods of disposal were available to reflect the gravity of their crimes. They come into the category of those sentenced to detention and serving over 12 months in custody, as shown earlier; in fact, they will normally serve longer than the two-year young offender institution maximum sentence, and in some cases may be detained for life. Excluding cases of murder, where a mandatory life sentence obtains, the courts' propensity to employ these lengthy sentence disposals has not diminished, even in the light of guiding principles set out in the Beijing Rules (United Nations 1986) and Riyadh Guidelines (United Nations 1990) to the effect that deprivation of liberty for juveniles should be a disposition of last resort, and then only for the minimum necessary period.

Comprehensive research was conducted during the 1990s on this small but singular group of young offenders, of whom there are in excess of 1,000 currently detained, many by now having reached the adult prison system (Boswell 1991,1995,1996). The earliest of these studies found the phenomena of background child abuse and traumatic loss repeatedly referred to, though they were not the subjects under investigation. Thus, it was decided to examine their prevalence in a statistically significant (one-third) sample of the s. 53 population. A detailed account of these findings, as they apply to the probation service, can be found in Boswell (1998). For the purposes of this chapter, they will be recounted briefly as a preface to considering other research findings relevant to the topic of dangerous offenders.

Researchers made a close examination of 200 centrally held files of s. 53 offenders, and noted down hard evidence in them relating to abuse or significant loss. Such evidence was derived from statements by qualified professionals, formal assessments, case conference notes and so on. Where evidence was partial or ambiguous, the offenders themselves were interviewed and asked about their experiences. Emotional abuse was found to have been experienced by 28.5 per cent of the sample; sexual abuse by 29 per cent; physical abuse by 40 per cent; organised abuse by 1.5 per cent; and combinations of abuses by 27 per cent. Of the total sample, 72 per cent had experienced one or more of these abuses. In respect of significant loss, 57 per cent had experienced bereavement of, or cessation of contact with, family or other significant figures in their lives. In only 18 out of 200 cases studies were there no recorded or personally reported incidents of abuse and or/loss. In other words, the total number of s. 53 offenders who had experienced one or both phenomena was 91 per cent. The total number who had experienced both phenomena was 35 per cent, suggesting that the presence of a double childhood trauma may be a potent factor in the backgrounds of violent offenders. The following case study serves to illustrate the way in which such ingredients may combine to lead to violent and dangerous outcomes.

Case study

Michael, now aged 32, was sentenced to a s. 53 discretionary life sentence 15 years ago for offences of grievous bodily harm and attempted rape. His background contains almost every kind of abuse, but the experience which is most significant to him is the loss of his father, who had left home when Michael was three years old, for reasons which Michael did not understand; they did not renew contact until relatively recently during Michael's prison sentence. The day his father left, his mother beat Michael, and such beatings continued several times a week, until he was taken into care at the age of ten years. He has very little memory of his life between the ages of five and seven years. His elder sister, however, tells him that he and she were both severely sexually abused by one of their mother's lovers during that period, and also that, on one occasion, Michael was nearly strangled. Michael himself has no memory of this incident, but does know that he has panic attacks and on some occasions blackouts, if ever anyone touches his neck. He also has nightmares about being strangled. One of his worst memories is of his mother locking him in the cellar for two hours. The cellar contained rats, and he recounts an experience of sheer terror as he tried to avoid them in the darkness.

Finally, at the age of ten, Michael was taken into care, but again found himself being consistently physically, sexually and emotionally abused. At the age of 14 he made the first of three unsuccessful suicide attempts. Long-serving staff at the children's home he was in have recently been convicted of abuse by the courts, though social workers at the time did not treat his allegations seriously. At the age of 15, Michael returned to his family home. He found work and spent most evenings out drinking so that he did not have to come into close contact with his family, particularly his mother and new stepfather, whom he strongly disliked. By this time, Michael was seriously disturbed and depressed, and in a state of mind which he, his probation officer and one of his doctors all later considered had led to his commission of a violent offence. The doctor judged that the offence was a specific acting out of aggression against Michael's mother. Michael himself has now made a deliberate decision to cease contact with her. However, his renewal of contact with his father has finally helped him to understand the reasons why his father left, an act which devastated Michael for years and removed from him the protection of an adult he trusted. During his 15 years of incarceration, there has been little sign of Michael receiving professional help to try to understand his violent behaviour and how he can avoid it in future. Instead he has turned to religion and believes that this has expiated his feelings of anger. A final, ironic ingredient is that his newfound father is now dying of cancer.

The findings recounted above reveal that a high proportion of young people who have committed violent or murderous offences, have themselves been the victims of childhood trauma in the form of abuse and/or loss, and frequently both. This does not mean, of course, that all youthful victims of trauma will become violent or murderous offenders in the way that Michael did. That is liable to depend on a whole variety of other variables, not least those related to socio-economic opportunity. These variables are sometimes known as 'protective factors' and may include, for example, biological predisposition, environmental factors, or a new and significant attachment figure, which can mitigate against earlier traumatic experiences in some cases (Garmezy 1981). However, it is very significant that many members of the sample had not been effectively helped to think through, interpret or resolve the traumatic event(s) which had occurred in their earlier lives, and that this help, such as can feasibly be offered within probation supervision (Renn 2000), could have provided a protective factor which might have made a difference to their later behaviour. It is also significant that such findings, as are available on early traumata are rarely cited when a violent offender of any age hits the headlines; partly, perhaps, because this is still an under-researched area, particularly in relation to physical and emotional abuse and loss, and post-traumatic stress disorder (Boswell 1998); though perhaps also partly because, as Miller says (1987, p. xvi):

> The general public is still far from realising that our earliest experiences unfailingly affect society as a whole; that psychoses, drug addiction and criminality are encoded expressions of these experiences. This fact is usually either disputed or accepted only on a strictly intellectual level. Since the intellect fails to influence the area of the emotions, the practical world (of politics, law or psychiatry) continues to be dominated by medieval concepts charac-terized by the outward projection of evil.

Perhaps this situation should not be a matter for surprise given that, as mentioned above, the 'battered baby syndrome' was identified only just over three decades ago (Kempe *et al.* 1962), despite well-known incidents of physical child abuse over the centuries. If Gelles and Straus's (1988) view, referred to earlier, is correct, that physical violence between family members is a normal part of family life in most societies, then perhaps there is a reluctance on the part of most people — researchers, criminal justice professionals and journalists alike — to acknowledge the threat that this 'normality' poses to all members of society as potential victims and offenders.

LINKING CHILDHOOD TRAUMA AND LATER VIOLENCE

While there is a plethora of published material on the effects of loss (in terms of failed or flawed attachment) and of child abuse (notably sexual), and plenty of literature on the genesis of violence and violent offending, historically there has been little attempt to link these phenomena. This section examines the evidence for such links, in respect of those who become violent offenders, whether in youth or adulthood.

Relating his comment to one of the killers of James Bulger, known to have been systematically bullied by his elder brothers, clinical psychologist Oliver James states (1994, p. 188):

> Of the 100-odd convicted violent men I have interviewed in depth, can think of only two who did not seem to have been physically abused as children. It can be said almost certainly that if the (name omitted) family had been poor but non-violent, James Bulger would be alive today. Despite a thorough search I have not found a single comment to this effect in any of the media coverage, not even in the *Guardian*, *Observer* or *Independent*.

James's penultimate sentence has to remain open to question, but his overall view is supported by Robert Johnson (1993), former consultant psychiatrist at Parkhurst Prison, whose report to the Reed Committee (1992) described his work with seriously violent adult prisoners suffering from the 'buried terror syndrome' induced by child abuse. The terror experienced by these men (one of whom, for example, was regularly used by his mother at the age of five as a human shield against his drunken father, who would beat them both with chair legs) became deeply buried for fear that its return to the surface would lead to its re-enactment. (This process is often known as a state of denial.) Any likelihood of this happening would precipitate an extreme, and probably violent, reaction based on the man's fundamental terror. The psychiatrist's job was gently and carefully to identify the terror and to show that it was now obsolete, a process which ultimately led to a recovery from violent manifestation. However, many of these men had spent decades in institutions without the questions being asked that could bring them to an understanding of their violent behaviour. Justice for them, as victims, had never been on anyone's professional agenda.

The transmission of violence

'Children are both victims and survivors of many violent acts ... whether within the family or outside it' (Yule 1993, p. 153). The phenomenon of transgenerational (or intergenerational) violence, in which abuse of one kind or another is transmitted from one generation to the next, has been described by Herrenkohl and Herrenkohl (1981), Rivera and Widom (1990), and Falshaw *et al.* (1996) amongst others. Widom, indeed, describes this transmission as 'the premier developmental hypothesis in the field of abuse and neglect' (Widom 1989, p. 160). A variety of explanations is offered for this process: for example, imitation of powerful adults by less powerful children; residual childhood anger of parents towards their own parents being displaced on to their own child (their parents' grandchild); projection of parental conflict on to the child; expectation placed upon the child to fulfil parents' own unmet needs, and violent reaction when they do not; the linking of parental stress and child abuse (Herrenkohl *et al.* 1983). Some or all of these may apply in different cases, but it is certainly arguable that 'many stresses on the family of origin may have elicited violent reactions in response to the frustrations generated, with violence then being incorporated by the children as a "coping strategy" for responding to stress in their current lives' (Herrenkohl *et al.* 1983, p. 306).

One of the variables in determining how a child reacts to parental abuse in the longer term is likely to be the way in which he or she perceives and interprets the abuse and uses this interpretation to form a rationale for the nature of subsequent disciplinary encounters with his or her own children. Herzberger (1983) describes the differential between 'sensitisation' (yelling and corporal punishment) and 'induction' (explaining, moralising) discipline techniques, and cites a study (Dienstbier *et al.* 1975) which showed that children falling within the second group tended to feel guilty, or culpable, and thus behave more responsibly, whilst those falling into the first group tended to feel shame, or humiliation, and thus behave less responsibly.

As well as constituting a further mechanism for transgenerational violence, this 'sensitisation' discipline also provides support for the suggestion that those who are regularly abused, in whatever form, become individuals with low empathy who, if they later become abusive and violent in their own right, view their victims as objects, for whom they have no feeling (Goddard and Stanley 1994). Such individuals clearly constitute a danger not only to their own future children, but also within society at large. Thus it seems not beyond the bounds of possibility that such a phenomenon applies not only at family level, but at community level also, which may help to explain the continuity of violent sub-cultures and of bullying behaviours in both education and employment sectors.

Violence at the family/community interface

The interface between family and community levels of violence is shown in the work of Bowers *et al.* (1992), who found that the kinds of children most likely to become victims at school or beyond were those who spent more time with their parents. Those most likely to become bullies tended to live with (male) models of dominance and aggression, who abused their power over their children. Similarly, it has been suggested that children who have been sexually abused and subjected to the abuse of authority, coupled with the perversion of physical intimacy, are conditioned to respond along a domination/submission continuum (Sanderson 1992). Bagley and King, in their search for the meaning that attaches to sexual abuse in childhood, provide a wide range of published personal accounts of such abuse, most of which have in common feelings of anger, rage and hate which, set against positions of utter powerlessness, have to be internalised, but nevertheless endure over time and surface in a variety of ways during adolescence or adulthood (Bagley and King 1991). Earlier, Miller had studied the childhoods of some authoritarian personalities, and in the case of Hitler, for example, responsible for mass oppression and murder, had traced his actions back to a physically and emotionally (and possibly sexually) abusive father, who persistently humiliated the young Adolf (Miller 1987). Such well-organised and unrelenting compulsive destruction has been described as narcissistic rage, an extreme form of self-defensive revenge against early childhood helplessness and humiliation (Kohut 1985; Wolf 1988).

An American study of particular interest (Corder *et al.* 1976) is helpfully described by Brufal (1994, p. 8) in relation to the case notes of ten adolescents admitted to a regional forensic hospital following parricide (the murder of a parent). In comparison with two homicidal control groups, a higher proportion of the parricidal group was found to be socially isolated in adolescence, having poor peer relationships and very little or no experience of dating. Interestingly, previous aggression, antisocial and poor impulse control patterns were far less frequent amongst the parricidal adolescents, leading Corder *et al.* to suggest that their offences may have resulted from gradual accumulation of stress, which they had not learned to discharge appropriately. (This, again, demonstrates that violent behaviour does not necessarily have violent antecedents to aid prediction.) The six murdered fathers were chronic alcoholics, who had abused their partners and children; the indications were that the four murdered mothers had sexually abused their sons. Those in the control groups (who had killed either strangers or other relatives) were described as having parents with antisocial, rather than abusive, behaviour patterns. Brufal's study (1994), however, sought to replicate Corder *et al.*s study in the UK by researching the case records of 11 male matricidal offenders admitted to Broadmoor between 1982 and 1992. They found similar patterns to the earlier study, but no statistically significant differences between the experimental and control groups. Notably, however, they found paternal loss via bereavement and divorce in over half the experimental group, and loss via care proceedings, or paternal absence following marital disputes, in over half of the control group. Significantly, also, eight matricidal and eight control group offenders had one either alcoholic or abusing parent, and six matricidal (though only two control) group offenders were subjected either to abuse or alcoholism from both parents. While there is scope for further investigation as to what causes some adolescents to kill their parent abusers and others to kill people apparently not their abusers, it is interesting that the more recent of the two studies identifies a high prevalence of abuse and loss in all homicidal offenders studied.

Victim becomes perpetrator

The range of findings described above begins to suggest a connection between children whose significant attachment figures either disappear, or abuse their positions as trusted adults to create a domination/ submission relationship, and some of those children's later entry into that small group of offenders who commit violent and murderous crimes, whether within their own subsequent families or beyond. For those who have been abused, if their parental role models dominate in order to gain control then, as time goes on, perhaps they too will find that part of their survival mechanism lies in gaining their own form of control in keeping with that pattern. If they have been denied their victim status by having no one to confide in about what has happened to them, it is possible that they will seek redress by finding their own form of domination, sometimes within the family but, where this is unfeasible, sometimes also as a 'displacement' activity beyond it. In attempting to illustrate the latter form of redress, Miller, for example, offers the speculation that millions of Jews might have escaped persecution, if Hitler had had children of his own, upon whom he could have taken revenge for his father's abuse of him (Miller 1987). Although speculative, this is nevertheless a sobering thought, which again leads back to a realisation of the crucial nature of preventative, protective action in the field of child abuse. It is also a reminder that many societal structures render it more difficult than it should be for an abusive act against a child to merit a formal response: 'Routine acts of minor violence such as bullying, chastisement or assault appear resistant to being defined as criminal when committed against children' (Morgan and Zedner 1992, p. 22). In more extreme cases of abuse, children have been likened to hostages or to concentration camp inmates, whose 'captors' are also their significant attachment figures and whose means of survival will often be a direct function of the only relationship dynamic they know — that of the captor/hostage relationship (Goddard and Stanley 1994). In such circumstances it seems not implausible that, without any intervention to tell them otherwise, children may come to believe that to take 'captives' for the purpose of physical, sexual and emotional abuse is the norm for adult behaviour. At the extreme of this spectrum (i.e., with no mediating factor to intervene), the victim may seek, at some later and not necessarily predictable point, to become the survivor by finding his or her own victim to dominate in turn.

SUMMARY AND IMPLICATIONS

This chapter has concentrated deliberately on the cultural legitimacy afforded to violence across the world, and on the prevalence of abuse and loss in the childhoods of violent young offenders, which is to be found in 'dangerous' offenders across the age spectrum. It is not suggested here that this is the whole story. There are other factors which may influence and combine to precipitate violent acts. The ingredients discussed above are, however, too often overlooked not just by the general public, but also by criminal justice professionals. The probation service increasingly is exhorted to concentrate on more immediate 'criminogenic need', leading potentially to the neglect of earlier life events which may, on the face of it, seem unconnected but, with sustained investigation, may prove to be more criminogenic than any peer group pressure or substance addiction.

The foregoing discussion highlights a number of prevention issues: the need for more effective mechanisms to enable victims to report abuse; the assessment and intervention requirements for a comprehensive understanding of the dynamics of domination and submission; and the necessity of supplementing existing gaps in knowledge as to the variables which intervene either to prevent or exacerbate the likelihood of violent offending. The probation service, in its crime prevention and multi-agency collaboration roles, could very importantly consider its contribution in these fields to the long-term reduction of victims who may later become perpetrators. A responsible use of the knowledge base described herein, for example, would be a pre-sentence report examination of known background factors in violent offending, which is clearly linked to sentencing proposals which address and seek to eradicate these factors, while providing an acceptable level of protection for the public. During custodial careers, provision should be made in sentence plans for interventions such as counselling, following child abuse and other background traumata. Both of these suggested practices require that professionals familiarise themselves with the features of such traumata, such as post-traumatic stress disorder (PTSD) (see Scott and Stradling 1992), so that when, for example, an offender starts to tell them about recurrent nightmares or flashbacks, they recognise these as symptoms of PTSD and, rather than let it pass, pursue it via sensitive questioning.

There is, however, a final message for those called upon to work with people who, for whatever reason, have become labelled as ' dangerous offenders'. Assessing and managing dangerousness has become a challenging and high-profile task for the probation service. It is not, by any means, impossible, but it should be approached with careful consideration of significant ingredients, which often lie hidden and upon which research findings beyond the What Works orthodoxy may well be able to throw light. In employing such an approach, probation staff not only afford greater protection to the public through being able to address these ingredients, but also provide the offenders themselves with a long overdue 'good authority' (Pitt-Aikens and Thomas Ellis 1990), within which their own victim experiences may finally be heard within a climate of compassion and understanding.

If the probation service can integrate its response to dangerous offenders through a research-based pinpointing of prevention, assessment and intervention techniques relevant to the complexities of contemporary social culture, then it will perform a major service for victims and offenders alike. However, information is power and interaction with local communities is also of the essence. The public is justifiably concerned about such offenders; its protection may better be served through straightforward explanatory dialogue and guidance than by some imagined fail-safe surveillance system. Justice for individuals and communities alike will only be served by assiduous attention to, and sharing of, knowledge about the ingredients which underlie and surround this elusive construct known as 'dangerousness'.

11   What Works: Have We Moved On?

Peter Raynor

A PREFACE WITH HINDSIGHT

When I was invited to revise my chapter for inclusion in the new edition of this book, I puzzled for some time about how I should go about it. Should I try to present these issues afresh, as they appear at the time of rewriting in the year 2001, or should I simply restate those parts of the argument which still seem relevant, with some comment on how they stand now? The more I thought about it, the more it seemed that the former strategy would result in a completely different chapter on rather different themes, while the latter would require a selection process which might be better carried out by someone other than the original author. In the end (after reflecting on the paradox that professional academics, supposedly paid to think and write, nowadays seem in practice to have remarkably little time for either), I decided that the best route might be, in effect, to re-present the original chapter and arguments, framed by some additional commentary to show how it was affected by the particular context of its time and how the same issues restate themselves in a different form in the new millennium.

Accordingly, the long central section of this 'new' chapter is in fact essentially the old chapter, with all its original imperfections: the reader may wish to imagine quotation marks around the whole section. It is a product of its time, and it is now preceded and followed by sections which comment on it for a new time.

The original version was written in 1994. In the previous year, I had written with some close colleagues a hopeful and optimistic book on probation practice (Raynor, Smith and Vanstone 1994). This was intended to show how the Criminal Justice Act 1991 could be used as a framework for a new era of constructive practice to rehabilitate offenders and promote social justice. By the time the book came out, Michael Howard had become Home Secretary, announced that 'prison works' and set about dismantling those progressive parts of the 1991 Act which had survived the attentions of his predecessor. The immediate outlook was bleak, relieved only by the fact that there would eventually have to be a general election, which this time the Conservatives were likely to lose. So the original version of this chapter was intended to point to some areas of emerging practice and research which still offered a slightly more optimistic outlook, and to suggest how we might understand them in the context of a critical view of the 'just deserts' principles which underpinned the 1991 Act. Whatever their drawbacks in detail, those principles offered some kind of moral framework for criminal justice decisions. My case is they should continue to do so, even though the 1991 Act itself has been much amended and, thus, weakened.

Now I am adding these new paragraphs on the eve of another general election, which seems likely to deliver an unprecedented second term for the 'New' Labour Government first elected in 1997; we have a new National Probation Service of England and Wales, and a series of new criminal justice statutes, designed to keep Labour in the public eye as the party that does something about crime. After tomorrow's election we can expect more, guided by a new criminal justice strategy and a review of the sentencing powers of the courts (Home Office 2000a). What Works is no longer a minority interest struggling for influence in penal policy, but an orthodoxy and a basis of policy, with all the benefits and costs which that implies (see, for example, Chapman and Hough 1998). At the end of the chapter, I make some comments about what these recent changes imply for its central themes of evidence-based practice and justice. In the meantime, here are the issues as I saw them seven years ago.

WHAT I THOUGHT IN 1994

The Chief Inspector of Probation began the 'overview' section of his 1993 Annual Report with the words: 'This is a difficult time to write the report' (Home Office 1993a). He went on to explore a theme which has become all too familiar to everyone connected with the probation service in recent years:

> Unfortunately too many users of probation services and the public appear unconvinced that current forms of supervision are either sufficiently rigorous to constitute adequate punishment or sufficiently effective to reduce criminal behaviour.

By 'users' of the service, one presumes that he meant sentencers rather than clients. This quotation neatly encapsulates the problem which this section seeks to explore. If probation is now to be seen as 'punishment', instead of in its earlier guise as an alternative to punishment, how do such punishments fit into the 'just deserts' sentencing models based on proportionality of punishment to offence, which many industrialised countries, including Britain, are adopting? And if 'effectiveness in reducing criminal behaviour' were to be pursued with a little more success than in the past, how would this fit, both conceptually and pragmatically, with a continuing concern for proportionality and justice?

At a strictly logical level, some difficulty of fit is inevitable. A strict 'just deserts' model is concerned with past actions only (Von Hirsch 1976), whereas the search for 'effective' sentencing measures is primarily a search for interventions that will influence future actions. Roger Hood, among others, argued 20 years ago that sentencing, which had forward-looking reductionist aims, whether based on deterrence or rehabilitation, risked injustice through over-intervention and departed from the only morally acceptable basis of sentencing, which he saw as a moral assessment based on the seriousness of the offence (Hood 1974). Others argued that a return to 'just deserts' models was needed to preserve the rights of offenders not to be coerced into programmes of 'care' or 'treatment' involving intervention beyond the level justified by the seriousness of the offence (for example, the American Friends Service Committee 1971), while British juvenile justice researchers were beginning to point out that 'welfare' based intervention in the lives of young offenders could prove counter-productive by exposing them to the risk of more coercive and more damaging intervention in the future (Thorpe *et al.* 1980). Within the probation sphere, it was argued by some practitioners (Bryant *et al.* 1978), and most cogently by Bottoms and

McWilliams (1979), that probation should no longer be seen as a 'treatment' process, in which the degree of intervention was determined by empirically dubious estimates of the likely response to treatment, but as a non-custodial penal measure offering a humane alternative to more coercive measures. Such arguments have been highly influential; the purpose of this chapter is to re-examine them in the light of current debates about 'just deserts' and What Works.

Current experience of what actually happens in penal systems underpinned by a rhetoric of 'just deserts' is certainly not uniformly encouraging. In the United States, 'back to justice' sloganising has been associated with a massive increase in imprisonment, particularly of poor and non-white Americans; and the general danger that 'just deserts' thinking can differentially disadvantage the poorest and least powerful has been thoroughly identified by Hudson (1987). In Britain, a carefully prepared attempt in the Criminal Justice Act 1991 to enlist 'just deserts' in the service of a rational and decarcerating penal policy was quickly blown off course by politicians using similar rhetoric to promote a policy of more severe punishment, as in the Home Secretary's speech to the 1993 Conservative Party conference (Howard 1993). Perhaps a sentencing principle so subjective and negotiable as 'seriousness' is particularly vulnerable to political perceptions of changes in the public mood or of electoral advantage, or even to Ministers' perceptions of their own prospects in party leadership struggles. Certainly, Ministers who deny the existence of socially discriminatory practices in the criminal justice system and of economic influences on crime (MacLean 1993) are not best placed to integrate the requirements of criminal justice with those of social justice. Quite small changes in the political message seem able to result in quite large changes in practice in volatile criminal justice systems (Zimring and Hawkins 1994). Perhaps we should not be too surprised that liberal academic criminologists and ambitious, but electorally vulnerable, politicians take different public stances about the seriousness of crime.

Strict 'just deserts' models are in fact subject to at least three significant criticisms. They run the risk of failing to take into account morally relevant differences in the social and individual circumstances of people who commit similar offences: are people, who have quite different levels of opportunity to avoid crime, equally blameworthy if they commit a crime (Raynor 1985)? They are also vulnerable on the question of 'dangerous' offenders, where likely future crimes are arguably a proper and necessary consideration, even if difficult to predict (Bottoms 1977); and the question of whether persistent offenders should be sentenced on the basis of the most recent offence, or in a way which recognises a pattern of offending, proved to be the Achilles' heel of the Criminal Justice Act 1991.

It can be argued that these criticisms are not necessarily fatal: for example, the 1991 Act incorporated the elements of a pragmatic accommodation to two of them. By emphasising the role of pre-sentence reports, it allowed at least the procedural space for consideration of individual and social circumstance in assessing the seriousness of crime; and it emphasised the need for an explicit basis and reasons, when strict proportionality was exceeded on grounds of dangerousness. It is also important to note that none of these criticisms offers support to discredited aspects of the rival 'treatment' model such as one-sided subjective diagnosis, open-ended intervention or the separation of consequences from judgments about the seriousness of the offence. However, the main focus of this chapter is on a slightly different problem: when advocates of justice models originally argued against 'treatment', they did so not simply because they expected the abandonment of treatment to lead to a general reduction in the severity of sanctions by putting an end to over-intervention, but also because they could find, and expected to find, no evidence of benefits from 'treatment'. It seems they were sometimes over-optimistic in the first of these expectations; are they still correct in the second? And if there is now rather more hope of using the criminal justice process to provide offenders with opportunities to offend less, how much difference does this make to their arguments?

The influential advocates of 'justice' models during the 1970s were writing in a context which was influenced not only by obvious excesses of 'treatment' (such as the linking of parole decisions in some American states to prisoners' consent to undergo unproven psychosurgical procedures), but also by a consensus among criminologists that 'nothing worked' in the treatment of offenders. In America, the terms of debate were set by Martinson and his colleagues in their famously negative review of correctional treatments (Lipton et al. 1975); in Britain, the Home Office undertook a similar review (Brody 1976) with similar results. Years of research on the effectiveness of probation finally ran out of steam with the discouraging IMPACT study (Folkard et al. 1976), after which the Home Office Research Unit virtually abandoned the issue of probation's effectiveness for more than a decade. It became a commonplace of criminological argument that decisions to allocate offenders to any particular programme could not be justified by expectations of benefit, and therefore needed some other justification, such as proportionality, or else the diversion of less serious offenders from expensive custody. Bottoms and McWilliams in 1979 took the ineffectiveness of treatment largely for granted, and penal reformers generally based their arguments on diversion or decarceration rather than rehabilitation; the belief that prison did harm proved more durable than the belief that probation did any good. Home Office researchers turned their attention to the evaluation of community service as an alternative to custody (Pease *et al.* 1977); juvenile justice researchers, alarmed by the consequences of the welfarist Children and Young Persons Act 1969, concentrated on diversion rather than reconviction (Thorpe *et al.* 1980); and practitioners sustained their optimism largely by a robust indifference to research. A few unconvinced researchers began local effectiveness studies in collaboration with probation services, but these were not to produce results until after substantial follow-up periods (Raynor 1988; Roberts 1989).

Interest in effective practice expressed itself largely in a search for useful techniques (notably those advocated by McGuire and Priestley 1985) and in the innovative forms of supervision developed in specialised facilities such as Day Training Centres (Vanstone 1993). A few writers (for example, Raynor 1985; Harris 1985) suggested that the requirements of 'welfare' and 'justice' might be reconciled by allowing proportionality to limit the scale of intervention (the 'size of the package' or the degree of interference with liberty), while considerations of potential effectiveness or helpfulness should influence the form of intervention (the 'contents of the package'); but claims about possible effectiveness remained very tentative.

In other countries, the position was rather different. Psychologically orientated correctional practitioners in Canada continued to develop and test programmes (for example, Ross *et al.* 1988), and 'intensive supervision' experiments in America, though largely negative in their results, produced interesting evaluation material (for example, Petersilia 1990; Clear *et al.* 1987). No doubt they were also aware of Martinson's recantation (Martinson 1979), which passed largely unnoticed in Britain. By the end of the 1980s and the early 1990s, research reviews were beginning to appear which gathered together evidence of effectiveness from a range of programme evaluations, often using the new statistical technique of meta-analysis to identify programme components which seemed regularly associated with positive effects (e.g., Andrews *et al.* 1990; Lipsey 1992). This work began to have an impact in Britain through research reviews (notably McIvor 1990) and through a series of 'What Works?' conferences inspired largely by probation services searching for meaningful programme content to fulfil the enhanced supervision role envisaged for them by the Criminal Justice Act 1991.

As a result of these and other developments, this author believes it is now possible to be a little less tentative about characteristics of effective programmes, which command some empirical support. It is not possible to do more here than summarise these characteristics, and some may prove in further research to be more firmly grounded than others. However, the following list is drawn from the contributions of a number of speakers to a conference on 'What Works: the Challenge For Managers', and represents some degree of consensus at least among those contributors. (The items relating to programme content are based largely on McGuire (1993) and Lipsey (1992); the more contextual items draw on Raynor (1988, 1993), Roberts (1989), McIvor (1990), Petersilia (1990) and Raynor, Smith and Vanstone (1994), but similar suggestions will be found in the work of a number of authors.) In the present state of our knowledge, it appears likely that the more effective programmes are those which:

(a)   target high-risk offenders, who are otherwise likely to continue to offend, rather than low-risk offenders, who may gain little benefit or be harmed;

(b)   focus on criminogenic need, i.e. those characteristics or circumstances of offenders which have contributed to their offending;

(c)   are highly structured, making clear and explicit demands and following a logical sequence determined by their learning goals;

(d)   use a directive working approach, so that participants know what they are meant to be doing;

(e)   use broadly cognitive-behavioural methods, to provide opportunities to learn new thinking and behaviour;

(f)   are located in the community;

(g)   have programme integrity, i.e. are delivered as intended, with procedures to ensure this;

(h) Have committed and effective management;

(i) Have appropriately trained staff, who believe they can be effective;

(j) Have adequate resources for continuity;

(k) Have integral evaluation and feedback.

One of the most comprehensive attempts in Britain to put these principles into practice was the 'Straight Thinking On Probation' programme (STOP), developed by the Mid Glamorgan Probation Service, based on the 'Reasoning and Rehabilitation' programme, devised by Ross and Fabiano in Canada (Ross and Fabiano 1985). The findings available from interim evaluation reports were broadly encouraging (Lucas, Raynor and Vanstone 1992; Raynor and Vanstone 1994a). Readers interested in the full detail are referred to the original reports, but in outline the evidence showed that the programme was effective in targeting high-risk offenders comparable to those receiving custodial sentences rather than to those receiving traditional non-custodial sentences; that it was feasible for the majority of offenders to undertake and complete the programme despite its quite high level of demand (70 hours of group sessions in 18 weeks); that completion rates were not worse than for comparable community sentences such as Day Centre requirements; that staff were on the whole supportive of the programme and delivered it with a high degree of programme integrity; that most participating offenders reported that they found it helpful; and that there were indications, from attitude-measurement questionnaires and from offenders' own comments, of some changes in thinking in line with the aims of the programme.

A follow-up of 12-month reconviction rates (Raynor and Vanstone 1994a), covering 107 probationers sentenced to the STOP programme in the first nine months of the experiment and 548 members of custodial and non-custodial comparison groups, compared expected and actual reconviction rates for standard list offences, and showed that those sentenced to STOP were reconvicted less than comparable offenders released from custodial sentences. (The predicted reconviction rate based on the Home Office's 'National Risk of Reconviction Predictor' and the actual reconviction rate were both 44 per cent for those sentenced to STOP, while members of the custodial comparison group had a predicted rate of 43 per cent and an actual rate of 49 per cent.) A further analysis of 59 probationers, who successfully completed the

STOP programme during the relevant period, showed a lower reconviction rate (predicted 42 per cent, actual 35 per cent); and members of this group who were reconvicted, tended to be reconvicted for less serious offences and to be sentenced less severely for them. Readers interested in the detailed figures, and in reoffending by other comparison groups, should consult the report (Raynor and Vanstone 1994a), which also registered some reservations: for example, the advantages of the programme are less clear for those who fail, for whatever reason, to complete it as planned, and it is suggested that methods of improving completion rates, including better matching to need, might be explored. However, it is fair to say that the majority of findings from the evaluation so far were consistent with the project's aims. It is particularly interesting, for example, that those who completed the programme were much less likely to be reconvicted for a serious offence (defined as a sexual or violent offence or a burglary); 8 per cent of them were reconvicted for such offences, compared to 21 per cent of those released from custody (see Raynor and Vanstone 1994b). There were signs instead of a shift to offences less damaging to other people, such as criminal damage or possession of drugs. One of the programme's aims was to promote victim awareness. The reduced seriousness of offending by those who completed the programme was also reflected in the fact that they were the only group in the study who received no immediate custodial sentences on reconviction.

Encouraging results emerging from this programme and others (Raynor 1988; Roberts 1989) suggested the possibility that even in Britain we might be moving beyond the era of 'nothing works' into a new period, when the question 'What works?' is at least worth asking. We need, of course, to beware of the opposite illusion that 'everything works'; not only is this unsupported by evidence, but it might encourage a fiscally attractive conclusion that further investment in effectiveness is unnecessary. Moreover, we must confront another question: If there are now signs that effectiveness at least might be achievable, how does this affect past arguments about just deserts and proportionality, which were based, at least in part, on the perceived ineffectiveness of penal sanctions in influencing offenders' behaviour?

Programmes like 'Reasoning and Rehabilitation' and STOP have in fact run into considerable criticism based on familiar arguments against the 'treatment' model, and these are reviewed in a paper (Raynor and Vanstone 1994b) which sought to re-evaluate and re-state the 'non-treatment paradigm' in a manner which does not presuppose ineffectiveness. One critic (Neary 1992), for example, argues that attempts to influence (or in his terms 'manipulate') offenders' thinking are reminiscent of 'Clockwork Orange', and that such programmes serve an ideological function in diverting our attention from the social context of offending. Such criticisms seem to be overstated: we all (including presumably Neary) try to influence people's thinking, and helping people to identify and act on more alternative options in the face of difficult social situations can be seen as a form of empowerment rather than manipulation. However, there are some more substantial concerns, which require us to think carefully about the place of such programmes within a 'just deserts' model. These direct our attention particularly to issues of proportionality, negotiability, social goals and alternative models of justice.

The principle of proportionality of sentence to offence requires that sanctions are limited to those justified by the seriousness of the offence: one of the strongest arguments against the 'treatment model' was the child faced with years of custodial 'care' for stealing a packet of sweets. However, a 70-hour programme as a condition of a probation order does not easily accommodate the idea that a person whose offence is less serious than the average for the programme, might be required to serve only 30 hours, or a particularly serious offender required to serve 140 hours and do the programme twice. This would have absurd consequences for programme integrity. A less pedantic approach to proportionality is required, which ranks sanctions in broadly comparable levels of seriousness (perhaps five, as in the Hampshire 'matrix': Hampshire Probation Service 1992) rather than in strict arithmetical equivalence. In any case, it is difficult for strict proportionality to allow for different perceptions by different offenders of the severity of the same sanction. (It is interesting and revealing that the most systematic attempt to do this, namely the unit fine system, was quickly abandoned in Britain, presumably because it required sentencers to impose fines of the same subjective severity on the rich, as they habitually impose on the poor.) Within such a system of broad comparability a reasonable degree of perceived fairness could probably be preserved, provided that one central principle was retained: no proportional sentence should be artificially inflated simply to make even a possibly effective programme available, since this would conflict both with the empirically-based principle of targeting high-risk offenders and with the moral principle of fairness or treating like cases alike. In particular, the presumed benefits of a programme should not be used to justify an increased sentence as being 'good for' an offender, since even where beneficial effects can be shown to be probable, they cannot be guaranteed for a particular individual. A related problem is posed by offenders who might qualify by reason of 'seriousness', but whose needs are different from those the programme is intended to meet: that is, in the language of Home Office National Standards, they are not 'suitable'. A developed system might require a range of programmes at a comparable level of seriousness to ensure reasonably equal opportunity of access to suitable programmes. Similar questions have repeatedly been raised about women's access to appropriate community service projects (Dominelli 1984).

The question of negotiability is potentially more problematic. Ideas about good practice with offenders, which grew out of the critique of the 'treatment model' (see particularly Bottoms and McWilliams 1979; Raynor 1985), rightly emphasised the principle of negotiation with offenders and informed consent to involvement in any process of supervision, particularly if this might make demands for active participation rather than mere passive availability. A 70-hour programme, which emphasises programme integrity and follows a particular sequence of modules and learning opportunities, presents problems for fully-informed consent to every detail, particularly in the context of preparing a pre-sentence report. However, many programmes present the same problem, perhaps particularly those whose content is unclear and which are devised in the light of available resources when the probationer is already under supervision. A more realistic model of consent would focus at least on clear explanation of and consent to the degree of restriction of liberty entailed (i.e., the time demands of the programme), its purpose, the type of participation expected or required, and the consequences of non-compliance. Intended benefits should not be highlighted in such discussions since consent does not guarantee their delivery. Many educational processes (including compulsory ones like school) are influenced, but not determined, by learners: the choice is not simply between officer-led and probationer-led agendas, since all programmes contain a mixture of these, but between a coercively imposed or openly negotiated initial agreement, backed up by an honest approach to respective roles and responsibilities. The responsibility for content and quality of programme opportunities rests with providers, and for compliance and participation with probationers. In practice, long and complex programmes often represent a continuing engagement with a probationer's partial, conditional and intermittent commitment to the goal of reducing offending. Bottoms' and McWilliams' notion of 'unconditional help' is perhaps too simple for the messy world of practice: what is needed is a continuing sensitivity to issues of consent and participation, combined with a commitment to programme quality. This is likely to be facilitated when programmes are seen and delivered as training, rather than as 'treatment'; for a fuller discussion of these problems, see Raynor and Vanstone (1994b).

The third problem is posed by the actual goals and purposes of such programmes: that is, their intention to be effective in helping offenders to reduce their offending, and their effectiveness, if this can be demonstrated, in achieving this with some offenders. If they are commended to sentencers and, by implication, to offenders on this basis, do they not infringe a basic principle of justice models, to which attention was drawn at the start of this chapter: namely, that sentences should be decided with reference to past behaviour rather than expected future behaviour? Does the re-entry of effectiveness as an issue in the sentencing debate undermine a large part of the logical basis of 'just deserts' thinking? Here common sense suggests one answer (of course we want sentencing to reduce crime as well as being fair), but the strict logic of proportional punishment based only on past offending simply excludes such issues from the argument. This problem exposes, in this author's view, some important contradictions at the heart of justice models, and requires some re-thinking about the form and content of the justice which these models offer us.

The rhetoric of 'just deserts' is a curiously abstract, formal doctrine, divorced from social context and from any vision of social objectives beyond 'law and order', which it does not obviously or easily achieve. In this it differs from its claimed neo-classical origins in eighteenth-century social theory: for writers such as Beccaria (1764) or Bentham (1789), proportionality had a social purpose and even a clear consequentialist element. Free and rational citizens, equal before the law, needed to be encouraged to make rational decisions to avoid crime, and this required the penalties (the 'cost' of crime) to be proportional, determinate and knowable in advance. If we divorce the notion of proportionate penalties from social context and social purpose, we are left with little more than punishment (or as Christie (1982) reminds us, the graduated infliction of harm or pain) without any clear vision of what it is trying to achieve. In particular, once we have deprived the offender of liberty or time, the pure justice model gives us no very clear idea about how to use it (again, it may guide us on the size of the package, but not on its content). The appeal of formal justice models may lie partly in their rejection of 'modernity' and their capacity for easy linkage to conservative appeals for the restoration of often imaginary traditional values and ways of life; however, their origins lie in early modern society rather than in pre-modern societies, and while they properly alert us to the dangers of positivist social engineering through uncontrolled 'treatment', they offer no new vision of desirable social goals or new bases of social order and harmony. In turning against the excesses of modernity, they may even help to invite the post-modern social fragmentation. One of the most telling criticisms of the 1991 Criminal Justice Act and its preparatory White and Green Papers was that they seemed content to attribute crime to individual wickedness and were largely silent on social causes or context. Perhaps this is best understood as a self-denying ordinance necessarily adopted by prag-matic Home Office reformers under a Prime Minister who believed there was 'no such thing as society'; however, the resulting version of 'just deserts' was decontextualised and not rooted in a wider social vision or a network of supporting social policies. When the content of 'justice' is so thinly reasoned and weakly supported, it easily collapses into 'punishment', and the penal policy agenda is rendered vulnerable to political hi-jacking by the Right. The difficulty of incorporating consequentialist notions like effectiveness within such a 'just deserts' model seems more a consequence of the narrowness and abstract nature of the model than of the inadmissibility of effectiveness. So, if we want to pursue both justice and crime reduction, and if we want effectiveness without the excesses of coercive treatment or disproportionate interven-tion, by what standards of justice or fairness should our efforts at effectiveness be judged?

In fact the criminological literature is not short of alternative visions of justice, which are more rooted in actual social practices and human needs. Christie (1977) draws his models largely from traditional and rural societies, and sees crime as a conflict or dispute which needs to be managed by a collective process of discussion and negotiation, which both clarifies social norms and reinforces social bonds; an important element is the restoration of the offender to full membership of the

community once appropriate reparation, whether practical o
has been made. (This is, of course, the proper meaning of
tion': the restoration or recovery of moral status as a member
community, rather than simply the cessation of offending.) In a more
modern-seeming vein, the 'republican' criminologists (Braithwaite
1989; Braithwaite and Pettit 1990) argue that criminal justice policy
should contribute to the attainment of social policy goals, which
both respect individual rights and contribute to the common good;
crime, they suggest, is controlled by 'reintegrative shaming', which
draws on shared values both to communicate disapproval of offending
and to offer the offender a route back to normal social status and
esteem, when the offence is accepted as blameworthy and regretted or
repaired. Effective penal sanctions, they argue, are reintegrative in
aim and effect, and they point to Japan (which alone among industrialised countries has experienced a long-term decline in crime) as an
example of a modern society which relies little on overt punishment of
offenders, but very heavily on communication of disapproval and on
encouragement to admit guilt and promise improvement. No doubt there
are cultural contexts and characteristics in Japanese society which are
not readily transferable; however, the principle that penal sanctions
should aim at reintegrative effects seems both persuasive and widely
applicable. Such ideas also offer a social rationale for offence resolution
by mediated agreements and symbolic or practical reparation, as
advocated by Wright (1982, 1991) and practised in a number of
innovative projects (Marshall and Merry 1990; Warner 1992). There are
also implications for community sentences: probation itself can be seen
as reintegrative, offering offenders an opportunity to take responsibility
for offending and to make a practical contribution to the reduction of
future offending.

Within such organic models of justice, which see penal policy as a
component of social policy and a contributor to the cohesion of social
life, the pursuit of effectiveness takes a natural place as an integral goal
of criminal justice alongside other goals, such as fairness, economy, due
process and compatibility with social justice. What such models offer is
a recognition of offenders as members of communities, and as having
much in common with other members; offending is not their only, or
their most important, characteristic. Control theories (Hirschi 1969)
also stress the importance of social bonds in restraining us from crime.
Such approaches to justice aim at reintegration and inclusion, rather

than at segregation and stigmatisation. The author is indebted to Sue Warner for drawing his attention to the writings of the Lebanese poet, Kahlil Gibran, on crime and justice (Warner 1993; Gibran 1991); here he offers another inclusive perspective:

> Oftentimes I have heard you speak of one who commits a wrong as
> Though he were not one of you, but a stranger unto you and an
> Intruder upon your world.

> But I say that even as the holy and righteous cannot rise beyond the
> highest which is in each one of you,

> So the wicked and the weak cannot fall lower than the lowest which
> Is in you also.

Effective programmes have their place within a model of organic justice, which aims at compatibility with social justice and communal solidarity. The conceptual problems arise mainly when 'justice' becomes a formal and abstract notion divorced from real human purposes and interests. Effective rehabilitation, if it can be achieved, serves the ends of justice by offering one route to the reintegration of some of our fellow citizens who are in trouble with the law; it also offers an alternative to non-integrative and stigmatising punishments, which achieve little change in attitudes or behaviour. The probation service needs to debate and develop its own models of justice and its own conception of its contribution to justice, if it is not to be blown off course by the temporary political preoccupations of Ministers. It could then develop a distinctive reforming contribution to a penal policy — a barrier against drifting towards a sterile preoccupation with ineffective punishment at a time when parts of our cities drift closer to the post-modern nightmare and the war of all against all.

WHERE ARE WE NOW? RISKS AND ACHIEVEMENTS IN THE NEW MILLENNIUM

That was how my chapter ended in 1994; the gloomy rhetoric of the conclusion expressed the despair which many felt when contemplating the sterility and destructiveness of social policy at the time, when individual competitiveness and greed were promoted as the chief public virtues and collective welfare provision by the state was seen as an anachronism to be progressively privatised into oblivion. Since then, obviously, much has changed, but many of the fundamental issues and arguments have not. This final section briefly reviews recent achievements and risks in three policy areas particularly relevant to the issues raised by this chapter: the implementation of What Works; the proposed changes in sentencing; and the reorganisation of the probation service itself. All this, of course, has taken place against the background of a new style of thinking in social policy associated particularly with 'New Labour' and different both from the previous Conservative regime and from previous 'Old' Labour Governments. Briefly, New Labour believes in collective provision and effective public services to give substance to the social rights of citizens, but it also emphasises what it sees as the corresponding social responsibilities, and this informs its approach to the unemployed and the delinquent. As Bill Jordan has pointed out (Jordan 2000), New Labour social policies are creating a range of services, settings and initiatives designed to influence people, by a mixture of persuasion, opportunity provision and coercion, to take action to resolve their problems and meet their social responsibilities. Sometimes this can have a quite moralistic and authoritarian flavour, and in the criminal justice field it is neatly expressed by the idea of being 'tough on crime and tough on the causes of crime'. New Labour penal policy has found it hard to leave behind the populist 'toughness' of the previous administration, and prison numbers have continued to rise. But alongside policies designed to display toughness, there is a genuine commitment to crime reduction and to the use of evidence-based effective methods to achieve this. This has had profound consequences for What Works in probation.

During the middle and late 1990s, the What Works agenda was championed and taken forward in the Home Office, particularly by the Probation Inspectorate, under the leadership of Sir Graham Smith. The final 'STOP' results (Raynor and Vanstone 1997) and other studies began to show how important assessment, selection and case management could be in making the difference between good and bad results, and a number of 'pathfinder' projects were set up to develop, pilot and evaluate effective approaches. Alongside this, a joint Accreditation Panel (Home Office 2000e) was established, building on existing practice in the prison service, to ensure that programmes used for offenders on probation or in prison would be, as far as possible, those which had the best demonstrable prospect of effectiveness in addressing their problems and helping them to reduce their offending.

Taken together, these developments and the resources they have succeeded in attracting from central government represent the best ever prospect for the probation service to become reliably effective in helping offenders to reduce their offending, to the benefit of themselves and the community. The risks are that such a strongly led central initiative (believed to be the largest experiment in effective correctional practice ever undertaken anywhere in the world) inevitably involves a strong element of prescription and (perhaps not so inevitably) a flavour of managerialism, which can get in the way of mobilising the enthusiasm and commitment of staff. The What Works movement grew out of the commitment and curiosity of pioneering practitioners, and it needs the same commitment and curiosity about results in order to flourish now. It is also important that the evidence-led approach extends across the whole range of policies; for example, the issue of enforcement is undoubtedly important for the public and political perception of probation, but it needs to be approached in a way which enhances rather than undermines the prospect of offenders completing effective programmes of supervision (Ellis 2000).

New enthusiasm about effective rehabilitation has also led to a new interest in more flexible approaches to sentencing, which are currently under discussion in the Government's review of sentencing. This seems certain to result eventually in new legislation designed to sentence offenders not simply for what they have done, but also in the light of the risk they present, the progress they may make on programmes and other similar considerations. A good example is the proposed 'custody-plus' sentence for those who currently receive short prison sentences with no follow-up supervision to assist in their resettlement. While this will make some assistance available to an otherwise neglected group (Maguire *et al.* 2000), it raises difficult questions about justice and fairness; for example, will people be released into community-based supervision earlier, if they show a good 'response' in prison, and how would this be decided? Will those who commit crimes but are assessed as having few 'needs', serve longer in prison because they are unsuitable for a post-custodial programme? As these proposals develop, they will need the kind of scrutiny that the 'just deserts' movement provided for earlier attempts at flexible sentencing, otherwise there is a risk that they will produce the kind of inconsistency and discrimination which undermines the perceived legitimacy of criminal justice.

Lastly, what of the probation service itself and its recent relaunch as a National Probation Service? Perhaps the simplest explanation is that the move to a national service simply follows from a loss of confidence in the capacity and willingness of locally organised services to deliver new services consistently in line with new standards and new knowledge. It also shows a real confidence that there really is something effective that can be delivered (otherwise the service would probably be moving towards abolition rather than reorganisation). In 1996–97, the Probation Inspectorate undertook a survey to see how far local probation services were applying and implementing the new knowledge about evidence-based practice, which was being disseminated during the early 1990s. The results were alarming: out of 267 projects and programmes, which Chief Officers claimed were based on principles of effective practice, only four could actually demonstrate effectiveness through methodologically adequate evaluation studies (Underdown 1998). The national unified service commended itself as a strategy to ensure more consistent implementation of policy and a faster route to the development of evidence-based practice. At the time of writing, we have only a couple of months' experience of how a national service will look and feel, so it is too early to reach any conclusions about it, except that considerable new resources have been raised from central Government, which would probably not have been provided to support the old system. The main risks seem to be that a system designed for the easier implementation of central policies can be used to implement bad policies as well as good ones; how would a service under direct Home Office control have fared in the Michael Howard era? The new area probation boards also face the challenge of ensuring that the new service is responsive to localities and to the small-scale social systems which actually carry most of the responsibility for crime control. In the past, local sentencers were well represented on probation committees, and they will not respond to the new probation service's ideas if they feel disenfranchised by the new approach to governance, which is exemplified by the new probation boards.

Through all this change, we also find strong continuities, and the final message of this chapter is the same as in 1994: if the new National Probation Service is to make a real difference, it must stand for something, and articulate what it stands for. Effective work with offenders and communities to reduce crime must be based on communication, dialogue, a recognition of common humanity and common human rights. We are not so different from 'offenders' that we can afford to ignore their similarities to us, and our similarities to them.

12 Community Service: Rediscovering Reintegration

Chris Johnson and Sue Rex

INTRODUCTION

In this chapter we wish to explore the renewed interest being taken in community service as a sentence, which can offer rehabilitation as well as punishment for the offender, and reparation for the community.[1] We come to the topic from different perspectives, one of us (Sue Rex) as an academic and researcher, the other (Chris Johnson) as an operational manager.[*] These viewpoints are reflected in the organisation of the chapter. Sue Rex begins by looking at the origins of community service before providing an account of recent research and theoretical developments. Chris Johnson then looks at the operational implications of these developments.

The interest arises in the context of the wider What Works movement affecting the whole of probation practice, and of the implementation of the Human Rights Act 1998, both of which have implications for

---

[*] The views presented in this chapter are the author's own and should not be taken to represent the views or plans of the national directorate.

[1] Indeed, it goes beyond mere interest. As one of its targets for the probation service, the Government expects the service to achieve 30,000 completions of an accredited version of community service by 2003/4, contributing to an overall reduction of 5 per cent in the two-year reconviction rates following community sentences. Funds have been made available to support implementation during this period.

community punishment orders which we aim to draw out. We are well aware of the irony, to put it no stronger, that we are writing this chapter just after the implementation of the legislation renaming the community service order as the community punishment order.[2]

ORIGINS: REINTEGRATIVE AND PUNITIVE THEMES

The current pursuit of a rehabilitative agenda for community service under the Crime Reduction Programme marks a return to its origins. It was the opportunity which it might provide for 'constructive activity in the form of personal service to the community and the possibility of a changed outlook on the part of the offender', that attracted the Wootton Committee in recommending the new court order (Advisory Council on the Penal System 1970, p. 13). Indeed, the importance it attached to the reformative value of performing unpaid work for the community led the Committee to envisage that community service would be undertaken, so far as practicable, in association with volunteer non-offenders. This aspect of the vision has not been realised; in practice, offenders usually undertake their community service hours in work parties with other offenders or in individual placements with voluntary organisations.

The Committee saw that the idea of offenders, performing work for the community would appeal to adherents of different penal philosophies:

> To some, it would be simply a more constructive and cheaper alternative to short sentences of imprisonment; by others it would be seen as introducing into the penal system a new dimension with an emphasis on reparation to the community; others again would regard it as a means of giving effect to the old adage that the punishment should fit the crime; while still others would stress the value of bringing offenders into close touch with those members of the community who are most in need of help and support. (Advisory Council on the Penal System 1970, p. 13).

---

[2] In the rest of this chapter we use the term 'community service order' when referring to the period before April 2000, and 'community punishment order' when considering current or future developments. We refer to the renamed combination order as the combined order. The outcome of debates about the scope of the change of terminology (for example in staff titles) is not yet clear. There is already evidence that some beneficiaries are unhappy with the idea that they might be providing 'community punishment'. We are sympathetic to the formulation that offenders perform community service as their punishment under a community punishment order. The difficulty we have experienced in adapting the language of this chapter reflects the semantic confusion of the new terminology.

Its ability to multi-task has undoubtedly proved to be one of the main attractions of community service, but at the cost of considerable 'philosophical confusion' (Mair 1997). As McIvor (1990) points out, the lack of clarity over its purpose has led to uncertainty over the place occupied by community service in the tariff, and the offenders for whom it should be used. Arguably, this is just one aspect of wider uncertainties about the role of non-custodial sentences, arising from their lack of a clear conceptual framework since the loss of faith in treatment (Rex 1998).

The Wootton Committee recognised that community service would necessarily be seen to have a punitive element, though it hoped that offenders would not come to see it as wholly negative and punitive (this was part of the rationale for suggesting mixed work groups of offenders and non-offenders). It has indeed been its relationship to 'punishment' that has predominated ideas about community service over the last 25 years. Coming at a time when non-custodial sentences were being conceptualised in terms of punishment, initially as alternatives to custody (the only 'real' punishment) and then as punishments in their own right (under the Criminal Justice Act 1991), it is hardly surprising that the reintegrative and rehabilitative potential of community service has remained untapped until recently.

Introduced in the Criminal Justice Act 1972, and piloted in six areas before its national implementation from 1975, the community service order was one element in the Government's strategy to offer courts alternatives to custody in an attempt to stem the rising prison population (see Bottoms 1987). However, even during the pilots, various indicators suggested that it was replacing custody in only half the cases in which it was imposed (Pease 1985). It soon became clear that the alternatives to custody approach was failing to have the desired impact on the prison population, which continued its upward trend and which the Government predicted would reach 70,000 by the year 2000 (Home Office 1988a).

Realising that a substantial rethink was necessary, if sentencers were to be persuaded to use options other than custody, the Government published the proposals which became the Criminal Justice Act 1991 (Home Office 1990a). Section 6 of the 1991 Act applied its deserts-based sentencing principles to non-custodial penalties; to mark their status as punishments in the community, they were renamed community orders and conceptualised in terms of restrictions on liberty commensurate with the seriousness of the offence. Two further changes underlined the point: making probation a sentence of the court; and introducing the combination order, which allowed probation to be combined with community service for a single offence and which the Government hoped would be particularly suitable for recidivist property offenders, who might otherwise have received a custodial sentence. In relation to community service, the Government stressed its reparative and reintegrative dimensions: it provided reparation to the community, and should be used in a way that strengthened, not weakened, offenders' links with the community (Home Office 1990a).

In practice, the impact of the 1991 Act has undoubtedly been to intensify the distinction between probation as rehabilitation and community service as punishment. In part, this was because the statutory rehabilitative criteria for probation helped to encourage probation officers to propose community service as a 'straight' restriction on liberty if someone was not suitable for probation (Rex 1998a). The creation of the combination order was unexpectedly popular with magistrates, because it enabled them to combine help (in the form of probation) with punishment (in the form of community service) — again, reinforcing the rehabilitation–punishment dichotomy. Following its introduction in October 1992, the use of the combination order has risen steadily, to reach around 4 per cent of those sentenced for indictable offences (Home Office 2000d).

It could be argued that community service, conceived primarily as a 'punishment in the community', has not fared particularly well, and this may help to explain why greater emphasis is now been given to its reintegrative and rehabilitative possibilities (as discussed below). Following a peak of 11 per cent in 1993, the proportionate use of community service for indictable offences has settled at 9 per cent over the last few years; the proportion of orders used for summary offences has risen from 10 per cent during the 1980s to two-fifths now (Home Office 2000d). It is still a volume sentence so far as the probation service is concerned — including combination orders, almost 70,000 orders are made annually. However, there has been a marked reduction in the use of community service for offenders with prior experience of custody — to a fifth — and an increase in its use for those with no prior conviction — to over two-fifths (Home Office 2001e). These trends suggest that community service has slipped quite steeply down-tariff, in the face of renewed interest in rehabilitation, and at a time when there has been a dramatic reduction in the use of the fine for indictable offences (from 40 per cent to 27 per cent over the last ten years. (Home Office 2000d)

The provision in the Criminal Justice and Court Services Act 2000 renaming community service orders as community punishment orders must surely re-emphasise the punitive, rather than the reintegrative, aspect of performing unpaid work for the community. It inevitably raises the question whether developing the reintegrative and rehabilitative aspects of undertaking unpaid work for the community might detract from the punitive, or reparative, elements of the order — the latter having undoubtedly won it considerable support from sentencers and the general public. Is there a possible conflict between those goals and developing elements of the order that are intended to influence offenders' behaviour, and which, incidentally, might be seen to benefit offenders — perhaps by increasing their self-confidence and chances of employment? This is a question to which we return below, but reintegrative aims need not preclude the reparation that community service offers to the community. There seems no reason in principle why the short-term benefit to the community of the unpaid work performed by offenders should be incompatible with the longer-term benefit derived from its positive impact on offenders' behaviour.

DEVELOPING IDEAS ABOUT EFFECTIVENESS

It was actually during its heyday as a punishment in the community (though arguably one that was being used for progressively less serious offenders) that attention began to return to the rehabilitative potential of community service. Research studies of reconviction following various community sentences published from the mid-1990s were beginning to hint that community service might reduce recidivism. Gill McIvor's study of community service in Scotland was already offering some insight into the mechanisms, by which their experience of community service might have a positive impact on offenders' behaviour (see McIvor 1990 for a full account of the Scottish study).

What Lloyd et al. (1995), Raynor and Vanstone (1997) and May (1999) all found in common was that the reconviction rate for community service was a few percentage points below the rate predicted on the basis of the offenders' sex, age and previous criminal histories. In May's study, this effect remained when pre-sentence social factors (principally drugs problems and employment) were added to the baseline prediction model. These results must be treated with some caution, as they may well be explained by some factor in the prior experience of the groups sentenced to community service that the prediction model failed to take into account (even May's study included only limited social factors). However, May still concluded that the fact that 'the low reconviction rate for (community service) could not be explained by the criminal histories and available social factors of offenders (suggests) that the sentence itself may have had a positive effect on reconviction' (May 1999).

McIvor's (1990) study offers some evidence that it may be the quality of their experiences in undertaking community service that has a positive impact on offenders. She found that people who viewed their experience of community service as very worthwhile (because it gave them the opportunity to gain skills, or because they could see that it benefited the community) had higher rates of compliance and lower rates of recidivism. As McIvor herself acknowledges, these findings are not conclusive, since some background factor might incline certain individuals both towards a positive view of community service and towards compliance with the requirements of the order. Nonetheless, it is interesting that the differences were particularly strong in the case of individuals who were unemployed, or who had a history of statutory social work supervision.

Killias *et al.* (2000) add a further dimension in uncovering a positive effect following community service compared with short periods of custody. Using quantitative data to investigate what it was about community service that might produce lower rates of re-arrest and reconviction, they found a strong statistical relationship between having served a prison sentence rather than community work and regarding the sentence as 'unfair'. However, no clear relationship emerged between the latter and recidivism, and the researchers were not in a position to examine the processes involved in community service. Could it be, as originally envisaged by the Wootton Committee, that offenders undergo constructive and reintegrative experiences in undertaking community work, and that accepting the sentence as 'fair' in the first place prepares them for these experiences?

The Pathfinder projects on community service now being sponsored by the Home Office under the Crime Reduction Programme, provide an opportunity fully to explore the reintegrative and rehabilitative potential of community service.[3] This is part of a larger What Works strategy, under which the Joint Prisons/Probation Accreditation Panel has been tasked with approving a core curriculum of demonstrably effective programmes for offenders.[4] The projects are being evaluated by the Institute of Criminology at Cambridge University in collaboration with the Probation Studies Unit at Oxford University, with a final report on intermediate outcomes due in March 2002 (if commissioned, a full reconviction analysis would follow in September 2003). Two key elements in community service are being developed through these Pathfinder projects: the use of pro-social modelling in supervising offenders undertaking unpaid work; and the development by offenders of employability skills, leading to further opportunities for training and employment. Below, each of these is examined in a little more detail.

Hitherto, it has primarily been in relation to probation practice that pro-social modelling has been conceived and developed.[5] Here, Trotter has defined pro-social modelling as 'the practice of offering praise and rewards for ... pro-social expressions and actions ... The probation officer becomes a positive role model acting to reinforce pro-social or non-criminal behaviour' (Trotter 1993, p. 4). The idea is to give the offender a definite lead, in a constructive and positive way; the approach combines elements of reinforcement through encouragement and reward, and modelling through positively exemplifying the desired behaviour.

The aim of the community service Pathfinder projects is to exploit what is seen as a natural environment for promoting the development of

---

[3] The projects are being undertaken by the following ten probation services, focusing on the listed components: Bedfordshire and Cambridgeshire (pro-social modelling); Gloucestershire, Norfolk and Suffolk (accrediting employability skills); Northumbria and Durham (skills accreditation and pro-social modelling); Leicestershire (using community service to advance the supervisory aims of a combination order); Hampshire (comparing agency and probation placements) and Somerset (targeting criminogenic need, e.g., through skills accreditation and pro-social modelling). At the time of writing, a further project is planned in Merseyside, in which community service would be used to reinforce the Think First probation programme for offenders on combination orders.

[4] See Probation Circulars 60/2000 for the What Works Strategy, and 35/1999 for the selection of community service Pathfinder projects.

[5] For example, it is described by HMIP's *Effective Practice Guide* as 'a necessary input for effective programme delivery' (HMIP 1998a, 49–50). It has been systematically developed in Christopher Trotter's work in Australia, which found that the breach and reconviction rates of offenders supervised by Community Corrections Officers (essentially probation officers) assessed as using 'pro-social' methods were significantly lower than those of similar groups of offenders (see Trotter 1993, 1996 and 1999).

socially responsible behaviour.[6] The performance of tasks in a practical setting can provide opportunities for offenders to be encouraged to practice pro-social behaviour — completing tasks, working as a team and learning from each other. In supervising offenders, community service supervisors can act as positive role models, showing offenders how to undertake the work and improve their performance, and themselves exhibiting a positive stance towards training and employment (perhaps playing the kind of role envisaged by the Wootton Committee for volunteer non-offenders — see above). As McIvor's (1990) study suggested, the work itself can offer immediate tangible rewards — a sense of achievement in doing something useful for the community. Here, the beneficiary plays a potentially important role — direct contact with community service beneficiaries enables offenders to see at first hand what people have gained from, and their appreciation of, the work undertaken for them. At its best, the performance of community service may engage offenders in the kind of altruistic activity that produces 'teaching points' similar to those in cognitive skills training, which 'emerge, however, from experience rather than academic training' (Toch 2000, p. 275). Indeed, interpreting her findings more recently, McIvor characterises the most 'rewarding' community service placements as reintegrative and entailing some reciprocity and exchange:

In many instances, it seems, contact with the beneficiaries gave offenders an insight into other people, and an increased insight into themselves; the acquisition of skills had instilled in them greater confidence and self-esteem; and the experience of completing their community service orders placed them in a position where they could enjoy reciprocal relationships — gaining the trust, confidence and appreciation of other people and having the opportunity to give something back to them. (McIvor 1998, pp. 55–56)

---

[6] Some evidence that pro-social modelling might have a positive impact, at least on compliance, has emerged from a small pilot study carried out jointly between the Institute of Criminology and Cambridgeshire Probation Service. In that study, offenders supervised predominantly by project CS supervisors were less likely than other offenders to have unacceptable absences or to be breached. They were also far more likely to select positive statements about their experiences of community service — that they were pleased with a job well done, were glad to have done something for the community and were pleased with what they had learnt (see Rex and Crosland 1999).

From the offenders' point of view, part of this exchange entailed their acquisition of skills (or perhaps the demonstration of skills), which produced what Toch (2000) would call 'grounded increments' in self-esteem. This seems somewhat reminiscent of the development of self-efficacy, or a belief in one's personal capability, as theorised by Bandura (1997). It brings the discussion to the other main element of the community service Pathfinder projects, the development of employability skills,[7] which is based on the finding that many offenders lack such skills, and on the statistically significant relationship between unemployment and reconviction found, for example, by May (1999). The thinking is that improving offenders' employment prospects might reduce their future offending.

There is some support for this proposition in criminal careers research, which points to the importance of improvements in offenders' social environments, specifically their employment situation, in their movement away from offending.[8] However, the evidence that giving offenders employability skills will lead directly to their employment and, therefore, lower rates of reconviction is scant (Palmer and Hollin 1995), perhaps because offenders' own community networks can be more successful in meeting their employment needs than efforts by social work agencies (Haines 1990). There is a chance that the skills developed in undertaking community service will assist offenders to obtain jobs through informal contacts, and increase their motivation to seek employment. Some attempts are also being made in the community service Pathfinder projects to offer routes into further training and employment, and Sarno et al. (2001) report promising — if inconclusive — findings from two probation employment programmes, involving practical measures to improve the employment and training prospects of 16–25-year-olds. The challenge for the evaluation of the community service Pathfinder projects will, therefore, be to establish whether, and how, offenders experience improvements in their employment status following participation in skills accreditation on community service.

---

[7] Supported by the allowance in para. D14 of the 2000 National Standards for 10 per cent of community service hours to be used for basic literacy training and the provision of qualifications (see Home Office 2000k).

[8] On the role of employment and job discrimination in ex-prisoners' ability to avoid offending, see for example Burnett (1994); Kendall (1998). More generally, see Sampson and Laub (1993); Graham and Bowling (1995).

PRACTICE IMPLICATIONS

What, then, are the implications of these ideas and findings for how community punishment orders might be delivered? There are four distinct but related strands to explore:

(a)   developing pro-social attitudes;
(b)   work placements which contribute to self-efficacy and a sense of citizenship;
(c)   developing cognitive (thinking) skills;
(d)   developing (and accrediting) other practical or vocational skills to enhance employability.

These elements are coherent and mutually reinforcing. Providing work experiences, which enable offenders to see that they can contribute something worthwhile and valued by the beneficiaries, complements and gives direct expression to work which supervisors may do to promote pro-social attitudes. Cognitive skills are an important part of the range of key skills which are essential building blocks towards employability. Linking the development of skills with providing rewards for deploying them in a pro-social way is both theoretically and intuitively a cogent approach to take. It is also one which connects very well with the models of change underpinning the cognitive skills programmes, which are being implemented throughout the probation service. This opens up possibilities for the creative use of combination orders (now community punishment and rehabilitation orders), which will be explored later in this section.

Pro-social modelling

Following Trotter's work, there has been considerable interest in the probation service in using pro-social modelling in a variety of settings, including hostels as well as community service. Tutors running accredited programmes are expected to be skilled in its use. 'But we do this anyway' is a common and understandable reaction of practitioners to the introduction of the concept. If it is to be fully effective, however, implementation needs to follow the What Works principle of delivery integrity, which would require at least that:

(a)   both elements are provided — the approach involves staff both acting as good role models of pro-social attitudes and behaviour, and reinforcing them in offenders (as well as helping to extinguish anti-social attitudes and behaviour); and

(b)   it is applied consistently over time, and by all staff.

These have important implications for implementation.

The two processes, of modelling and reinforcing behaviour, involve different change mechanisms, although both work towards the same goal. While it is relatively easy to train someone to reinforce effectively and appropriately, it is much more difficult to train to be a good pro-social role model, which is likely to be linked with established patterns of thinking and behaving. This would suggest a strategy of selecting for appointment those who show the potential to be good role models (amongst other criteria), and training them in the necessary reinforcement skills. Such an approach would apply to all probation service staff, not just those supervising community punishment orders.

Trotter's original work relied on training, and follow-up workshops for practitioners to achieve consistency of delivery. Much can be achieved in this way: workshops not only maintain a focus on the topic, but also enable staff to develop routines — ways of handling common work situations in a pro-social way. These can then be internalised, both for the individual staff member and for the organisation. Other approaches also need to be used: although video monitoring of the whole of every work session may not be feasible, parts of sessions could be covered in this way and supplemented by direct observation by other staff. Feedback from offenders can also be used in a systematic way to give staff a measure of what they are doing well and what badly. Appraisal can provide a framework for gathering and using all this evidence. It is precisely because pro-social modelling covers such a wide range of behaviour that we need to ensure that it is being delivered as intended.

Placements

McIvor's work leads to a very different view of the role of the beneficiaries in community service work. Instead of being simply passive recipients of work done by offenders, they potentially become partners in a social contract, along the lines of 'in return for you doing this work for me (or my organisation) I will value you and your work as making a worthwhile contribution to society'. They therefore carry a powerful reintegration message, and as a bonus they may often act as good pro-social models themselves.

From this perspective, the task of setting up a work placement is really about negotiating a contract, specifying and agreeing not only the work to be done, but also the roles of offender, supervisor and beneficiary. Where the work is a service direct to an individual, the process may be straightforward. In other situations, however, it may mean negotiating for a representative of the benefiting organisation to visit a work site, at agreed intervals, to see the progress being made and to discuss its significance with those doing the work. Ingenuity may be needed: for example, when the project involves helping a charity with fundraising (through charity shops or collecting items for sale), part of the induction could be ensuring that workers understand the aims of the charity, and what the money raised would be used for. However it is done, the key is that offenders understand the significance of what they are doing, and how and for whom it is of benefit. It is worthwhile exploring, as part of an allocation decision, an offender's concerns or interests — some types of work may capture his or her imagination more readily than others. In fact, the placement characteristics, which McIvor found led to a positive impact on some offenders, are very close to those which management theory sets out as essential elements of good job design.

Such an approach may be particularly powerful when offenders undertake work in the communities where they themselves live, and where members of that community are directly involved in deciding on the work to be carried out. This can establish a new relationship between the offender and local role models, which can continue after the end of the order and provide a counterbalance to the anti-social influence of others who may be powerful in sustaining criminal activity. The potential of the approach to promote social inclusion is shown by an example from West Yorkshire. As part of a general programme of estate regeneration, groups of offenders (largely from the area themselves) worked under the direction of a residents' association. Members of the association complained to probation service staff that they were being too rigorous in enforcing orders, and were not showing sufficient understanding of the problems the offenders faced — a nice demonstration of how community service brought about changed attitudes towards offenders, as well as changes in them.

There is no reason why this approach to placements should conflict with the recent growing interest in using work done on community service to contribute to community safety and to Crime and Disorder Partnerships (set up following the Crime and Disorder Act 1998). Indeed, such work may offer particularly powerful experiences when the beneficiaries are themselves victims of crime, though these placements need to be arranged with particular sensitivity to the needs and perspectives of victims.[9]

Cognitive Skills

The research which shows that offenders can improve their cognitive skills through modelling and reinforcement — the same processes used in pro-social modelling — has yet to be applied in this country, though its potential is clear (see, e.g., Fabiano *et al.* 1996). While it can be used as an approach in straight community punishment orders, there are particularly exciting possibilities in community punishment and reha-bilitation (combination) orders, where it could support and enhance learning from general cognitive skills programmes being undertaken as part of the probation element.

Implementation raises issues analogous to those affecting pro-social modelling — how to ensure integrity and consistency of delivery by supervisors and other staff. There are similar implications too for the recruitment and training of supervisors, though here we have an existing assessment centre model of selection and training of tutors for accredited programmes, from which to borrow.

Developing Work Skills

The opportunity to develop new skills was one of the features which McIvor found led offenders to value their community service place-ments. While such opportunities occur naturally in many work situations, two developments have enabled a more formal approach. First, there is now a wide range of qualifications covering both general

---

[9] The Wootton Committee (Advisory Council on the Penal System 1970) discounted the use of community service to provide direct reparation — that is, work done by an offender for a victim of his or her offences. However, the development of reparation orders for offenders under 18 provides a stimulus for further exploration of this for adult offenders. Victims need to be safeguarded in this, and the criterion for success defined — is it victim satisfaction with the outcome, or impact on offender attitudes and future behaviour? To be able to achieve both would be a bonus. Current pathfinders are not exploring this approach.

and vocational skills at different levels, which can be used to give recognition to and certification of what an offender has learned. They are readily accessible, either through partnership with an institution such as a college of further education, or by a probation area establishing itself as an assessment centre. They are subdivided into units, one or more of which can be completed within the timescale of most orders. Secondly, the most recent version of National Standards allows for up to 10 per cent of community punishment order hours to be devoted specifically to activities aimed at improving an offender's employability — time which can be used, for example, in preparing portfolios as well as in direct learning. (This is, incidentally, important formal recognition of the legitimacy of using community punishment orders in part to pursue rehabilitative aims.)

Given the two possible mechanisms by which skills accreditation might affect future behaviour (developing self-efficacy, or increasing the likelihood of an offender successfully securing a job), the choice of qualification may be important. Thus:

(a)   it should extend existing skills (to offer a qualification well below the level of current skill risks being demotivating rather than positive; to offer it to someone already in stable and suitable employment, may be a waste of resources);
(b)   it should be a qualification recognised by potential employers.

Qualifications covering general employability or key skills have some advantages in the context of community punishment orders compared with vocational awards: they can be demonstrated in a variety of different placements, do not require supervisors to hold specific vocational qualifications themselves, and, arguably, match what employers say they want (see, e.g., Gillis *et al.* 1996). In addition, key skills include general problem solving, which makes a natural link with cognitive skills modelling by supervisors outlined above. On the other hand, practical or vocational skills may be more useful in the informal labour market, which may be more important than formal routes. We have as yet no information on employment or offending outcomes from such schemes, on which to make a soundly-based choice between the options.

It is not enough to provide offenders with a qualification: if employment is the outcome sought, they need help in how to progress, whether to further training, or to the job market. Without this, they may develop expectations which will not be met, leading to disillusionment and perhaps increased offending. Schemes linking with colleges may have advantages here, as such guidance should be routinely available to all those registered for an award, and options for continuing training readily accessible. All schemes should make the provision, which would be another way of using the 10 per cent hours allowance.

Community punishment and rehabilitation (combination) orders

The discussion so far has focused on the community punishment order as a stand-alone order. As part of a combination order, it still provides the element of punishment which the court was no doubt seeking in making the order, but it also has the potential to contribute to the rehabilitative component. In terms of the factors which affect the likelihood of reoffending, it can help address:

(a)   anti-social attitudes and behaviour;
(b)   poor cognitive and interpersonal skills;
(c)   employability;
(d)   predominance of anti-social role models;
(e)   lack of pro-social models.

It can be deployed, therefore, as part of the plan to bring about changes in these factors — not in isolation, but strengthening and reinforcing other work. The accreditation of skills can form part of a wider set of interventions aimed at helping an offender into sustainable employment. The cognitive skills and pro-social modelling can reinforce and provide opportunities for practising learning from a general offending behaviour programme, particularly where the community service work can be timed to run alongside the programme. For this to be effective, supervisors would clearly need to have a good understanding of what the programme was teaching, and be able to use the same conceptual framework. A work placement involving victims as beneficiaries can play a part in enhancing awareness of the impact of crime on victims.

This approach provides a sound basis for regarding the order as an integrated whole, for not only is enforcement coordinated, but each part also contributes to the effort to change behaviour. We could expect an enhanced impact, either in effect size, or in its length of duration — but there is, as yet, no direct evidence that this will be realised, nor about what implementation problems have to be overcome to achieve it. Conclusions will need to await the outcome of the combination order projects still running at the time of writing.

IS IT FEASIBLE?

The view of community service/punishment outlined so far is, if not so different from its original conception, more demanding and more costly than the practice prevalent during a period of financial constraints and rehabilitative pessimism.[10] Could such a model now be established as standard?

Perhaps the first question should be whether such elaboration is always required. Current sentencing practice has seen community service used increasingly for first-time offenders.[11] the majority of whom will be unlikely to reoffend. One of the principles of effective practice, as currently understood, is that the intensity of intervention should match the risk of reoffending — intervening with low-risk offenders is at best likely to have no effect, at worst can increase reconviction rates. While positive placements and good staff modelling and reinforcement seem prima facie unlikely to be negative in their effect on any offenders, they may be unnecessary for the low-risk group.

This would suggest a two-tier model of community service/punishment: one in which placement selection was not critical, and where, though staff might be trained in pro-social and cognitive skills modelling, delivery integrity would not have to be monitored; and the second, where placement quality and staff behaviour were assessed to ensure delivery as planned, and where skills accreditation was provided. Selection between these two possibilities would be based on level of risk (of reoffending) and assessed offender need. The model readily accommodates the use of individual placements, where someone not directly employed by the probation service (usually from a voluntary sector organisation) carries out the supervision; as now, these could be used for the lower-risk group. They have the added advantage of

---

[10] Though there were honourable exceptions, where enthusiastic staff and imaginative management kept faith with the potential positive impact of community service.
[11] The latest *Probation Statistics for England and Wales* (Home Office 2001e) show that in 1999, 42 per cent of those starting community service had no previous convictions.

avoiding the possible negative influence of higher-risk offenders on lower-risk offenders.[12]

It might be argued that such a model breaches any commitment to equality of opportunity. It does indeed provide differential treatment, but this is quite congruent with the approach taken with community rehabilitation (probation) orders, where lower-risk offenders do not normally take the accredited programmes provided for those of higher risk. A differentiated approach, based on risk and need, is a fundamental element of evidence-based practice.

There are important staffing implications to be worked through. The task of supervising groups of offenders, often in public view, and maintaining the standard of work done has always been difficult, and has usually been undervalued. Additionally, the expectation that supervisors will play a significant part in changing behaviour, and will have the necessary skills, must have implications for their status in the organisation, and is likely to have implications for pay and grading. The two-tier model suggested above would probably require two grades of supervisor, with different levels of training and responsibility — a break with current practice, but one which should be readily accepted, provided staff are given opportunities for progression.

JUSTICE AND PUNISHMENT: THE HUMAN RIGHTS ACT AND DIVERSITY

So far in this chapter we have focused on the development and practice implications of ideas of effectiveness in community service/punishment. We need to consider how far this agenda meets the requirements of a justice perspective — that is, that the community punishment order, as a sentence, is fair in its treatment of individual offenders, and that it is used in an equitable way for different groups, particularly women offenders and those from minority ethnic groups. This leads us to a discussion of the Human Rights Act 1998, and diversity issues.

The incorporation of the European Convention on Human Rights into UK law on 2 October 2000 caused anxiety — not to say panic — in some quarters about its impact and likely level of use within the criminal

---

[12] Though some argue that the lower-risk group can have a positive influence on the higher; no doubt that is possible, but the evidence suggests the predominant direction of influence is the other way (Trotter 1993).

justice system. Several of the Articles were identified as having potential application to community service, and as leading to possible challenges. The main Articles, as identified in guidance promulgated to the probation service by the Home Office in Probation Circular 59/2000, were as follows:

(a) *Article 3*, prohibiting inhuman or degrading treatment or punishment. Could this apply to offenders being required to undertake menial work on community service, or to the oft-mooted, but never yet implemented, plan to make offenders on these orders wear uniforms? Suggested counter-arguments were that work which is socially useful and within the capability of the individual to perform, could not be regarded as inhuman or degrading. Although the work has to be rigorous and demanding, offenders are sentenced to the order as punishment, not for it. The uniforms issue has yet to be put to the test.

(b) *Article 4*, prohibiting slavery and forced labour. Some initial advice to sentencers wrongly suggested that, because of this provision, a community service (punishment) order could be made only with the consent of the offender (a requirement of the original legislation removed by the Crime (Sentences) Act 1997). However, the Article itself provides exemptions for work done 'in the ordinary course of detention imposed according to the provisions of Article 5 ... or during conditional release from such detention'. This, translated into a British context, covered community service, it was argued, and the advice to sentencers has been altered accordingly.

(c) *Articles 5 and 6*, providing for the right to liberty and security, and to a fair trial respectively. The protection here for the service comes from the legitimacy of the court, an independent and impartial body, determining the level of punishment and deprivation of liberty, not the officer responsible for the order; and determining whether or not there has been a breach, and, if so, what the penalty should be. Carrying out procedures in accordance with National Standards would be a further protection, since a court would regard these as part of the regulations governing the order.

(d) *Articles 9 and 14*, providing for freedom of thought, conscience and religion, and the prohibition of discrimination. These Articles will require staff, when they give work instructions, to respect the religious observance requirements of all recognised religions — already part of good practice. Article 14 applies only to the enjoyment of the rights and freedoms set out in the Convention. Although the European Court has interpreted the Article broadly, it is likely to be less demanding than existing UK legislation, which covers discrimination on the grounds of disability, gender or race — recently extended by the Race Relations (Amendment) Act 2000 to cover both direct and indirect discrimination and applicable to all government bodies.

(e) *Article 1 of Protocol 1*, which provides for the protection of property, which has been interpreted as covering the right to pursue one's business or trade. This reinforces the importance of respecting work commitments in organising placements.

Despite the fears, the initial Home Office advice — that all current probation activity, if conducted within the framework of the law and National Standards, would withstand challenge — has so far proved sound: in the first nine months of the Act, no challenge to community service orders or community punishment orders came to court on human rights grounds.

This initial defensive reaction is understandable, but altogether too negative. The 1998 Act and the Convention itself provide a welcome and supporting ethical framework for the reintegrative approach to community punishment order practice which has been outlined in this chapter. They complement the more pragmatic, evidence-based approach derived from What Works, and help ensure into the future that offenders will be sentenced to a community punishment order as punishment, not for punishment.

The extension of UK race discrimination legislation (see above) raises more sharply concerns about the patterns of use of community punishment orders for offenders from minority ethnic groups — and by implication, women. Compared with its use for white males, as a sentence community service has been underused for women offenders (while the probation order has been overused) and overused for ethnic minority offenders (while the probation order has been underused),[13] though it is not clear how far this reflects differing patterns of offending. Studies of sentencing have focused on the custody decision and suggest

---

[13] See Probation Statistics for England and Wales 1998: in that year 20.7 per cent of Probation commencements were on women offenders, against 9.9 per cent of CS commencements; and 10.1 per cent of CS commencements against 7.4 per cent of Probation commencements were on minority ethnic offenders. The latter figures in particular need to be treated with caution because of the relatively large number of cases where data on ethnicity was not available.

that, once the seriousness of the offence and previous record are taken into account, women receive similar sentences to men, or are treated more leniently. For a summary of the recent studies, see Hedderman and Gelsthorpe (1997), who also found that magistrates regarded women as 'troubled' rather than 'troublesome' and were, therefore, inclined towards probation rather than community service. One problem has been a shortage of the types of project that magistrates see as suitable for women (Barker 1993). There is some evidence of a reduction in the disparities in the sentencing of women and ethnic minority offenders to community service (Home Office 2001e), but it is not possible to tell whether this has resulted from efforts to tackle the apparent discrimination, or from changed patterns of offending.

The practical implications of tackling the sentencing disparities for women and ethnic minority offenders set out above have already been well explored (Barker 1993; HMIP 2000f; Howard League 1999). They include responsiveness to child care demands; ensuring the appointment of women and those from a minority ethnic group as supervisors; challenging gender based assumptions about suitability for community punishment orders; ensuring a supportive composition of work groups; ensuring that minority ethnic groups are appropriately represented as beneficiaries; and increasing the confidence of probation staff in working with minority ethnic offenders on community rehabilitation orders.

Pursuing a rehabilitative and reintegrative agenda for community punishment orders throws up a new set of questions and challenges:

(a)   What rates of compliance do these orders achieve with different types of offender?

(b)   What impact do they have on dynamic risk factors and subsequent reoffending; and how, if at all, is this different for women and offenders from minority ethnic groups?

Answers to these questions will need to take account of the different risk and needs profiles of the offender populations. For example, if a higher proportion of women offenders on community punishment orders are in the lower-risk group, fewer would, on a two-tier model, go into the enhanced version. However, where there are relevant needs, for example in relation to skills development, it is important that access is fair and progress supported. There are also questions about the effectiveness of some of the mechanisms described above: is pro-social modelling more effective when supervisor and offender are from the same ethnic group or of the same sex? Is the reintegrative effect of a placement more powerful if the beneficiary (individual or organisation) is from the same ethnic group? We are a long way from having sound evidence on these questions, though the pathfinders may offer some first indications. Practical choices may not be straightforward: would we want to make a presumption that offenders would work for beneficiaries of similar ethnic origin, if the evidence supported this; and would this apply equally to white offenders? We may decide that promoting an inclusive society is more important here than pursuing effectiveness.

As in the case of the Human Rights Act 1998, we can say that current legislation on discrimination reflects and promotes that best practice to which the probation service aspires. If the service fails to deliver, it can look forward to the scrutiny of the courts to guide and stimulate its continuing efforts.

CONCLUDING THOUGHTS

One recent difficulty faced by community penalties has been the lack of a sustained idea as to what they are intended to achieve, and therefore their place in the range of sentencing options. The What Works strategy gives strong impetus to the development of community-based programmes, and for exploiting the unique reintegrative and rehabilitative potential of this kind of work. However, the intellectual framework needs to keep pace, if such initiatives are to stand the test of time; and we need to resolve questions such as the reconcilability of reintegrative work with offenders with the self-proclaimed status of the community punishment order. Given the current trend towards combining different types of conditions and orders,[14] it is even more important that such conditions cohere as an overall package: the work on the combined community punishment and rehabilitation orders, which is outlined above, provides a model of how this can be achieved.

In setting out the strands and implications, theoretical and practical, of a reintegrative approach to community service and, now, community

---

[14] For example, the Criminal Justice and Court Services Act 2000 allows any requirement of any order to be enforced through electronic monitoring, and a Community Rehabilitation Order (previously a Probation Order) to include conditions of drug abstinence, curfew and exclusion.

punishment, we want to stress that we see them as additional to its punitive and reparative elements, not as replacements for them. Nothing suggested here takes away from the work delivered to the community, or makes it any less demanding physically or emotionally for the offender; rather the reverse — if society can have its correctional cake and eat it, why not?

Lastly, let us emphasise that, while there is some evidence to support the developments we have described, it is far from conclusive. Community service has, in this country and abroad, been a much under-researched intervention. The Pathfinder study, currently under-way, should add considerably to our knowledge; but even when it is available, there will remain much to do, in research as well as implementation.

Acknowledgements

Both the authors would like to acknowledge their debt to staff involved in the Community Punishment and Combined Order Pathfinders, who have contributed to the development of the ideas set out in this chapter, and who have been testing them out in practice.

13   Just Practice in Probation Hostels

Paul Thurston

INTRODUCTION

This chapter explores the unique contribution that approved hostels make to the system of justice, and also some of the challenges facing hostels in delivering a just — i.e. fair — service. It has been written at the dawn of the new National Probation Service, and we therefore speculate on how hostels could affect the two key outcomes set by the National Director:

(a)   to achieve a reduction of 5 per cent in the re-conviction rate of offenders subject to supervision by 2004;

(b)   to be recognised as a top performing public service by 2006.

As any student of hostel practice will quickly discern, there is a paucity of scholarly endeavour in this field. Hence, this chapter is a very personal view, based on the author's 12 years' professional experience as a residential social worker, the manager of an approved hostel, the senior manager responsible for a group of six hostels, and a former involvement at national level as Chair of the Association of Chief Probation Officers' Housing and Hostels Group.

HOSTELS AND THE SYSTEM OF JUSTICE

When Her Majesty's Inspectorate of Probation (HMIP) conducted a national review of hostels in 1993, it discovered a professional world characterised by under-occupancy and lack of constructive engagement:

> The original rationale for approved hostels (as temporary accommodation for young petty offenders, who went out to work during the day) was no longer valid. Hostels were struggling to find a regime suited to the new rationale, defined by National Standards in terms of offering an enhanced level of supervision within a structured and supportive environment. Many residents had very restricted access to educational, training and leisure opportunities and the boredom and lack of purpose they experienced militated against the maintenance of a constructive atmosphere in the hostel. (HMIP 1993)

This resulted in the catchphrase, 'If you don't use them, you will lose them', and indeed, several hostels were subsequently closed.

When the Inspectorate undertook another review of hostels in 1998, it reported a very different outlook:

> Significant progress has been made by approved hostels since they were last inspected in 1993, especially in the extent to which they were providing the enhanced level of supervision required by National Standards ... The public could be greatly encouraged by many of the findings of this inspection. (HMIP 1998c)

So why the change? Well, survival is a strong motivator, but does not provide a complete explanation. Within the probation services, a much more profound change was under way — a shift from a collusive to an inclusive agenda; a move from seeing probation as the apologists for offenders to recognising that probation also had a responsibility to victims and the general public — in short, the emergence of a new role for probation as a major contributor to public protection. Public protection work requires on-going risk assessment, regular supervision, monitoring and enforcement. If there was ever a remit better suited to hostels in search of an identity, it was this. Hence the Association of

Chief Probation Officers' (ACOP's) strategic statement on the role of hostels published in 1996:

> Decisions about appropriate accommodation for offenders need to be made within the context of a commonly accepted framework for risk management. The higher the risk, then the greater the level of oversight and support required ... Probation/Bail Hostels should be targeted at statutory cases, which are assessed as high risk, temporary high risk (respite/emergency care) and uncertain risk (a need for a more thorough assessment in a stable environment). (ACOP 1996)

Unlike other offender accommodation providers, approved hostels are a recognised part of the local criminal justice network, particularly important for enforcement purposes. Compared with other community disposals, hostels — by virtue of the residency requirement — are uniquely well placed to deliver on the other components intrinsic to effective public protection, namely continuing assessment, surveillance, curfew and developing pro-social attitudes/behaviour.

This focus for the role of hostels is enshrined in the latest National Standards:

> The purpose of approved hostels is to provide an enhanced level of residential supervision with the aim of protecting the public by reducing the likelihood of offending. Approved hostels are for bailees, probationers and post-custody licensees, where their risk of causing serious harm to the public or other likelihood of re-offending means that no other form of accommodation in the community would be suitable. (Home Office 2000k)

Helpfully, the National Standards go on to insist that hostel managers should not refuse cases based on the type of offence, but only on the grounds of risk to the hostel resident himself or herself, other hostel residents, hostel staff or the local community. This makes perfect sense from a hostel management viewpoint, but is not a judgment easily accepted by other 'customers' like supervising officers, service managers, the Dangerous Offenders Unit and Home Office Ministers, particularly when it comes to placing a high-risk, high-profile case. Here is a professional conundrum: hostels are best suited for the high-risk cases, but some of these pose too much of a risk for hostels to manage.

Part of a longer-term solution would be a change in legislation so that dangerous offenders, who showed no indication of reduced risk to the community, could be detained in custody. That is the only 'safe' option from a public protection viewpoint. Perversely, this is the arrangement made for Sidney Cook, a notorious paedophile, at the unit inside Nottingham Prison, albeit on a voluntary basis. Justice demands, however, that once a prisoner has been released, he or she is entitled to a degree of liberty. Hostels cannot be expected to provide a totally supervised and risk-free option. They are not prisons.

Another strategy has been to give hostels additional moneys, for example, to employ extra staff in order to manage such difficult cases more safely. In practice, however, many such cases have ended up being placed in independent sector accommodation. Personally, this author does not see this necessarily as a bad thing — some cases might respond more positively to a less institutionalised regime. A package of additional public protection safeguards can still be provided, albeit by other providers, e.g., electronic tagging, police surveillance, regular probation supervision contacts. Local authorities still have a responsibility to address homelessness and have acquired a new duty for those leaving institutional care. Indeed, the truth of the matter is that most high-risk cases do not live in hostels and do live in the community — that is the norm.

This last point is an important one. There are 101 hostels currently providing a total of 2,251 bed spaces. Each year, the probation service commences the supervision of 170,000 offenders. (Wallis 2001). So, the hostel resource has to be targeted appropriately. In addition, hostels are designed as a short-term staging post and not as a long term accommodation solution. Hence, even when cases are admitted, consideration for the most appropriate move-on accommodation is an immediate issue. Hostels therefore need to be placed strategically, as just one part of a much broader accommodation continuum culminating for most, but not all, in access to fully independent living.

Having attempted to describe how approved hostels can add value to the system of justice, it is also necessary to raise the issue of whether they represent value for money. Matthew Taylor (2000), Director of the Institute for Public Policy Research, asserts that publicly managed services are still on trial with the current Government. There has been a recent substantial investment in establishing a National Probation Service and also for enhanced service delivery. However, if publicly managed services fail to deliver then a second term Labour Government would be less sympathetic. What has this got to do with hostels? Well, like the prison service, hostels are already a mixed economy, with 12 of the 101 hostels being managed by independent committees representing voluntary organisations. The funding mechanism is also about to change. From April 2001, probation managed hostels will appear in area budgets, and therefore be open to local scrutiny and challenge in a way unheard of under the direct Home Office funding system, and hostels are an expensive commodity. The National Probation Service will also be subject to the Government's Better Quality Service (BQS) test, which is designed to ensure that the public receive the kind of service they require, to a quality standard which is acceptable, at a price which is fair. BQS requires a review of all services over a five-year period, against the following criteria:

- Challenge: is the service needed?
- Compare: is the service meeting targets, and who is performing better?
- Consult: what do customers, users, stakeholders and staff think about the service?
- Compete: who is best able to deliver the service — public, private, voluntary sector?
- Collaborate: who else has an interest in this service, and how can we share responsibility?

The National Director has already intimated an intention to select three aspects of probation service activity each year for BQS. Inevitably, hostels will be caught up in this rigorous process, and it could result in all of them being managed by the private or voluntary sector. Having spent seven years of his professional life managing hostels in an area where half of them were in the voluntary sector, this is an issue very close to this author's heart! His plea is twofold: first, when comparing unit costs, make sure you are comparing like with like and that any formula takes account of surpluses as well as expenditure. Secondly, even if hostels are operated by the independent sector, make sure that firm links remain with the local probation area — both at a governance level and at an operational level. Fortunately, shared governance is currently secured through the Probation Hostel Rules (Home Office 1995d). These require local probation committees to approve the written constitution of a voluntarily managed hostel. They also require such a hostel to have representation on its management group by a probation committee representative and a senior probation manager. These rules are currently being revised to accommodate the new National Probation Service, but no doubt similar safeguards will remain. More importantly, it is vital that — at an operational level — hostels retain the services of a seconded senior probation officer as manager. In part, this recognises the close service links required for assessments, supervision plans, interventions, enforcement action, public protection, reports and — increasingly — IT systems, all of which contribute towards National Standards compliance and the achievement of key performance measures. It also recognises the need for career mobility and a belief that managers should not get stuck in one role, particularly the institutionalised one of a hostel. This model of secondments is the one recommended by Janet Maitland (1997) in her helpful guide for voluntarily managed hostel committees.

HOSTELS PROVIDING A JUST SERVICE

Hostels are not prisons in the community, but they do represent the most intrusive option currently provided by probation by virtue of the residency requirement and the curfew. Consequently, while they may not be total institutions — as described by Goffman (1968) — they are, nonetheless, institutions. This fact poses big challenges about the appropriate use of authority. The stakes are high because personal liberty is at issue. At its crudest, a bailee required to live in a hostel could find himself or herself arrested by the police, produced before a court and remanded in custody simply on the strength of one telephone call from a night duty member of hostel staff. Unfettered power is likely to lead to abuse and to decisions based on the interests of the institution and comfort of staff, rather than on the interests of those for whom the institution is supposed to provide a direct service — the hostel residents. This has implications for the governance of hostels. There needs to be a system of internal checks and balances in the operational processes, so that an individual staff member cannot unilaterally decide on somebody's fate — and this includes managers too. Ideally, there needs to be an external scrutiny too, whether this is supplied by a more senior manager or via a routinised accountability to the committee/board via reports and inspections to ensure healthy functioning. It also requires developing a regime in which the hostel residents feel empowered and not oppressed; where their views are sought about the functioning of the hostel; and, most critical of all, one in which they feel able to use a complaints procedure in the knowledge that this will result in a fair determination. This is not to say that this is an easy task; there is often a chasm between the value system of residents and those of the hostel staff. Indeed, such a truism probably goes to the heart of the professional quest — to promote pro-social attitudes and behaviour. All the more vital then that the staff themselves model pro-social attitudes and behaviours. As Shakespeare shows in *Macbeth*, failure has dire consequences:

> That we but teach bloody instructions, which, being taught, return, to plague the inventors; this even-handed justice commends the ingredients of our poison'd chalice to our own lips.

Badly-managed hostels, where decisions are either avoided, are idiosyncratic or are simply oppressive, are corrupting places both for the staff and the residents who have the misfortune to be sent there. Well-managed hostels are characterised by timely and defensible decision-making regarding the discharge of authority. In such an environment, both staff and residents feel safe and can engage purposefully in the quest for promoting positive change. If the justice of this position requires any further endorsement, surely it comes with the advent of the Human Rights Act 1998. Hostel staff need to ensure that the decisions taken about the residents are defensible professionally, and also that residents comprehend the reasoning behind them.

A second challenge for hostels in providing a just service is how they can tackle institutional racism, as defined by the Macpherson Inquiry into the death of Stephen Lawrence. The basis of this assertion is the fact that minority ethnic people are over-represented in custody and under-represented in hostels. Martin Todd's research discovered a hostel world in which staff had received little anti-racist training and seemed wary of addressing minority ethnic issues. The hostels seemed to 'operate in a vacuum removed from the ethnic minority communities they claim to serve' (Todd 1996). Consequently, minority ethnic residents had little confidence in the ability of the hostel to provide a service to meet their particular needs. Adapting to the cultural needs of residents was viewed by many hostel staff as an additional and time-consuming task. This negative culture was also discerned by Tuklo Orenda Associates (1999), who described the following self-fulfilling cycle: absence of appropriate provision for minority ethnic residents — we don't have much call for it — fewer referrals of minority ethnic cases — the occasional minority ethnic admission likely to fail — even less perceived need to accommodate diversity — fewer or no minority ethnic referrals.

All of this was shockingly familiar to the West Yorkshire hostels, which had attempted to 'do the right thing' by accommodating difference, but without ever impacting on the low referral rate of minority ethnic cases — and this in an area with a significant minority ethnic population. The imaginative leap was to shift from a mindset which accommodated difference, to one which genuinely celebrated diversity in a pro-active way. To break the mould, the six local hostels jointly funded a Black/Asian Support Worker post, the purpose of which was to drive up the admission rate for suitable minority ethnic cases and to develop best hostel practice. The six hostels also funded a complementary piece of independent research from the University of Huddersfield (Kazi *et al.* 2001). This would identify best practice, and additionally provide credible staff and resident survey tools in order to gauge progress and the quality of service. The hostels agreed that two out of the six would become semi-specialist minority ethnic facilities. In part, this reflected a desire to establish a 'critical mass' of Black/Asian residents, so that they did not feel isolated. It also reflected a desire to equip the hostel staff teams with the confidence and skills to engage in a positive way and establish a 'critical mass' in the minority ethnic staff complement too.

Tuklo Orenda Associates were right — this pro-active approach is working. Admissions of Black/ethnic minorities have doubled within the first year. A culture which genuinely celebrates diversity is being established via diet, reading materials, positive images and individual support. The surveys confirm that residents feel their needs are being met and, interestingly, staff are now more aware of the further learning required by them.

Of course, this raises a third important issue for a 'just' hostel service — should they be generic providers of a universal service, or is some degree of specialisation required? Certainly, the 'critical mass' issue was an important aspect in developing the Black/Asian initiative in West

Yorkshire, and was itself founded on the experience of improving services for women in hostels locally. The idea, therefore, that appropriate services are likely to be provided on the basis of just one or two women or minority ethnic residents in otherwise all-male or all-white hostel communities does seem fanciful. Hence the conclusion that, for women and minority ethnic residents, totally specialist or semi-specialist hostels are required. Then it is properly a matter of choice in terms of which one suits an individual best, rather than a debate about which model is right or wrong.

When it comes to other specialisms based on crime-related needs, the author finds himself floundering in a professional mire. Should there be specialist drug misusers hostels? Drug misuse is so ubiquitous amongst hostel residents that most hostels will need to be able to access good quality, community-based services in collaboration with local health service providers. In fact, the question might more usefully be asked: 'Should some hostels be designated as drug-free to help those who have stopped misusing drugs and protect the few who have never started? Should there be specialist mentally disordered offender hostels?' There is already a process under way to replicate West Midlands' Elliott House model in both the South and the North of England, to provide three centres nationally. The author's personal struggle with this is that he still sees approved hostels as short-term provision. In that case, residents in such hostels would have to move on to community-based provision to meet their long-term needs. All hostels need to be able to access emergency mental health services when required, but whether the primary care for mentally disordered offenders should more properly rest with health providers assisted by probation rather than vice versa is, it is suggested, debatable.

What about specialist hostels based upon offence type, e.g., sex offender hostels? Many of the post-release through-care cases will be in this category. Of course, from an internal hostel management point of view, this would be quite a compliant place to run. Sex offenders, however — like sex offences — are not an homogeneous entity. There would be concerns about internal networking. In addition, the risk management issues to the immediate local community would be enormous, particularly if the hostel residents moved on to settle in long-term local accommodation. And of course, when a hostel resident re-offended, the media fall-out would be horrendous. In an inclusive service, concerned with public protection, this would be an act of professional suicide. Hence, the sense behind ACOP's strategic statement on *Housing Sex Offenders in Approved Hostels*, which advocates equitable burden-sharing of such cases across the hostel estate, using local public protection mechanisms to gatekeep the admissions (ACOP 1998).

How can the National Probation Service develop the appropriate specialisms? Certainly not by continuing to regard hostels as the exclusive property of the area in which they happen to be located. This author has been fortunate to work in an area with six hostels, and this has enabled us to explore all kinds of service improvements, from shared research, training and recruitment to semi-specialisation. If there was ever an aspect of service delivery which lent itself to strategic management at a regional level, hostels are it. Not only would it challenge the isolation of a singleton, generic hostel, it would promote continuous improvement in the quality of service provided and — importantly — provide such services within a reasonable proximity of family/community connections. Such a mindset would contribute to a more just service. It would also align hostels with the prison service's aim of greater regionalisation and facilitate collaborative strategic management in pursuit of the joint re-settlement performance targets.

Lastly, a recognition of the strategic importance of securing appropriate move-on accommodation for hostel residents. This is important, given the premise that hostels are a short-term and not a long-term intervention, more to do with promoting positive change than meeting a long-term accommodation need. Again, we need to anticipate a significantly changing world. Currently, probation areas can enter into direct contracts with local housing providers to ensure suitable access for offenders, using the moneys allocated by the Home Office under the former Purchased Accommodation Grants (PAGS) Scheme. From 2003, such moneys get subsumed into a much larger fund for supported housing administered by the local authority. Probation will cease to be a direct contractor and become a joint commissioner instead. How will the interests of hostel residents, who are difficult to place by virtue of the risk they present, be met under this new arrangement, particularly when the probation contribution to pooled funding is likely to be quite marginal? In addition, local authorities are now being encouraged to outsource the management of their own housing to independent registered social landlords. Consequently, deals struck by probation areas with the local authority about their proper involvement in public protection processes and the defensible longer-term housing of high-risk hostel cases, will have to be renegotiated with the new management bodies. These include local tenant representatives on their governance boards. Legislative changes also empower local authorities or the police to seek anti-social behaviour orders against tenants who are creating a nuisance. All these factors could conspire to make the move on of hostel residents to long-term tenancies in their own right, more problematic. It is vital for the National Probation Service and local areas to appreciate what is at stake and invest in the resources necessary to turn a potential threat into an advantage, so that the access right of offenders to mainstream housing is improved rather than diminished by the new arrangements. The joint ACOP/Home Office/Department of the Environment, Transport and the Regions initiative is to be welcomed, in sponsoring nationally appointed secondees to lead on the strategic positioning of area services with their respective local authority housing providers.

HOSTELS AND REDUCING CONVICTION RATES

How can hostels contribute to the national objective of reducing conviction rates by 5 per cent? Our basic assumption is that hostels are not essentially just an accommodation resource, but rather one service option that is equally concerned with promoting positive change. Clearly, the belief is that this target will be achieved by offenders completing a national curriculum of programmes based on accredited What Works interventions. Many of these programmes cannot be deployed within the hostel setting. Hostels can, however, play a unique role in complementing such programmes by offering booster programmes to reinforce changes in thinking, behaviour and motivation, as well as addressing basic literacy/numeracy deficits and life skills. Hostels are particularly well placed to deliver on the pro-social modelling agenda of What Works, and this presents a big challenge as to how hostel staff conduct themselves professionally. Cricital to success is that a hostel contribution to positive change is cemented in a jointly agreed supervision plan with the supervising officer and the offender — an interesting challenge, since the National Standards currently set different time limits for hostel staff and field staff in the completion of this task.

In one regard, however, hostels have a unique contribution to make. In office or prison settings, offenders subject to change programmes can 'talk the talk' but can never be effectively tested as to whether they can also 'walk the walk' in more normal social settings. The residency element of hostels enables this to happen. Ultimately, the aspiration should be to develop effective hostel practice criteria, which would result in the overall regime being accredited, rather than individual programme elements.

HOSTELS AND ACHIEVING EXCELLENCE

If hostels are about promoting positive change for residents then, equally, the staff must be committed to continuous improvement if the National Director's target is to be achieved. This is a big challenge for hostels — as institutions, they can become very insular and set in their ways. Even when they do compare favourably with other hostels, the European Excellence Model implies that there is still scope for further improvement. The model is results driven. At present, hostel performance is measured by occupancy levels (an input) and, to a lesser extent, successful completion of a period of residence (an output). Currently, however, there is no outcome measure, i.e. the longer-term impact of the hostel residency in affecting positive change. What would it be? Presumably, it would have to measure both the stability of the move-on address and the reconviction rate at intervals post-departure from the hostel. The results would then have to be compared with a control group with similar offending histories, who were not hostel residents, to gauge the net impact. Unfortunately, efforts to fund such research at a national level have so far fallen on deaf ears. Application of the European Excellence Model would also lead to comparative performance measures — benchmarking — and, in particular, unit cost data. It also places a premium on customer-driven service, and this would require systematic feedback from residents, staff and other stakeholders about the quality of service provided, as well as gauging their views about what ought to be provided. How many hostels could sign up to this agenda now without having to undergo a radical cultural shift?

CONCLUSION

So what does the future hold? It seems clear that well-run hostels still have a unique contribution to make for greater public protection and effective practice within the justice system. Who runs them — the public or independent sector — and how they are managed — nationally, regionally or locally — is all up for grabs. So too is whether the hostel estate expands or contracts. In a professional environment, in which service quality becomes more transparent, hostels which consistently under-perform are likely to close. Securing planning permission for new building is notoriously difficult, the hostel becoming the focus of the local community's fear of crime. Progress will therefore require both strategic vision and political will. Whatever the resolutions, hostels must be seen as part of a much larger accommodation network, if they are to remain as a short-term resource promoting positive change, rather than a long-term housing option.

Acknowledgement

Particular thanks to my colleagues Dick Marsh, Peter Johnston, Rosemary Heal, Ralph Brown and Derek Kettlewell for their well-informed comments about the first draft of this chapter, and to Margaret Flint for being such a willing accomplice in word processing the various proofs.

14 Controlling Drug Use: Where is the Justice?

Ira Unell

INTRODUCTION

> Society cannot exist unless a controlling power upon will and appetite
> be placed somewhere, and the less of it there is within, the more there
> must be without. It is the ordained in the eternal constitution of things,
> that men of intemperate minds cannot be free. Their passions forge
> their fetters. (Edmund Burke, 1791, quoted in Szasz, 1975)

This chapter considers the role of the state in controlling the use of
drugs. The perception of drugs and drug users over the last century has
changed significantly. Along with those changes, new forms of control
and treatment have been developed. New treatments have brought with
them new ethical problems, and these have yet to be adequately
addressed. Furthermore, medical treatment and criminal punishment
have recently formed a new alliance within the criminal justice system.
The probation service is at the heart of that new alliance. The age-old
controversy of 'care' versus 'control' has found a new battleground.

THE ROLE OF THE STATE IN SANCTIONING DRUG USE: FREEDOM VERSUS LICENCE?

John Stuart Mill, one of the founders of liberal political philosophy, was a champion of the individual and one's right to make decisions in what one sees as one's best interest without the interference of the state (Himmelfard 1974). The only valid principle of interference is to protect a third party. Other considerations should not interfere with this principle. Mill, in On Liberty, said:

> The only purpose for which power can be rightfully exercised over any member of a civilized community, against his will, is to prevent harm to others. His own good, either physical or moral, is not a sufficient warrant. (Moore 1993, p. 226)

If an individual (with the exception of children, or those who are mentally incapable) wished to use a drug, even if it were not in his best interest to do so, the state should have no right to prevent him, unless it could be demonstrated that it would harm a third party. At least potential harm could be shown in some circumstances, i.e. when someone is driving a motor vehicle under the influence of a drug. In this instance, the state would have a duty to try to prevent this from happening. It is less clear that the state has such a duty when the individual uses a drug in his own home and there is no clear danger to another party.

Others, like Gerald Dworkin, have argued differently. He stated that there should be a limited 'paternalism' practised by the state where there is agreement that an individual may, at times, be unable to make a decision in his own best interest (Beauchamp and McCullough 1984). An example of this may be where someone is clearly under the influence of alcohol and has a serious injury needing immediate medical attention. While that person may make a decision to refuse treatment while sober, Dworkin says that until he achieves sobriety, others (i.e. doctors) should make the decision for him.

More recent philosophers have argued that justice cannot be found in structuring social institutions to protect individual rights, but rather in the development of social institutions which reflect the community's understanding of what is good and right for an individual and the community (Moore 1993). This argument might sound attractive until it deals with an issue where there seems to be less than universal agreement, such as the rights of individuals to use drugs.

DRUG USE AND PROBLEM DRUG USERS

There is little doubt that illicit drug use is gaining popularity at a fast rate. Recent surveys suggest that in urban areas in the United Kingdom, lifetime use for adults ranges from 32 per cent to 52 per cent of all adults (Leitner *et al.* 1994). It is now commonly accepted by experts in the field that experimental and recreational drug users rarely come to harm and the majority are not in need of treatment: 'Much of the widespread recreational drug use may produce no discernible social problems, with the exception of the consequences of legal sanctions' (Seivewright 2000, p. 4). At the same time, there is good evidence that more and more people are suffering from the consequences of problem drug use, as the numbers of people presenting to drug treatment services is increasing yearly (House of Commons 1998).

The remainder of this chapter will consider problem drug users (that is those who use drugs and as a result suffer from social, legal and health problems) and not those who use drugs without problems.

THE VILIFICATION OF DRUGS AND DRUG USERS

In the last part of the nineteenth century, the medical profession was at last having success in discovering the source of some diseases. Cholera and typhoid are but two examples of diseases of which the causes were identified and measures taken to control them. The prestige gained from these enterprises gave the medical profession increasing influence over many areas of life. The nineteenth century was optimistic on the progress made by science, and this extended to all fields where science could be seen to play a part.

At the same time, the spread of 'opium eating' by the working class, middle class bohemians and artists drew moral condemnation, especially from the growing middle class of professionals. As doctors became ever more involved in treating those physically dependent upon drugs, 'addiction' was reframed from a moral weakness to a medical disease.

The vilification of some psychoactive drugs, such as opiates (an example of which is heroin), began towards the end of the nineteenth century. Stories of the power of the drug to enslave the drug user have been told in both the popular press and government reports for almost 100 years. This view of opiates was not always prevalent.

Heroin is derived from the poppy plant and is similar to (but much more powerful) than opium. The uses of opiates were well known by British physicians from at least the sixteenth century. Opiates were seen by many doctors as a virtual panacea because of their pain killing and sedating qualities in an era where there was little useful prevention or treatment of disease. Thomas Sydenham, one of the founders of British medicine, said of laudanum (tincture of opium in alcohol and water):

... here I cannot but break out in praise of the great God, the giver of all good things, who hath given to the human race, as a comfort in their afflictions, no medicine of the value of opium, either in regard to the number of diseases it can control or its efficiency in extirpating them ... Medicine would be a cripple without it. ... (Berridge 1999, p. xxiv)

A recognition of the dangers of opiates, which led to the Pharmacy Act of 1868, allowed them to be sold only by registered pharmacists, but this was not part of the criminal law. The new Pharmacy Act was a result of the 'professionalisation' of medicine, which was slowly but surely granting a monopoly to train and license doctors, pharmacists and (later) nurses (Berridge 1999).

By the turn of the century, the perception of those who used drugs such as heroin had also undergone a transformation. The increasingly influential medical profession had been developing its own notions of addiction and its social control. Even after the Dangerous Drugs Act (1920), doctors were still allowed to prescribe whatever drug they wanted for the purposes of medical treatment of disease. The treatment of addiction was, however, another matter. In 1924, after lengthy negotiations between the Home Office and the Ministry of Health, Sir Humphrey Rolleston, President of the Royal College of Physicians, was asked to chair a committee to 'consider and advise as to the circumstances, if any, in which the supply of morphine and heroin ... To persons suffering from addiction to those drugs may be regarded as medically advisable ...' (Trebach 1981, p. 90). The Rolleston Committee adopted a 'disease model' (rather than a 'criminal' model) of addiction. Addiction was seen as a 'neurosis'. The final report put the position succinctly: '... the condition must be seen as a manifestation of disease and not as a mere form of vicious indulgence' (Ministry of Health 1925, p. 11). The medical profession, along with its allies at the Ministry of Health, was not prepared to leave the social control of drugs solely to those concerned with law enforcement. Its concern was in the interests both of its patients and its profession, which was not prepared to sacrifice its monopoly on medical matters. The issue of compulsory treatment was considered by the Rolleston Committee, but rejected as being too Draconian and dangerous to the doctor/patient relationship. The Committee wanted to avoid the situation in the United States, of which it was well aware, where a federal law enforcement agency prevented what it saw as the legitimate medical treatment of addiction.

Addicts in the 1920s were mainly middle class, often professional doctors or nurses, and did not publicise their habit. They did not commit crime to pay for their drug use. They were not part of a criminal fraternity. They may have been 'neurotic', but at least they were 'one of us' and deserved some sympathy. Addiction was at worst a private vice to be treated by a doctor — in private. This set the stage for the continuing conflict between social control of drugs through health agencies (physicians) and their advocates in the Department of Health, and legal sanctions represented by law enforcement agencies (police, customs and excise) and their advocates in the Home Office. This conflict continues today into the twenty-first century.

The recommendations of the Rolleston Committee in 1925 stood unchallenged until 1958, when they were reviewed by the newly appointed Interdepartmental Committee on Drug Addiction. Appointed by the then Minister of Health, Derek Walker-Smith, the Committee was to consider the changes (i.e., new drugs such as amphetamines becoming available and new forms of treatment) which had occurred during the last 32 years. The so-called 'Brain Committee' (named after the Chair, Sir Russell Brain, not the organ) did not report until 1961. The Committee confirmed the view that addiction 'should be regarded as an expression of mental disorder rather than a form of criminal behaviour' (Ministry of Health 1961, p. 9). Again, compulsory treatment was considered but rejected, for essentially the same reasons as in 1925. The evidence presented to the Brain Committee was based upon the current situation: few known 'addicts', no relationship to crime, few convictions under the (now several) Dangerous Drugs Acts. Even as the Committee met, the seeds of the 1960s revolution were sprouting under their very feet, in nearby Soho.

The Brain Committee was recalled less than three years later to reconsider its advice. Several factors were taken into account, which led to the recall of the Committee. The given reasons were the increasing number of 'addicts' known to the Home Office (454 in 1959, 753 in 1964) and the uncontrolled prescribing of addictive drugs by a small handful (a total of six) of doctors (Trebach 1982). The unfettered use of drugs by some young people within an 'alternative' culture, which tolerated if not advocated drug use, must have also played on the collective mind of the government. The noise from the party in Soho could not be ignored by the Committee. It interviewed 'witnesses' to find out what was happening:

> Witnesses have told us there are numerous clubs, many in the West End of London, enjoying a vogue among young people who can find in them such diversions as modern music or all-night dancing. In such places it is known that some young people have indulged in stimulant drugs of the amphetamine type. Some of our witnesses have further maintained that in an atmosphere where drug taking is socially acceptable, there is a risk that young people may be persuaded to turn to cannabis, probably in the form of a 'reefer' cigarette. There is a further risk that if they reach this stage they may move on to heroin and cocaine. (Ministry of Health 1965, p. 12)

The new wave of drug use was no longer restricted to the professional and respectable middle class. There was an alarmingly democratic openness to the 'new club'. Anyone could join, even those of lower social classes. This change in the perception of addiction was noted by some authors such as Philip Bean (1974), but was largely ignored by other observers.

A simultaneous spread of addiction and the threat to the young was enough to precipitate a change in the conception of addiction. Up until then it was a personal vice, practised by those with a 'mental disorder' — a cause for concern for the health of the individual, but no threat to the fabric of society. Now addiction was different. The new Brain Committee (1965) recommended that doctors should be required by law to notify addicts to the Home Office, as they would be required to notify those with an infectious disease under the Public Health Act: 'We think the analogy to addiction is apt, for addiction is after all a socially infectious condition and its notification may offer a means for epidemiological assessment and control' (Ministry of Health 1965, p. 8). Previously, notification of addicts by doctors to the Home Office did not have the force of law to secure their cooperation. The new Brain Committee now changed their recommendations in favour of social control (i.e., restricting the number of doctors able to prescribe heroin and other controlled drugs for the treatment of addiction, establishment of treatment centres in NHS hospitals instead of general practices, etc.) instead of individualised medical treatment. The advice of the previous Committee was overturned and compulsory treatment was recommended where addicts 'may wish to break off treatment after they have embarked upon it' because of the discomfort of withdrawal (Ministry of Health 1965, p. 9). New legislation would be required to enact this recommendation. While virtually all of the new Brain Committee recommendations were accepted, the recommendation for compulsory treatment was rejected by the then Home Secretary, Jim Callaghan.

The notion of compulsory treatment for 'addiction' again came to be considered during the debate surrounding the Mental Health Act 1983. This time, recommendations for compulsory treatment were firmly rejected, because dependence on drugs was not defined as a 'mental disorder', 'severe mental disorder', 'mental impairment' or 'psychopathic disorder' (Mental Health Act 1983, Pt 1). Also, it was suggested that treatment was difficult, if not impossible, without the cooperation of the patient, and compulsion was not the best way to form the necessary 'therapeutic alliance'.

The fear of the spread of the HIV/AIDS virus from drug user to the public at large, reinforced the notion that problem drug use (the new accepted terminology replacing the terms 'drug misusers' or 'addicts') was mainly a public health issue. From the mid-1980s until the early 1990s, government policy changed significantly in favour of a 'public health' view of addiction. The main risk from addiction was now as a means of spreading HIV/AIDS.

A major part of the new social policy was to encourage untreated addicts into treatment centres with free injecting equipment provided with few controls, more 'flexible' (read liberal) prescribing programmes, and shorter waiting periods. Compulsory admission was considered yet again in the late 1980s and early 1990s in relation to the

HIV/AIDS epidemic. The compulsory treatment of drug users who were infected with the HIV virus was debated and finally rejected on the grounds that the threat of compulsory treatment would act as a barrier to some drug users to come for help, if they thought that they might be detained against their will. Untreated addicts were to be persuaded by appeals to their own self-interest to change their behaviour to prevent the spread of the virus. Subsequent experience has shown that compulsory detainment of HIV infected drug users was unnecessary.

The next change in the perception of problem drug use came at the end of the Conservative regime in Great Britain with the publication of *Tackling Drugs Together*, the new national framework for drug policy, which succeeded in attracting all-party support. Where previously, public health concerns were the main stated considerations behind drug policy, now drug use by young people and drug-driven crime became the new driving force. Years of trying to 'prevent' young people from even experimenting with drugs through education and special pro-grammes proved to be less than successful. Year by year, the proportion of young people who had tried illegal drugs had been rising, and only in the last few years have the increases slowed (Wright and Pearl 2000). Despite the rhetoric, public spending on drug policy has gone towards law enforcement rather than prevention and treatment. More effort and considerable resources are now being developed within the criminal justice system.

By what right does the state use coercion to treat drug users? If drug use (or even addiction) were a mental illness, it could be argued that in some cases enforced treatment might be necessary. However, even though drug use may have in the past been considered a form of mental illness, this is no longer the case: 'With the demonstration of increased prevalence of drug use, including school surveys, the activity can be said to be becoming normative' (Seivewright 2000, p. 3) The current view that at least some types of drug use (mainly compulsive heroin or cocaine use) are 'driven' by crime has some merit, but requires closer examination. Compulsive drug use of any type is expensive, and there is good research evidence that often (though not always) acquisitive crime pays for most of the drugs being consumed. The larger question to be considered is that of choice. At times it may seem that at least some drug users behave in a way which suggests that they lose control of their capacity to make choices, i.e. when the user sells all his belongings, acquires debts which cannot be repaid, and commits crimes when previously he was not a criminal. Did he choose to do these things, or did he have to do them? The consequences for him of not obtaining drugs would be that he suffers withdrawals, which are often uncomfortable, distressing, and even painful. They are not, however, life-threatening. It is rarely, if ever, the case that withdrawals from illicit drugs are fatal. Fatalities from withdrawals from alcohol or prescribed drugs are more common.

Clearly, the compulsive nature of some types of drug use is not driven by fear of loss of life. Do problem drug users who are 'addicted' lose their capacity to make choices for other reasons? This question has been considered by authors such as Stanton Peele (1985) and John B. Davies (1993). They both accept that people who continually and compulsively use some types of drugs are likely to continue to choose to behave in that way as long as the behaviour serves a purpose. They continue to make a choice to use drugs, and it may be the case that the longer they use compulsively and the more drugs they use, the more difficult it may be to make other choices, i.e. not to use. That is not to say that they have lost their capacity to make a choice, only that it becomes more difficult to make other choices.

The concept of 'addiction' is compelling. As an explanation for behaviour, it is limited in value and meaning when it is universally applied. Note the recent expansion of the meaning of addiction into other fields of endeavour. Now the rich are treated for 'sex addiction'; radio channels broadcasting in shopping malls in Los Angeles advertise (with no sense of irony) treatment for 'Shopaholics'. Addiction may have use as a descriptive term, but loses much of its meaning when used as an explanatory term.

TREATMENT COERCION THROUGH THE CRIMINAL JUSTICE SYSTEM

The first real attempt at making treatment a part of the criminal justice system was the use of the s. 1A order, a probation order with a condition of treatment, under the Criminal Justice Act 1991. Magistrates' courts and Crown Courts could attach a 'treatment order' to a probation order, if the court believed that the offending was linked to the drug use of the offender. The 'treatment order' could be imposed only with the agreement of the offender and of a treatment agency. Soon after the new law took effect, it became clear that it would not make a major impact on the criminal justice system (Harrison 1993). Many probation officers, mainly through their union, the National Association of Probation Officers, protested against the imposition of this new power of the courts. Probation officers questioned the ethics of making failure to succeed in treatment punishable through the courts, which could in theory breach the probationer, if they failed to comply with treatment. 'Breach' meant that the offender had to return to court for sentencing. (In many cases this did not result in the custodial sentence which many probation officers had feared.)

Many treatment agencies, both in the NHS and the voluntary field, questioned the utility and ethics of treating or helping a patient or client, with the powers of the court to be used in the event of non-cooperation. This was especially true of community treatment agencies, which had a tradition of separateness from the criminal justice system. Treatment agencies within the NHS were bound by regulations on confidentiality and informed consent, which at least provided a basis for their reluctance to be seen as an instrument of the court.

Within a short time, it became clear that this measure was less than effective. In some areas, such as Leicestershire, no orders for a probation order with a condition of treatment were granted. Lack of cooperation from probation officers and reluctance of community treatment agencies to accept the role of agents of the court made the imposition of the order impossible (Harrison 1993). This was the last resistance to the marriage of drug treatment and the criminal justice system. The Home Office accepted defeat, but soon returned with a new marriage contract, which has found wide-ranging acceptance, the drug testing and treatment order.

THE CARE AND CONTROL CONTROVERSY IN THE PROBATION SERVICE

Working with offenders who problematically used drugs brought new dilemmas to the care and control controversy in probation. Early attempts by probation officers to work with problem drug users resulted in their advocating that probation officers should work in ways were which acceptable to their drug using clients, rather than requiring their drug using clients to conform to standards imposed by the probation service and the courts (Dawtry 1968, p. 14):

During probation supervision the drug abuser who is often nocturnal, nomadic and anti-authoritarian, will find major difficulties in conforming to probation requirements — changing address frequently or living rough, not working industriously, failing to accept treatment, not reporting when told to do so, and continuing to use illicit drugs. To work effectively and objectively with such a client should not the probation officer put his major role of authority on one side at times, forget the idea of casework by formal office interviewing, and become more identified with the drug abusers by meeting them in their pads, speaking and understanding drug lore, and being available to them in their periods of mental and physical agony — often at night time?

The casework framework referred to by the author was heavily laden with psychoanalytic theory. Much blame was laid on early parental rejection, unsuccessful competition for parental approval with a more successful sibling, and ambiguous emotions of love and hate towards parents. In the late 1960s, problem drug use within the offender population was, however, rare. This was soon to change.

Over the next 20 years, problem drug use by offenders became much more common. Alcohol was (and still is) most heavily associated with crime, especially serious crime. Probation officers, realising that most drug use is not associated with acquisitive or violent crime, concentrated on offenders who used drugs problematically, and where they could demonstrate a firm link between the offending behaviour of the offender and their drug use.

By the early 1990s, the probation service was starting to undergo changes imposed by the Conservative Government. These changes came as a result of rising crime statistics, high re-offending rates and, most importantly, the public perception that ordinary citizens were in danger of becoming the victims of crime. Previously, many probation officers had perceived their role as that of a case worker and advocate providing 'care', rather than as an officer of the court and agent of the state imposing 'control'. Many probation officers defined their role as a helping agent for their offending clients, believing that by providing that help they would be promoting their clients leading crime-free lives and therefore protecting the public. Directives from the Home Office (such as National Standards) reframed the role of probation and gave greater emphasis to their role of protecting the public. It was no longer acceptable that protecting the public was a mere side-effect of helping the offender with social and personal problems. Public protection was now at the heart of the probation service.

DRUG TREATMENT AND THE THERAPEUTIC STATE

Until the 1960s, doctors claimed the right to treat those with drug problems as patients, but they had little in the way of pharmacological help for their treatment. They could give them decreasing quantities of opiates, like heroin or morphine, to 'detoxify' their patients and help minimise their withdrawal symptoms. They could also symptomatically treat other withdrawals with yet other drugs, i.e. sedatives, to help sleep. There was no pharmacological 'fix' for the psychological problems of drug dependence, until two American doctors, Vincent Dole and Maria Nyswander, discovered that a heroin substitute (methadone), taken from a German pharmaceutical company after World War II, was longer-acting than heroin. Heroin, if injected intravenously, causes instant euphoria and, depending on the dose and tolerance of the user, slowly fades away over several hours. Methadone was found to last up to 24 hours. It had other advantages as well. It could be taken orally, eliminating the need to inject (arguably the health risks from injecting heroin are of greater danger than the drug itself), and lasted all day, allowing the heroin user to pursue other activities besides taking drugs to escape from withdrawals. Furthermore, methadone did not cause the euphoria associated with heroin, making it more acceptable to clinicians than a drug which could otherwise lay them open to a charge of giving 'addicts a good time'. Dole and Nyswander claimed that heroin users who were prescribed methadone did not suffer from the 'cravings' which were described as part of a withdrawal syndrome. Methadone could be used in two ways: (i) as a means to detoxify safely, over days or even months, those with heroin habits; and (ii) to 'maintain' heroin addicts who were not willing to stop using drugs *per se* but did not want to continue to use street drugs, thus allowing them (in theory) to find jobs or education and start a long process of rehabilitation.

Many doctors found it easier to prescribe methadone than heroin. Methadone had a lower street value than heroin. Also, with prescribing facilities increasing, it soon became apparent that NHS drug services offering treatment in the community needed to prescribe substitute drugs in order to attract heroin users. As the spectre of an AIDS epidemic caused public and governmental concern, enticing drug users (as possible carriers of the disease) into treatment had a key public health role. Methadone prescribing had one more advantage — those on methadone committed substantially less crime than those who used only street drugs (Department of Health 1998).

Methadone prescribing started in New York in the 1960s and spread to the United Kingdom in the 1970s. Within a few years, most doctors (mainly psychiatrists) treating heroin users in the UK had switched from prescribing heroin to prescribing methadone. Many of their patients preferred the prescribed heroin which they received (for the 'buzz'), but this was more than outweighed by what most doctors saw as the advantages of methadone.

Critics of methadone prescribing ask, 'In whose interest is it being prescribed?'. It is a popular drug for heroin users, who often come for treatment and ask for a methadone prescription. (If heroin were on offer, many, if not most, would ask for it instead of methadone.) But it also serves the purpose of the state, i.e. it lures people into treatment, gets them in touch with rehabilitation services, reduces illicit drug use (though it does not usually stop other illicit drug use) and reduces crime (Department of Health 1998). No doubt there are many benefits for drug users who come for treatment, including better health, less time in prison, etc., but the advantages to the state should never be overlooked.

Most people in receipt of a methadone prescription continue to use at least some illicit drugs and, while crime is reduced, it is rarely stopped entirely. In practice, few patients on methadone prescription find regular, gainful employment, and few complete training courses. Many remain on a 'maintenance' prescription for years, and some have commented that long-term prescribing could prolong drug habits by providing a free source of drugs with relatively little commitment to change. Most heroin users complain that it is more difficult to withdraw from methadone than heroin. At least, it seems that withdrawals take a longer time on methadone, but they may also be less unpleasant.

Prescribing opiates for the treatment of problem drug use has always included an element of social control. If patients failed to meet enough appointments, returned too many urine samples containing street drugs, or failed to attend group or individual therapy, prescriptions could be cut or stopped entirely. There may be good clinical reasons to alter or stop prescriptions (i.e., how ethical is it to continue to prescribe a powerful drug, if the patient is not regularly monitored or if other drugs are being used?), but it is also a means of social control. The state may be taking on a therapeutic role beyond the limits of what J.S. Mill had in mind. The social control element may also be enlarging. New drugs, such as naltraxone, can prevent relapse for newly abstinent problem drug users (in this case heroin) by blocking the effects of opiates such as heroin. Some have even reported withdrawal, when using heroin after they take naltraxone. More to the point are the recent partnerships with the probation service. The line between treatment and punishment becomes thinner year by year, as treatment services focus more on crime prevention and perhaps less on health.

SOCIAL POLICY AND THE THERAPEUTIC STATE

The conflict between the Home Office and the Department of Health over who would take the lead in the social control of drugs has been well recognised for many years. Recognition that we may not all be 'singing from the same song sheet' brought about an attempt to end those differences though the creation of the United Kingdom Anti-drug Coordinator (UKADC) in 1997, the office of what has become known as the Drug Czar. The new Drug Czar, Keith Hellawell, would be responsible to a high-powered Cabinet Committee, composed of Senior Ministers from all relevant Government departments.

The intention of the UKADC was to combine all of the resources of the state in the 'fight against drugs'. The aims and objectives of the reconstituted fight against drugs were made explicit in the White Paper, *Tackling Drugs to Build a Better Britain*, published in 1998. This time everyone would be focused: 'By March 1999: all agencies should realign their priorities, resources and operational focus in line with this White Paper and produce their forward plans.' (House of Commons 1998, p. 6)

Eventually, all spending on drug misuse was channeled through the office of the Drug Czar. Not much happened during the first two years, but by 2000, very substantial sums of money were made available to increase service provision for problem drug users. The way the money was spent is indicative of the trend towards combining the forces of medical treatment and the criminal justice system. The first large sums went directly into the prison system to provide assessment, counselling and referral upon discharge to community agencies (the CARAT programme) and provision of in-house therapeutic programmes. Also, large sums were provided for every part of the country to develop arrest/referral schemes to allow offenders early access to treatment and counseling, and finally to drug testing and treatment orders. There are increases for health-orientated advice/counselling and NHS treatment services, but these are receiving much lower priority. Despite increased funding, treatment facilities will always be under pressure, and some advocates of a health-orientated treatment system point out that a logical outcome of an increasing commitment to a criminal justice-orientated system may be that problem drug users who want help, will have to commit crime in order to avoid long waiting lists for more voluntary entrance into the treatment system.

The best example of the merging of drug treatment and punishment is to be found in the Crime and Disorder Act 1998. Under the provisions of the Act, magistrates and judges are empowered (as of October 2000) to impose a sentence of drug testing and treatment, if the offender 'is dependent on or has a propensity to misuse drugs' (Home Office 2000o, p. 3) and is susceptible to treatment. The offending must be having a 'disproportionately disruptive effect on their communities' and the offender must be motivated to undertake treatment. The purpose of this order is clear: 'The primary (*sic*) aim of the drug treatment and testing order is therefore to prevent further offending' (*ibid*). Note that the purpose is not to treat the offender's drug problem *per se*, but rather to ensure that he no longer offends. This lays the way open for goals other than the achievement of abstinence, i.e. long-term methadone prescribing (which has proven effectiveness in reducing crime), which may prolong the offender's drug problem. The long-term methadone prescribing could well have health benefits for the offender in terms of harm reduction and improved health, but under the Crime and Disorder Act 1998 these will be secondary gains.

Furthermore, the courts are to play an active role in monitoring the treatment order. Monthly reports to the court by the probation service (who manage the orders and fund the treatment) are mandatory. Attendance for counselling and urine testing are also mandatory, and failure in either can lead to breach proceedings, where the court could decide to continue the programme or to impose a custodial sentence, if the offence warrants it.

THE HUMAN RIGHTS ACT AND IMPLICATIONS FOR THE SOCIAL CONTROL OF DRUGS

The European Convention on Human Rights came into force in 1953. Since that time it has been adopted by over 40 sovereign states, which are now signatories. The Convention has been expanded over time and now includes not only the Articles which set out the rights of individuals in relation to the state, but also Protocols, which give guidance on how the Convention should be implemented. The United Kingdom was one of the first signatories. Until 1998, though, United Kingdom courts were allowed to consider the European Convention on Human Rights only in very limited circumstances. Those who believed their rights were infringed under the Convention could remedy the situation only by taking their case to the European Court of Human Rights. Under the Human Rights Act 1998, public authorities are now required to act in a way which is compatible with the European Convention. Claims can now be heard in domestic courts as well as in the European Court.

At least two of the Convention Articles may be relevant to the social control of drugs. The first, Article 8 (right to respect for private and family life), could be used to question the legitimacy of the control of some drugs (such as cannabis) under the Misuse of Drugs Act 1971. Article 8(2) provides:

> There shall be no interference by a public authority with the exercise of this right except such as is in accordance with the law and is necessary in a democratic society in the interests of national security, public safety or the economic well-being of the country, for the prevention of disorder or crime, for the protection of health or morals, or for the protection of the rights and freedoms of others.

Under the proposed changes to the Mental Health Act 1983 (Department of Health 1999a), the Government aims to broaden the definition of a 'mental disorder' to include some cases of a diagnosis of alcohol or drug misuse which are currently specifically excluded. This could enable the state to admit compulsorily to hospital and/or treat those with alcohol or drug problems. Under Article 5 (right to liberty and security), it may promote this extension of the Mental Health Act because of the specific exclusions:

Everyone has the right to liberty and security of person. No one shall be deprived of his liberty save in the following cases and in accordance with a procedure prescribed by law ...

There are six exclusions to Article 5 (cases (a)–(f)). Most of these cases include those who have been convicted of a criminal charge by a court of law, those not granted bail and minors (to allow them to attend school, etc.). Case (e) is of particular significance:

(e) the lawful detention of persons for the prevention of the spreading of infectious diseases, of persons of unsound mind, alcoholics or drug addicts or vagrants ...

This particular clause of the European Convention on Human Rights harks back to the Poor Laws of the eighteenth and nineteenth centuries, when poor people were grouped together for the purposes of detention and work.

While the Human Rights Act 1998 could thus be used to challenge the right of the state to categorise certain drugs as dangerous, it might also be used to enhance the right of the state to detain (and possibly treat) those with drug problems.

CONCLUSION

The Misuse of Drugs Act 1971 clearly states that the purpose of the Act is to prevent the non-medical use of selected drugs within the United Kingdom. If the Act has been successful then it would be reasonable to expect that the number of people who have been convicted under the Act should have decreased. This has hardly been the case to date. In 1973, there were a total of 14,977 convictions (Department of Health and Social Security 1982). In 1999, there were 120,007 convictions (Home Office 2001c), an increase of over 800 per cent in 26 years. The failure of the Misuse of Drugs Act to carry out its primary aim can be explained in many ways. The increased production of illicit drugs worldwide, the fall in the price of drugs, changing attitudes to drug use and drug users, increased global travel and trade, have all played their part. Drug use has become a fact of life for many individuals; no individual and no community is immune.

Social controls of drugs by means of prevention and education campaigns have also been tried, with little success, if we are to gauge success by the numbers of people who have used drugs, even if only once. Treatment for problem drug use can be effective over the long term; instant cures have been tried and failed the test of time. The combination of the criminal justice system and drug treatment, which represents the way forward in the current government strategy (House of Commons 1998), has yet to be assessed. The new approach presents difficult ethical problems for those working in the new systems. Are we treating individuals, or are we preventing crime? The issues are not always entirely clear.

Perhaps it is time to take a broader look at the application of the criminal justice system in relation to drug use. There are no easy options awaiting us just beyond the horizon. Already, several European countries and several states in the United States have started to change their laws and practices in relation to at least some illicit drugs. There are even signs that the new Bush Administration in America may be rethinking what once seemed like a policy set in concrete, i.e. that drugs are best controlled through the criminal justice system.

Control of illicit drug use through the criminal law has simply not worked. Criminal laws, which are now openly disregarded by a large part of the population, may not be enforceable. If they are enforced, it is often those with the least influence in society who end up in court, not those with money and power. No law is ethical, if it is not applied equally.

While some people would be prepared to argue the case for ceasing all criminal regulation of illicit drugs (Szasz 1996), many would at least consider making the response of the state less punitive to the use of some drugs (i.e. cannabis) by decreasing the penalties for possession. Coercion into treatment through the criminal justice system may seem a viable alternative to punishment alone. While treatment can be effective in the long term, for many people it is not. In the final analysis, how can we justify coerced treatment for 'a disease (addiction), which may not exist, by treatment methods, which are only effective for some' (Cameron 2001)?

15   Rights, Probation and Mentally Disturbed Offenders

Rob Canton

INTRODUCTION

They called me mad, and I called them mad, and damn them, they outvoted me. (Nathaniel Lee 1649–1692)

Visited Peckham asylum (a private madhouse) on Saturday last. Long affair — six hours. What a lesson! How small the interval — a hair's breadth — between reason and madness. A sight, too, to stir apprehension in one's own mind. I am visiting in authority today. I may be visited by authority tomorrow. God be praised that there are any visitations at all; time was when such care was unknown. What an awful condition that of a lunatic! His words are generally disbelieved, and his most innocent peculiarities perverted; it is natural that it should be so; we know him to be insane; at least, we are told that he is so; and we place ourselves on guard — that is, we give to every word, look, gesture a value and meaning which oftentimes it cannot bear, and which it would never bear in ordinary life. Thus we too readily get him in, and too sluggishly get him out, and yet what a destiny! (Lord Shaftesbury 1844, quoted in Porter 1991, p. 1 and, p. 4)

Many people will have shared Lord Shaftesbury's unease at the 'hair's breadth ... between reason and madness'. One familiar way of managing the discomfort this engenders is to emphasise the difference between those who are mentally disordered and the rest of us. Stereotyped imagery of mental disorder comes to our aid, representing 'mad' people as unpredictable, out of control, violent; as sad and bewildered; as irrational or stupid.

Such stereotypes, embedded in our culture and often assimilated in childhood, 'are not discarded, but continue to exist alongside medical conceptions, because the stereotypes receive almost continual support from the mass media and in ordinary social discourse. They are peculiarly resistant to change because 'they are functional for the current social order and tend to be integrated into the psychological make up of all members of the society' (Scheff 1984). One of the functions that the stereotype serves — and this is substantially true of all stereotypes — is that of helping to define ourselves by contrast with 'them'. We define ourselves in the comparison — mad is what we are not. While 'functional' in this sense, these stereotypes distort our understanding of ourselves, at the same time as excluding and oppressing 'the other'.

Offenders play a similar role in our self-definition. One of the illusions conjured by political rhetoric about crime is that offenders are 'other' — not friends, neighbours or members of our families, and least of all 'us'. This illusion is maintained even when research demonstrates that, while only a small fraction of all offences lead to a conviction, even so one-third of all males has acquired a conviction by the age of 40 (Home Office 1999c).

Mentally disordered offenders are doubly censured. They are 'other', both among offenders and among the mentally disordered. Unpredictable, deluded and uncontrolled offenders, they cannot be managed in the criminal justice system: untrustworthy and delinquent, they are less deserving of health care.

These deeply embedded, if usually unarticulated, attitudes regularly result in ironic outcomes in the implementation of policy. For example, a strong policy commitment to diversion notwithstanding, it is often easier for mentally unwell offenders to become involved in the criminal justice system. Prosecution may be seen as the best way of securing treatment. The irony is that, to qualify for diversion, the defendant must first be seen as a mentally disordered offender, but this designation — because of anxiety about risk or a need for treatment, often aggravated by the unavailability of the specialist resources that this 'group' is felt to need — commonly precipitates people into penal custody rather than health care (Canton 1995). This is especially true of black people (Cope 1989; Browne 1990; Fernando *et al.* 1998).

Not the least of the reasons for the study of the sociology of deviance is that it illuminates the character of conformity and the reproduction of social order. Infraction casts the rules in high relief. In much the same way, mentally disordered offenders, a doubly deviant group, pose questions not only about their 'management' and their rights, but also, by implication and contrast, about 'normal' offenders too. For example, conceptions of criminal responsibility and the justifications of punishment are put to the test by the consideration of offenders who are not (or not fully) responsible. Later in this chapter, in discussing the contemporary probation agenda in relation to mentally disordered offenders, it is suggested that the discussion raises hard questions about probation policy and practice much more generally.

DIVERSION

For at least the first half of the 1990s, there was a strong policy commitment to diversion — the idea that mentally disordered offenders should receive care and treatment from the health and social services, rather than being dealt with in the criminal justice system. The authoritative Home Office Circular 66/1990 identified the points at which this diversion might take place. This policy, often qualified but never disowned, finds a contemporary restatement in *Reform of the Mental Health Act 1983* (Department of Health 1999a).

The policy of diversion, however, was never sufficiently scrutinised (see Prins 1992; Canton 1997). The target group was inadequately defined, the rationale under-examined, performance measures rarely specified and the effect of the strategy incompletely evaluated. The term 'diversion' is itself misleading: just a minority of defendants sent for psychiatric assessment end up being dealt with under special mental health provisions. Most do not leave the criminal justice process at all. Theirs is the motorists' diversion, a different route leading to the same destination. In these circumstances, 'diversion' amounts to the (sometimes temporary) involvement of another agency:

> ... the simple view that in principle all those who are mentally disordered ought to be diverted from the criminal justice system into

psychiatric care in the health service is both impracticable and fails to take into account the heterogeneity of psychiatric conditions and clinical needs. It is an aspiration with a long history of failure. The policy question cannot be framed as: 'How can we achieve the diversion of the mentally disordered from the criminal justice system?' rather, the questions are 'What kinds of mentally disordered offender should be diverted?' 'Under what circumstances?' 'At what stage in the criminal process?' 'Within what legal framework?' 'To what provision?' And, crucially, 'What should be done to meet the needs of those who are not diverted and remain either in the penal system or are simply released back to the community?' (Grounds 1991, p. 38)

PARALLELS BETWEEN 'DIVERSION' AND 'ALTERNATIVES TO CUSTODY'

There are some suggestive parallels between debates about diversion and criminological discussions about 'alternatives to custody'. There are several examples of projects where imaginative and skilled workers can clearly demonstrate considerable success in diverting mentally disturbed people from prison (Cavadino 1999; Geelan *et al.* 2000). Equally, there are ready examples of schemes that can be shown to have displaced offenders from custody (Mair 1997, for discussion and references). Yet as a strategy, diversion, like alternatives, has everything to prove. The proliferation of alternatives notwithstanding, the prison population increases; diversion schemes operate variably, but there is no evidence of a reduction in the numbers of mentally disturbed people in prison.

The analogy could be extended. We are by now familiar with the argument that the language and mindset of alternatives undermine the strategy itself, not least by privileging prison as the standard case, against which other measures must be appraised. In the same way, the language of diversion assumes untenable distinctions between the mentally disordered and 'normal' offenders, urging different paths for different people. It identifies a distinctive group — mentally disordered offenders — supposes that this group is in need of special resources or facilities and then discovers that such facilities normally do not exist.

The analogy could perhaps be stretched further. As alternatives and imprisonment have been taken to function symbiotically in an extension of social control (Cohen 1985), so might diversion have a role as the beneficent face of the criminalisation of mental illness. It is only when mental health needs, hitherto neglected, manifest themselves in offending, that treatment can be accessed through 'diversion'. For some, the criminal justice process is the only accessible gateway to mental health care — already a usual experience for many black people (Fernando *et al.* 1998).

FROM DIVERSION TO INTER-AGENCY WORKING

Misgivings about diversion may have influenced the Home Office to shift its emphasis to inter-agency work in the 1995 Circular (Home Office and Department of Health 1995). Conceptually, this is progress. Instead of an artificial construction of separate routes, inter-agency working calls on the respective contributions that the different agencies and disciplines can make to a collective and complementary endeavour.

It is characteristic of mentally disordered offenders that their clinical conditions are diagnosed imprecisely (Blackburn 1993). Probation officers may encounter offenders who are found to be suffering from a formal mental illness, but the experience of loosely specified, contingent and variable mental disturbance is much more common. Regularly, this type of mental distress is not taken to amount to disorder within the meaning of the Mental Health Act 1983, so that some of the diversionary options are foreclosed. The promise of a complementary and flexible network of inter-agency support seems a much better 'fit' with the predicaments of probation practice, than does the mindset of diversion.

The recognition that the legal definition of mental disorder excluded many of those who caused such concern led NACRO to favour the more general expression 'mentally disturbed offenders', and to formulate this definition:

Those offenders who may be acutely or chronically mentally ill; those with neuroses, behavioural and/or personality disorders; those with learning difficulties; some who, as a function of alcohol and/or substance misuse, have a mental health problem; and any who are suspected of falling into one or other of these groups. It also includes those offenders where a degree of mental disturbance is recognised even though that may not be severe enough to bring it within the

criteria laid down by the Mental Health Act 1983. It also applies to
those offenders who, even though they do not fall easily within this
definition — for example, some sex offenders and some abnormally
aggressive offenders — may benefit from psychological treatments.
(NACRO 1993)

This definition is much more serviceable for people working with
offenders. It is inclusive, perhaps too inclusive, and refers to the
contributions which different disciplines might make to care and treatment.

The *Learning and Development Programme for Work with Mentally
Disordered Offenders* promotes this approach (Home Office 1999a).
The Programme encourages workers to translate problems of identification (how do I know if this person is mentally ill?) into questions of
referral (when and how should I seek the involvement of another
agency?). Referral is made, then, not in the implausible belief that the
problem will be taken away and conclusively dealt with by another
agency, but in recognition that a complex set of needs requires a
correspondingly sophisticated intervention.

This approach fitted well, too, with the probation service's commitment to working in partnership, which emerged in the late 1980s. It also
chimed with case management approaches to mental health care — the
idea that mentally ill people (non-offenders) should be supported
through a network of health and social services agencies providing
community care (Shepherd 1993; Pilgrim and Rogers 1999).

Yet despite the undoubted vigour and success of some initiatives
(Bhui 1999), the Social Services Inspectorate has found many shortcomings in provision for mentally disordered offenders (Watson 1997).
As Shepherd astutely observed, inter-agency initiatives may highlight
and exacerbate differences, rivalry, suspicion and boundary disputes
among agencies (Shepherd 1993). Harding, considering the needs of
young offenders, speaks of probation staff:

caught up in diagnostic debates, which normally proved a barrier to
service, access and this was particularly the case where substance
misuse was a co-existing factor. They were also involved in dialogue
about the lack of resources and the priority of allocating resources to
this group. Inter-service co-operation was poor and attempts to pull
agencies together were thwarted by what can only be described as
professional rivalries. (Harding 1999a, p. 86)

DUAL DIAGNOSIS

Reference to 'where substance misuse was a co-existing factor' introduces the problem of what has come to be known 'dual diagnosis'. Dual diagnosis (or co-morbidity) refers to the co-existence of mental illness and substance misuse (Watkins *et al.* 2001). The phenomenon is a case study in the potential and the shortcomings of inter-agency work.

Some combinations of mental disorder and substance misuse greatly increase risks of offending (NACRO 1998, Chapter 4; MacArthur 2001). It would be reasonable to anticipate that this problem would be met by combining the skills and resources of mental health and substance abuse workers in a complementary response. Instead, the experience of many community justice workers is that hard-pressed agencies defend their boundaries and engage in unproductive speculation about whether the individual is really or primarily mentally disordered or a substance misuser. The very real needs of these individuals and the significant risks they often present may be aggravated by the organisational arrangements.

A service user reports:

I was pushed around like a tennis ball. The alcohol people said I had a mental illness and the mental illness group said I had a drink problem. Neither of them did much. (MIND 1998, p. 7)

While misuse of certain substances can produce signs of mental illness, people who are mentally disturbed are at least as likely as anyone else to misuse substances (Watkins *et al.* 2001). Typically, neither problem can be understood without an appreciation of the other: it is precisely the interaction that exacerbates the distress and the risk.

Dual diagnosis is not, of course, a single clinical condition, but encompasses a wide (and contestable) range of needs and behaviours. In this respect, it is like the 'term mentally disordered offenders'. These expressions have much less to do with the lived condition of the client group and much more to do with the division of labour among agencies. While their application should enable individuals to have access to services that meet their complex needs, in practice it becomes the occasion for their rejection.

ISSUES OF DEFINITION AND REMIT

One of the shortcomings of inter-agency practice, as demonstrated in numerous inquiries in mental health and in child abuse, is failure of communication (for example, Prins 1999, pp. 127*ff*). This has been plausibly associated with differences in professional culture and remit, and discrepancies in expectation among agencies (Prins 1999, *loc. cit.*; Peay, 1993, 1997; Watson and Grounds 1993).

Peay (1997) points to differences of definition as an obstacle to inter-agency work. There are, notoriously, competing vocabularies of madness in law, medicine and ordinary discourse. These vocabularies overlap in denotation and connotation, but are not co-extensive. At a deeper level, it could be said that definitions will inevitably fail to coincide because the definition is shaped by the interests and purposes of the definers, and different agencies and professionals have different (and sometimes opposing) reasons for ascribing or resisting the designation 'mentally disordered offender' (*cf.* Allen 1987).

Neither is definitional dispute the whole of the problem. Prins notes the challenges of inter-disciplinary work, in which personnel with differing professional education, culture, status and roles have to establish and implement a common approach (Prins 1999, pp. 127*ff*). This challenge can be met, and it is wise to remember that we are more likely to hear about failures here than success, but the challenge must not be under-estimated either (Preston-Shoot 1999). A group of professionals, for example, may have to work hard at negotiating a shared understanding of what it means in practice to make an assessment, or to monitor a person or state of affairs. This effort has to take place at a local level, and it remains an open question about the extent to which local practice may be distorted by drives towards consistency from a national agency.[1]

The values and purposes of an agency will (or should) make a difference to its own practice and to the principles it brings to inter-agency work. In the 'post-diversion' era, agencies must negotiate and implement coherent understandings of how they are to work together, transcending stale debates about who 'owns' mentally

---

[1] This may be an example of the tensions inherent between the Crime and Disorder Act emphasis on local responses to crime and, on the other hand, the setting of standards nationally. Some local variations are appropriate and functional.

disordered offenders. The National Probation Service, affirming enforcement, rehabilitation and public protection, has consciously reconstructed probation practice, repudiating social work and the language of care. As patients, however, offenders, like other citizens, have an entitlement to health care, which should be, 'wherever possible, provided on an informal basis with full agreement between the patient and care team' (Department of Health 1999a). How is the probation service, then, to position itself in the context of the provision of an inter-agency care plan? How do its priorities fit with the remit of other agencies? What are these other agencies to expect of it? What will enforcement, rehabilitation and public protection entail for its work with people who are mentally disturbed?

REHABILITATION — WHAT WORKS

NACRO's definition included '... those offenders who ... may benefit from psychological treatments' (see above). This definition was formulated in the early 1990s. Since then, evidence has been emerging that particular types of psychological treatment — not only but especially cognitive-behavioural methods — are effective with most offenders (Chapman and Hough 1998). NACRO's definition now plausibly includes the majority of offenders.

Leach has identified some of the hazards of a rigid, or over-simplistic, reliance on the Effective Practice Initiative (Leach 1999). He notes that the approach risks overlooking the social factors which are known to be associated with offending (May 1999), including accommodation, substance misuse and unemployment, but beyond the purview of cognitive-behavioural programmes. While the 'wiser authorities' (Leach 1999; cf. McGuire 2000) recognise this, there is no doubt that the effective practice debate has much more to say about the cognitive shortcomings of offenders than the social circumstances so frequently associated with their offending (Gorman 2001; Drakeford and Vanstone 1996, 'Introduction').

The particular relevance of this to the position of mentally disturbed offenders is that the expression itself — the very terms in which the 'group' is identified — invites an understanding of their (mis) behaviour in terms of their mental state. Despite the complexities of establishing an association between mental disorder and offending (Prins 1995,

Chapter 4), Shaftesbury is right that the behaviour of mentally disturbed people is normally seen through the lens of their madness. Familiar human motivation is superseded and in this way the mentally disturbed are literally dehumanised (Canton 1995).

The 'loss of the social' — or at least its subordination to 'the clinical' — has profound implications for working with mentally disordered offenders. Keyes found that:

> The 'mentally disordered offenders' we have encountered have carried enormous burdens of social and psychological deprivation. These are lives of material and spiritual poverty — lonely, disenfranchised, angry.... It's not the whole picture, of course, but I cannot accept that these powerful factors are not intimately connected to the 'mental distress' in which much offending behaviour takes place. (Keyes 1995, p. 3)

Other studies have emphasised this social deprivation, especially in relation to homelessness (Burney and Pearson 1995; Kennedy *et al.* 1997). The increased likelihood that mentally disordered offenders will have nowhere to live, together with known correlations between homelessness and remand into custody, give another instance of the way in which mentally disturbed offenders are precipitated into the penal system.

Debunking the 'treatment model' of offending used to be a routine undergraduate exercise. Are cognitive-behavioural approaches anything more than a contemporary restatement of this model? The answer to this innocent-looking question is probably more complex than it appears. This understanding of human (mis) behaviour has brought clinical psychology and work with offenders closer together. While quasi-medical terms (dosage, relapse) are to be found in the offending behaviour literature, the language of education is more characteristic, with emphasis on learning, skills acquisition and understanding. In clinical psychology, while behaviourism may deal with patients — people as acted upon — cognitivism requires an appreciation of meaning, implying an educational mode of intervention (Tyrer and Steinberg 1998; Pilgrim and Rogers 1999; McGuire 2000). The identification of deep-seated pathologies and disease entities, especially as 'causes of crime', has been displaced by the assessment of often quite specific cognitive-behavioural dysfunctions.

It may be premature, as well as too general, to say that 'treatment' for mental disorder (except of course where medication is prescribed) and 'working with offenders' deploy the same techniques, but there is no doubt that this is becoming progressively more true. Cognitive-behaviourism, moreover, recognises 'no dividing line ... between so-called normality and abnormality' (McGuire 2000, p. 23), so that any dysfunctional behaviour is amenable to its methods. McMurran has challenged her colleagues in forensic psychology to learn from the evidence-based programmes being developed in the prison and proba-tion services (McMurran 2000).

There is, then, a deep irony that the early editions of manuals for general offending behaviour programmes are typically expressing caution about admitting mentally disordered offenders on to the programme at all. This raises some sharp questions for treatment managers. For example:

Are all 'mentally disordered offenders' to be excluded? Who? Those who are suffering from depression, anxiety and stress? (How depressed, anxious, stressed must they be to be disqualified?) People with learning disabilities? (How severe?) People with a history of schizophrenia — or only those with current symptoms? People with personality disorders? Why are any of these people to be excluded? How will these judgements be taken and by whom? Does the research show these programmes to be less effective for mentally disordered offenders? If so, for whom exactly? If not, what is the case for exclusion? If courts believe that participation in certain programmes is so effective that they are persuaded not to send some offenders to prison, what are the likely consequences for defendants so excluded?

Unless these decisions are taken individually — not because of assumed membership of a group — any strategy of exclusion is unfairly and inappropriately discriminatory. This is quite as true for mentally disordered offenders as for black people or for women.[2] If, on the other hand, decisions are to be taken person-by-person, then this should be so for all offenders and not just those believed to be mentally disturbed.

---

[2] Both black people and women offenders are more likely (than white men) to have their offending perceived in terms of mental disorder (Canton 1995 and references there cited).

ENFORCEMENT

Enforcement is a defining function of modern probation. Punishment cannot be just, or intervention effective, unless the order of the court is implemented.

Hedderman and Hearnden, however, have asked whether more rigorous enforcement sits quite as comfortably with effective practice as has been assumed (Hedderman and Hearnden 2000). After all, if the programme of intervention is prematurely curtailed, for whatever reason, it cannot have its full effect. Georgiou, unconvinced by the claim that contemporary enforcement practice has shown itself to be (reductively) effective, has developed this point (Georgiou 2000). There is a possibility that effective becomes a coded term for punitive. Neither should claims for effectiveness suppress considerations of justice.

A national audit exposed shortcomings in enforcement practice (Georgiou 2000 and references there cited). Research audits, however, typically attend to countable phenomena — how many appointments were missed and with what result, how often were absences recorded and so forth. By these measures, practice is not up to standard, though improving. But while these findings raise questions about accountability, there is a need for a much more subtle qualitative evaluation of enforcement, centring on the matter of how officers decide if an absence is or is not acceptable.

A number of probation areas set out a presumption that absences are unacceptable — the burden is on the probationer to demonstrate that there was a good and sufficient reason for absence. Many areas too have gone on to stipulate what will be allowed to count as an acceptable reason, although these instructions vary between areas — probably beyond justifiable limits (Dersley 2000).

Sameness is not to be mistaken for justice. Since there are indefinitely many ways in which circumstances may vary, National Standards have always allowed that there may be a departure from the standards in appropriate circumstances, normally to be approved by a senior officer. The circle, which the National Standards cannot square, is how to ensure that practice can be sufficiently flexible to be fair and decent, without admitting unwarrantable discrepancies.

Mentally disordered offenders highlight these difficulties. Some probation areas explicitly identify them as people for whom proper exceptions in enforcement might be made, and in his research Georgiou found that mental health issues were adduced in 17 per cent of cases in which officers had departed from National Standards (Georgiou 2000).

Finding a (rare enough!) example of a case in which a service had, in its opinion, been over-zealous in instigating breach action, Her Majesty's Inspectorate of Probation refers to the probationer's mental ill health and drug use. It adds:

> This does not mean that all offenders who are mentally ill should be regarded as incapable of reporting as directed. However, there may be individual cases that contain complex factors that justify a more flexible approach to enable regular contact to take place. (HMIP 2000b, section 3.28)

This is sensible and humane. Yet the principle applies just as much to every probationer. Consideration of enforcement with mentally disordered offenders raises the same kinds of questions as effective practice. Most pointedly, what can be the grounds for granting exemptions to mentally disordered people that do not apply with just as much weight to other people similarly circumstanced?

RISK AND PROTECTING THE PUBLIC

Volatility, unpredictability and dangerousness are among the stereotypical attributes of people who are mentally disordered. Agencies charged with making judgments about risk — for example, the Parole Board — are likely to take mental disorder as a factor that increases risk (Pitchers 1999).

In a judicious review of the literature discussing the association between mental disorder and crime, Prins (1999, Chapter 3) concludes:

1. Most mentally disordered people do not present an increased risk of violence to others
2. The strongest predictors of offending are the same for mentally disordered offenders as for others
3. People with a functional psychosis may present an increased risk of harm to others when they have active symptoms, especially if they are also substance misusers
4. By definition, people with severe personality disorder present an increased risk of violence. (Prins, *op. cit.* p. 66)

So, while conscientious application of the usual risk assessment instruments may serve probation officers well enough (point 2.), they need to make sure that they are close enough to the people they supervise to recognise and respond to the development of 'active symptoms' (point 3.). (*Cf.* Taylor and Monahan 1996.)

Yet many of the recent changes in probation practice have tended to formalise and distance officers from the people they supervise. Emphasis on punishment and strict enforcement potentially transforms the character of the relationship. This 'distancing' may be literal as well as figurative. Home visits are much less common nowadays and are normally undertaken merely to verify residence. This makes it very much harder for the officer to appreciate the lived reality of the individual's circumstances, which may be crucial to the assessment of risk.

Families and friends, who might well be enlisted in support of a care effort centred on helping the probationer to avoid offending, may be less enthusiastic recruits to an intervention which emphasises the priority of punishment. Peay (1995) detects as a principal theme in many inquiries following grave crimes, that relatives, uniquely placed to detect changes or deteriorations, were not listened to. Contemporary policy and practice will not improve this.

Grounds has written:

Supervision is not primarily a surveillance and crime control process, but a framework of support. Monitoring depends centrally on the maintenance of a relationship with the patient, with every effort being made to achieve cooperation, openness and trust. Surveillance that is onerous and outside a framework of support may reduce the cooperation and disclosure on which effective continuing risk assessment depends. (Grounds 1995)

In consideration of risk, as with enforcement, attention to the particular position of mentally disordered offenders leads to wider questions about probation practice much more generally. It is possible that inflexible enforcement makes it less likely that orders will be completed, and that undue emphasis on punishment and risk can interfere with effective risk management. Practice can in this way become ironically self-defeating. But the broader point is that practice cannot be reduced to a relentless pursuit of effectiveness. There may be approaches that 'work' that are morally unacceptable and even, with the incorporation into United Kingdom law of the European Convention on Human Rights, legally challengeable. These questions are raised starkly by the Government's proposals for managing dangerous people with severe personality disorder (Home Office/Department of Health 1999).

PERSONALITY DISORDER

Gunn's influential (1991) survey of psychiatric morbidity found that 10 per cent of the (sentenced male) prison population had some form of personality disorder. Commenting on the difference between this and his 1972 finding (22 per cent), Gunn suggested 'the low reliability of clinical criteria' as the most likely explanation (Gunn *et al.* 1991). This must also explain the finding of the 1997 survey by the Office of National Statistics, that fully 64 per cent of (adult, male, sentenced) prisoners had some personality disorder. In this survey, 49 per cent of sentenced male prisoners were assessed as having anti-social personality disorder, while one in five prisoners had anti-social and another personality disorder (Singleton *et al.* 1998).

Overlaps in personality disorder call into question the existing framework of categories. DSM-IV Axis II has already formed the categories into broader clusters of disorder to move closer to clinical reality, while Tyrer has recently taken this further by arguing that categories are inappropriate for personality disorder 'because the subject naturally fits into dimensions' (Tyrer 2000).

Thus we arrive at a concept of severe personality disorder. This term, not found in standard diagnostic classifications,[3] seems to have appeared first in 1996, but has been taken up widely (Manning 2000). Government proposals in managing dangerous people with severe personality dsorder (Home Office/Department of Health 1999) suggest that there are just over 2,000 people, who are 'very seriously disordered and who pose a very high risk to the public'. The Government proposes that there should be powers to detain these people, while they continue to pose a high risk of serious harm. Although most people so designated are

---

[3] The principal international diagnostic standards are the *Diagnostic and Statistical Manual of Mental Disorders*, 4th edn (DSM-IV), published by the American Psychiatric Association, and the *International Classification of Diseases* (now in its 10th edn) of the World Health Organisation (ICD 10).

already in prison or secure hospital, people might be detained indefinitely even without offending.

One context for this proposal is the Government's view that 100,000 persistent offenders can be identified, who commit half of all crime (Home Office 2000c). These offenders are to be targeted and given longer sentences. The Home Office recognises that they

are also a highly fluid group: this year's 100,000 will not be the same as last year's 100,000 or indeed next year's. Perhaps a fifth of them will stop offending each year, though a fresh cohort of criminals graduating from intermittent to highly persistent criminality will soon take their place. (Home Office, *op. cit.*, section 1.31)

The consequence of incapacitative sentencing is a very substantial increase in the prison population, with unpredictable and probably relatively modest effects on the incidence of crime (Cavadino and Dignan 1997, p. 38 and references there). The idea that a group of offenders can be identified and incapacitated, however, is politically seductive.

The proposals for managing people with severe personality disorders, then, represent an attempt to identify 'the core of the core' — the very small number of those responsible for so much serious crime and likely to continue to perpetrate it.

Why should this core of dangerous offenders be regarded as mentally disordered? The question is especially pertinent when the psychiatric profession itself is divided on the question of whether personality disorder is an illness and, if so, treatable (Mann and Moran 2000). Barbara Wootton over 40 years ago warned of 'the circular process by which mental abnormality is inferred from anti-social behaviour while anti-social behaviour is explained by mental abnormality' (quoted Prins 1999, p. 60).

Personality disorder, the Government's paper reminds us, is not a mental illness, but can be considered an instance of 'unsound mind'. This expression, not common in forensic or general psychiatry, happens to be the term used in the European Convention on Human Rights. Under Article 5 (right to liberty and security), the lawful detention of 'persons of unsound mind' is one of the specific exceptions to the principle that people should not be deprived of their liberty. (Lawful detention after conviction is another circumstance, but this would not

cover the Government's proposal to detain severely personality disordered people, who have committed no offence.) It is for this reason
that these proposals have been denounced as 'unethical proposals for
preventive detention', designed to circumvent the European Convention
(Mullen 2000).

These are clear trends:

- a political aspiration to target persistent offenders
- an extended application of the diagnosis of personality disorder that
  has resulted in a majority of prisoners being assessed as personality
  disordered
- a move to conceptualise personality disorder in dimensional rather
  than categorical terms
- a move to allow the preventative detention of individuals whose
  personality disorders are severe.

This is not to deny the utility of a concept of personality disorder,
(although it is not a concept that is favoured in cognitive-behavioural
approaches (McGuire 2000, p. 37)). The diagnosis of severe personality
disorder, however, not to be found in the standard international
classifications and quite insufficiently specified, lacks the reliability and
validity to support preventive detention (compare Mann and Moran
2000). Since the category is so loosely specified, it is not easy to
anticipate how many people it may come to include. And, for much the
same reasons, it is likely to be difficult for a prisoner/patient to
demonstrate that the disorder has come to an end. Shaftesbury's words
echo again: 'Thus we too readily get him in, and too sluggishly get him
out . . .'

HUMAN RIGHTS

The rights of mentally disordered people are always precarious. The
belief that they lack the mental competence to make judgments about
their own interests leaves them uniquely vulnerable to the infringement
of their rights and disqualifies their objections (Cavadino 1997).

Punishment involves the withdrawal of certain rights. The incorporation of the European Convention into United Kingdom law will
progressively allow the courts to test what rights may lawfully be taken

away and which must remain. The incremental effect of the censure of mentally disordered offenders makes their rights even more precarious. For mentally disordered people, uniquely, rights may be compromised not merely for social defence, but 'in their own interests'.

Failure to recognise the distinctive needs of mentally disordered people demonstrably leads to distress for them and for others. Yet the way in which we think about these matters may be as much part of the problem as a solution. It is not, it is suggested, possible to identify a 'group' of mentally disordered offenders, whose members have as much in common with one another as to constitute a group, or are sufficiently different from many offenders excluded by the definition. This is partly because of the enormous range of conditions encompassed by the expression 'mental disorder', but also because so many of these conditions are more or less extreme instances of familiar human experience.

In the post-diversionary phase, what is needed is a complementary inter-agency and inter-disciplinary endeavour, which enables access to services in response to need and risk. The identification of groups (for instance, people with 'dual diagnosis') seems more likely to lead to exclusion and denial of service. At the worst, identification of people with distinctive needs becomes the occasion for special control (Peay 1997, p. 697).

Those unconvinced by this understanding of mental disorder will still need to ponder how the modern probation service is to fit into inter-agency networks. Should enforcement, rehabilitation and public protection mean something different for people who are mentally disordered? Effectiveness, as well as justice, requires that differences of approach are reasoned on the basis of distinctive need or risk and not on stereotypical conceptions of mental disorder and 'normality'. Neither is effectiveness more important than justice.

The development of cognitive-behavioural approaches in probation practice means that we are more than ever inclined to understand offending in psychological terms. While this need not entail a disregard of the socio-economic context of offending, the significance of 'the social' may need to be defended and re-affirmed. Meanwhile, the Government's aspiration to identify a core group of persistent offenders — and within that group a core of grave offenders, identified in psychiatric terms — follows a similar trajectory.

At the centre of this strategy is a putative group of people with a 'condition' not known to standard diagnostic classifications. Most of them will have anti-social personality disorder (typically accompanied by other disorders), a category that has shown itself to be inclusive and expansive (as witness its fivefold increase in the prison population in less than a decade). We seem increasingly disposed to understand offending not merely in psychological, but in psychiatric terms. Our history of promoting the rights of people who are mentally disordered, should make us wary about what these trends could entail for offenders.

16   Case Management: Shaping Practice

Paul Holt

INTRODUCTION

While it may well be true that probation practitioners have operated a form of case management for some years, especially regarding prioritisation and the use of specialist provision, it has been brought into sharp focus by the advent of effective practice. In addition, although the implications for probation of the Human Rights Act 1998 are not yet fully appreciated, practice will be placed under the spotlight in an entirely different way (Scott and Ward 1999). What follows, therefore, is an attempt at locating the probation case management discussion in the broader context of anti-discriminatory practice, human rights, and justice for the individual offender.

To begin with, case management as a method of service delivery will briefly be explored, followed by a similarly succinct review of the events that have given case management such prominence (at least in theory) in probation practice. In so doing, some of the main issues concerning case management in probation practice will be identified. It will then be argued that the case manager occupies the key role in furthering human rights concerns, especially in regard to countering discrimination and monitoring equality of access to justice.

WHAT IS 'CASE MANAGEMENT'?

Historical background

Case management has been described a being 'part of the history of social work' (Miller 1983, p. 6). Emanating mainly from the United States, it came about largely as a response to two post-war phenomena. First, although human service provision mushroomed at this time, much of it focused on individual issues (for example, homelessness). It was uncoordinated, 'sprawling and fragmented' (Intagliata 1992, p. 28), and often inaccessible to those with multiple needs. Secondly, the discovery of psychotropic drugs in the 1950s led to the de-institutionalisation agenda in mental health (Rubin 1992). These two developments took place against a background of the increasingly complex needs of service users, too complex in fact for agencies dedicated to single-issue provision to deal with. Thus, the need was recognised for a 'generalist worker', whose function was to coordinate services. Accordingly, a specific service component, termed 'case management', came into use during the 1970s to enable service users to access provision (Intagliata 1982).

The de-institutionalisation agenda in mental health also stimulated the growth of case management in the UK, although it took longer to develop (Barton 1996; Challis *et al.* 1990; Corney 1995). Following numerous enquiries into the provision of care, the same concerns over fragmentation and lack of coordination in delivery were identified. The subsequent NHS and Community Care Act 1990 partly enshrined in legislation the need for greater organisation in service delivery. Indeed, the Care Plan Approach (Department of Health 1990) care management (Department of Health 1991), and the practice of Community Mental Health Teams all have their roots in case management.

Core functions — diversity of practice

As a generic name for a method of service delivery, case management combines the core functions of assessment, planning, linking and monitoring into a process designed to be integrating and facilitative (Agranoff 1977). To these four functions is sometimes added a fifth, namely advocacy (Rubin 1992), which relates specifically to service user empowerment and is thus a critical component of anti-discriminatory practice. Alongside these core tasks, the literature identifies a range of additional functions which case managers may sometimes need to undertake, relative to the needs of individual cases; for example, advocacy for service users, monitoring both the take-up of service and the outputs of other providers.

There is a wide miscellany of models in use in other human service agencies. Space does not permit a detailed survey of this diversity (see further Holt 2000a), but it is noted in passing that the term 'case management' is used to describe a variety of models, each with differing emphases. Agencies have developed the model(s) they use relative to their goals. In consequence, the definition of case management cannot simply be assumed, neither can one model be translated uncritically from one setting to another. In other words, within the broad framework of case management, there is a need for specificity as to its exact purpose.

THE EVOLUTION OF 'EFFECTIVE PRACTICE'

It is now necessary briefly to review the evolution of the effective practice agenda in probation in order further to appreciate the emergence of case management as the preferred model of service delivery in current practice.

Research findings from Canada came to be known in Britain, particularly through McIvor's study (1990) suggesting that the previously received wisdom that 'nothing worked' in reducing recidivism could be challenged (Raynor 1996). Initiatives by the Home Office, the Association of Chief Officers of Probation (ACOP) and the Central Probation Council (CPC) resulted in two conferences during 1995, entitled 'Managing What Works' and 'Quality and What Works': these were followed by a Probation Circular (Home Office 1995b) advertising the major components of the What Works approach.

Although the importance of What Works principles in practice was beginning to be recognised at least from 1995, the evidence suggests that the implementation of effective practice was uncoordinated and piecemeal. For example, each one of four of Her Majesty's Inspectorate of Probation (HMIP) thematic inspections made comments and recommendations with a strong What Works flavour, but unsurprisingly only in relation to the aspect of practice under inspection. As an example, the report of the Inspection into *Probation Orders with Additional Requirements* (HMIP 1996a), while observing the need for services to make greater use of research findings in planning interventions with offenders, drew attention to deficiencies in assessment, in particular concerning offenders' suitability for specific interventions. Weaknesses in assessment were also identified in a further Inspection report during 1996 (HMIP 1996b), especially concerning supervision planning, recommending that interventions should be more clearly outcome focused.

With the publication of National Standards in 1992 (revised in 1995 and 2000), the focus was 'on the management of supervision rather than its content' (Worrall 1997, p. 73), the discretion of the individual supervising officer being considerably limited in the process, albeit in the context of accountability.

The What Works Project

Following the 1995 series of inspections and conferences disseminating elements of practice based on What Works principles, Sir Graham Smith, the Chief Inspector of Probation, announced the commencement of the What Works project in January 1996. Its brief was to

provide best practice guidance to probation areas with regard to effective types of programming appropriate for supervising offenders in the community and advice on the management arrangements needed to promote and support their effective supervision. (from CPO letter January 1996, quoted in HMIP 1998c, p. 16)

Andrew Underdown, a senior manager with Greater Manchester Probation Service, was seconded to the Home Office to lead the project. Its report, *Strategies for Effective Offender Supervision* (HMIP 1998b) was launched by Sir Graham Smith at the HMIP annual conference in February 1998. In his remarks, he highlighted the report's findings, in particular the inconsistency and variation in scope of direct work with offenders already apparent amongst services. He emphasised the report's recommendations, in particular the desirability of more structured assessments, a 'menu' of supervision options, and better reviews and evaluations of supervision quality.

A feature of the report was its bringing forward six 'agendas for development', progress in which would progress the implementation of effective practice; one of these concerned case management.

Four months later, HMIP's Effective Practice Initiative had been developed into a National Implementation Plan, to be led, managed and coordinated by a Steering Group, where members from ACOP, the Prison Service and the Home Office joined those from HMIP (Home Office 1998c). Later in 1998, a further volume entitled *Evidence Based Practice* was published (Chapman and Hough 1998), providing further development of the effective practice themes. What Works had come to stay.

ENFORCEMENT: THE CONTEXT FOR CASE MANAGEMENT

The implementation of practice based on What Works is one of the three prongs of modernisation, the others being the creation of the National Probation Service and the achievement of improved enforcement practices in line with the new National Standards (Home Office 2000k). The policy context has increasingly been dominated by enforcement and compliance issues. A number of reasons lie behind this, amongst them a Probation Circular emphasising the need for practice concerning judicial and non-judicial enforcement to be in accordance with National Standards (Home Office 1999d) and evidence from HMIP's inspections revealing 'evidence of unsatisfactory performance by services in enforcing orders to National Standards', with 'an undoubted need for enforcement practice to improve' (HMIP 1999d). The emphasis on enforcement received a ministerial imprimatur with Paul Boateng's pronouncement that 'We are an enforcement agency ... this is what we are, this is what we do'. It is clear, therefore, that any model of case management adopted by the service must also have utility in enhancing compliance and completion rates amongst offenders.

CASE MANAGEMENT AT CENTRE STAGE?

The implementation of effective practice has therefore given case management a key role (HMIP 1998a; Chapman and Hough 1998).

However, despite this central position, with a few notable exceptions, little had subsequently been written to expand and develop the notion for the probation service (Oldfield 1998; Holt 2000a). Equally, only very recently has the Home Office become involved in researching case management, with a view to establishing some best practice guidelines (Home Office 2000f). Nevertheless, in the meantime, many services implemented their own models, with such a consequently wide variety that developing a typology of models has not proved an easy task (Home Office 2001g).

One result of this uncoordinated activity would seem to be that some fundamental questions have gone unaddressed, of which two seem critical. First, although the What Works project placed considerable emphasis on design issues, in that programmes of interventions with offenders should be based on a model of change for which there is research evidence, similar attention does not seem to have been given to the matter of design in case management. Thus, the question arises as to the level of congruence between programmes of intervention and the case management model developed to support them. Secondly, 'evidence-led practice' is fundamentally concerned with demonstrations of effectiveness; the pathfinders, the Accreditation Panel and the establishment of the core curriculum of programmes of intervention are all key elements of this approach. Indeed, a poorly designed activity cannot be readily evaluated (Challis 1993). Regrettably, it seems rare for a case management model to have been designed with sufficient methodological rigour that ready evaluation is possible (see further Holt, forthcoming).

CASE MANAGEMENT IN THE DELIVERY OF EFFECTIVE PRACTICE

It is important at this stage to reflect that effective practice assumes a situation where the caseholding practitioner is not the sole provider of service. On the contrary, others are to be involved in delivering the various outputs of the supervision plan, a state of affairs often referred to as 'differential supervision'. Supporting, optimising and 'seamlessly integrating' interventions are roles assigned to the case manager (Chapman and Hough 1998). Underdown set down six core tasks of the case manager in the delivery of effective practice:

- Risk assessment and management,
- Supervision planning and review,
- Referral and allocation of resources used in supervision,
- Coordination and sequencing of work through the Order,
- Managing contact, attendance and enforcement,
- Prioritising within the caseload. (HMIP 1998b)

Two major issues arise from this: first, case management is distinguished as both a system and a process; and, secondly, great emphasis is clearly placed on the role of the case manager.

System and process: the whole, not simply the parts

The case management literature also distinguishes between system and process, agreeing that the core functions of assessment, planning, linking and monitoring are combined into a process designed to be integrating and facilitative (Agranoff 1977; Moxley 1989; Rose 1992). Decisively, therefore, it is not as a sum of parts that case management principally operates, but as an integrated and integrative whole — one function, spanning boundaries, drawing together service provision and providing a single context for the whole process of service delivery (Bachrach 1983). Case management is, therefore, a dynamic intervention in its own right, a contextual system within which important processes take place.

Each element has a distinct effect on outcome. If by 'system' we mean a logical, coherent relationship between inputs and outputs, this must relate to the way in which resources are deployed (i.e. inputs), with a corresponding influence on the effectiveness of the outputs deliver. Similarly, 'process' issues relate to the mechanics of delivering outputs (the 'how'), including quality. For this distinction to find operational expression, it would appear of fundamental importance to recognise the practice of case management as also a whole service issue, and not simply an activity performed by practitioners alone.

It has been proposed elsewhere that there should be a high level of congruence between programmes of intervention and the methods of supervision that support them. Processes should, therefore, be designed to support inputs and integrate outputs so that the result is a coherent, meaningful and therefore effective programme of supervision (Holt 2000a). One way forward is to embed the system of case management in key process variables; in particular, consistency, continuity, consolidation, as 'features of support most likely to produce positive outcomes' (Downing and Hatfield 1999), based on the cognitive-behavioural components in Adult Learning Theory, identified as being necessary supports for learning changed behaviours (Holt 2000a).

However, the reality of differential supervision 'on the ground' may be experienced by an offender as fragmentary. For example, in some services it is not unknown for an offender to have contact with four or five different 'providers' during the first 12 weeks of the court order. This may create the possibility that, without a 'point of stability', not only are important advantages to community supervision lost (for example, continuous assessment), but also a range of Human Rights Act provisions could be breached, if service is not provided appropriately (for example, Articles 2, 5, 8 or 14: Scott and Ward 1999).

The case manager: the 'human link'

The pivotal importance of the case manager in the delivery of effective practice is clearly recognised by the report of the What Works project (HMIP 1998b), and emphasised in the companion report *Evidence Based Practice* (Chapman and Hough 1998). For example:

> Case managers form the key relationship with the supervised offender. In this way, they come to represent the probation service to the individual. (Chapman and Hough 1998, p. 44)

Intagliata observes that:

> Case managers are the most critical components in the case management system. They serve as the human link between the client and the system. (1992, p. 31)

The case management literature describes this linkage role in terms of boundary spanning (that is, identifying service for multiple needs from a range of different providers), drawing together provision into a single context (Hasenfeld 1983). The impact of differential supervision and its potential for creating a fragmented (and therefore deficient) experience of being supervised creates a challenge for the case manager, which will be discussed further below.

Case management, as it has developed in other human service agencies, also recognises that, in order to provide continuity and coordination, 'strategies focused solely on organisations are not enough, *a human link is required*' (Miller 1983, as quoted in Barton 1996, p. 5, emphasis added). Thus it has been argued that:

> The most influential aspect of the case management process is the quality of the personal commitment that case managers develop towards their clients. The human relationship ... should be considered a fundamental strength of the case management system. (Intagliata, 1992, p. 33)

This foregrounding of a high-quality working relationship is also explicit in the effective practice literature. Chapman and Hough consider that amongst its characteristics are safety, consistency, reliability and firmness (1998). To this list may be added a high level of engagement (Pritchard *et al.* 1998), stability, continuity and reassurance (Rubin 1992). Indeed, the provision of the conditions conducive to the development of an effective working relationship is axiomatic to pro-social modelling, particularly in regard to clarity of role, the use of constructive empathy and collaborative goal-setting (Trotter 1999).

CASE MANAGERS, JUSTICE AND EQUAL OPPORTUNITIES

It almost goes without saying that, once an offender has been dealt with by the court, the service has a responsibility to deal with the offender in such a way that he or she is not discriminated against on 'any improper ground' (Criminal Justice Act 1991, s. 95). Thus concerns about justice do not end with the imposition of a sentence; it is self-evident that fairness must lie at the heart of supervision practices.

That there is discrimination against minorities at all levels in the criminal justice system has been well rehearsed, thus it seems impossible to separate an emphasis on fairness as a component of justice from anti-discriminatory practice. Addressing and combating discrimination is also a whole service issue, and practitioners are well aware of their responsibilities under service equal opportunities policies. Nevertheless, as has been seen, the advent of effective practice has significantly altered the role of practitioners, so that case managers (as they are or will become) have additional opportunities both to contribute to discriminatory practice and to challenge it. Before considering this further, it is worth exploring how effective practice may unwittingly have created windows for potentially compounding existing levels of discrimination.

An anti-discriminatory critique of the What Works literature would be bound to observe that serious difficulties arise, if generalised findings from research are assimilated uncritically. For example, the meta-analyses produced results predicated largely on the behaviour of males (Howden-Windell and Clark 1999) and arguably present as gender-free and race-neutral. It would appear that none of the meta-analysts controlled for difference. A commitment to equal opportunities implies an anti-oppressive stance in regard to interventions that, through the adoption of design features that favour the existing cultural hegemony of white masculinity, may further compound the impact of discrimination. It is proposed to examine this issue in relation to women and black offenders and to argue that case managers' attention to difference in assessment practices and in the construction of supervision plans is more than simply a responsivity issue. It will also be argued that attention needs to be given to developing offenders' literacy skills if they are to make optimum use of cognitively based programmes.

Women offenders

It is a commonplace that the vast majority of offending is carried out by males. Consequently, attempts at understanding women's offending have been comparatively recent and much rarer (for example, Eaton 1986, Chesney-Lind 1997). The reasons for this are no doubt complex, but it may partly be due to the fact that 'female crime, as a social phenomenon, is no threat to society' (Worrall 1997, p. 41). However, attempts have been made to identify women's criminogenic needs in order to develop appropriately targeted interventions. For example, Hannah-Moffatt's list includes low self-esteem, dependency, suicide attempts, self-injury, substance abuse, parental death at an early age, constant changes in foster care and living on the streets (1997, as quoted in Kendall 1998; Howden-Windell and Clark 1999). Other studies have recognised that criminogenic factors associated with male offending are relevant to women, but that women's offending is less the result of isolated factors and more that they are 'people with life histories'

(Chesney-Lind 1997, quoted in Howden-Windell and Clark 1999, p. 3). In addition, the extent of the overlap in criminogenic need factors between females and males is still problematic (Koons *et al.* 1997); indeed, a recategorisation of needs in the criminogenic–non-criminogenic continuum may be required for female offenders. For example, self-esteem (noted above) would not be considered a criminogenic need for males (Andrews and Bonta 1998).

Research dedicated to What Works with female offenders has been small (Morash *et al.* 1997). A recent study identified 67 other studies reporting encouraging findings, but only 12 of these included an outcome measure, and in no case was recidivism considered (Morash *et al.* 1997). Dowden and Andrews (1999), in a recent meta-analysis of over 220 primary studies, found that there was support for the risk, need and responsivity principle (and thus confirmed existing theory, such as Andrews *et al.* 1990a), but importantly none of the studies focused entirely on the list of female-related criminogenic needs, as described above, in particular, self-esteem. Dowden and Andrews did not

> ... examine whether making the treatment programme more responsive to the specific learning styles of women offenders (i.e. relationship-oriented treatment) had any impact on recidivism. (1999, p. 450)

Thus the effects of gender, as a 'specific responsivity consideration', remain to be explored. Indeed, on the basis of research findings described above, a strong case could be made for providing scope — within a standardised, unitary, risk/needs assessment tool — for the criminogenic needs which are more often associated with female offending, to be addressed (see further below).

Black offenders

There are complex reasons why black people are over-represented in the criminal justice system (Reiner 1989; Denney 1992). For example, black people run a higher risk of imprisonment even when they are convicted of similar offences as white offenders, and once imprisoned are there for longer (Hood 1992). The criminal justice system is dominated by white people (including the probation service) (Denney 1992), to the extent that the Home Office has recently set targets for the recruitment, retention and promotion of black staff (Home Office

1999b). Structural discourses note the (relative) powerlessness of black people in any event (and by extension, offenders) in analyses of power relations (for example, Dominelli 1988).

Probation officers routinely 'explain' offending behaviour to the court, especially by means of the PSR. It has been found that individual officers' understanding of oppression will have a bearing on how a black person's offence is analysed and presented. A failure to locate this in the 'blackness' of a black offender's experience (which includes their experience of institutional racism) has been noted as one reason why stereotypes have gone unchallenged and oppression continues (Denney 1992). As Denney notes, it is in this area that tendencies towards generalised understandings of offending behaviour (and regarding 'what works' in reducing it) are not only imprecise, but may also run the risk of contributing to oppression. Of note is the recent legislative development concerning racism (ss. 22–25 of the Crime and Disorder Act 1998, creating new offences of racially aggravated assaults and racial harassment) and the scope within the unified risk/needs assessment tool for specific reference to an offender's experiences of racism and its (possible) connection with offending.

The What Works project's pilot study did not scrutinise any programmes for black offenders, for the same reasons as given regarding programmes for women. The need has been recognised for a more thorough understanding of criminogenic need in relation to black offenders, that locates offending in the specificity of being black, so that programmes of intervention can bring influence to bear without compounding existing experiences of oppression. To this end, further ethnographic studies amongst black offenders would also assist (for example, Harris 1992).

Stephen Lawrence was a black teenager murdered in 1993. Four years later, the Home Secretary's Inquiry (chaired by Sir William MacPherson) brought into sharp focus the extent of racialism in the criminal justice system, in particular the institutional racism in the Metropolitan Police. Its report made 70 recommendations, which were taken up in the form of an Action Plan announced by the Home Secretary to Parliament in March 1999 (Macpherson 1999; Home Office 1999g). Amongst other objectives, the 'framework for change' aimed at increasing trust and confidence in policing, especially amongst ethnic minority communities. An immediate inspection of the Metropolitan Police by Her Majesty's Inspectorate of Constabulary was ordered, as a first step to restoring public confidence. Importantly, provision was also made for a tighter definition of 'racist incident' and a more broadly-based training in racism awareness and valuing cultural diversity. The Home Secretary also made a commitment to producing an annual report to Parliament on the progress made in implementing the Action Plan. Advances are being made. For example, the first progress report showed an increase in the recording of racist incidents (Home Office 2000r).

Although not singling out the probation service in particular, the Inquiry's report identified complacency in many aspects of the criminal justice system, and called upon all agencies to be seen to be demonstrating fairness in matters of race. Following this, in February 1999, ACOP, along with CPC, the Association of Black Probation Officers (ABPO), the National Association of Asian Probation Staff (NAAPS) and the Home Office, set up a working group to examine the recruitment, retention and progression of ethnic minority staff. It reported in July 1999 (Home Office 1999b), offering 22 recommendations, including the development of a national strategy to improve retention and progression of ethnic minority staff, a review of the funding of ABPO and NAAPS, and a renewed commitment to race equality at all levels of the probation service.

It was also recommended that a Race Equality Implementation Group be established to take forward the report's recommendations. In addition, the Probation Inspectorate was to undertake a thematic inspection on race equality, to report between March and August 2000 (HMIP 2000f).

Offenders with low levels of literacy

In a 1994 survey, one in two inmates amongst 400 prisoners received into 16 prisons had a low level of literacy, compared with one in six of the general population (ALBSU 1994). The STOP project in Shropshire, reported by Davies and Byatt (1998), found that 33 per cent of offenders could not read above Foundation Level, and that 45 per cent were at this level in respect of writing (Foundation Level being Level 2/3 of the National Curriculum). On the basis of these and similar findings, Caddick and Webster (1998) argue that improving the literacy levels of offenders could be a crucial aspect in reducing the risk of their reoffending, and as such is a prime candidate for inclusion in a discussion of criminogenic need.

In their discourse, literacy is seen as fundamental to the kind of 'cognitive processing' implicit in the use of cognitive-behaviourally based interventions with offenders. For example, literacy can be seen as an important part of the process whereby an offender is encouraged to be aware of thinking and to link thoughts with behaviour — in the sense that the complex relationship between language, thinking and writing, and the derivation of meaning from text, strengthens the capacity to make sense of the world (Olson 1994). Thus, in enabling an individual to make connections with the 'communicated thoughts and experiences of others', literacy ensures that cognition is not simply the result of an offender's own experience. Literacy is also 'a core element in the development of a feeling of inclusion' (Home Office 1997, quoted in Caddick and Webster 1998), as opposed to isolation and disconnectedness. This latter has manifestly clear implications for community reintegration (objectified in the effective practice agenda) and a hoped-for desistance from offending.

Hayden *et al.* (1999) found that the presence of considerable literacy difficulties amongst the offenders with whom they worked in Cambridgeshire, encouraged them to review how to communicate ideas effectively. They considered that an incorporation of ideas from the creative arts provided 'a dynamic environment for active learning' (Hayden *et al.* 1999, p. 44). Several theatre companies have collaborated with services not simply in the delivery of diversions from an otherwise slow-paced session, but in providing drama as an enhancement to learning. The Geese Theatre Company, for example, has specialised in the development of 'cognitive metaphors', by means of which offenders can conceptualise important issues as a prelude to re-learning appropriate behaviour.

The development of an anti-discriminatory stance in the delivery of effective practice seems critical in the light of what has been discussed above. It is noteworthy that the most recent edition of the What Works strategy document locates anti-discriminatory practice squarely in the effective practice discourse, thus:

The needs principle requires that the criminogenic needs of all groups of offenders are identified; the responsivity principle that methods of delivery are designed so that all can access the service; equality of opportunity that all offenders have access to services designed to meet their needs; evaluation that programmes achieve planned outcomes with all groups of offenders. (Home Office 2000s, p. 7)

For reasons of completeness, it is important to note the most recent developments (at the time of writing) regarding provision for minority groups of offenders. That female offenders may have certain criminogenic needs in addition to those of male offenders (notably current abusive relationships) has been acknowledged, together with the question whether 'there are unique criminogenic needs relating to race' (Home Office 2000s, p. 14). Both issues are currently being researched at the Home Office. An adapted version for female offenders of a violent male offender programme entitled 'Focus on Violence' is due for accreditation in March 2001, and a programme focusing on persistent female acquisitive offenders is due in October 2001. Research pathfinders are examining programme adaptations and various other models of service delivery in connection with offenders from ethnic minority groups. Also of note is the programme for racially motivated offenders currently under development (Home Office 2000s). Improvements in literacy, where appropriate, have been adopted as an outcome measure for the effectiveness of programmes in recent official guidance (Colledge *et al.* 1999).

THE CASE MANAGER — 'CHAMPION' OF ANTI-DISCRIMINATORY PRACTICE?

In addition to the policy developments described above, it is suggested that the arrival of the Human Rights Act 1998 (and the possibility of court action under Article 14 of the European Convention) may prompt the development of an anti-discriminatory practice 'champion' at the level of individual service delivery, to be pro-active in much the same way as the implementation of effective practice requires an 'internal champion' at senior management level (Gendreau 1996). With the case manager having overall responsibility for an offender's passage through the court order, it would seem that he or she would be ideally suitable for the task. It is suggested that the key stages of supervision (coincident with case management's core functions) provide ready opportunities for vigorous anti-discriminatory activity, in particular assessment, planning, implementation, review and evaluation. While all are of critical importance, it is proposed to focus on three areas, namely assessment, planning and review.

Assessment

At this initial stage of involvement the case manager, as the 'human agent' who represents the probation service to the individual, is well placed to become acutely aware of difference (and the possibility of disadvantage and inequality of access to service). Assessments should manifestly not be race and/or gender blind, neither should literacy difficulties be ignored. While the assessment process is greatly assisted by the use of combined needs/risk assessment tools (soon to be standardised), there remains considerable scope for professional judgement. This will remain, even when comprehensive targetting matrices are rolled out (as referred to in Home Office 2000s), especially when applying suitability and exclusion criteria for accredited programmes. While the use of standardised assessment and targetting tools should vastly reduce the scope for (unwitting) discriminatory practice by limiting practitioner idiosyncracy, assessments made in this way will only be as accurate as the case managers making them. Thus the need for vigilant anti-discriminatory practice is in no way diminished.

Developments in IT will also assist the assessment process, especially those associated with IAPS (Interim Accredited Programme Software). This system, when fully implemented, will (amongst other things) provide practitioners with assistance in assessing offender's suitability for a programme, record the progress of offenders through programmes and monitor the quality of programme delivery (Home Office 2000s).

Planning

The 'boundary spanning' role of the case manager was noted above, especially in regard to moving across agency boundaries and identifying resources from a range of providers. However, the literature also identifies case management's double focus, both on the individual service user and on the systems in society of which they are part (for example, family and community (Rose 1992)). That there is a system focus at all is a corrective to the view that the practice of case management is 'simply an administrative function designed to process service users more efficiently' (Moxley 1989, p. 22).

The systems focus implies a proactive stance by case managers, both with regard to an overly individualistic assessment of an individual offender, and also with regard to the availability of provision. This latter takes account of whether appropriate provision is available in the first place, and whether the quality of what is provided is acceptable. Indeed, one writer states: 'Case Management must become a system reform strategy with responsibility for direct practice with individuals ...' (Rose 1992, p. viii)

The systems focus is a corrective to an 'individual defect' model of service users (Rose 1992, p. x), where interventions are planned on a quasi-diagnostic (and therefore very limiting) basis, sole attention to which will leave the system unchanged. A systems focus strengthens anti-discriminatory practice amongst case managers, preserving a holistic view of an individual and a clear recognition of difference.

A systemic, ecological focus can require the case manager to be pro-active in changing systems that are discriminatory, perhaps through their inaccessibility to service users. It can also mean that provision is made for rehearsal opportunities in supporting newly learnt behaviour (Chapman and Hough 1998). Additionally, in line with the need for community reintegration by offenders, a systems focus will entail identification and consolidation of community support (Pincus and Minahan 1973; Seed 1990).

The system focus of case management also provides an illustration that its practice is a whole service issue. For example, it may be that gaps are identified in service provision, for which a remedial strategy is required. A Partnership Strategy is already underway as part of the What Works implementation (Home Office 2001d), and includes attention to the development of basic skills and employment services, as well as sustaining existing provision for debt advice and accommodation needs. However, it is interesting that this Circular roots the system focus, described here, in the model of service design for effective offender supervision set out in the 1998 HMI report, rather than more appropriately in case management developments. As Rothman suggested, case managers could well monitor other agencies' outputs (1991). Indeed, such information from case managers supplied to partnership and implementation managers would assist them in their planning activities, especially concerning the quality of partnership output.

Review

Evaluation is fundamental to evidence-led practice: it is of critical importance to know whether an intervention has achieved its objective.

So far, the evaluation of case management has been approached in two main ways, one described by Merrington and Hine (2001) and the other by Holt (forthcoming). In any event, given the proposition that case management is both a system and a process (and also a whole service issue), it seems reasonable that both elements should be evaluated, as well as the contribution of the service at strategic and operational level.

Quality issues are one set of concerns that are close to the heart of working for justice, inevitably and necessarily taking into account what offenders have made of the supervision process. It was noted above that an unintended outcome of differential supervision may be fragmentation. Should this unplanned negative outcome occur, it may compound offenders' existing fragmented thinking patterns, leading to the possibility that key messages from cognitive-behavioural programmes may be undermined or lost. In addition, an offender may experience such fragmentation as 'pass the parcel', and thereby as degrading. The failure to guard against this possibility, as well as to provide a coherent experience of supervision, may even lay a service open to challenge in the courts under human rights legislation. It is suggested that both negative outcomes could be avoided if services develop a case management model, where the system is embedded in a process designed to limit the possibility of fragmentation.

CONCLUSION

This chapter set out to explore the development of case management as a service delivery strategy, and in particular to give an account of its prominence in the delivery of effective practice. Attention has been drawn to the need for a consideration of design issues, especially in the light of the imperative of evaluation. Given the current wide diversity in case management practice, it seems particularly important to give further clarity to case management tasks and role, emphasising the separate importance of both system and process issues. Of equal consequence is the need to identify how the case manager role can be developed to take account of the need to counter discrimination in the criminal justice setting, with the necessary vigilance that should characterise anti-discriminatory practice. Some suggestions have been made as to how this might be taken forward, in particular identifying the key role case managers occupy at the assessment, planning and review stages of supervision. It has also been observed that case management is a whole service issue, and not simply an activity limited to case managers; they require resourcing, monitoring and appraising if they are to deliver. The overarching concern has been to identify the opportunities case managers have in working for justice. It may well prove to be the case that the human rights legislation may refresh the statutory context within which case managers operate, by providing a fresh impetus for the task. In any event, the importance of the human link in the strategy can never be overlooked — discrimination is a human creation and its eradication remains an urgent human task.

17 Training for a Modern Service

Charlotte Knight

INTRODUCTION

In July 1997, the Home Secretary, Jack Straw, made an announcement about the future of probation training. This brought to an end a long period of uncertainty that had prevailed under the previous Conservative Government (Ward 1996). A Diploma in Probation Studies would be put in place, which would combine a National Vocational Qualification (NVQ) to be achieved in employment, and an undergraduate degree to be awarded by universities. The new arrangements were to be employment led and delivered by consortia of probation services using the services of higher education institutions. The curriculum would be based on occupational standards and the NVQ part of the diploma was set at Level 4, a standard identified as compatible with undergraduate degree level education. The new award was to be accredited by a new awarding body, the Community Justice National Training Organisation (CJNTO), to give the qualification an identity distinct from the Diploma in Social Work. This distinctiveness had also to be reflected structurally in the format of delivery and assessment within any higher education institutions involved.

A consultancy was awarded to devise, with reference to all interested parties, a 'Core Curriculum' (Senior 1998b) for the degree and a Regulatory Framework (Senior 1998a) for the management and award of the combined diploma. The occupational standards competences framework was completed after thorough consultation. The CJNTO was to incorporate a wide range of interests across the voluntary and statutory sectors in relation to community-based responses to crime. While the new diploma presented an immediate area for activity, both the diploma and the probation service would sit within a much wider span of responsibility. Probation higher education interests would have a place on the CJNTO board of directors (Knight and Ward 2001).

This chapter traces the background to the current training arrangements and addresses some of the themes that arise for qualifying training from the development of the What Works project within the probation service (Home Office 2000s) and in the context of the Home Office Crime Reduction Strategy. It suggests that the development of a new training provision has suffered from a lack of clarity about the intended role of the probation officer at the point of qualification. A new and complex training provision has been put in place before the Home Office or the probation service could clearly identify the role and tasks of the qualified probation officer within the new National Probation Service. It suggests that, nevertheless, programme providers have a key role to play in shaping and influencing how the new National Probation Service evolves, by providing programmes that encourage staff to be critical, reflective, evidence-led and just practitioners. It is to be hoped that these are qualities that will continue to be valued in the emerging service.

CONTEXT AND BACKGROUND OF PRE-QUALIFYING TRAINING

The probation service, since its inception in 1907, has placed a high value on the need to employ staff with the skills and knowledge to work effectively with offenders. From as early as 1922, an agreement had been reached that the qualification for probation officers should be located within the social science discipline in higher education, and in 1930 the Home Office introduced the first probation officer training course. In 1946, a training centre was established at Rainer House, in Chelsea. By the 1950s, the Home Office monopoly on probation officer training was being challenged by universities, as they began to offer diploma courses in probation work. Subsequently, probation training became located within social work education, via the Certificate of

Qualification in Social Work (CQSW) and more recently the Diploma in Social Work (DipSW) (Pillay 2000).

Since the mid-1980s, questions had been asked about the quality of probation training within social work programmes, and despite overall satisfaction by employers, the reviews and the debates continued. In 1988, Colin Thomas, Chief Inspector of Probation, indicated his belief that the overall structure of probation training was sound and that there were no plans to move it away from social work training (Thomas 1988). However, by 1993 there were indications that the Home Office was not satisfied with the content of the DipSW course, with particular disquiet about the focus on anti-racist and anti-discriminatory practice (Pillay 2000). In the summer of 1994, a review of probation officer recruitment and qualifying training was undertaken by the Home Office (Dews and Watts 1994), which signalled the Government's intention to abolish the requirement for probation officers to hold a social work qualification on the grounds that other disciplines were relevant to the work and that the existing arrangements restricted the intake of applicants with appropriate experience. The Dews Report proposed a two-tier system, with most probation officers being recruited directly as trainees by probation services and selected students sponsored by the Home Office for a two-year Masters degree at a small number of universities (Dews and Watts 1994, pp. 3–6).

The sense of injustice felt by most of the probation service organisations at these proposals — both the de-valuing of the current training and the scarcely concealed discrimination implicit in the reference to over-recruitment of young, female and black staff — had the effect of galvanising action. A concerted campaign against the proposals and for the retention of university-based education ran from 1996 up to the General Election in 1997. The history of the campaign mounted by all the interested parties to maintain a formal structure for probation training is well documented (Pillay 2000; Knight and Taylor 1996; Ward 1996). The commitment to a joint strategy was first incorporated in a joint statement made by the Committee of Vice Chancellors and Principals (CVCP), Association of Chief Officers of Probation (ACOP), and the National Association of Probation Officers (NAPO).

There was a commitment to educational principles that outlined the core position of providing teaching which is developmental; that is building on previous teaching and knowledge in such a manner as to broaden and deepen a student's understanding — delivered in such a way as to develop students' critical and analytic skills. (Spencer 1998)

Spencer also identified that the seizing on an NVQ framework by NAPO was an attempt to persuade the Government that this was a national training framework that could be successfully applied. The work was begun on developing occupational standards for the sector long before any clarity had emerged about how this might apply to training.

During the process of the campaign to reinstate the need for a common framework for learning and assessment, work was commenced on developing the NVQ to reflect the needs of the probation officer role. The Criminal Justice NVQ Level 3 had had partial take-up since its inception, but the work on defining occupational standards for the sector as a whole was still in its infancy. Both NAPO and higher education interests, represented through the Standing Conference of Probation Tutors, worked hard to influence and guide the development of the occupational standards at this time. However, the efforts to try to find some acceptable compromise with the Home Office met with little sympathy from Home Office officials, and none at all from Ministers (Pillay 2000). The impasse continued until the run-up to the General Election, when Baroness Blatch, Home Office Minister of State, announced that meetings were to be suspended pending the election.

Concurrent with the development of the new training programme, described in the opening paragraphs, has been the changing shape and focus of the probation service in recent years. When the previous Conservative Government made the decision to change fundamentally the nature of probation training, it was in the context of anticipated changes to the structure and philosophy of the service, in the absence of any clear blueprint for the new model:

... a review of probation training, which appears to have an inbuilt assumption that the DipSW and higher education have failed to deliver. (Ward and Spencer 1994, p. 98)

Thus decisions were made on the basis of what the Government did not want, a training programme located within social work and higher education, rather than a training programme to meet the needs of a newly structured service. It appeared to be a desire to remove the professional status of a service, which seemed ill-advised at a time, when the service was increasingly being asked to work with high-risk offenders, and other organisations, such as nursing, were becoming increasingly professionalised. However, the probation service had, for too long, in the eyes of the Government, been allowed to dictate its purpose, be largely unaccountable to the Government or the public, and too soft on criminals. The driving force behind these proposals lay in the belief that probation practice needed to be shifted fundamentally from the traditional 'advise, assist and befriend' remit to one of control, monitoring, surveillance and discipline. The Government of the time was seeking to re-capitalise on the law and order ticket that had brought them into power in 1979, and remind the public that they were the party tough on crime. The probation service had largely failed to deliver in terms of evidence that it was effective in reducing crime through its traditional 'social work' and helping methods, and the time had come for a re-branding, and restructuring of the service. Training was a soft target, and it had proved relatively easy to remove Home Office sponsorship from programmes (Home Office 1995c) and effectively end the existing provision. In December 1995, Probation Rules (secondary legislation) were amended to remove the requirement for probation officers to hold the DipSW (or equivalent). The National Association of Probation Officers sought to have this overturned through judicial review, but on 12 February 1996, NAPO was informed that it had lost (Pillay 2000).

FOR WHAT PURPOSE WAS THE DIPLOMA IN PROBATION STUDIES ESTABLISHED?

The recent history of the probation service, since the 1971 requirement that all probation officers should be trained alongside social workers with a common award of the CQSW, has been that of a substantially qualified workforce at probation officer level. The roles and responsibilities of the probation officer were clearly defined within a professional framework for practice. Probation officers were responsible for writing reports for courts and parole boards, supervising offenders on community-based supervision orders and on license from prison, and undertaking family court welfare work. Significant numbers of 'unqualified' workers had always been employed in the service, undertaking a range of tasks alongside probation officers and generally supervised by them. These included undertaking court duty (but not writing reports), managing community service projects, supervising money payment supervision orders and performing a range of assistant roles. The role boundaries between the two positions were clearly demarcated and policed by the union, such that any attempts by services to cross boundaries and use probation assistants to undertake probation officer tasks were strongly resisted. While seen as a necessary process to protect the profession, it also left a growing workforce of unqualified staff feeling under-valued and lacking any formal career structure or training opportunities for their role. Amongst this workforce was an increasing number of black staff: an acknowledgement of the growing demand that the staff group should better reflect the offender population. However, with no clear career progression or training structure in place for these staff, it was a fairly arbitrary process that saw some gain places on DipSW programmes and others remain frustrated in their attempts to move forward in their careers.

There has been a profound shift in these boundaries in recent years, and it is not altogether clear what has been the main driver for this. One view is that the increasing erosion of the role of probation officer, by the allocation of much of their previous domain to the role of probation service officer (PSO), has been economically and politically driven, rather than aimed at meeting the professional needs of the service. The current recruitment shortage of qualified officers within the service can be directly attributed to the decision of the previous Government to withdraw sponsorship for probation students from DipSW programmes in 1996, and the two-year vacuum before the new training programme was established in 1998. In the absence of qualified officers, the service has had to find staff to plug the gaps, and so large numbers of 'unqualified workers'[1] have been appointed. This also accords with the view that the agenda of the Home Office, initiated by the previous Administration and reinforced by the Labour Government, has been to de-professionalise the service and remove the degree of autonomy previously exercised by probation officers. An alternative perspective is that the evolving National Probation Service has begun to identify the

---

[1] Many recent appointments to the role of PSO have included graduates in other disciplines such as psychology, and with a range of work experience including running groups and working in related fields.

degrees of complexity of a range of tasks and to respond to this by introducing a multi-layered workforce, which is allocated work appropriate to the different roles and qualifications. Certainly there is a great deal of routine and relatively unproblematic work within the service, which can be supervised and carried out appropriately by staff who do not hold the probation officer qualification. An effective model of case management enables, in principle, such staff to be managed and supervised to work with these tasks, thus freeing up the more highly-trained staff to work with the higher-risk, higher-complexity cases.

The Home Office decision in 1998 to identify NVQ Level 3 as the appropriate standard (and qualification) for workers to run accredited, core offending programmes for medium-risk offenders, raised concerns about the extent to which the proper analysis of levels of 'difficulty' had been undertaken. The impression at the time was that this was a pragmatic response to the dearth of qualified officers and a confirmation of an overall downgrading of the professional role of probation officer and of the skills and knowledge required to undertake group work with offenders. A more generous interpretation was that it freed up qualified staff to undertake group work and one-to-one work with the most serious and high-risk offenders. To test which of these perspectives holds the most currency would require evaluation of accredited, core offending programmes run by NVQ Level 3 staff compared with those run by qualified probation officers, and there are no current plans to do this.

The recent developments of the NVQ 3 and the Certificate in Community Justice for staff working as probation service officers has been a welcome one for a workforce that, as previously indicated, has felt itself to be under-valued and lacking in training opportunities. These developments are seen to be part of a continuum of training that offers all staff within the service career opportunities and qualifications that reflect their role. The Diploma in Probation Studies (DipPS) was presented as a core part of the development of a suite of awards that would reflect the training needs of the entire probation service workforce. Some of the difficulties faced by areas interested in developing the Certificate are linked to the urgency with which the DipPS programme was established in 1998. This urgency meant that there was little opportunity to undertake the necessary concurrent thinking and planning to map the continuum of awards, from Certificate through DipPS to post-qualifying routes, in their entirety, before one element, the DipPS, was introduced.

CORE FEATURES OF THE DIPLOMA IN PROBATION STUDIES PROGRAMME

Some issues raised by the new model of training and identified by Knight and Ward (2001, pp. 176–7) include:

- The link with an NVQ: what would be the implications of an occupational standards and competences led approach, and what place for intellectual openness and critique? How would theory and practice inter-link? The NVQ/degree combination is very complex. Is its management overly resource demanding/too expensive? Does the NVQ bring down standards to the minimum necessary as opposed to striving for best quality?
- The introduction of a contractual purchaser/provider, time-limited relationship with service consortia. How would university management view the arrangement? What scope would there be for academics to contribute proactively to the training and development of the profession?
- A new employer-led awarding body. How far would academic values and concerns figure in its interests and the requirements it would set?
- Managing the student/employee combination. Would the freedom to question, to make mistakes, be stifled? What is shared between employers and university about a trainee's progress? What happens to failing trainees?
- The majority of trainees recruited have first degrees already. How do you teach a mixed ability group? What are the consequences of the two-year time-scale in this context?
- A smaller number of programmes to cover large geographical regions. Is distance learning the answer? What are the implications of introducing distance learning into this education/training area?

If it is accepted that the NVQ structure, as a formal, national framework for learning and assessment in employment, is here to stay, the question is how to ensure that it moves in the direction of compatibility with good educational principles (Elliot 1997). Concerns expressed about the NVQ within an academic context include the fear that it brings standards of practice down to the minimum necessary for competence, rather than aiming for best practice, and knowledge requirements to the instrumental, rather than the critical. Early experiences of working with the NVQ framework have not altogether dispelled these concerns. The bureaucratic nature of the NVQ framework lends itself to very detailed attention to the minutiae of the guidelines on how to ensure that all the elements, performance criteria and range statements are met. Thus an assessment process can become preoccupied with the pedantic need to check every detail, and can miss the holistic and rounded assessment that is also required to ensure the professional role is being fulfilled. PDAs trained in the previous era of practice teaching have a firm grasp of what is required of the total assessment process. However, there is some concern that new PDAs, trained only in the NVQ assessment processes, might lack the broader perspective and be seduced by the mechanical nature of NVQ compliance into missing some of the larger concepts related to reflective and analytic practice, including the integration of theory and of values.

> NVQs are employer led and, in a managerial age, management can be reduced, as McWilliams put it, to a 'second-order activity' a conduit for implementing populist political policies, and there is a need for alternative power bases that are not so directly beholden to their political bosses. (Elliot 1997, p. 207)

The NVQ framework is not, in itself, a training or educational process, it is an assessment of competence within a work setting. Nevertheless, with progression up through the levels, the expectations of the occupational standards for the NVQ require ever-increasing levels of skills, knowledge and understanding. The underpinning knowledge required at Level 4 of an NVQ, while not directly comparable with degree level education, nevertheless has some very direct correlation. Underpinning knowledge at this level becomes a synthesis of theoretical insights and practice wisdom. On this basis, and in line with the Regulatory Framework (Senior 1998), some universities incorporate the NVQ assessment process completely within the degree structure and award it academic credit. Others have identified units of academic assessment which form the underpinning knowledge for the NVQ, and award these assessments the academic credit. While there is debate and disagreement about the differences between, and values of, these models, the issue is far from resolved, and comparative evaluation of outcomes remains to be undertaken to discover if there is any quantifiable difference. Neither of these models awards qualitative grades for practice, and it is not possible, therefore, to ascertain the quality of practice undertaken by trainees at the point of qualification, other than that competency has been achieved. Students working under intense pressure, and keen to obtain levels of 'excellence', will see that, whatever endeavour they invest in their practice, they will gain only a 'pass' or 'competent' result, whereas tenacity with academic assignments may result in a higher degree classification. This anomaly may be of concern on a programme that in other respects is striving to produce practitioners who can operate at a high level of both knowledge and skill in practice.

One of the key features of the new award was the development of the role of the PDA. Programmes have developed the role in different ways to meet the needs defined by their structures. The development of a national PDA Award may go some way to confirming core elements of this role. However, one important, emerging component is the way in which PDAs enable trainees to balance the tensions of being an employee and a student, a worker and a learner, and to mediate their learning needs within the service:

> The boundaries between theory and practice can be dismantled by PDAs who have the time (one day per trainee per week) to help their trainees make the theory to practice links come alive. It also means that debates and teaching on valuing diversity, developing equality of opportunity and practicing anti-discrimination, are part of an interactive and shared process within the programme. (Knight and White 2001, p. 207)

Perhaps the most exciting and challenging development has been around the integration of theory and practice. While the potential for disaggregation of theory from practice through the independent assessment of the NVQ was of major concern, in reality this has posed a very creative dynamic (Knight and Ward 2001), and PDAs are central to this development.

A notable improvement of the new programme from the 'old' has been the collaborative nature of the work between Higher Education Institutions (HEIs) and consortia. The new arrangements have required a real sharing of responsibility, rather than the rhetoric of partnership which, for example, left many DipSW programmes struggling to find sufficient placements to meet the demands of student numbers. The implications of both the NVQ and the fact that trainees are employees, are that the provision of practice opportunities is a service responsibility. Universities are no longer faced with the responsibility for providing placements without command over the requisite resources.

The contractual nature of the new arrangements required that the nine national consortia specified the work to be undertaken and that the HEIs delivered — a purchaser/provider arrangement, with the concept of 'partnership' not considered appropriate. In reality, the programmes could not have been established and successfully operated without the spirit of partnership in operation at each stage. Probation services, keen to regain a primary role in the training of staff, had historically been somewhat marginally involved in the previous training arrangements,[2] and initially were not well equipped to establish the rigorous, quality assured programmes required to meet the standards set for the new qualification (Knight and Ward 2001, p. 179). This sharing of responsibility is proving complex and costly in terms of human resources, and there are some indications of concern that the new scheme may prove to be 'too thorough and complex, and perhaps too expensive' (Schofield 2000, p. 256). However, it does seem more likely to produce the desired outcomes in terms of qualified workers, valued by employers who have been closely involved in their training and have made a substantial resource investment.

Trainee probation officers are service employees with all the normal terms and conditions of employment. However, they also need to be equipped to study at degree level. Probation services have not had the same experience of recruiting for potential as opposed to actual ability in their staff members, as HEIs, for whom it is key business. Probation services have also been concerned to secure staff who ideally will remain with them after qualifying, whereas HEIs' traditional responsibility ends with the completion of the programme. Balancing these two positions has required careful and continual negotiation and respect for the validity of the two positions.

The responsibility for assessment of practice has traditionally rested within the remit of practice teachers, supported by tutors and practice assessment panels on DipSWs. In the new arrangements, on most

---

[2] Probation services were members of Programme Provider Boards of the DipSW under the previous arrangements, and had scope to play an active part in course recruitment, design and delivery, but in practice they rarely developed this role to its full, active potential.

programmes, PDAs hold primary responsibility for assessment of practice through the NVQ structure, although in the initial/foundation phase of the programme, the university holds primary responsibility for assessment. The extent to which the university has a role to play in the development and assessment of professional standards in practice, is a matter of debate across the HEI programme providers. Some universities see it as a core element of their role in delivering vocational training, while others consider it should rest within the remit of the employing agencies. Some of these differences fall between the 'new' universities, which have a background of vocational training in their former lives as polytechnics, and the 'old' universities, with a more traditional focus on academic achievement, for whom competence-led NVQ structures are problematic within academic frameworks. However, this issue does not fall neatly between such a divide of 'old' and 'new', but is part of a complex and far-reaching debate about the role and purpose of vocational training within higher education.

The resolution of difficulties and problems which might arise for individual students on a DipPS programme, is an area that is increasingly being tested as the programmes evolve. Drawing up a complaints procedure that meets the requirements of the consortium, the probation service and the HEI is complex. Trainee probation officers are both students and employees. This can sometimes create an uncomfortable dynamic. While the university may be clear that they are students, with all the opportunities for learning, testing out, reflecting, challenging and making mistakes that this role entails, probation services want workers who understand the boundaries of their role and can function within these. Students may make mistakes in their practice that, from an educational perspective, constitute a good learning opportunity; but from an employer's perspective this may signal failure to meet guidelines and standards. A student may be performing competently in the workplace, but failing academically. Universities need to encourage trainees to develop their learning and analysis of their practice using appropriate strategies that enable them to develop their competency, and not leave them isolated with their 'mistakes'. Services need to recognise the validity and relevance of academic assessment and offer support, not collusion, to students who struggle with this. These issues are not always easily resolved, and these tensions are inevitable and to some extent a healthy dynamic of the new programme. Where they prove the most challenging is when a student is assessed as failing one or other element of the programme. The PDA role can be pivotal in determining how these challenges are mediated.

How to define equivalence across very different learning arenas has been variously interpreted across the different consortia areas. Probation service managers may want and expect to see their trainees in the workplace for most of the working week. Universities know that in order to study at degree level students need time, space, learning opportunities and learning resources. Some programmes have adopted a sequential model of practice blocks interspersed with academic blocks. Others have adopted a concurrent model of practice interspersed with academic teaching and study time. Inevitably, whatever structure is imposed will not necessarily meet the learning needs of all individual students, or all the service expectations of different probation areas. The extent to which students are able to integrate effectively theoretical learning within practice experience, may vary depending on their learning needs. However, experience of the part-time route for social work training has generally highlighted the ability of these students to take their academic learning directly into their employment situation more effectively than students who have been absent from practice for some months. This aspect of 'integration' would be worthy of further evaluative study.

Issues of who determines workload also vary across programmes and consortia. Probation managers are generally keen to see their trainees undertake a full range of work experience and play their part in the team. PDAs and tutors may argue that this needs to be carefully managed and controlled, with the trainee's learning needs taking priority over any service-led expediency or work demand. Trainees on most programmes are in the workplace over a longer period of time than former students on DipSW placements, and, in the concurrent models of programme delivery, are also continually juggling academic with practice-led demands. The actual numbers of cases and reports have to be carefully managed to reflect the stage the trainee is at on the programme, balanced against his or her need to undertake the full range of work. The active involvement of the line manager, and indeed work colleagues, in the training process, is crucial to the successful management of this issue.

The concept of distance learning, as a model for delivering the training across a wide geographical area, has been developed by universities in some consortia areas. Distance learning has a great deal to commend it, not least its flexibility to meet a range of learning needs and its openness in terms of curriculum design and delivery. However, without a good supportive infrastructure, that also allows trainees to come together for elements of their learning, there is a risk of isolation and fragmentation for the student learning experience. While there is clearly scope for considerable development in open, distance and e-enabled learning for the whole suite of awards in the community justice sector, early experience suggests that interactive and face-to-face teaching and learning should remain an essential component for particular stages within the educational process. Probation areas will need to move rapidly towards a comprehensive inclusion of Web-based access to resources and learning opportunities, if they are to stay abreast of national and international developments.

The identification of the qualification at undergraduate level was contentious for some, who felt that the opportunities for students with first degrees, to obtain a post-graduate award, should be maintained. Others considered it entirely appropriate that the qualification, like other professional qualifications, should be located for all at undergraduate level, with opportunities for post-qualifying awards developed at post-graduate level. Teaching a mixed ability group of students, some of whom have first (and indeed masters) degrees in social science/criminology subject areas, and others of whom have no formal higher education academic experience but years of practice experience, is challenging. However, with appropriate recognition of the value of both, and sharing across the learning group, these differences can be managed creatively. The process of accreditation of prior learning does allow for students to have validated prior learning, in both academic and practice arenas. An introduction of a post-graduate route carries the risk of reinstating a two-tier system, with Masters degree students having a greater likelihood of obtaining employment in a competitive employment field, as happened under the DipSW probation route.

At a time when, for example, social work training is moving to a three-year degree programme, with the recognition that the previous two-year Diploma and Masters programmes were insufficient in length to cover the range and depth of the subject matter, the creation of a probation degree programme that can be completed within 24 months has set a precedent which has to be carefully monitored. Trainees on current programmes find the intensity and volume of the work to be undertaken overwhelming at times. Certainly, there is little space for additional needs, such as study skills development, family commitments or ill health, to intrude without serious consequences. There is also little time for the depth of reflection and analysis normally associated with degree level education. There are moves to shorten programmes still further through the increased use of accreditation of prior learning, and it is crucial that if the quality of training and education is to be preserved, further 'short-cuts' to qualification are resisted. The question remains as to how just it is to expect this particular group of qualifying professional workers, albeit salaried trainees, to complete their course of study under greater time pressure than other comparable fields of study?

WHAT IS THE ANTICIPATED OUTCOME OF PRE-QUALIFYING TRAINING?

In the context of the above developments, what might training providers expect to be the outcome of their endeavours within the new DipPS programmes? What exactly should probation officers be able to do at the point of qualification?

The developments in the probation service nationally are set within the Government's overall aim for the criminal justice system, which identifies targets against which performance can be measured (Home Office 2000q). The *What Works Strategy for the Probation Service* (Home Office 2000s) identifies the plans for meeting these targets and outlines the design for service delivery. A complex model is presented of the interrelationship between all the different component parts, and builds on the model provided by Underdown (1998) for effective service delivery. Underdown identified the crucial role of case manager for integrating service delivery by sustaining motivation in offenders, managing risk and coordination of service delivery, and monitoring and evaluating outcomes. Within the model, service delivery, primarily via cognitive-behavioural programmes of intervention (both group and individual), formed the core tasks of the service. Programmes were, additionally, to be linked to interventions that would help offenders to address associated personal factors, such as substance misuse, mental health and relationships, and reintegration factors, such as accommodation, basic skills and employment, and would also include plans for accredited community service (re-named community punishment orders from 1 April 2001). Much of the work in the area of associated personal factors and reintegration factors would be undertaken by partnership agencies. Crucial to the model of service delivery was the core task of assessment, and work has been undertaken to devise a common assessment framework for both prison and probation service use (OASys).

It could be fairly assumed from this model of service delivery, that the role of the probation officer is to undertake the case management task, with all its complex organisational and facilitative implications, and to undertake the core offending behaviour programmes with offenders considered to be 'medium' to 'high' risk. Offenders with secondary needs and/or assessed as low risk, might be expected to be supervised and assisted by partner agencies and/or probation service officers. Such an allocation of work would underline the need for highly-trained workers, able to respond flexibly, creatively and with professional judgement to the range of complex, often contradictory and frequently very sensitive issues that arise in work with offenders assessed to be high risk and often vulnerable. The emerging picture suggests some different interpretations of what constitutes the most complex tasks within probation practice.

The drive from the Home Office, through the Accredited Programme rollout, (Home Office 2000s), is for probation staff to be able to deliver accredited group work programmes. However, as indicated earlier, the Home Office took the decision that the majority of these programmes would be run by staff trained to NVQ Level 3, the grade identified as probation service officer, and not probation officers. The latter would be confined to running group work programmes for the most serious offenders, such as sex offenders, and working on a one-to-one basis with offenders not thought suitable for group work programmes. The introduction of unit D308, managing accredited programmes for low- to medium-risk offenders, to replace E04 on group work, within the designated units for trainee probation officers, confirms the core nature of this work. However, although trainee probation officers are to learn how to run core offending, accredited programmes as part of their qualifying training,[3] they will not, as qualified officers, be expected to run these programmes. This may be a lost opportunity to test out the extent to which the training provided on the DipPS is in fact core to the ability to run these group work programmes.

---

[3] They are unlikely, however, to have the opportunity within the time span of the programme to gain their own accreditation, which requires them to run two full programmes.

The evolving role of the case manager, as identified within the What Works development, has also remained ill-defined and imprecise in its implementation (Holt 2000b). While it is possible to see it as a core and crucial probation officer task, it is currently being implemented in a range of different ways. Thus, while DipPS programmes may believe this is what they are training students for, the trainees' experience post-qualification may be very different.

The publication of the report on the Stephen Lawrence Inquiry in 1999, and the subsequent publication of the Thematic Inspection Report, *Towards Race Equality* (HMIP 2000f), have also had a significant impact on policy development within the probation service, and have been influential in the consideration of the work of the probation officer. The Inspectors concluded that race equality could not be seen as an optional extra, and that it is synonymous with good practice and is central to the core business of the probation service in addressing risk and protecting the public (HMIP 2000f). There is some irony in the fact that probation training programmes had been criticised in the Dews Report for their emphasis on anti-racism, and yet some six years later probation services are criticised for failing to address race equality adequately. The Thematic Inspection Report recommends that probation committees and chief probation officers should ensure the inclusion of appropriate mandatory training for all staff to promote race equality in annual training and staff development plans from 2001. This gives a clear message to DipPS programmes to ensure that their curriculum includes such training as core. There is, however, much less clarity about the need for staff (and students) to be trained in other equality areas, such as gender, sexuality and disability.

Eithne Wallis, Director of the National Probation Service, speaking at the Trainee Conference in 1999 on aspects of the Government's modernisation agenda that related to the probation service, referred to the effective practice agenda as involving a cultural shift in terms of structured programmes and evaluation, enforcement and the McPherson Report. She talked of the importance of training that focuses on breaking down the hard edges of some traditional approaches, and equips staff to work in the 'collective melting pot' of developing methods of service delivery. She also made reference to the importance of moving from an adversarial context to a restorative and problem-solving approach (Pillay 2000, p. 64). Her views suggest that DipPS programmes need to equip students with the skills, knowledge and awareness to work flexibly with change and innovative developments. Her words lend credence to the recent growth of restorative justice in the UK, and teaching the theoretical components of this model could be seen as core to the DipPS programme.

The speed of the developments, since the formation of the What Works project by HMIP in 1996, has been such that, while training programmes have been expected to include these changes within the curriculum, they have lacked guidance on the expected outcomes of the programme in relation to the role of probation officer. The lack of clarity in this debate is a reflection of the changing role of the probation officer and the structure of staffing within the new National Probation Service. So the extent to which trainee probation officers are being trained to be case managers (Holt 2000a), or to deliver accredited group work programmes (as opposed to one-to-one programmes within the case manager role), remains unclear. What does seem clear is that the ability to integrate theory with practice will be fundamental to the role of qualified officer, however this is defined, and of course links directly with the drive for evidence-based practice. Probation officers will increasingly need to be able to understand, interrogate and develop for themselves, the research that underpins effective practice (Knight and White 2001). This can only be achieved by practitioners who have learnt how to integrate and apply theory to practice and *vice versa*.

WHAT ARE THE KEY PRINCIPLES OF AN EFFECTIVE TRAINING PROGRAMME?

Given all the uncertainties identified above, including the still-evolving shape of the new National Probation Service, are there, nevertheless, some guiding principles on which qualifying probation training programmes should be based?

Spencer, introducing the Conference on Community Justice run by the Standing Conference of Criminal and Youth Justice Tutors in 1998, identified the themes of partnership, anti-discriminatory practice, the need to broaden and deepen knowledge, to take account of a student's previous experience and knowledge and the ability to understand and apply research (Spencer 1998). Building on these themes, annual inspections by the CJNTO reveal that the current provision does contain all of these elements and is producing probation officers of a high calibre, who are well regarded by their services. The programmes are managed successfully in partnerships between consortia and higher education, although Spencer's definition of partnership also included the wider community justice sector and, as yet, most degree programmes that include the DipPS are run predominantly for probation trainees. There is merit in training probation officers alongside workers from other disciplines, as was the case when it was located within social work training.

Anti-discriminatory practice, now frequently renamed 'working with diversity', continues to be taught, practised and assessed with considerable variation, but since the McPherson Report, has regained some of its lost status. However, 'working with diversity' risks being relegated to the same territory as 'multi-culturalism' in the 1980s — a cosy ideal that fails adequately to address the realities of disadvantage, discrimination and oppression within British society. The Thematic Inspection Report, *Towards Race Equality* (HMIP 2000f), had some hard-hitting things to say about the failure of services to address race equality adequately, and sets some rigorous targets. With this as a backdrop, maybe programme providers will find more recognition and validation of their endeavours to teach students about structural oppression and power imbalance, as it is played out within the criminal justice system; and the role of the probation officer in either perpetuating or challenging this. Similarly, the Human Rights Act 1998 has many potential implications for probation practice and for probation training. Already probation trainees are raising issues of concern related to the rights of offenders: for example, to look for and undertake paid work, when they are compelled to complete long hours of community service and accredited programmes. Students on training may be more sensitive to the implications of human rights, having the space and opportunity to test these out in academic debate, than will be their colleagues in the workplace. Services need to be able to hear the concerns raised by their trainee employees.

The need to broaden and deepen knowledge seems axiomatic, and entirely supported by the drive for evidence-based practice, which places a premium on the use of research in practice. The political drive to be seen to be reducing crime, through a largely unilateral route of accredited programmes based on a cognitive-behavioural model of change almost to the exclusion of any other approach, may be seen to compromise an open mind on effectiveness. Students completing DipPS programmes need to have highly developed critical faculties, as well as the knowledge to equip them to undertake current interventions. They need to be presented with a range of models of intervention and the theory under-pinning them, in order to sustain the eclecticism that is essential when working with complex and diverse human problems. The service needs to learn from earlier failure to evaluate practice critically, and not to stifle both potential dissent and new approaches that may emerge over the next few years.

Taking account of a student/worker's previous experience is built into the DipPS programmes through the potential for accreditation of prior learning and experience. However, of equal significance is the development of a continuum of training provision and the mapping of learning opportunities, from the first point of entry into the service, as a volunteer or probation service officer, through to post-qualifying and Masters programmes of study, which build on the Government's commitment to 'life-long learning'.

The ability to understand and apply research is assumed within the context of broadening and deepening knowledge, but has not always occurred within the history of the service. What is additionally needed is the knowledge to evaluate research critically, which is most effectively carried out when there is a sound understanding of research methodology; an essential component of the taught curriculum on the DipPS. Also needed is the encouragement for practitioners to undertake research in practice alongside academic colleagues. This will do much to enhance the credibility of the findings, to instil a culture of research within service delivery, and to debunk the myth that research only happens in the ivory tower of academia and is, therefore, unlikely to have much to say that is helpful to practitioners. While students need knowledge as information to perform tasks — the knowledge of data and facts — they also require a broad and deep understanding of the 'how' — methods, techniques and procedures — and the 'why' — a range of theoretical perspectives that will inform their professional development, as well as their day-to-day practice. There is now the potential on DipPS programmes for academic and practice institutions, working in harness, to cease to be precious about their own remits, and to be prepared to stray into one another's territory, if this enhances programme delivery (Knight and White 2001).

The increasing use of information technology and the electronic campus on programmes has generally been seen as a welcome and enhanced opportunity for students to learn. Probation services have been slow to seize on the opportunities available from access to the Internet and have been overly concerned about the potential for misuse of these systems, to the detriment of opportunities afforded. As students have demonstrated, the access to worldwide resources can only enhance learning and development, with very little evidence that access is misused:

> Equally at the heart of New Labour's mission is the pursuit of the post modern experience: Information Communication Technology (ICT) for all ... Without virtual reality systems it is unlikely that joined up thinking would ever have become a reality. (Schofield 2000)

CONCLUSION

Perhaps, finally, programmes need to develop and enhance a student's desire and thirst for learning and for the creation of new knowledge. Sadly, in times of excessive work pressure and low morale arising from the pace of change and lack of consultation, workers frequently lose this thirst for knowledge and give up on the process of 'thinking'. The importance of enabling probation trainees to be students is critical to this process. As employees, they are bound by codes of practice and an institutional culture that can limit and restrict their ability to develop their critical faculties. As students, within a higher education environment, and trainees, supervised and supported by experienced PDAs, they have permission to think the unthinkable, to challenge current orthodoxy, and to hear the views of a wide range of academic staff and experienced practitioners, who feel free to express their opinions on current developments. Programmes need to help students develop strategies for survival, not just for their health and well-being in the workplace, but also for their spirit of curiosity and desire to improve the service they offer.

18   National Standards: Defining the Service

Keir Hopley

The key role of National Standards in delivering a consistent service to the public and to offenders

INTRODUCTION

To those of us accustomed to operating in the modern National Probation Service, and used to its role as a law enforcement agency and to its ethos as an effective and efficient delivery organisation, it comes as something of a shock to discover that National Standards were introduced only some ten years ago. This chapter takes a brief look at the introduction of the first two versions of National Standards; describes in more detail the aims and gestation of the 2000 version, placing these standards in the context of the effective practice initiative and legislation that created the National Probation Service; looks to the future for further likely developments; and argues that strict adherence to National Standards is in the interests of the general public, of offenders, and of the service itself.

DEVELOPMENT OF NATIONAL STANDARDS

Today, National Standards are the rock upon which effective service delivery is moored. It is against those standards that Her Majesty's Inspectorate of Probation (HMIP) measures areas, and it is for the attainment of those standards that the Home Office provides funds to areas. And yet for most of its history, the probation service managed to operate without any National Standards and survived. Why, it might legitimately be asked, should so much emphasis be placed on National Standards now? Why could not the service carry on as before?

The author does not propose to enter a debate on the performance of the probation service throughout most of the twentieth century. But it is abundantly clear that, whatever its successes — and at the level of individual offenders, or 'clients' as they were then known, there were many — the service failed to convince the Conservative Government of the 1990s that it fulfilled a function that deserved investment. National Standards were introduced as a measure to try to achieve consistency of performance, and to guide the service in ways that would be likely to command public support. National Standards were not welcomed by some staff, neither were they always treated seriously. This further damaged the service's reputation with Ministers, who were inclined to believe in the value of imprisonment and to want to concentrate their resources in that direction. This failure to persuade politicians of the service's value cost it dearly in the 1990s, most starkly when recruitment policies were changed, in effect depriving the service of a whole tranche of staff that it misses to this day.

Opposition to National Standards consisted — and still consists in isolated pockets of antediluvian officers — of two main strands. First, staff did not like to be told what to do, not by their own management, and most certainly not by Government. The second limb of this view was shared by many local senior managers. Secondly, there was distrust of anything that tried to impose consistency, or uniformity, as its critics would say: National Standards, it was argued, led to cloning of probation officers and stifling of individual ideas and creativity. As a slight variant of this theme, it was alleged that measurement was inappropriate, that 'clients' were all different and needed to be helped, fulfilling the old duty to 'assist, advise and befriend' that was contained in probation legislation since the start (Probation of Offenders Act 1907) and was swept away only with the creation of the National Probation Service. This was an attitude representative of some unionised staff in the 1980s and early 1990s across all sectors of the economy, that was memorably typified in a poster produced by the Home Office branch of the CPSA[1] that simply read 'Say no to objectives', in this context, specific objectives in staff appraisals.

So officials introducing the first version of National Standards in 1992 (Home Office 1992b) had to tread very carefully. They were trying to set standards and to achieve consistency, but they were doing so in a very difficult context, where operational management, staff and unions distrusted them, were wary of Government intervention, and in many cases were not keen on the concept in the first place. So it is not surprising that, compared with the current version, those standards are long, timid and less than precise in a number of areas. They read more as guidance than as requirements, even allowing for characteristic Civil Service style where 'you may care to consider going' means 'go'. The updated version, produced in 1995 (Home Office 1995a), was somewhat shorter and more *dirigiste*.

When the new Labour Government came to office in 1997, Ministers were prepared to look more favourably upon the probation service. They did not have the same attitude that 'prison works', and the implied corollary that community punishment does not. Rather, the Home Secretary, Jack Straw, repeated on many occasions that he had no ideal prison population figure in his mind. Who was sent to prison was a matter for the courts to determine. The Government's job was to deliver the sentences pronounced by the courts, both custodial and community.

It became very clear that Ministers' desire to improve public services extended to probation. Ministers were prepared to invest, but only if they thought there was a better than even chance that they would get some worthwhile return on their investment. So, in order to attract resources, the probation service had to demonstrate that it could help to deliver the Government's agenda. In particular, it needed to make a worthwhile contribution to the achievement of Home Office Aim 4 — 'effective execution of the sentences of the court so as to reduce reoffending and protect the public' (Home Office 2000k).

---

[1] Civil and Public Services Association, the trades union for Civil Service clerical staff, now part of the Public and Commercial Services Union.

In order to deliver this aim, a broad offensive was opened on two main fronts. First, great attention was paid, by the then Probation Unit of the Home Office, by HMIP and by individual services, to developing the effective practice initiative, now better known by the shorthand of What Works. Secondly, a much more robust approach to performance management was required, particularly in the area of enforcement, where the probation service's record was abysmal. Both these fronts came together in the 2000 version of National Standards (Home Office 2000k).

What Works challenged two credos that had become popular during the 1980s and early 1990s. First, there was the belief that nothing worked. Despite increased investment in the police, the introduction of flash new technology for investigating crime and political rhetoric about being tough on crime, crime figures continued inexorably to rise: a graph of crime figures since the First World War shows virtually a straightline increase throughout the period. Therefore, there was no point putting resources into dealing with criminals when sentenced; the best thing to do was keep them locked up for a period so as to provide some respite for the crime-weary general public. What Works sought to dispel this belief by examining the evidence of effectiveness of various interventions in terms of their effects on reconvictions, the best proxy measure that has so far been devised for reoffending, and then devising programmes designed to address the criminogenic needs identified.

Secondly, What Works challenged the practice of individualism that had been embedded in probation services since time immemorial. In general, each service had its own programmes, which were seldom evaluated and could not be proven to work — or otherwise. There was not even consistency within individual probation services, as separate offices (or indeed members of staff) pursued their pet theories and beliefs. It is easy to be scornful of this now, but nothing better was known, and many offenders were helped not to reoffend and to improve their lives. But something more was needed to satisfy Ministers, who believed that all offenders under probation service supervision should be dealt with in such a way as to increase the likelihood that they would not reoffend.

The logic of What Works was that all programmes should be evaluated. Those that were proven to work would be replicated throughout the country; those that did not would be abandoned. In other words, interventions with offenders should be restricted to the ones that were scientifically proven to be effective. Moreover, research showed that 'programme integrity' — that is, delivering exactly the prescribed programme in exactly the prescribed way — was crucial to effectiveness. So the aim soon became to develop a core curriculum of effective programmes that could be delivered throughout the country. Despite the existence of dedicated accreditation machinery for What Works, it can easily be seen that there is a clear link with National Standards, which are themselves trying to deliver national consistency.

If What Works, along with the developing role in public protection, particularly from dangerous offenders, is the jewel in the probation service crown, its Achilles' heel was clearly enforcement. By the late 1990s, sentencers were frustrated by their inability to pass a community sentence knowing that it would be administered effectively. The general public, helped by the media headlines along the lines of 'Bloggs walks free from court with a probation order', believed that community sentences were not effective punishment, and Ministers, not surprisingly, believed that the service was massively underperforming. So Ministers launched a major offensive on enforcement, challenging the service to raise its game. This challenge was accepted by the Association of Chief Officers of Probation (ACOP) and its then Chair, Geoff Dobson. ACOP conducted an audit in January 1999 as to services' performance against the National Standards (1995 version), and took the brave step of publishing the results (ACOP 1999). These results were bad: on the key indicator of breach at third failure to comply with the order, they showed that only 44 per cent of cases were indeed breached, with properly authorised management discretion not to breach for exceptional reasons being exercised in a further 7 per cent. And the level of inconsistency was staggering: in one area, only 8 per cent of cases were breached.

Clearly, action was needed quickly. ACOP realised that it had to concentrate all its efforts on improving enforcement if the service were to have any credibility with the general public and with Ministers. A major improvement campaign was therefore put in place, with active encouragement from Ministers and the Probation Unit. Considerable improvement has been made, with performance rising to 66 per cent in a second audit carried out in September 1999 and to 70 per cent in a third in September 2000 (ACOP 1999, 2000, 2001). The third audit measured against the new National Standard, of which more below.

NATIONAL STANDARDS 2000

The rollout of What Works and the increased emphasis on enforcement caused a fundamental review of National Standards to be begun in late 1998. The aim was to complete the work that had only partially been done in the previous two versions in setting absolute standards that the Government would expect the service to meet: only those items that were mandatory would be included in the Standards themselves; guidance would be kept separate and issued as such. And aspirational *obiter* would be edited out ruthlessly.

The author led the team that reviewed the 1995 National Standards and drafted the 2000 version. While his initial target of reducing the length of the document to 12 pages of A4 (as opposed to some 75 pages of A5 in the 1995 version, and more than 120 in the 1992 edition) was certainly not achieved, the Standards are now much clearer in what they require, and shorter and sharper in the way they are expressed. Areas are left in no doubt as to what is required, and on what they will be assessed by the Inspectorate.

The 1995 National Standards predated What Works. The 2000 version, in contrast, embraced the principles and identified good practice. So, for example, much is made of risk assessment, the central role of the supervision plan, and accredited programmes, with the central importance of protection of the public and reduction of reoffending running like strong threads throughout the document.

Another key difference from earlier versions is that the 2000 National Standards place the emphasis firmly on those things that are within the control of probation areas. So, for example, the Standards now specify the number of appointments to be offered, rather than the number to be attended, because whether or not the offender turns up is his or her responsibility, not that of the service. There has been some criticism that this puts the emphasis on process rather than results. But that is wide of the mark: if an offender does not turn up, National Standards require appropriate enforcement action to be taken.

The type of action to be taken and the timescale for that is very clearly set out in the 2000 National Standards. Ministers took a deliberate policy decision to use the new Standards as a mechanism for tightening up the enforcement of community sentences. Whereas the 1995 version required breach action to be taken no later than the third failure to comply with an order, the 2000 Standards require action no later than the second failure.

So Ministers now clearly see National Standards as an essential weapon in their armoury for driving up performance across the probation service. This is itself an essential part of the modernisation strategy for the service that has three prongs, as described by the then Prisons and Probation Minister, Paul Boateng, in 1999. First is What Works. This is the essential positive work that is being developed in the service to improve the product that is delivered to offenders, so as to reduce the likelihood that they will reoffend and to increase public protection. Secondly, there are improvements to the regulatory framework in which the service operates. National Standards are the key here, setting the parameters for all major aspects of the service's work. Lastly, there are changes to the infrastructure, so as to enable the other two prongs to work more effectively.

The order of the three prongs is important. Although structural reform has had the greatest public attention in recent months on account of the passage of the Criminal Justice and Court Services Act 2000 and the establishment of the National Probation Service for England and Wales with effect from 1 April 2001, Ministers always saw this as being in support of the primary purpose: embedding What Works and improving performance, so as to deliver Home Office Aim 4.

The 2000 Act does show, however, how deeply the approach and rationale adopted by National Standards have become embedded in thinking about the service. The 2000 National Standards have a preliminary sheet that contains a quotation from Paul Boateng: 'We are a law enforcement agency. That is what we are. That is what we do' (Home Office 2000k). Boateng used those words very deliberately to signify the change in culture from a social work or welfare-based organisation to one whose aims indeed were to reduce reoffending and protect the public. That philosophy has been carried forward into the legislation, which for the first time clearly defines the purposes, aims and functions of the service:

1.—(1)   This Chapter has effect for the purposes of providing for—
    (a)   courts to be given assistance in determining the appropriate sentences to pass, and making other decisions, in respect of persons charged with or convicted of offences, and
    (b)   the supervision and rehabilitation of such persons.
  (2)   Subsection (1)(b) extends (in particular) to—
    (a)   giving effect to community orders,

    (b)   supervising persons released from prison on licence,

    (c)   providing accommodation in approved premises ...

2.—(1) This section applies to—

    (a)   the functions of the Secretary of State under this Chapter,

    (b)   the functions of local probation boards, and officers of local probation boards, under this Act or any other enactment, so far as they may be exercised for the purposes mentioned in section 1.

    (2) In exercising those functions the person concerned must have regard to the following aims—

    (a)   the protection of the public,

    (b)   the reduction of reoffending,

    (c)   the proper punishment of offenders,

    (d)   ensuring offenders' awareness of the effects of crime on the victims of crime and the public,

    (e)   the rehabilitation of offenders.

3.—(1) The Secretary of State has the function of ensuring that provision is made throughout England and Wales for the purposes mentioned in section 1 ...

The duty to assist, advise and befriend was repealed by the 2000 Act.

It is, of course, impossible to predict the future with accuracy. No one can be certain as to the identity and approach of Ministers to come, let alone the impact of seminal events in criminal history. But one can extrapolate from the history of National Standards and the 2000 Act in a couple of areas.

First, it is clear that performance management culture is here to stay for the foreseeable future. Not only did the 2001 Labour Party Manifesto (Labour Party 2001) continue to place much emphasis on improving the quality of public services, but policies issuing from the new National Probation Directorate also point in this direction. There is now a Head of Planning and Performance at senior civil servant level, and the intention is to put in place a performance management framework that will measure all aspects of areas' performance, with particular emphasis on National Standards. Performance against a basket of National Standards measures will also count for 50 per cent of the performance link being introduced into probation area funding. In other words, for the first time, grants to individual probation areas will depend to some extent on their performance against National Standards.

Moreover, National Standards may well themselves be given statutory backing. By virtue of para. 12 of Sch. 1 to the 2000 Act, the Home Secretary has the power to direct local probation boards as to the way in which they fulfil their functions. It is possible that the general instruction to follow National Standards may become a formal direction using these powers.

The author would argue that greater consistency of approach through What Works, and more effective administration of community sentences through tougher and clearer National Standards and the creation of the National Probation Service are self-evidently good for the service. This approach gives the service its best chance of making a difference to and with offenders and, at the same time, increasing its own professionalism and credibility in the eyes of sentencers, the general public and Ministers, including Treasury Ministers, who will look very hard at competing demands for resources. While not all who work within the service would necessarily be enthusiastic about the change of direction, few would seek to argue against the logic of the approach.

The benefits to the courts, the general public and Ministers would also seem fairly obvious. The courts have a right to expect that the sentences they impose will be administered properly, and that offenders will be held to account for their attendance, behaviour and performance. The general public want to be reassured that community sentences really do make a difference to offending behaviour. And both they and Ministers will benefit, if there is an effective alternative to custody that is considerably cheaper. Ministers too need to be satisfied that any institution into which they invest public money, is likely to give a good return on that money.

But what of offenders? How should they regard what is generally viewed as a toughening of the approach to community sentences? Prima facie, they should be worried. Ministers have signalled their intention to ensure that community sentences (and licences) are properly enforced, and offenders will come to realise that community sentences are not a soft option. This will become even more so when s. 53 of the 2000 Act is implemented and sanctions for breach of community sentences become more severe, with imprisonment more likely to result.

But there is also great potential benefit for offenders. For those who do not want a life of crime, it is an advantage that the work the probation service will do with them is based on something that is proven to work, rather than on whatever interests the probation officer responsible for their supervision. Effectiveness in supervision, accredited programmes, work as part of a community punishment order or a community punishment and rehabilitation order, and effectiveness in basic skills provision can all make a major difference to an offender's chances of finding employment and avoiding further offending.

Secondly, offenders can now have a much better idea as to how they will be treated by the probation service, wherever their offending has taken place. A nationally consistent approach to enforcement means a much more level playing field for offenders: they know that, if they behave in certain ways, they will face sanctions; and they know that, if other offenders behave in those ways, those offenders too will face sanctions. The lottery of a hard or soft probation officer, office or area will be removed, and offenders will all be treated fairly in accordance with open and transparent Standards that are published, have a basis in law, and are freely available. This is very much in line with the principles of the European Convention on Human Rights.

Thirdly, the development of a core curriculum, with National Standards for the number of appointments to be offered and other contact levels, means that an offender who transfers from one part of the country to another, will find it much easier to take up where he or she has left off in attending a programme; and he or she will know what to expect from the staff who are supervising him or her and what they will require of him or her. In time, closer links with the Prison Service and commonality of accredited programmes will mean that those released on licence will be able to fit into appropriate programmes in the community within their home area, regardless of whether they have been released from Acklington Prison in Northumbria or from Albany on the Isle of Wight.

National Standards require all offenders to be treated fairly, irrespective of race, religion, ethnicity, sex or sexual orientation. The National Probation Directorate is looking to develop accredited programmes dealing with the criminogenic needs of women and ethnic minority offenders, and is monitoring the attendance at and performance on accredited programmes by offenders according to race and sex. While there is still a long way to go in making sure that all offenders are treated equally and receive an equally good service (HMIP 2000f), again, the publication of transparent, clear and unambiguous National Standards ensures that performance can be assessed easily and lessons learned.

So the author concludes that, while offenders are placed in potentially a more punitive position and culture than previously by the greater emphasis on compliance and enforcement in the 2000 National Standards, a more consistent approach will mean that they are treated more fairly, and that those who want to benefit from probation service supervision and be helped to turn away from crime, will be more able to do so.

While National Standards are the responsibility of Ministers, in working up the 2000 edition, the Home Office was assisted by a steering group comprising representatives of all interested parties, in the probation service and in the wider criminal justice system, including, *inter alia*, sentencers, the police and the voluntary sector. While, unsurprisingly, there was not unanimity on every point, neither was there any major disagreement. And even those parts of the service that would have preferred to see less emphasis on law enforcement, nonetheless welcomed the clarity that the new Standards offered. All of which suggests that National Standards, and central regulation through them, are very much here to stay.

19   Probation Service Performance and Accountability: the Role of Inspection

Jane Furniss

INTRODUCION

Our parents grew up in the generation which displayed a generally grateful and unquestioning acceptance of services provided by the state — our justice system, National Health Service and state education were seen as the best in the world. Doctors and teachers (among other public service professionals) were seen as figures of status in society, who had only the public interests at heart. By comparison, our children belong to the generation of the Internet and the mobile phone, and expect fast and individual attention delivered to fit in with their needs — NHS Direct, telephone banking and call centres, for example. They are also less likely to believe in altruism, and are more questioning about both the motives and competence of public servants. We no longer believe the state knows best; no longer willing to 'trust me, I'm a doctor'. High-profile cases — miscarriages of justice, Stephen Lawrence and the Bristol heart doctors — undermine faith in those traditionally seen as trustworthy. What role can inspectorates play in ensuring that public expectations are met and confidence in public services built and improved?

The 1980s saw a growth in the number of independent regulator bodies designed to focus on performance and sharpen accountability.

As more and more targets and standards were set centrally, based on thinking that those responsible for implementation were the opposition, who need to be controlled by a mixture of carrot and stick, regulators were seen as a response to service delivery failures, inefficiency and lack of probity. There has been a plethora of reports and recommendations emanating from audit, inspection and regulatory bodies designed to tackle these perceptions of public services.

But the golden era of the inspector/auditor may be coming to an end. There are signs that central Government's love affair with the regulator may be on the wane. Increasingly questions are being asked: What do we get for our investment in audit and inspection? Is there any evidence that the UK's high ratio of auditors/inspectors to those engaged in service delivery has done anything for improving performance and raising standards? Does the emphasis on faults and errors create a blame culture and inhibit learning from mistakes? Does the focus on processes and the 'rules', on the *minutiae* rather than strategy, hinder innovation? Is the regulatory burden on managers and practitioners too heavy? Given the recognised need for joined-up delivery, does it make sense to have such a range of inspection and audit bodies responsible for different public services, and are they inconsistent in their methods and the standards they use for measuring and judging performance? *Quis custodiet ipsos custodes!*?[1]

Her Majesty's Inspectorate of Probation (HMIP) is an independent inspectorate, originally established in 1936, and given statutory authority in the Criminal Justice Act 1991. The Criminal Justice and Court Services Act 2000 renames HMIP, 'Her Majesty's Inspectorate of the National Probation Service for England and Wales'. The Inspectorate is funded by the Home Office and reports directly to the Home Secretary. It is a fundamental principle that it retains its independence from both the policy-making and operational functions of the National Probation Service for England and Wales. It has a wider remit than merely inspection, and its current strategic statement, agreed by the Chief Inspector with the Home Secretary, states that its purpose is to:

(a)   report to the Home Secretary on the extent to which the National Probation Service for England and Wales is fulfilling its statutory duties,

---

[1] 'Who will watch over the watchers themselves?' (Juvenal, *Satires*, VI, 347).

contributing to the achievement of Home Office aims and meeting performance targets as required;

(b) demonstrate that inspections improve the performance of the National Probation Service;

(c) contribute to sound policy and effective service delivery by providing advice and disseminating good practice based on inspection findings to Ministers, the National Directorate and probation boards/areas; and

(d) promote actively race equality and diversity in the National Probation Service.

HMIP combines a professional development and disseminating best practice responsibility with its inspection duties and, on the basis of both, advises Ministers and officials and contributes to sound policy-making for the work of the probation service. It aims both to account for the performance of the probation service to Ministers and the public, and enable the service to develop and improve its performance.

So how does HMIP meet its aims and respond to the challenges set out above?

WHAT DO WE GET FOR OUR INVESTMENT IN INSPECTION? IS THERE ANY EVIDENCE THAT HMIP HAS DONE ANYTHING FOR IMPROVING PERFORMANCE AND RAISING STANDARDS?

HMIP's budget is small in itself — approximately £1.3 million for 2000/01 — and as a proportion of the total national cash limited probation budget (approx £380 million in that year). This does not include all the costs of the Inspectorate, as the budget is not fully devolved. Accommodation and some related costs for the Queen Anne's Gate offices are met centrally from the Home Office wider budget. Based on the devolved budget, an inspector day rate comes out at around £430. Based on the budget and the inspector day rate, the cost of a probation area inspection ranges between £19,000 and £35,000, depending on the size of the local area and the number of inspector days required. The cost of a full, large-scale national thematic is around £150,000, while a more limited piece of work (the inspection of the Langley Trust Hostels) costs approximately £35,000.

Does the public get value for its money? To answer that question we need to know how to measure the effectiveness of inspection activity, and compare the performance of HMIP and the cost of its activity with similar bodies. No such exercise has been undertaken, although in 1997 the Home Office did carry out an internal (unpublished) benchmarking exercise of its inspectorates. As a result, HMIP was judged to be an organisation which completed a very full inspection programme at a low cost. But the exercise was a limited one, and there was no attempt made to judge the impact of our work on probation service performance.

In the same way that in recent years Ministers, officials and the probation service itself have become clearer about how to judge the service's performance, so has HMIP. While HMIP does not have the responsibility for making policy, deciding strategy or determining the standards for the service's work, it has a key role to play in all those processes. Based on our inspection findings and professional expertise, we provide significant advice to Ministers and officials who make the decisions. It is important, however, that the setting of the policy expectations and National Standards is separate from the judgement (through inspection) of implementation. Ultimately the former is a job for Ministers, advised by officials; and the latter is a job for HMIP.

In planning its inspections, HMIP establishes a set of standards and criteria, against which the service's performance will be judged. These standards, which are published, are based on the current legislation, policy, National Standards, key performance indicators and targets, which are set by the Home Secretary and supplemented, when appropriate, by what is regarded as good professional practice, including that which research indicates is likely to be effective.

HMIP judges its own effectiveness by its impact on service performance and on the extent to which the recommendations in its reports[2] are implemented. The recommendations made in the area quality and effectiveness inspections became, over time, more outcome focused. When areas received their follow-up visit to inspect progress, in 1999/2000 it was judged that on average 96 per cent of recommen-

---

[2] All HMIP inspection reports are published and available to the public. See website at www.homeoffice.gov.uk/hmiprob.htm for details.

dations had been fully or partially implemented.[3] In the current performance inspection programme (PIP), the extent to which area performance improves against the Home Secretary's expectations and standards, is central to our overall judgement of both service performance and our own effectiveness. Our recommendations are very clearly outcome/performance focused, and are aimed at ensuring that a local area's performance is improved against those expectations and standards. It is early days to make judgements, as at the time of writing few areas have been re-inspected following the PIP. The evidence, however, to date is that in the follow-up inspection, we are finding that the majority of probation areas show evidence of progress, with many having made significant efforts to implement the recommendations, with evidence of impact in improving performance.[4]

Clearly the responsibility for implementation of inspection recommendations and improvement of performance lies with the local chief officer and probation board, but it is also a measure of HMIP's performance. If our recommendations are not implemented and our inspections result in little or no improvement, Ministers, the service and the public have a right to ask questions about our effectiveness.

A further criterion, by which HMIP would judge its effectiveness, would be the extent to which the Inspectorate ensures the dissemination of best practice and contributes to organisational professional practice development. In this regard HMIP has a sound track record, particularly through its thematic inspection programme. For example, the thematic inspection on *The Victim Perspective* (HMIP 2000e) identified a lack of policy and guidance within the Home Office for the work of the probation service, and has since resulted in significant policy development. The thematic inspection *Towards Race Equality* (HMIP 2000f) made a series of recommendations for improvements in employment practice and work with offenders, all of which were fully accepted by Ministers and officials and resulted in an action plan to ensure implementation nationally and locally. HMIP advice and expertise, based on our inspection knowledge, is therefore called on in relation to both inspection reports and subsequent programmes of work to improve policy, practice and performance.

---

[3] See HMIP Annual Report 1998 and 1999/2000, and individual quality and effectiveness inspection reports and follow-up reports.
[4] See performance inspection reports and follow-up reports.

It is HMIP's role over the last four years in the What Works initiative, which is arguably its greatest achievement. During a period when there was no formal central leadership of the probation service, HM Chief Inspector of Probation frequently played the role of 'head of the profession' as well as its regulator. The production of the report *Strategies for Effective Offender Supervision* (Underdown 1998) and the *Evidenced Based Practice Guide* (Chapman and Hough 1998), plus HMIP's role in the initial development of the pathfinders, were pivotal, and there is little doubt that the effective practice/What Works initiative would not have developed nationally without HMIP's leadership (Nutley and Furniss 2000).

Both offenders and victims have a right to a probation service which performs in ways that the evidence suggests will best meet their needs, by reducing crime and protecting victims. They also have a right to know just how well the service is doing against those expectations. For the future, as the National Probation Directorate rolls out an increasing number of evidence-based offender supervision programmes, HMIP will audit and inspect how local areas are performing against the methods and standards set by the Joint Accreditation Panel, which the research indicates will lead to lower re-offending and improved community integration of those being supervised by the probation service.

In the past the Home Office Probation Unit took a relatively neutral approach to a probation service which HMIP found to be repeatedly performing below standard. In the future, the new National Director, who is accountable to Ministers for the overall performance of the service, will not be neutral. Probation areas are likely to be asked to produce action plans setting out how they intend to bring about improvement, and the Director and her staff will want to see evidence of progress before the inspectors return. HMIP will need to judge the effectiveness of the action plan, how well it has been implemented and what impact it has had on the performance of the probation area. A judgement will also need to be made about the effectiveness of the National Director in overseeing and ensuring the required improvements. The Criminal Justice and Court Services Act 2000 provides the Home Secretary, for the first time, with powers to intervene in a probation area, and for HMIP to be asked to undertake a specific inspection to ascertain whether this is necessary.

IS THERE TOO MUCH EMPHASIS ON FAULTS AND ERRORS AND A BLAME CULTURE, WHICH INHIBITS LEARNING FROM MISTAKES?

There has been over the last ten years, alongside the growth of public regulators, a growing recognition in the public sector of the need to develop a culture of no blame and learning from mistakes, as a necessary way of improving performance. If staff cannot admit to making a mistake in case they are subjected to disciplinary procedures and dismissal, they will play safe, take no risks and cover up mistakes in a way which is unhelpful and even dangerous. While they should not condone wilful rule-breaking, public organisations need to create a safe environment, which allows for human error and for mistakes to be acknowledged and seen as beneficial to organisational development. The probation service needs to develop formal ways of learning from mistakes. The serious incident reporting process has not adequately provided this, for reasons documented elsewhere (HMIP 2001), and has on occasions been used by the press as a stick with which to beat the service (*The Guardian* 2001).

There has been much talk of the OFSTED model of inspection, which is seen as the archetypal 'brutalised naming-and-shaming model of inspection' (Travers 2000) and necessarily something to be avoided by other inspectorates. Chris Woodhead and his style of inspection are seen as to blame for low morale, a mass exodus from the teaching profession, a lack of new recruits and even for individual cases of suicide. Whether the perception is accurate has become almost irrelevant. The Chief Inspector of Prisons' reports have highlighted appalling standards of performance, and newspapers regularly headline 'Report slams failing prison ...', but Lord Laming's Report (Home Office 2000j) indicates, and even Sir David Ramsbotham himself believes, that little within prisons has improved as a result.

The accusations against HMIP have been less dramatic. In the distant past, if its existence was known, it was seen as at best worthy but dull — an irrelevance to most probation managers and practitioners. More recently, it has been accused of being primarily negative. Inspectors are seen as being rigorous in finding out and enthusiastic in finding fault, but grudging in giving praise. Even though it is recognised by service mangers that HMIP has played a significant role in identifying and promoting best practice in its inspection reports, and led the development of the What Works initiative, it is the critical reports which get most press coverage and arguably have most impact on service managers.

A key role for any inspectorate is public accountability — publicising information about the service's performance. The public have a right to know the extent to which their local service is delivering. This may be of particular importance for a probation area, as the profile of the service is low and most members of the public would not regard themselves as 'receiving' its services. By comparison there is huge public interest in prisons and their inspection reports are widely reported in the press — even if the public are divided between those who are outraged on human rights' grounds at the findings, and those who believe that the shocking findings are no more than prisoners deserve.

Publication of inspection reports, which reveal to the public, stakeholders and users how poorly some probation areas are performing, risks undermining confidence in the probation service itself and, therefore, damaging its place in the criminal justice system. Is publication of high-profile and critical reports, with league tables which 'name and shame' followed by press calls for the sacking of the guilty managers, the way to improve performance? Is the 'Rottweiler inspector' an effective way to get poorly performing probation services to improve and raise their game? Is it possible for the same organisation to 'praise and acclaim', disseminate and inspire best practice, as well as 'name and shame'?

HMIP believes it is not only possible, but also vital. The public have a right to know how their local service compares with the standards set centrally and with other similar services. This is why HMIP in the performance inspections has adopted the practice of publishing comparative tables and grading the overall standard of an area's performance. Areas are graded 1, when judged to be performing generally satisfactorily; 2, when it is judged that weaknesses and strengths are fairly equally balanced; and 3, when weaknesses outweigh strengths. The category then determines the type of future inspection, which takes place to follow up implementation of our recommendations.[5]

Delivery of public services always depends on staff, managers and the organisations to which they belong. Inspections which leave

---

[5] See full description of categories and the follow-up inspections in Chapter 8 of any performance inspection report.

managers and staff feeling only criticised and blamed for poor performance, are unlikely to produce insight and staff motivated to change, improve and perform as required in the following weeks and months. It is, after all, those managers and staff — not the Home Secretary, the National Probation Director or HM Inspectors — who will be preparing the court report, assessing that dangerous offender or running the offending behaviour course next week and next month. Excessive central direction, which undermines the proper use of professional skills, the exercise of discretion and judgement, will ultimately fail. We need probation staff who know when to follow the rules to the letter and when to use their judgement because the rulebook does not help. An inspectorate must be able to inspire the highest standards and be the disseminator of good practice, as well as the organisation which exposes the service and holds it publicly to account for poor performance.

This is a delicate balance, and HMIP seeks to achieve it by adopting a style which 'enables' as well as accounts for performance. It is our expectation that our staff are able to conduct themselves in a way which is rigorous and evidence-based, provides clear and critical feedback about an area's performance against the standards expected, and does so in a way which inspires managers and staff and helps them to change and improve. If managers and staff want only to 'shoot the messenger', little will be gained, however evidence-based and rigorous the inspection. Inspection and audit findings need to be delivered in a manner which makes clear that poor performance is unacceptable and will not be tolerated. Equally, inspectors need to demonstrate that they believe in the organisation's ability and willingness to improve, and that the Inspectorate can provide the support and assistance to help put things right, based on our knowledge of best practice and what works.

For the future, HMIP will be examining local area performance within the framework of national direction, policies and strategies. It will be important that we are seen to be as robust in our approach to the Directorate as we are to local boards, identifying those issues in which we see poor performance at the centre as well as in the local areas, and focusing attention on how performance overall can be raised and improved. The thematic inspection on information and technology is an early example of how our inspections can report on poor performance by the Home Office (HMIP 2000b).

DOES HMIP FOCUS ON PROCESSES AND THE 'RULES', ON THE MINUTIAE RATHER THAN STRATEGY AND HINDER INNOVATION?

Although it is not the role of HMIP to set the standards for the work of the service, it has over the years played a key role in helping to establish policy, standards and best practice. It would be foolish to pretend we do not have a body of wisdom and a national picture based on our inspections about current practice — what is working and what is not, and more importantly why. We also have a group of inspectors who have sound experience of probation service practice and management, which can be used to good effect in establishing what policy should look like, what strategies will assist and what standards will help us all to know whether we are on track.

One of the criticisms of auditors and inspectors is that they know how to count, but don't know what counts. They focus — the theory goes — on measuring what can be counted, rather than on what counts and will make a difference. They are too focused on processes rather than on outcomes, on the *minutiae* of the rules rather than on strategy. They are too keen on the *status quo* and skewed against innovation, and are always against taking a risk. The enforcement agenda is used to illustrate the point for HMIP by some pundits.

Since 1992, probation services have been expected to supervise offenders to National Standards (Home Office 2000k) set by Ministers following full consultation with service managers and staff and on the advice of both Home Office officials and HMIP. Sentencers and other stakeholders are also consulted in the process. Over recent years, HMIP's inspections have repeatedly shown poor performance against these Standards in many probation areas, particularly in requiring the offender to report to the expected frequency and taking the appropriate steps if he or she fails to do so. Ministers have seen improvement in this as being a litmus test of the service's willingness to change from a social welfare organisation 'on the side' of the offender to one which put public protection and law enforcement at the top of its priorities.

HMIP has focused significant attention on measuring and reporting the service's performance against the National Standards, and not just on those that can be 'counted'. We have used our professional judgement to examine, for example, how well probation staff have challenged offending behaviour, sought to develop some awareness in the offender of the impact of crime on victims and ensured that public protection is given the highest priority. We have tried to ensure that the focus is on ensuring compliance — getting the offender to report regularly — rather than merely breach action — returning the offender to court when he or she fails to report. But perhaps inevitably the message is heard as being 'breach offenders' instead of 'ensure you offer them something worthwhile, chase them up when they fail to report, engage them in the process of supervision and use the discipline of the order to get them to work with you, because the evidence is that, if you do, you will help to reduce offending'.

In conducting its inspections, HMIP makes widespread use of service staff to assess the work being scrutinised. Within a region, local staff are recruited and briefed to assist in file-reading exercises and in observing probation staff working with individual and groups of offenders. This has a number of benefits, as it ensures that the judgements made include the views of the practitioners who work with offenders day to day. It also means that lessons learned from the process can be fed back to the service by those staff to assist learning and improve practice. The inspection findings and judgements are more likely to be based in the 'real world' that staff inhabit, and are less likely to feel as if the work of staff is being judged by 'the Home Office inspector'. A further spin-off is that services gain a group of staff who have learned some rigorous inspection skills for future local use.

HMIP has worked hard not to become seen as an organisation which takes a tape measure to the service and finds it failing because it does not measure up. We need to balance measuring the 'what' and the 'how' and focus mainly on the what (the outcome) and only on the how (the process) when there is sound evidence that one method is demonstrably more effective than another. We also need to allow for/encourage innovation and learning/development for the future. Measuring services' performance against current expectations only, can be stultifying. We need to be evidence-based — where there is evidence that an approach or approaches are more effective, or where there are clear ministerial/public expectations, we should be absolutely rigorous in expecting these to be followed; but where there is no such evidence, we should be neutral and enquiring on methodology. We aim to be open and encouraging about the development of new methods, to accept that in order to learn and develop, some risk may need to be taken. At the same time, we should expect managers to monitor and evaluate both the outcome and process, so that the approach is one of proper experimentation, innovation and learning, not idiosyncratic practice.

IS THE REGULATORY BURDEN ON PROBATION MANAGERS AND PRACTITIONERS TOO HEAVY? DOES IT MAKE SENSE TO HAVE 6 INSPECTION AND TWO AUDIT BODIES RESPONSIBLE FOR THE DIFFERENT PARTS OF THE CRIMINAL JUSTICE SYSTEM AND ARE THEY INCONSISTENT IN THEIR METHODS AND THE STANDARDS THEY USE FOR MEASURING AND JUDGING PERFORMANCE?

During the last three to five years, most probation services have received an inspection visit from HMIP at least every two years, and many annually. Every service was inspected during the five-year quality and effectiveness programme, and received a visit some two years after report publication to follow up progress. Additionally around 10–15 services have been visited for each of the national thematic inspections, of which two or three have been undertaken each year. Ministers were keen to see this level of scrutiny because of the lack of central control and accountability for probation, because of concerns that performance against Ministerial expectations was poor and because local chiefs and committees were seen as exercising a high degree of autonomy not to implement central dictates.

In addition, there was a lack of information nationally, and ineffective national technology systems to provide data to the centre to help Ministers and officials feel more confident. (A small number of probation areas had invested time and effort in developing effective information systems, of which they made good use to improve performance: HMIP 2000g.) Inspection findings became the main source of reliable data, often for the local probation services as well as nationally for Ministers and officials. Three *ad hoc* audits of elements of the National Standards, organised by the former Association of Chief Officers of Probation (ACOP 1999, 2000, 2001), were the only sources of national information, and were validated by HMIP in order to reassure Ministers that the findings were reliable. Although the exercises had a positive impact on overall performance, they were very limited and focused primarily on the enforcement and breach aspects of the Standards.

So, although many may have complained that the level and frequency of inspections were burdensome, they were nevertheless the main source of information available about probation service performance. Local staff need access to regular, routine and comparative monitoring information, which they produce for themselves, if they are to believe and 'own' it and use it to improve their own performance. We know from our inspections that involving local staff in case file-reading exercises often produces both shock at the findings and a determination that lessons should be shared with colleagues so that improvements can be made. The kind of self-assessment and regulation which the introduction of the European Excellence Model aims to create, will be vital if probation staff are to learn, improve and strive for excellence.

There is little doubt that more work could be done jointly by inspectorates in examining the work of their agencies, particularly where policy delivery is required across service boundaries. Where policy expectations are joined up, inspection and audit need to enhance and contribute to this, not hinder. Inspectors also need to model the behaviour and approach that we expect from our services. We deserve to be criticised for the times that we have followed the trail of the Audit Commission (or *vice versa*) into a probation service, asking for broadly similar information but in a slightly different format for a slightly different time frame.

Amongst the criminal justice inspectorates — HM Inspectorates of Constabulary, Prisons, Magistrates' Court Services, Crown Prosecution Service and the Social Services Inspectorate — HMIP has been one of the pioneers of joint work. Over recent years, we have worked jointly with all the inspectorates to produce thematic inspections and to undertake one-off pieces of work. We have also worked jointly with the Audit Commission to develop our work on value for money, and with the National Audit Office (NAO) on our information thematic. But a good deal more could be done; particularly to examine how well our relative services are together meeting the Home Office Seven Aims, the Criminal Justice Business Plan and related common objectives. This is why the six Chief Inspectors have proposed the setting-up of a joint inspection unit to plan and coordinate inspection work across the whole system. Some limited funding has been provided, and during the coming months the unit will be established.

For the future, the National Probation Service will be independently inspected nationally and at local board level by HMIP; it will be externally audited locally by the Audit Commission and nationally by the NAO. Additionally, local and national internal audit is likely to be undertaken by the Home Office Audit and Assurance Unit. This is a significant inspection and audit machinery for a service, the total national budget of which is less than £500 million.

In order to manage this machine in a way which is coordinated and coherent, avoids duplication and encourages a joined-up approach, HMIP has taken the initiative to establish the National Probation Service for England and Wales Inspection and Audit Forum, which aims 'to enable improved ministerial accountability to Parliament by delivering effective, integrated inspection and audit oversight of the performance of the National Probation Service'. The relevant bodies will meet quarterly to 'coordinate inspection and audit programmes (method and timing) where possible in order to ensure "added value" and to minimise any possible disruption to service delivery'.[6]

QUIS CUSTODIET IPSOS CUSTODES?

Over the past three years, the author has been asked 'Who inspects HMIP?'. A good question. The nature of our work means that it is all subject to scrutiny. In relation to the probation service itself, we provide many opportunities for the service to examine and comment on our work. We consult about the standards and criteria against which we judge services, and these are published. We give notice to probation areas about our intention to inspect and the programme we intend to follow. We provide our inspection findings to areas well ahead of publication. Our reports are always provided in draft, and are often amended in the light of comments made. Areas are notified of publication dates and provided with a copy of the press notice in order to consider their own response. Lastly, we encourage feedback — have reported on one formal consultation process (HMIP 2000a) — and we have a complaints procedure, which has been used (though rarely) by services to highlight occasions when it was felt inspectors got it wrong and the lessons to be learned.

We are directly accountable to Ministers, who are our key stake-holders, and all our work is reported to them. The author's personal

---

[6] A draft and as yet unpublished statement from the Forum due to be publicised during 2001.

experience of working for two Home Secretaries and four Ministers is that they are never reluctant to let one know if they are dissatisfied. The evidence is that they are more than satisfied with HMIP's performance; and as a result, confirmed and enhanced its status in the Criminal Justice and Court Services Act 2000 — an opportunity, if they had wished to take it, to abolish or reduce the Inspectorate's role.

The public generally know little about both HMIP and the service itself. As indicated previously, the profile of both is significantly less than that of either the Inspectorate of Prisons and the prison service, or OFSTED and schools. We seek to ensure that our work is accounted for publicly by publishing all our inspection reports — no piece of work goes unreported and all reports are published, by making them available widely, including on the Internet. Additionally, we involve members of the public in many of our thematic inspections and all our area inspections, recruiting people for their local knowledge, or expertise, to bring an external eye to our work. Their questions result in changes and improvements to our methodologies and approach.

There is no doubt that HMIP could benefit from further external scrutiny. The approach we are increasingly taking, of working jointly with other inspectorates and the audit bodies, will provide an opportunity for us to re-examine our effectiveness and learn by comparing ourselves with others.

CONCLUSION

An inspectorate needs to be tough but fair, rigorous but practical, independent and helpful. 'Tough' means that we need to be clear about the expectations and standards of the service, and that we must publish our results against those without fear of favour. But we need to ensure fairness, by setting those results in context — the difficulty of the task, the particular challenges the area faces, its successes as well as its failures.

'Rigorous' means that we need to have sound, demonstrable evidence for our judgements: an inspectorate which relies on impression and observation will not be respected; but we need to be practical and realistic in our recommendations, concentrating on the critical few which will make a difference to performance.

'Independent' means that we must comment robustly and in a balanced way on the policy, as well as its implementation, and on the role of the centre, as well as local performance. But being independent does not prevent us helping to get the policy and implementation right, where we have based our inspections on information, expertise and evidence.

The public have raised and increased expectations of public services, which we expect to give us more choice, to meet high standards and be of good quality, and be accessible to us, where and when we want to use them. The Government too has high expectations, and it is frustrated by the slow pace of change and modernisation of public service and what is seen as the too frequent failure to deliver. Both the Government and the public want those services to perform and be accountable. Inspection is seen as one of the ways both to check that this is happening and to ensure that it does happen. The promise is that, if public services deliver, more resources and investment will follow; the threat is that, if they don't, someone else, who can deliver, will be found.

20 Modernisation and Criminal Justice

John Raine

INTRODUCTION

It took about two years to gestate, but by the middle of Tony Blair's first term of office, 'modernisation' had emerged as the 'big idea' and leading project for the New Labour Administration. And by the beginning of the second term, almost no corner of the public sector had been untouched by the 'M' word and the associated determination to review and renew the public services and processes of government (Raine 2001b).

In some respects, there has been much commonality between what modernisation has meant in criminal justice — the subject of this chapter — and what it has meant in other governance and public service contexts. But in other respects there have been some distinctive issues, which are examined below. The chapter also explores the extent to which the rhetoric about modernisation in criminal justice has been matched by the reality of change, and in what ways the New Labour agenda is impacting on the agencies that 'work for justice'. Most important, it also offers a perspective on what now needs to be done to minimise the risk of disappointment at the outcomes and legacy of the current agenda of modernisation in criminal justice.

MODERNISING CRIMINAL JUSTICE

Few, if any, of those who knew criminal justice in England and Wales at the end of the twentieth century would argue against the proposition that all was not well and that reform, at least in some fundamental respects, was required. Despite successive organisational upheavals and revisions of the legislative framework of criminal justice under almost two decades of Conservative political leadership, old problems remained intractable and new ones had begun to be apparent. Serious miscarriages of justice continued to surface. The charge of institutional racism still haunted the agencies. Her Majesty's Inspector of Prisons continued to produce damning reports of conditions in the jails. The legal professions continued to operate in ways that seemed to put their own interests ahead of those whom they represented. Centrally controlled and bluntly designed funding regimes continued to hamper both opportunity and inclination to challenge the *status quo* and to innovate. Comparatively few of the attempts to respond to criminality and to change patterns of anti-social behaviour seemed to work. And public confidence in the criminal justice process appeared, if anything, to be falling in the wake of ever-deepening gloom at the scenarios of increasing violent crime, apparently growing indiscipline among young people and the menace of drugs.

Such was the background against which New Labour set about modernising criminal justice. Indeed, much of the tenor of the reform programme, particularly in relation to youth justice and the resourcing of crime prevention (as opposed to crime management), was voiced ahead of the 1997 General Election. Here the manifestos drew heavily on the tide of thinking that was emerging from both the policy 'think tanks' and the more pragmatic, managerial perspectives within government (e.g., the Audit Commission 1997). But what was not so apparent until well after the Election was the full extent of what was to become a much wider modernisation programme for criminal justice. This gradually emerged as having at least five main facets, highlighted in Figure 20.1, which we will examine in turn.

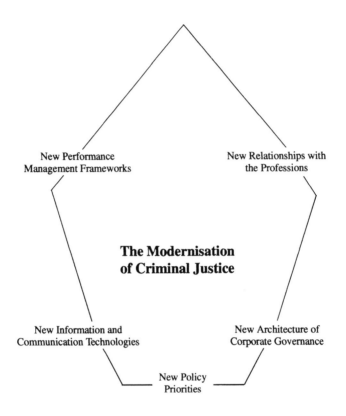

Figure 20.1   Facets of modernisation in criminal justice

NEW POLICY PRIORITIES

Probably the most discussed facet of the modernising agenda in criminal justice has been the cluster of policy and practice developments that New Labour has pursued. These have taken two main forms. On the one hand, there have been the reviews of and revisions to substantive policy in criminal justice — what the agencies would be expected to do — while on the other, there have been the shifts in approach and practice, which have been mirrored across the spectrum of governance activity, not just in criminal justice, and which relate to how the agencies would be expected to work.

With regard to the substantive policy shifts, undoubtedly the key area on which New Labour has focused to date, has been youth crime and youth justice. The roots of this policy concern lay in a string of influential reports published ahead of the 1997 General Election (Audit Commission 1997; Allen 1997; Bright 1997; LGA 1997; NACRO 1997). Once in office, the new Government responded with a raft of proposals, most of which found their way into the new legislative framework for youth justice and for crime and disorder (Crime and Disorder Act 1998). Equally important was the increased commitment to pilot projects in restorative justice and other alternatives to the traditional prosecution route. Similarly, a number of important other policy reviews were commissioned, reflecting governmental instincts for change and policy shifts in specific areas. For example, policy reviews were commissioned both of the criminal justice process as a whole (Auld Report) and of probation services (Home Office 1999f).

Two other key policy issues, which were the subject of reviews, concerned the judiciary in the magistrates' courts and the sentencing framework. The former study (Morgan and Russell 2000) was set up to compare the costs and benefits of stipendiary (district judge) full-time professional magistrates and part-time lay justices. The latter (Home Office 2001h) was commissioned to take a fresh look at the sentencing framework for the first time since the Criminal Justice Act 1991, particularly in the light of arguments that previous criminal records ought to be a more explicit factor in the sentencing of offenders.

But alongside such policy reviews has been a set of subtler, but nonetheless very significant, shifts in approach and practice in public policy generally but which, as indicated, has also had resonance in criminal justice. Indeed, these may well eventually prove to have been the more durable legacy of New Labour 'modernisation'. Here we refer to the new emphasis (quickly enshrined in a new vocabulary) on policy outcomes (as opposed to outputs); on evidence-based practice and What Works (as opposed to what practitioners or Ministers choose to do); on cost effectiveness (as opposed to cost efficiency) as the critical test of worthiness; and of a 'joined up' approach to policy and practice (as opposed to 'silo' mentality), which in the criminal justice context has meant both closer relations between agencies working for justice and addressing crime more as one interlinked aspect of the social policy agenda. Although it tended to receive rather less significance within criminal justice than in other arenas, such as local government and health care, a further new policy emphasis was on consultation as a process prerequisite.

From outputs to outcomes

The emphasis given to policy outcomes seems obvious from where we now view policy. But, despite longstanding advocacy by management accountants and academic commentators of the case for focusing more on the impacts of policy (i.e., what was actually achieved as a result of the interventions made, for example, in terms of reduced crime levels, rates of recidivism, etc.), the world of practice in criminal justice — as most elsewhere in public management — had hitherto seemed more preoccupied with lower order measures of output (e.g., numbers of client referrals made, numbers of case disposals, levels of prisoner overcrowding, etc.) and with inputs (i.e., size of budgets and other resources involved in making different interventions). Of course, the new emphasis on outcomes was not so much a replacement for the concern with inputs and outputs, more an additional focus. But that addition has arguably already begun to have a profound effect on the nature of discourse in criminal justice and on expectations about policy. The quest is now on, as never before, to measure and assess the impacts of criminal justice practices and policies, although there is a danger that, in the current political climate of impatience for results, the measures chosen and the assessments made prove inadequate and too short-termist, failing properly to reflect and capture the full policy objectives and their longer-term implications.

From habits and hobby horses to what works

In much the same way, the phrases evidence-based practice and What Works have joined the vocabulary of everyday criminal justice debate, and are having significant impacts in terms of moving attention on from the hopelessness of 'nothing works' to an altogether more engaging climate of monitoring and learning about the effects of practice. Certainly, there are grounds for concern that the reality will be less than the rhetoric of 'evidence-based practice', as much depends on the capacities and inclinations of service managers to challenge and change their preconceptions and practices. Likewise, there are grounds for concern that hobby horses (whether of politicians or practitioners) will still play roles in dictating what is funded, done and given the stamp of approval, as much as any objectively gathered scientific evidence. Nevertheless, the new vocabulary has already shown itself to be capable of challenging any tendencies towards inertia among practitioners and of encouraging a stronger spirit of learning and interest in disseminating the lessons of experience. Although a still low-trusting central government has been largely instrumental in managing this learning and dissemination process (for example, in the world of probation practice through a new Home Office 'National What Works Newsletter'), it is also clear that local agencies have been granted the licence to try things out and to exploit the new opportunities provided by the considerable extra funding afforded in the Spending Review of 2000.

From cost efficiency to cost effectiveness

The important qualification to the What Works issue has inevitably been that of affordability, and here another key phrase of modernisation has been 'cost effectiveness'. This represents the new calculation of impact in relation to price, and as such has become the main criterion determining what gets done (what gets funded from among the competing spending priorities). While this might well mean ruling out the most expensive interventions, even though they may be known to be very effective, the criterion would probably seem to most practitioners altogether more suitable than the 'cost efficiency' that had tended to dominate under the earlier managerial values, and which simply pitched costs against lower order output measures (e.g., the amount of work undertaken, as opposed to the impact of that effort).

From 'silo' services to joined-up approaches

Perhaps the most discussed of the new watchwords of modernisation in criminal justice — as elsewhere in the public policy arena — has been that of 'joining up'. This concept, too, has quickly had impact on thinking and behaviour in relation to policy-making and practice. Of course, the rhetoric of holistic thinking and of collaborative and inter-agency approaches to problem-solving was hardly new, but the particularly strong emphasis given by Government in recent years to 'joined-up' approaches, has undoubtedly provided fresh legitimacy and impetus to the challenge of partnership working between organisations and to tackling some of the key obstacles in this respect. In contemporary criminal justice, the widespread expectation is now much more strongly based on joint approaches, with plenty of illustrations of new preparedness of agencies to work together. For example, there are pioneering multi-agency initiatives in relation to drug problems, including special drugs courts operating in parts of the country. There is closer conjunction between the probation and prison services, and many front-line CPS prosecutors are now being relocated into police stations to work closer to the officers investigating and preparing the cases. All such initiatives are helping to break down inter-organisational barriers and to build more of a sense of common purpose and shared responsibility for problems in criminal justice.

But, perhaps particularly for criminal justice, where 'independence' has long been regarded as a fundamental value, these developments also carry risk of damage to the integrity and impartiality of the agencies in their distinctive tasks and responsibilities. This is particularly so in relation to the courts, where the concept of judicial independence is so precious. And as has been argued elsewhere (Raine 2001a), it is worrying how the meaning of 'judicial independence' is gradually being downgraded from its traditional status, as of institutional significance in relation to the doctrine of the separation of powers, to one of individual case significance, in which it is simply seen as a duty in relation to each hearing in the courtroom. The concept of 'independence' is important and should be cherished by the other agencies as well, since each has a distinct purpose to pursue and a particular perspective and set of values to be applied (the police to investigate; the CPS to prosecute; the courts to adjudicate and dispense justice; the probation service to supervise offenders and assist in their rehabilitation; the prison service to provide secure and constructive regimes for those committed to custody, and so on). The danger is that, in the rush to 'join up', the value of independence is eroded to the point where we may unwittingly end up with a monolithic criminal justice process; one that lacks the healthy tensions that safeguard the integrity of the process and which give vital reassurance and confidence to the public as to the quality of justice.

NEW INFORMATION AND COMMUNICATION TECHNOLOGIES

A second facet of modernisation in criminal justice concerns the impact of new information and communication technologies (ICTs) on the development of the process. This, of course, has been widely seen as a key aspect of modernisation in public policy generally. For example, its centrality to public service modernisation has been particularly strongly projected in the Government's White Paper, *Modernising Government* (Cabinet Office 1999). Here targets have been set that imply an extraordinary scale and nature of transformation in ways of working (e.g., that 90 per cent of interactions between public service organisations and their customers will be by electronic means by 2004).

Within criminal justice, however, the story so far seems mixed. There have been, to be sure, significant developments in the use of ICTs in all of the agencies. Yet at the same time, mostly these have been about 'automating' existing processes, or introducing electronic information and measurement processes ('informatising' developments), rather than real 'transformations' or re-engineering of the approach to criminal justice (Bellamy and Taylor 1998). Perhaps the most significant developments to date have been in the direction of establishing electronic intercommunication between the agencies as the principal means of transferring information and case data from agency to agency. A major programme of work has been in progress under the banner of the initiative, the 'Coordination of Computerisation in the Criminal Justice System' (CCCJS), which has been focused on the interoperability of the separate systems and on the flows of information between agencies through the building of 'electronic bridges'. This has been in addition to a series of developments within each agency that providing new information management systems to address agency-specific requirements and performance monitoring needs (e.g., the Phoenix system for police intelligence and criminal records, the NAFIS system for fingerprint identification, the LIBRA project for the magistrates' courts, the CREST case management system in the Crown

Court, the SCOPE system for the CPS, the CRAMS system for the probation service, and the LIDS system for the prison service).

Along the way, a number of challenges have had to be tackled, some technical, but many more about the politics of funding, human and organisational issues. A key factor affecting the pace and path of development of ICTs in criminal justice has been the Government's preference for a private finance initiative (PFI) approach, as the basic organisational and financial arrangement for large-scale investment in this respect. This has simultaneously caused both delay and stimulation to the development process. On the one hand, the decisions about financing have taken longer to reach than traditional public expenditure decisions, and compliance with the complex procedural requirements of PFI has proved more demanding. On the other hand, the nature of PFI contracting has arguably served to encourage a more innovative approach (with the risk lying principally with the private sector consortium) than would have been likely with conventional public finance.

The process of extending the use of ICTs in criminal justice has also been complicated by the different stages of development of the different systems in place at each agency and questions about who should pay for the links (given that their benefits would be shared). There have been issues to be confronted about sub-optimal solutions for some agencies being the necessary price for overall system-wide benefits. And there has been much uncertainty created for staff, not least because of the potential implications for job security of PFI deals. Inevitably, this has all affected morale and motivation. There have also been issues to be confronted about confidentiality, privacy and legitimacy in data sharing, which would always be particularly acute within a context like criminal justice. And, inevitably, there has been institutional inertia and resistance to be tackled concerning the sharing of information, mostly based on perceived threats to organisational power/status and fears of possible consequences of disclosure.

As indicated, however, the main question about modernisation through ICTs in criminal justice relates to the extent to which the opportunities have been taken for using new technology for process transformation or re-engineering. The issue here is less to do with developing capacity in relation to existing functions and ways of working, but more about harnessing the potential of ICTs to define new ways of conducting criminal justice that are qualitatively different in terms of the prospective outputs and outcomes.

To date, progress in this regard has been very limited, two notable exceptions being the advent of electronic tagging as a form of supervised home curfew, and the introduction of video-links between remand prisons and courts to save time escorting prisoners. Otherwise, despite the potential of fields in relation to on-line conferencing, networking, tele-voting etc., the criminal justice process has continued to develop largely in its traditional modes of working, for example, with juries of 12 still being assembled at courts on a daily basis, with delays in scheduling cases still tolerated because of the continued expectation that all parties must simultaneously appear in person in the courtroom, and with continued listing of cases at the court in the locality where the alleged offence took place, irrespective of the potential inconvenience this may cause to the parties.

All this contrasts starkly with other contexts, where ICTs have played a more fundamental part in the design or redesign of service processes. One such example is the London Parking Appeals Service — not itself part of the criminal jurisdiction, nor indeed a court of appeal, it being a tribunal system, but nevertheless a very relevant comparator in a number of ways. Here, for example, the nature of the judicial process (quite as much as the supporting administrative processes) has been significantly changed from its traditional courtroom manner through the deployment of ICTs in the front-line adjudication process, not just for back-line administration. The process, as a result, has been made more accessible and comprehensible to users by creating an across-the-table, interactive process, in which adjudicator and appellant view together the same computer screen and together go through the evidence before the adjudicator decides the appeal (Raine 2001a). The process encourages participation and involvement on the part of the appellant and, in so doing, arguably contributes greatly to the building of confidence in the process and to a new form of accountability. This is modernisation indeed, when compared with the style of conduct of such appeal proceedings when previously they were undertaken in the more formal and austere setting of a magistrates' court.

NEW ARCHITECTURE OF CORPORATE GOVERNANCE

The predecessor Conservative Administration had been generally wary of structural reorganisations of public services. Mindful of the possibility of unanticipated costs of such reorganisations spiralling out of control (as for example, with the local government reorganisation in 1974), and chastened by the criticisms that had dogged the Crown Prosecution Service (CPS) relentlessly since its establishment in 1985, the preference latterly was to use other levers, notably tight cash-limited funding, to press the public agencies in the direction of structural change. Thus it was that the Conservative Lord Chancellor in 1992 had been recommending a reduction in the number of magistrates' courts committee areas, and the Home Secretary was advocating greater co-terminosity between the organisational boundaries of criminal justice agencies but not actually demanding the change.

But the New Labour Government adopted a more assertive stance on such issues and established a new momentum to the reorganisation of the architecture of criminal justice, a further facet of its modernisation agenda. Two particular (and somewhat contradictory) aspects charac- terised this reorganisation. On the one hand was the clear commitment to establishing the police areas as the new template for the modernised local criminal justice organisation. This was reflected, for example, in the reorganisation (yet again) of the CPS on to the territorial organisa- tion of 42 police areas (a decentralisation from the 13 territorial units of the CPS that had only recently been established). It was also apparent in the requirement for a series of magistrates' courts committee amalgamations, again to fit the police area map. On the other hand, a nationalisation strategy was chosen for the probation service (albeit again with a substructure of 42 local areas). This no doubt reflected Ministers' keenness to ensure a more concerted and managed approach from the service in its newly redefined and tripartite roles of enforce- ment, rehabilitation and protecting the public. In so doing, a further aim was to bring it more into line with the already nationalised prison service, with which it was expected to develop closer relations. Nationalisation, as an organisational strategy, also seemed a step closer in relation to the magistrates' courts, with increasing discussion in Whitehall and in submissions to the Auld Review of the case for a unified court system, bringing the magistrates' courts (with their traditional local management ethos) into a closer relationship with the Crown Court (which had been nationally organised since its inception).

A further important expression of the modernised organisational architecture under New Labour concerned the establishment of a number of new units, each with a single purpose to undertake. Some were specifically tied into the criminal justice process, such as the Criminal Cases Review Commission, established in the light of a series of notorious miscarriages of justice, and the more recently proposed Independent Police Complaints Commission. Others, such as the Social Exclusion Unit within the Cabinet Office and the Drugs Tsar, were set up to 'join up' criminal justice with other social policy areas (e.g., education, employment, health, housing, etc.); for these developments, recruitment from all the relevant agencies was seen as essential.

Alongside these more specific and visible reforms and additions to the organisational structure of criminal justice, modernisation has involved a further category of architectural reform, concerning the processes of corporate governance. Here the reforms were largely predicated on the goal of enhanced accountability and transparency in ways of working. This was evident, for example, in the reform of judicial appointments through the creation of a new commission. Enhanced public accountability was evident in the establishment/ development of more inspectorial and regulatory regimes, such as a new CPS Inspectorate. And it underlay the new machinery put in place for coordinating strategic policy at the highest levels (i.e., between the three leading departments of state — the Home Office, the Lord Chancellor's Department and the Office of the Attorney-General).

The desire to modernise organisational processes in criminal justice has also found expression in some of the new legislation, not least in the incorporation into UK law of the Articles of the European Convention on Human Rights (Walker and Raine 2001). At face value, the Human Rights Act 1998 could simply be seen as allowing the kinds of challenges which had hitherto required a trip to Strasbourg, to be made in the domestic courts (the UK having been a signatory to the Convention from the outset). But on reflection, there was the possibility that the move would herald a new, more 'rights orientated', culture, not only in criminal justice, but also in public life generally (since all public authorities were bound by the new law, not only the courts).

In fact the Human Rights Act issue could be viewed as just one aspect of a broader modernising shift towards a more ethical approach in public policy, including criminal justice, of which other notable examples were the legislation to establish independent Standards Committees in local government and the overhaul of the House of Lords (where the main aim was to disenfranchise the hereditary peerage in the legislative process). Intriguingly, however, the same modernising Government responsible for these constitutional changes failed to include in its programme any reform to the office of Lord Chancellor. For here perhaps was constitutional oddity indeed, with the office holder being simultaneously head of the judiciary, president in the upper chamber of the legislature and a member of the Cabinet at the heart of HM Government. This tripartite role has seemed to most commentators to be quite at odds with the doctrine of the 'separation of powers' (which demanded clear separation between the judiciary, legislature and executive arms of the state). Still more intriguing was the failure to address this ethically questionable state of affairs, even under pressure of media revelations about the Lord Chancellor's personal invitations to large numbers of leading lawyers (many of whom were eligible candidates for judicial appointment) to attend a fund-raising dinner for the Labour Party.

NEW PERFORMANCE MANAGEMENT FRAMEWORKS

Although the 'die was cast' well before the New Labour came to power, the impetus given to performance management has been another key facet of modernisation, and one which seems set to continue to shape the nature of criminal justice management in the years ahead. From the outset, Prime Minister Blair invited the public to 'judge us by our results', and impressed upon the public services the need to improve their performance. Over the past four years, the work that had been commenced under the previous Government, in establishing performance targets and developing measurement and reporting systems, has been firmly ratcheted up as a priority across the spectrum of public policy organisations.

This has been evident in the proliferation of performance measures and targets generally, and particularly in the developing 'statistics industry' within the Audit Commission. The nature of these measures and targets in criminal justice has steadily evolved from initial preoccupations with agency case-management efficiency (unit costs and the like) to more sophisticated outcome measures such as 'change in public confidence in criminal justice', as measured in the bi-annual British Crime Survey (though such measures would always be potentially problematical to interpret and susceptible to influence by particular events and individual headline-grabbing cases, e.g., the James Bulger murder or the Guilford Four miscarriage of justice).

The new status for performance management in criminal justice has also been evident in the establishment of new inspectorial regimes and in the extended role of those already in existence. It has been particularly strongly reflected in two major public policy initiatives: on the one hand, the development of Best Value, both as a driving philosophy and practical requirement for many local public services; and on the other hand, the establishment of a new regime of 'public service agreements' that explicitly links the privilege of access to additional funding opportunities to attainment of performance targets.

The introduction of Best Value, which in criminal justice is now a formal requirement for police forces, has been particularly interesting. This started out as little more than a political necessity to replace the previous Conservative Administration's regime of Compulsory Competitive Tendering (CCT) in local government. In identifying a replacement, it was necessary to appease both those in local government, who wished for the complete abolition of the CCT regime, and those who were doubtful about New Labour's credentials in relation to the national economy and management of efficient public services. However, Best Value, a notion initially borrowed from across the Atlantic, has quickly built up its own momentum and developed into a highly-tuned performance management regime, which, rather ironically, has already had far more widespread impact in local authorities than its predecessor could ever have had. This is because, under Best Value, those organisations covered by the new legal duty are expected to apply continuously the principles and practices across all areas of their responsibility and be subject to a rigorous Best Value inspection process (managed by a new inspection service within the Audit Commission).

Within criminal justice, although the new regime is (so far) strictly only applicable to the police (though that in itself accounts for about half of the overall budget), there were bound to be widespread 'spill-over' effects into other agencies, which means that, in practice few, if any, criminal justice organisations are not complying with at least the philosophy and general expectations of Best Value.

The other broad public sector-wide regime of significance in this context — public service agreements (PSAs) — seems destined to have similarly profound implications for criminal justice. Here, while the initiative was at first introduced for certain central government units and departments, and then extended to embrace key local government services, there is clearly now the potential for it to be rolled out more fully across the public sector as a key part of public spending control strategy. Crucially, PSAs seem set to challenge the traditional needs-driven philosophy of public funding of services, in so far as they make 'performance' a key criterion in resource allocation processes, and in so doing, challenge the hitherto powerful equity ethic underpinning traditional public funding regimes. For criminal justice, as elsewhere, it could well invite increased variance (and conflict) over standards of provision, since the high-performing agencies would, as rewards, be eligible for extra resources to enable further improvements. Meanwhile, the less successful ones could struggle to live up to expectations and so fall into the trap of 'failing services'.

More generally, the considerable emphasis on performance as an element of modernisation in criminal justice has brought both benefits and disbenefits. In terms of benefits, it has certainly brought to the fore many issues of quality, particularly in relation to user experiences of service provision that had for too long been neglected. Standards of service responsiveness, treatment of victims and witnesses, and infor-mation provision generally, all have advanced greatly, as a result of the greater emphasis on measurement and reporting, and much of the old complacency associated with provider-driven services has given way to a more concerted commitment to the notion of continuous improve-ment.

On the other hand, the general approach by which performance management has been developing in criminal justice, as in other public policy contexts, has certainly not been unproblematic. For example, many of the Government's targets — particularly for delay reduction — have not so far been met. Not least, this has been because the targets are not always sufficiently within the agencies' sphere of control. There are also important questions to be asked about the net benefit of the performance management preoccupation. Certainly, alongside the quality 'gains' for criminal justice, another story has also often been apparent, of year-on-year pressure for budget savings as often as not forcing service rationalisation (e.g., closure of police stations, local courts and probation projects) and therefore 'losses' in terms of access to service. At the same time, despite much talk of more 'joined-up' and 'cross-cutting' approaches, another reality of performance manage-ment in criminal justice has been heightened 'organisational individual-ism' and self-centredness, and a tendency for contracting relations to take hold where once collaborative relations were the order of the day between the agencies.

A further set of problems has arisen because of the essentially more short-term perspective that performance management has tended to encourage. Impatient politicians wanting results to demonstrate their competence in tackling crime, for example, would always be more likely to support short-term perspectives and outputs, and in so doing could easily distort priorities away from longer-term, and fundamentally more satisfactory, approaches and outcomes. There has been evidence, too, of how the relentless emphasis on performance measurement has encouraged partial, or worse, dishonest, reporting (e.g., the deliberate manipulation of crime statistics in some police forces to portray more favourable clear-up rates). Of more widespread significance, there have been serious problems for the senior management in the various agencies in winning front-line and supervisor-grade staff commitment to the cause of delivering on the performance measures, which are almost invariably conceived without consultation with the front-line on a largely 'top-down' basis (Raine and Willson 1997). Until it is learned that the 'top-down' approach to performance management needs to be complemented with more 'bottom-up' approaches, it seems likely that the impact of this particular strand of modernisation will remain limited and potentially outbalanced by the negative aspects of excess paper-generation and the sapping of staff morale.

NEW RELATIONSHIPS WITH THE PROFESSIONS

The fifth key facet of modernisation that is identifiable in criminal justice concerns relations between Government and the practitioner community. Compared with the general position under the preceding political Administration, New Labour modernisation has been marked by a generally less antagonistic relationship. To some extent, this must have been facilitated by the comparatively favourable national economic climate of recent years and the extra funding opportunities that this has afforded. But as important in the process of change has been the instinctively more sympathetic outlook of the new team of Ministers towards public service practitioners — in some contrast with the climate of suspicion that had characterised relationships between Government and the professions in the previous decade. The new relationship has by no means been tension-free for any of the criminal justice agencies. But the past five years have certainly seen a significant rebuilding of more trustful relations, reflected, for example, in the preparedness of local probation chiefs to work constructively with the Home Office on the formation of a new national service.

Two key facets can be identified as hallmarks of the new relationship between Government and the practitioner community of criminal justice. First is the continued supremacy of the management perspective in setting the agenda and shaping professional practice. As in the previous decade, the top jobs in criminal justice are almost invariably being filled more according to managerial track records and credentials than professional experience. Indeed, an increasing number of senior appointments are now purposefully being made from outside the particular professional group, often from outside the public service. In the case of the magistrates' courts, for example, the new Government quickly asserted the strength of its commitment to managerial values, first and foremost, by redefining the role and responsibilities of justices' clerks (traditionally, not only the professional legal advisers to magistrates but also the heads of court administration) to exclude administrative and management roles. These roles are now enshrined in law as the province of the new cadre of justices' chief executives (who are not required to have either legal qualifications, or previous court administrative experience).

Secondly, professional discretion continues to be curbed; a trend again established under the Conservatives, but now continued apace by tight control of budgets, by explicit prescription of methods of working, and by detailed specification of expected outputs and outcomes (as targets). Despite the relatively healthy state of the public finances throughout New Labour's first term, there has been no let-up in the disciplines of cash-limited budgets and built-in annual efficiency savings. This has meant that most new projects or initiatives (and there have been plenty) depend more heavily than ever on Government sponsorship and support. A significant example here has been the range of new projects instigated under the Crime Reduction Programme — a commitment of some £250 million to identify What Works in tackling crime, but which has been very tightly selected and managed by the Home Office. Likewise, in terms of methods of working, the debate about practice, once the province of the professional associations and staff representative bodies, continues to be led and dominated by

Whitehall policy-makers through the ever-increasing volume of 'best practice' guidance notes and pamphlets. These tend to follow a 'one-size fits all' approach; and, despite their official status as 'advisory and guidance' documentation, in truth, it is a brave or foolhardy local service chief who deviates 'off message', given Whitehall's general predisposition to expect compliance. Whatever the benefits of centralisation in terms of overall consistency and relief from individualised whimsy and idiosyncrasy, the colour, diversity and local character of criminal justice (as in education and other professional practice) has been leeched away.

Increasingly, then, the criminal justice agencies are operating as agents of Government in the centrally defined tasks of 'working for justice'. It is the Government which is 'calling the shots' in most respects and, increasingly, in determining preferred practices, not only with regard to executive branch responsibilities — policing and sentence management — but also in the judicial branch. In so doing, it is inevitably downgrading the concept and reality of judicial independence and the separation of powers. Moreover, while the rhetoric of New Labour modernisation has made much of the importance of innovation and learning, in reality, the culture of 'working for Whitehall' is providing little incentive to do much other than follow the lead given by the centre.

WHERE NEXT FOR MODERNISATION?

As argued at the outset, despite all the political kudos attached to the notion of 'modernisation', in many respects, the agenda of change that it has represented to date has been little more than an extension of the developments which were already apparent in criminal justice. That said, it is also clear that the fresh emphasis given to those developments, and the adoption of the 'M' word itself, has created new momentum to the process and served to stir and stimulate a still-emergent change agenda. The five dimensions discussed in this chapter have each been of significance as particular strands of development in criminal justice organisation and practice. And while some inherent tensions and contradictions have been apparent between the different objectives and priorities in the early years of New Labour modernisation (for example, between the continued focus on individual agency performance on the one hand and a more joined-up criminal justice process on the other), arguably there is now emerging a greater sense of overall coherence and direction to the changes taking place in the sector than for a while. In this respect, more than anything, it is argued, 'modernisation' has represented a significant broadening from the largely managerialist and rather short-termist perspective of the past decade towards an approach which encompasses a wider set of values and which is arguably more sustainable.

Almost a decade ago, in writing about the transformations then taking place in criminal justice, Raine and Willson (1993) drew on the 'metamodel' of organisational cultures of the American management scientist, Robert Quinn, to describe the pattern of changing priorities in criminal justice. This model charts the broad journey of development (the life-cycle) that any organisation might expect to travel in its life. As such, it provides an insightful description of the story of the development of criminal justice (and indeed, of the wider public sector). Over the past decade, that journey has been made from the administrative bureaucratic tradition, through the managerialist drive for greater efficiency, towards a more outward-orientated, competitive market model, in which entrepreneurial skills and a predilection for innovation and change have been among the defining hallmarks, and onwards to the world of partnership building and the establishment of more collaborative relationships with other organisations.

Some ten years ago, the shift towards such partnership working was still largely to come. Now, arguably, we are seeing the symptoms of further progression round the life-cycle, in the form of new traits of administrative bureaucracy and greater preoccupation with internal process issues (performance management, best value, information management systems and the like). This, of course, does not quite amount to 'revisiting' of the environment and style of criminal justice two or more decades ago. But the basic circularity of the Quinn model does seem to ring true, and there are many signs to support the proposition that criminal justice is modernising in the direction of a new form of bureaucracy and with a new preoccupation with internal processes. And the key question which this prompts is: 'Could it be otherwise?'

21 Organisation and Management: a Changing Agenda

Norman Flynn

INTRODUCTION

In chapter 20, John Raine has shown how the Government has applied its 'modernisation' agenda to the criminal justice system. This chapter looks specifically at the changes in the organisation and management of the probation service, and asks what style of management has been designed for the service. It does not take the modernisation agenda as its starting point, and argues that the changes since 1997 are the extension of a process begun by previous Home Secretaries.

This chapter analyses the management style for the newly organised service, and asks what is the likelihood of success for the service within the centralised structure and processes adopted. The Home Office does not have an unblemished record of management achievements: the prison service is run in a way that is very similar to the new arrangements for probation, and has proved notoriously troublesome to manage to produce a uniformly quality service.

WHICH MANAGEMENT MODEL?

One problem facing anyone designing a management system in the public sector is that the tasks and the professions and occupations involved are very varied. Public sector activities range from very high to very low discretion, risk is very variable, confidence in the effectiveness of particular practices is uneven. The political saliency is also very variable, and affects the degree to which politicians want to be in control or be seen to be in control.

Because of this variety, it is unlikely that a standard set of solutions will be either easily implemented or successful. The post-1997 Government adopted a set of management and governance principles that were applied in many different contexts. The principles presented were those identified by Raine: a focus on outcomes, evidence-based, cost effectiveness, joined-up and consultative. The principles underlying the modernisation efforts include a distrust of professionals, a desire for standardisation and centralisation, numerical targets for everything, heavy reliance on audit and inspection as control mechanisms, and threats to replace poorly performing managers.

CONTROLLING THE 'PROFESSIONALS'

Changed mission

All politicians have periods of frustration with the departments and services over which they nominally rule. From 1980 onwards, successive Conservative Governments tried to take power and influence way from professionals, mainly by imposing management structures to control them. General management, and then markets, were introduced in the NHS; a national curriculum and stricter inspection in the school system; quality instruments for teaching and research in the universities; the introduction of privatisation and competition in many local government services and the prison service.

The extra emphasis on measurable targets that the Labour Government brought to its first term of office gave a precision to the causes of frustration. The shortlist of promises in the manifesto for the 1997 Election grew into thousands of targets through Public Service Agreements and targets agreed in agencies' business plans, corporate plans and other control documents. Not only were targets established, but league tables were also published to compare how individual units, such as schools and hospitals, were performing.

Assuming that data can be collected accurately and honestly, specific targets make politicians vulnerable, if they are not reached. The natural response is to blame the professionals, and the Labour Government was no exception to this rule. The Prime Minister famously referred to the 'scars on his back' from his dealings with public sector professionals (in that case the British Medical Association) and the 'forces of conservatism' among the professionals and other workers in the public sector. The whole 'modernisation' campaign was presented as if public services were hopelessly out of date: local authorities were described as having structures and processes from the nineteenth century; the NHS as not having changed since it was founded. Professionals were part of the old ways to be swept aside by the new. What this meant in relation to management was that steps had to be taken to bring the professionals under control.

In the case of probation, this was made especially hard by the fact that the purpose and values of the service were disputed between the Home Secretary and the Home Office on one side and the probation officers on the other. The dispute was reflected in Michael Howard's time by public confrontation between the Association of Chief Officers of Probation (ACOP) and the Home Secretary, serious reluctance to participate in electronic tagging and, during Mr Straw's time, in a dispute about the name and, more importantly, the purpose of the service. Apart from the name, the profession mostly lost — 'advise, assist and befriend' went the way of Clause IV and was replaced by punishment in the community. Social work values were out, and interventions to punish and reform, based on cognitive behaviourism, were in. The clash was in practice less stark than this, since many probation officers' practice had been developing the sorts of programmes approved by the new regime. The change was recognition that the 1907 Act values had officially been replaced.

Even the most Messianic manager would see that as a challenge. It is one thing to improve management in a situation where all the participants agree on the purposes and the generally accepted methods to achieve them; it is quite another to manage when some members of the organisation have different ideas not only about what works, but also about what the aim is. One of the problems in managing the prison service is that in many cases the prison officers have different and deep-rooted ideas about the purposes of the prison service, as well as how it should be run.

Standardisation

A basic characteristic of a profession is that its members are autonomous; their working practices emerge from their profession and not from the organisation they work for or in. What coordination or supervision is required is done through mutual adjustment and conversations between people who have equal or close professional status. If politicians or 'the management' want professionals to do something different, they have to find alternatives to the professional method of supervision. There are three options: change and standardise the 'inputs', or the processes, or the outputs (outcomes).

It is at least debatable whether probation was a profession, in the sense that the training and self-managing standards standardised practice to such a degree that the profession ran itself. The DipSW/CQSW qualifications could be argued to have provided a pre-professional training, but many aspects of the job had to be learned though practice under supervision. Supervision was always a mixture of managerial supervision, concerned with matters such as how much work has been completed and how workloads are distributed, and professional supervision. The latter contained elements of training in how to do the job, not just checking.

So, the question is whether the abandonment of the social work qualification, as an essential entry requirement in England and Wales, constitutes a rejection of standardised 'inputs' or characteristics of the workforce? If so, standardisation of inputs would have to be replaced with standardisation of some other aspect of the work. If not, then the new management arrangements can be seen as correcting the gap left by the fact that training did not produce a universally accepted set of standards and ways of working, which could be maintained effectively through a system of professional supervision.

What Works provides one answer to the problem of standardisation. If probation officers cannot be relied upon to adopt those practices that produce results, there will be a national set of practices. It is a risky management idea, since it puts all its money on there being a set of programmes that will be transferable from where they were developed to every other part of England and Wales, and, perhaps more importantly, that no other practices will be allowed. Apart from that, of course, the process of accreditation is slow, and it will be a long while before there are sufficient approved programmes. In any case, What Works is looking for solutions for the long term and, therefore, longitudinal studies have to be followed through to determine the real impact.

The Correctional Policy Framework issued by the Home Office, put What Works at the centre:

Correctional policy is driven by What Works principles. This means that offending behaviour programmes should involve planned interventions over a specified period of time, which can be shown to change positively attitudes, beliefs, behaviour and social circumstances. Usually, they will be characterised by a sequence of activities designed to achieve clearly defined objectives based on a theoretical model or empirical evidence. There should also be a capacity to replicate the programme with different offenders to achieve the same results. (Home Office 1999e)

What Works was not new but was the continuation of an older initiative, the Effective Practice Initiative, renamed by the incoming Government.

Another, earlier attempt at standardisation was the development of National Standards, launched in 1992, which simply set out in some detail what probation officers were supposed to do. Less ambitious than What Works, the Standards are simply a rule book, standing in place of reliance on good practice. The rules are about what should be done, by whom and when, and can therefore be monitored by counting. They refer mainly to report writing and the correct procedures for orders, rather than to the programmes with which What Works is concerned.

Together the two initiatives represent an attempt to standardise work practices, because of a lack of confidence in the standardisation of inputs, especially the skills and knowledge of the practitioners.

UNIFIED MANAGEMENT STRUCTURE

The pre-April 2001 service was organised as 54 probation services, linked to, and partly funded by, local authorities, although they were also linked to the Home Office's C6 division, known as the Probation Unit. The areas had a governing committee, to which the chief probation officer was locally accountable. Her Majesty's Inspectorate of Probation (HMIP) was always an important part of the accountability structure.

On 1 April 2001, the National Probation Service was launched for England and Wales. The Probation Unit of the Home Office became the National Probation Directorate. A new National Director, Eithne Wallis, was appointed head of the service, and local area probation boards replaced committees. The boundaries of the 42 new areas were coterminous with police authority boundaries, in an effort to make collaboration between the criminal justice agencies easier.

The link with local authorities was broken and the new structure is a unified, hierarchical service operating in England and Wales. Accountability of the service is through the National Probation Directorate to the Home Secretary.

EUROPEAN BUSINESS EXCELLENCE MODEL

Soon after she was appointed, Eithne Wallis announced that the service would work towards European Foundation for Quality Management (EFQM) accreditation, and set the service a target score of 700 within five years. The EFQM model covers nine aspects of management, divided into 'enablers' — leadership, policy and strategy, people, partnerships and resources, processes and 'results' — people results, customer results, society results and key performance results. The winner of the EFQM award for large organisations in 2000 was Nokia. The first public sector winner was the Inland Revenue Account Office in Cumbernauld. A target score of 700 is ambitious and shows a commitment to quality management, but not to a narrowly defined approach, as the EFQM allows a variety of approaches within each of its nine criteria.

The framework for the EFQM model is shown in Figure 21.1. An aspect which will be of particular interest to those who work in the service, will be where the leadership comes from. Past experience has indicated a battle for leadership among the Minister, the Permanent Secretary and the head of the service. There are important questions to ask about where policy and strategy are made, in what sort of style, and how innovation and learning can take place. The desire for a highly centralised service implies a model of learning, policy and decision-making which is based on the idea that all information should be passed upwards for decisions about strategy, and that judgements about the best way forward should be passed downwards. It also implies that innovation and learning are highly centralised. While the EFQM model makes no explicit judgement about how these things should be managed, it will be interesting to see whether such a large organisation will be judged as a quality organisation with such a high degree of centralisation of management.

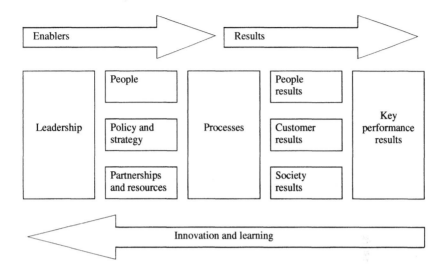

Figure 21.1   The European Foundation for Quality Management Model

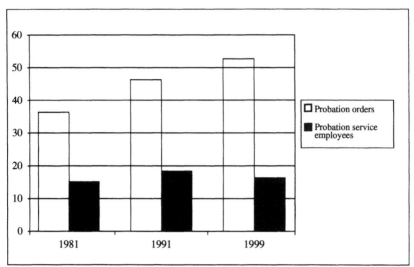

Source: Social Trends (2001) 31, sections 9.3, 9.19 and 9.23.

Figure 21.2   Probation orders and probation employees

MORE STAFF

Probation officers' workload has increased greatly. Figure 21.2 shows the number of probation orders and the number of probation staff from 1981 to 1999. While the control over their work was tightened through the National Standards, the volume of work increased to produce long working hours and a stressful environment.

This increase in workload was the main feature of probation officers' working life. Perhaps the most significant feature of the newly-established National Probation Service was the announcement, in September 2000, of the projected recruitment of 4,500 extra staff over three years, to include 1,500 probation officers, 2,500 probation service officers (assistants) and 500 support staff. It was later announced that there would be an additional 3,000 staff in the first year of the new service. Given that the new qualification requires two years' training, it is likely that the early recruits will not be at qualified probation officer level.

TARGETS

The high-level 'outcome' target for the service is that there will be a 5 per cent reduction in the re-conviction rates for offenders supervised by the service by 2004. The old service had adopted nine key performance indicators in its three-year plan. There is a national target for the time taken for young offenders to be tried, part of which concerns the time taken by the service to write reports on the arrested individuals. There are also targets for the recruitment of people from ethic minorities.

It is not yet clear what will be the consequences of failing to meet targets. In the case of Executive Agencies, targets change regularly, not always to make them harder to achieve in subsequent years. While there is no suggestion that the 5 per cent reduction in re-conviction rates will be changed, what will happen if the target is not met? Will interim achievement be published? What will happen if the trend is in the wrong direction?

INFORMATION MANAGEMENT

The service has had a sorry history of information management and information and communication technology, along with other Government departments. The National Probation Service Information Systems Strategy was to be implemented partly through an integrated case record system, CRAMS. Unfortunately, CRAMS joined the list of central Government experiences with the IT industry which have resulted in delays, cost over-runs and failure to meet the original specification. The National Audit Office report on the procurement process diagnosed a lack of leadership, continuity of staffing and of resources as the main reasons for the failure. The report also urged the Home Office to persist in completing the system, since it is essential for the success of the new probation service.

Information management will be a vital tool in the new organisation. Not only will it allow people to do their job, but it will also enable managers to see whether they are meeting their targets.

Assessment

The management of the new service have taken on a big task. The governance arrangements are new, the boards having replaced the old probation committees. The management will need to work hard to establish the role and ways of working with the boards. The old network of chief probation officers, with their dual accountabilities to the locality and the Home Office, has been replaced by a group of 42 chief officers accountable to the new National Director. Many of the experienced chief probation officers have taken the opportunity to retire or pursue their careers elsewhere. Management methods will have to be developed for the new unified service. The creaky IT systems will have to be completed and made to respond to the needs of the service. New staff have to be recruited to meet the greatly expanded workload, and the newly qualified professionals will have a recently introduced qualification, the Diploma in Probation Studies (DipPS).

Risks

The most obvious risk in the new set up is that the management arrangements might not be adequate to deliver the ambitious targets. At the time of writing, it is too early to assess the likely effectiveness of the unified command structure. The Home Office has a mixed record of operating command structures. The prison service is organised in a similar way to probation and has serious problems in trying to control what happens in individual prisons, in a direct hierarchy from prison governors, through area managers to the head of the prison service. A thorough and outspoken inspectorate backs up the hierarchy. Almost all of the features of the new probation service management arrangements are reproductions of the prison service, except the probation model has regional managers, who will provide 'a light regional touch'.

The prison inspectorate has repeatedly identified the turnover of prison governors as a problem for the prison service. The new management of probation needs to make sure that the same does not happen at the area level of the new service.

Another recurring theme of prison inspectorate reports is the growth of targets sent from prison service headquarters to the prisons, some contained in business, corporate and strategic plans, and some attached to initiatives. The targets are part of a stream of instructions issued from various levels of the hierarchy. Despite these, reports indicate that individual prisons manage to develop and maintain their own cultures, often negating the proclaimed goals of the service and impervious to both management and inspection.

The other main risk is the heavy dependence on the What Works programme as the basis for service development. One commentator has remarked that the least we can do at this stage is to realise that what we are undertaking is a huge criminological experiment (Merrington and Stanley 2000). The dependence has two effects: (i) local development of services for local circumstances will now be seen as a research and development role for the national service; (ii) work that is specifically local, whether in the form of programmes or individual work, will not receive national accreditation and will therefore not be permitted.

This is a very centralised definition of evidence-based practice. It is similar to the operation of the National Institute for Clinical Excellence (NICE) in the NHS, in that what counts as evidence is nationally collected and interpreted information on the results of particular treatments or actions. The medical analogy is not perfectly replicated here, in that the accreditation programme is based only on small local trials and not equivalent to national epidemiological data. Various doctors have complained that the NICE approach devalues local experience and individual knowledge of 'what works' for individual patients. In the probation case, the argument is similar in that local probation officers can no longer rely on their own experience and initiative, unless it is to start a programme, which may then get national accreditation.

There are practical problems with a national accreditation system as a policy and management tool: the process takes a long time and will in future be required to change in response to changing patterns of crime. In the past, local services have produced, for example, car projects to respond to outbreaks of 'taking without consent' on their patch. In future, the increase in a particular form of crime will presumably have to wait for a pilot to be run, the evaluation done and permission given.

The third risk of reliance on What Works is timescale. Whereas the NHS equivalent of accreditation relies both on short-term recovery statistics and longer-term morbidity and mortality data, long-term statistics on re-conviction (never mind re-offending), which are the measure of effectiveness in response to different punishment in the community programmes, will not be available before the end of the period that the first re-conviction reduction targets have to be met. The gamble, therefore, is that the panel will make good enough judgements to direct the resources into programmes that produce the desired results. Part of the judgement will inevitably be 'professional', in the sense that it will rely on experience of what has worked elsewhere as well as what works in the schemes being accredited. Presumably, this was the reason for employing panel members from overseas.

The final major risk is that the various national systems that the service now relies upon do not work as well as they should. The information strategy is the most obvious one, but there are various others, such as the system for finding places in secure units, which used to rely on local contact networks and which now is managed through national systems. The gamble is that what worked reasonably well at local level can be transferred to a national, centralised system.

CONCLUSION

Society places great reliance on the probation service. The recent changes in the organisation and management of the service are the end point of a long journey of nationalisation and standardisation. The methods that have been devised to manage the service include a range of standardisations of processes and programmes and a move away from standardisation of the background and qualifications of the staff. They create a unified, hierarchical service and a set of management instruments, including targets and inspections. There is an ambition to overlay these processes with the European Business Excellence Model.

It is an ambitious project especially as the changes in organisation and management have been introduced after a change in the mission of the service to one of punishment in the community. Many of the values and traditions of the old service will therefore not be available to the new hierarchy of managers and their boards.

The task has been taken on in parallel with the Home Office's ambition to bring about change in the prison service as part of the same agenda of reducing re-conviction rates. Prisons will be called upon to do more re-education and rehabilitation work with inmates.

One cannot help feeling a certain irony that much the same management structures and processes will be used to encourage the prison service to do more rehabilitation as have been devised to get the probation service to do more punishment.

22   Probation, Partnership and Civil Society

Mike Nellis

'PARTNERSHIP' POLICY 1990–1997

The probation service has a long, if largely undocumented, history of links with voluntary organisations, but it was only in the early 1990s that the term 'partnership' formally entered probation vocabularies. It was used to designate this relationship in a 'discussion document' and in a 'decision document'; both called *Partnership in Dealing with Offenders in the Community* (Home Office 1990c, 1992c). These sought to promote, extend and modify joint working between local probation services and a range of voluntary and private organisations, which they sometimes glossed as 'the independent sector', a term seemingly intended to contrast the assumed dynamism of such organisations with apparently moribund state bureaucracies, but which actually blurred important legal, administrative and cultural differences between the two types. Both documents appeared in the midst of the 'punishment in the community' initiative, at a time when the Home Office was seeking to push the probation service away from its social work traditions, to shift the role of probation officer towards that of case manager rather than all-purpose service provider, to adopt a tougher and more controlling approach to community sentences and, thereby, help to reduce the prison population. Four benefits were claimed for partnership working:

(a)   for the community (utilising its resources);

(b)   for the offender (facilitating reintegration);

(c)   for the probation service (improved efficiency and effectiveness); and

(d)   for the independent sector itself (increasing its opportunities and capacities).

In the Home Office (1993b) circular which followed up 'the decision document', partnership was defined very loosely as 'relations between the probation service and the private and voluntary sectors, whether on the basis of grants or payments, or services in kind or joint working relationships'.

The partnership initiative in probation owed more to managerialism than to a shift towards punishment. It was consistent with broader developments in public policy, notably the influence of the new public management (NPM) strategy, which, in the name of economy, efficiency and effectiveness, encouraged (among other things) community empowerment, contracting out, outsourcing and the creation of quasi-markets (Osborne and Gaebler 1992). It placed an overriding emphasis on securing 'value for money' and the use of compulsory competitive tendering (CCT) to select partners, as opposed to the traditional statutory strategy of grant aiding. A 'contract culture' had already developed in the community care field by the time the probation partnership papers appeared; local authorities were being required to purchase from others services they had hitherto provided 'in-house' to the old, the disabled and the mentally ill. NPM needs to be understood in the context of the general Thatcherite mission to 'roll back the frontiers of the state' (ostensibly to increase freedom and democracy), although this imperative was always more muted in the criminal justice than in the community care field, because a manifestly 'strong state', even when it cannot deal with crime alone, remains ideologically indispensable in public debate on law and order.

Public sector reaction to contracting out was largely negative, and the probation service was no exception. It feared job substitution — loss of jobs, loss of professionalism and a diminished service to offenders, delivered either by 'amateurs' in the voluntary sector or by profit-seeking entrepreneurs in the private sector. Some commentators worried that partnership with voluntary agencies was merely a precursor to the full or partial privatisation of probation and, indeed, there was at this time a barely veiled threat from Government that if the probation service did not shift from social work to punishment, it would be replaced by another, more compliant organisation. In practice, there was nonetheless a degree of goodwill on the part of the probation service towards many voluntary organisations which worked with offenders, so long as they presented no threat to the service's perceived professional responsibilities. Some services had created their own Care Trusts to access charitable funding, and individual officers had often stimulated the development of local voluntary bodies, including branches of victim support. For the most part, established voluntary organisations in the criminal justice field were disinclined to usurp probation functions; the Home Office underestimated their own commitment to humanistic ('social work') values and overestimated their aptitude and capacity to 'threaten' the service. Neither probation nor the voluntary sector was comfortable using the term 'partnership' normatively, to convey an ideal of positive and constructive cooperation, regardless of the power differentials that might prevail between the 'partners' in a contract culture. The voluntary sector resented use of the term 'independent', not least because of worries that its traditional independence to set its own goals and priorities, and to voice social criticism, would be lost if it became too embroiled in service delivery on behalf of state or-ganisations (Kay 1992). Private organisations themselves actually played little part in the partnership debate, although voluntary or-ganisations generally were being encouraged, and sometimes being assisted, by private organisations to become more 'businesslike' in the new culture.

In practical terms, there were several elements to the partnership strategy. Local probation services were required to spend 5 per cent of their cash-limited budgets on non-statutory service providers, and to consult widely with potential providers in their areas. They had to take over the Probation Supervision Grants Scheme (PSUGS) from the Home Office; a devolution strategy consistent with the decentralising impulse of the NPM, although tight oversight of local partnership plans remained at the centre. PSUGS was an amalgamation of several earlier Home Office schemes for grant-aiding specific voluntary organisations on the recommendation of local services. From the standpoint of large, national voluntary organisations with projects in several local areas, the earlier arrangement had the advantage of having only one contact point. After devolution, the large, national voluntaries had to draw up contacts with however many services they were involved with. The same applied a year later when the Probation Accommodation Grants Scheme (PAGS) was also devolved to local services, and the spending requirement was raised to 7 per cent. Lastly, local probation staff were required to withdraw from all voluntary sector management boards with which they were involved, in order to give a fair, competitive chance of funding to all potentially relevant service providers in a given locality (Home Office 1993c). This initially met with resistance, not only from probation services, but also from voluntary organisations — particularly those where there was never likely to be competition for their services, such as Victim Support — who found the presence of a probation officer on their boards helpful. To facilitate local liaison, most probation services set up a 'partnership forum' or 'partnership strategy group', building on pre-existing forums in the employment and accommodation fields, or creating new ones (Smith, Paylor and Mitchell 1993; James and Bottomley 1994).

For a handful of people in both the probation service and the voluntary sector, partnership offered an opportunity to pick up on, and pursue further, the service's brief experimental forays into community work and community development (Broad 1991; Sarkis and Webster 1995; Nellis 1995). The three-year plan for the probation service 1994–97 even seemed to hint at this, but in the main, these hopes were stillborn; this is not what partnership turned into. The ascendancy of managerial imperatives, and an ethos of value for money, ensured that what happened in practice was organisational capacity building — using voluntary and community organisations to help achieve service objectives — rather than community capacity building, the regeneration of supportive resources and networks — the 'social capital', which could both dampen criminal proclivities and provide incentives to law-abiding behaviour. Rhetorically, the construction of probation partnerships had a clear affinity with revitalising civil society, but in reality there were other tendencies in play as well, with probable outcomes very different from what revitalising civil society usually means.

But even as partnership practice was taking shape on the ground, the policy context, in which the idea had originally been rooted, was changing significantly, particularly for the probation service, but also — though less so — for the voluntary sector itself. After a distinct rightward shift in the Conservative Government in 1993, the Home

Office abandoned its commitment to penal reductionism; the ideals of punishment in the community and the break with social work remained, but emphasis shifted subtly towards a discourse which encompassed public protection and risk management as well as punishment, and in which increased prison use was openly countenanced. The probation service finally acquiesced in the 'punishment in the community' agenda, hoping to do so on its own terms, by staking its future on the What Works developments, evolving a steadily sharper distinction between addressing offending behaviour (a probation task) and meeting criminogenic need (a task for partners, who could perhaps keep social work values alive). The Home Office itself came to recognise that crime-focused voluntary organisations were even more reluctant to embrace 'punitiveness' than the probation service itself, and such organisations were never again to figure explicitly in policy discussions about the management of offenders in the community. The sense of threat-to-probation that had been implied in the original partnership documents had receded by the mid-1990s, although local services still experienced strong central direction, and pressure to take CCT more seriously, from an Inspectorate Report (HMIP 1996b). Although mutual trust was mentioned, there was a clear expectation in this report that voluntary organisations were expected to be passive service providers, and that the probation service should be the dominant partner.

Apart from reservations about the seriousness with which CCT was being taken, the Inspectorate was complimentary about the ways in which partnership had developed, emphasising particularly the effective managerial control which the service had over its partners. A clear and unsurprising national picture had emerged of the kind of voluntary organisations with which the service was working. The fields of work in which partnership was being developed in 1996–97, listed in order of the amount of money being spent in each field nationally, was as follows: drugs and alcohol; employment/education and training; accommodation; multicore programmes; family court welfare work; motor projects; financial advice; sex offenders; community service; outdoor activities; crime prevention; throughcare; bail; violence/anger management; mentally disordered offenders; project evaluation; victim support and involving offenders in voluntary work (Home Office 1998b). This pattern owed a great deal to existing patterns of voluntary sector provision, and filled obvious gaps for probation. There was a marked preference for service involvement with small local voluntary bodies, as opposed to branches of larger nationals; whether this expressed a preference for easier-to-control groups, or a gesture towards local community development, or both, is not clear — the motive may be different in different fields of work, even in the same service.

In the later years of the Conservative Government there was a discernible retreat from the hardline criticism of the public sector — centred on its allegedly inherent ineffectiveness — that had so energised Mrs Thatcher. The corollary of this, however, was the belief that with better, tougher management, statutory organisations could actually become more efficient and effective. They were thus required to accept more central direction, and to act in an even more regulatory fashion with such partners as they had. As Nicholas Deakin (2001, p. 28) was later to put it, there was in this period some recognition in Government that voluntary bodies could not simply substitute for statutory ones; their organisational forms, financial regimes, internal procedures and cultures were often dissimilar in ways that might crucially affect their capacity to undertake new tasks. A very probation-specific version of this same argument was put by Geoff Dobson (1997), ACOP's then lead officer on partnership, who mapped out more carefully than anyone had done hitherto, what the precise disadvantages of contracting out were in the context of public protection, and what the case for in-house provision in probation actually was. But the rethinking, of which Dobson was a part expressly, did not augur a return to pre-Thatcher days, and certainly not to the ideal of an autonomous voluntary sector, for independence seemed now to be the last thing for which it was valued by Government.

The growing anxieties which the sector had had about its increasing cooption into an ever more regulatory state — its relegation to a mere 'third sector' providing services alongside the state and the market — found expression in the Report of the Commission on the Future of the Voluntary Sector (1996) (the Deakin Report). This remains the most cogent defence to date of voluntary organisations as expressions of an independent civil society free in part to conceive and pursue purposes independent of the state. This is a vital indicator of democratic health. Voluntary organisations should be free to enter into service-providing partnerships without losing their right to act as advocates of reform or as critics of the state. While having to accept standards of good practice, the sector should not be pressured into taking on functions best performed by the market or the state. These were fine affirmations, but as the Report itself recognised, easier said than done; the 'institutional isomorphism' — the steady succumbing of voluntary bodies to the managerialist ethos of the state — which DiMaggio and Powell (1983) had famously anticipated, was increasingly apparent.

THE DEVELOPMENT OF PARTNERSHIP IN PRACTICE

This section reviews, somewhat selectively, three major pieces of research on partnership that were undertaken in the 1990–97 period. Although activities on the ground may have moved on since they were completed, they constitute the empirical bedrock from which our thinking on partnership needs to proceed. Bev Cross's (1997) research was undertaken in two probation service areas in the north of England between 1991 and 1994. Anita Gibbs (1999, 2001) researched three such areas in the southwest between 1993 and 1996. Judith Rumgay (2000; see also Rumgay and Cowan 1998) undertook a national survey and then a more focused study of substance abuse organisations and their links with probation services between 1994 and 1997. Between them, they advance our knowledge of partnership in practice enormously, but diversity of approach and attitude within the 55 probation areas that existed at the time, as well as diversity within and across different fields of voluntary activity itself, require us to be cautious about making generalisations.

Both Cross and Gibbs were interested in what services and voluntary bodies themselves defined as real and meaningful partnerships, and both found instances of working relationships, even within contractual frameworks, based on equality of respect. But within any given probation service there was a range of interrelationships — the tone of the relationship varied according to the field of activity and the personnel involved — and not all could accurately be characterised as partnership in the sense of mutuality. Gibbs distinguished four primary discourses on these interrelationships, each clustered around a distinctive issue. The first corresponded to the official contracting-out model. The others centred on:

(a) an ideal of interdependency and mutual reliance (without necessarily expecting equality);

(b) an ideal of equality and reciprocity; and

(c)   a commitment to empowering service users;

and, within the discourse — in all cases — attention was drawn to the discrepancy between the ideal and the reality.

Respondents often felt that the Government framework for partnership development had fallen short of the partnership ideal and had not paid sufficient regard to notions of equality and fairness. Voluntary sector respondents in particular felt aggrieved that they had to enter into unequal partnerships, where the probation service set the agenda. A few respondents felt that the influence of new public managerialism and the purchaser-provider split had led to the voluntary sector being 'used and abused'. The probation service allocated most of its money to the organisations which could best show value for money and were more likely to view service users in terms of their offending behaviour rather than more holistically, as many of the voluntary organisations preferred to view them (Gibbs 2001)

In general, for the voluntary sector, the contract culture had meant more intense competition between organisations (which had been muted in the days of grantaiding), a more business-like approach to strategy, performance and evaluation, and the complexity of developing service level agreements with a range of different bodies and organisations, to whom services were being supplied. Management boards had become much more aware of their legal and financial responsibilities. There was less of an emphasis on unpaid volunteers and more on paid members of staff (posts funded by the probation service or other statutory body, or by trusts). Voluntary organisations became part of the statutory process, being obliged to inform probation services if clients attending their programmes failed to attend or cooperate, in ways which can lead to breach. There was no unanimity of response to these developments in the voluntary sector, with some seeing traditions threatened and ideals corrupted, while others, often newly created, sought to seize fresh opportunities. 'The pragmatic approach of some voluntary organisations enabled them to have more influence upon the specification of service level agreements and be clearer about what they would and would not offer' (Gibbs 2001, p. 20).

Rumgay's is the most subtle and fine-grained research on partnership practice to date. It looks particularly at the substance abuse field, and its conclusions may hold good for this field only and not necessarily for probation partnerships in other fields. It involved a national survey, followed by a more narrow focus on 25 partnership projects (in 16 probation services and 24 voluntary substance abuse agencies) and nine in-service only projects, and concluded with a very specific analysis of three projects (two partnership and one in service). Rumgay's first major finding was that, in the substance abuse field, voluntary sector partners consider themselves to be in a position of strength, and rarely fear the loss of specific contractual partnerships; there will always be other sources of funding for services to drug users. 'The scarcity of voluntary sector providers at local level,' Rumgay (2000, p. 247) writes, 'strengthens the position of those which do exist'. Secondly, there was in the main, in the successful projects, no enmity from probation towards the project workers; they worked with 'clients' in a treatment-orientated way, which probation officers found acceptable and consistent with their own beleaguered professional ideals, 'enabling officers to avoid entrapment in narrow roles of correctional enforcement' (p. 249). The substance abuse agencies understood well enough the tougher approach, which the Home Office expected them to take, but because of their position of strength felt able to resist the worst excesses of this, and to offer client-centred services which kept coercion to a minimum. Probation services were happy to let them, and actively encouraged them, believing that this was the best, most effective way to help individuals and reduce drug-related crime. Thus, in this research, 'partnership' genuinely meant sharing, support and empowerment; the relationship may at base have been contractual, but this did not prevent 'value-based, informal and creatively collusive inter-agency negotiations' (p. 251) from shaping good work. Rumgay eloquently sums up:

> It is overly simplistic to view the contractual relationship merely as one in which a weaker voluntary agency yields degrees of autonomy to, and fulfils only those tasks which are determined by a more powerful statutory one.... More sophisticated and helpful analyses appeal to the interdependence of different organisations, embedded within a network of relationships, which necessarily involve mutual alliance, reciprocity, assistance and trust. (2000, p. 251)

Such creativity does indeed invite commendation, but some reservations are nonetheless required. In her conclusions (if not in the text itself), Rumgay tends to underplay the extent to which probation and voluntary sector workers achieved success by going against the grain of the prevailing managerial and crime control culture; while it is important to know that both the opportunity and the motivation existed to do this, its precariousness needs also to be acknowledged. It should also be noted that Rumgay's research was undertaken before the advent of New Labour (before the Effective Practice Initiative; before drug treatment and testing orders — a sentence with some in-built voluntary sector providers; before the tighter National Standards issued in 2000) and the approach to partnership in the probation service may have changed in the intervening period; there have been no comparably sophisticated research projects to ascertain this. In addition, as she, and others, point out, the relationship between statutory and voluntary agencies can vary across different fields of activity (and, they might add, over time). The dynamics that apply in the substance abuse field may not apply elsewhere, and may not last forever. A brief perusal of partnership in the race equality field will demonstrate this and, at the end, return us to the inescapable issue of 'community'.

RACE EQUALITY AND PARTNERSHIP

Cross noted in her study that voluntary agencies in the black and Asian communities, which tended to be small and very localised, while keen to influence probation practice, did not necessarily share the service's or the Home Office's view of priorities. They did not find it as easy as more professionalised voluntary groups to relate to statutory agencies, funding applications, in particular, being time-consuming and over-complicated. Neither crime control *per se* nor value for money were likely to be the starting points for such groups: 'they may consider it more important to address underlying structural issues,' Cross (1997, p. 74) wrote, 'for example, unemployment and lack of social facilities for youth, to say nothing of the institutionalised racism that tends to criminalise and punish them disproportionately to their white counter-parts'. A much more recent study of ten local services, by the Probation Inspectorate, in Autumn 1999, undertaken in the aftermath of the MacPherson Report, suggested that too little had changed. Nationally, 32 of the 55 services had not allocated any of their partnership budget to minority ethnic service users, although this did not mean the services were not working with ethnic community groups, or that black and Asian offenders did not benefit from other partnership projects.

Nonetheless, two rural services were specifically criticised for failing to pay attention to the needs of the very small minority groups within their boundaries, and there was a general sense that many more services had made insufficient effort to consult with relevant minority groups on matters of strategy and service delivery:

> It was apparent from discussion with representatives from community groups that all services had considerable work to do to improve their standing and to gain the confidence of the local ethnic minority community, both in terms of work with offenders, and as a potential employer. Although perceptions varied, common themes emerged and it was apparent that the representatives interviewed from the local minority ethnic community saw the probation service as an institutionally racist criminal justice organisation. (HMIP 2000f, p. 87)

Taylor (2001, p. 101) observes generally that 'black voluntary organisations did argue that there was systematic discrimination' among statutory agencies, but the use of the blanket term 'local minority ethnic community' nonetheless suggests a flaw in the Inspectorate's own reasoning — there is no single such community, nationally or (often) locally. It is the very existence of diversity and, indeed, conflict within and between different minority groups that can make relating to them so difficult for statutory organisations. Issues of representativeness, who speaks for whom, continually arise. At local level, for example, the Commission for Racial Equality is not always accepted as representative of all minority group interests. The critical edge of the term 'institutional racism' will be blunted, if gradations and types of racist expression are not acknowledged, and if organisational and political factors, operating separately from racism, are not given their due weight as obstacles to good partnership practice. It is these factors, which Cariba, an African-Caribbean group in Coventry, seems to be identifying, insisting that partnership ought to be about ceding at least some influence to some people at the grass roots in local communities:

> There should be more liaison conferences with the probation service and the community in order for both sides to work more closely together and also complement each other, not for one party feeling as though they are big brother and the other is a 'Do as I say' organisation. I believe it is a fact if you take away all the voluntary

organisations from working with the probation service then the agency will not cope by itself. We know how the grass roots work, where probation officers coming in and out of a town area into a new area would not know the community as well as we locals. (Cariba, quoted in HMIP 2000, p. 87)

Cariba gives clear expression to the communitarian ideal and to the view that civil society — at least as much as the state — should play a significant part in preventing and responding to crime. It is by no means an unproblematic ideal — communities can be destructive and exclusive, and there are forces within civil society that are deeply hostile to liberal and humane responses to crime, which can only be checked by the state. But a great deal more thinking has been done since the partnership debate began as to how civil society might be mobilised constructively, centred particularly around the ideas of 'restorative justice' and 'community justice' (Clear and Karp 1999; Nellis 2000b; Braithwaite and Strang 2001), and it is within these frameworks that the partnership debate now needs to be recast. The advent of a modernising New Labour Government in 1997 hinted faintly at the possibility of such recasting, but despite adding — or rather augmenting — an important new dimension to partnership practice, it has so far fallen short.

NEW LABOUR: CRIME AND DISORDER PARTNERSHIPS

Despite signing a National Compact on Government-voluntary sector relations (inspired by a recommendation of the Deakin Commission) in November 1998, New Labour policy on the voluntary sector has been in many respects a continuation of Conservative policy, slightly more empathetic in tone, but still emphasising the importance of voluntary and private sector service provision, the demonstrable need for efficiency and effectiveness, and the necessity for regulation and monitoring. New Labour's pledge to 'put voluntary action at the heart of restoring civil society' was arguably more deeply grounded in deeper communitarian influences than the Major Government's half-hearted rediscovery of 'active citizenship' had been, but it had the same managerial overlay, expressed in this instance as commitment to 'joined-up thinking' and 'joined-up government', i.e. stronger communication and collaboration between statutory agencies as well as

' voluntary, private and community ones (Scanlon 2000).
ur also developed a new quality control strategy — 'Best
which supposedly muted the worst excesses of compulsory
e tendering on voluntary organisations, albeit with ambivalent results. Tony Blair has argued personally that 'the third sector' —
a term connoting service delivery rather than independence — is
essential to the Third Way (New Labour's ideological reference point,
see Giddens 2000) as a means of revitalising community, and although
the tensions between this position and seeing voluntary organisations as
the backbone of civil society remains, New Labour has taken some steps
in the right direction — particularly in the community safety field — as
well as in the wrong direction.

Certain aspects of the Crime and Disorder Act 1998, the legislation
with which New Labour sought to give expression to its manifesto
promise to be 'tough on crime and tough on the causes of crime', have
much to recommend them. Building on pre-existing developments in
multi-agency crime prevention (Crawford 1998), the Act placed a legal
duty on the police and the local authorities to undertake detailed audits
of local crime problems and, on a three-year cycle, to work collab-
oratively with other organisations to devise community safety strategies, among them health authorities and probation committees (now
probation boards). The Act also required that two specific voluntary
groups — Neighbourhood Watch and Victim Support — were involved
in each local authority area, as well as 'groups established in the
interests of women, young people, the elderly, the disabled, ethnic
minorities, gay and lesbian people, religious purposes, residents,
shopkeepers [and] cooperatives'.

In research terms, little is known about the workings of crime and
disorder partnerships. Hester (2000) has surveyed the nationwide
involvement of voluntary and community groups in the audit and
strategy-making processes (many are involved, providing specialist
information on harder-to-reach groups). The Probation Inspectorate has
examined the contribution of probation to the partnerships, in ten areas
of the country (HMIP 2000d; see also Home Office 2000b). It found that
probation services were occasionally regarded as the lead agency on
specific aspects of the strategy, e.g., West Yorkshire in respect of house
and commercial burglary, and domestic violence, Hampshire in relation
to racially motivated crime and harassment, sometimes in conjunction
with voluntary sector partners. The Inspectorate's earlier report on race

equality was complimentary about both actual and potential probation service involvement in crime and disorder partnerships, not least because they had been strongly endorsed by the MacPherson Report as means by which cultural diversity might be promoted and racism challenged (HMIP 2000f, p. 85). It is in these forums, rather than in the probation service itself, that 'the absence of a strategic vision about community engagement' (p. 87) could most usefully be addressed, because as both Sibbitt (1997) and Bowling (2000) have argued, any adequate response to racial harassment and violence must address the broad community context in which racist attitudes are formed and sustained, as well as the specific actions of convicted perpetrators.

This point can in fact be made about crime in general, and returns us to the community capacity building dimension in the original probation partnership concept. Key thinkers and researchers repeatedly acknowledge that, while meaning can indeed be given to the term 'partnership' and satisfying things done in its name, it is still falling far short of what it needs to be, or could be, if its potential is to be realised. The practical emphasis needs to go beyond organisational capacity building to community capacity building; the vision needs to be less probation-centric and more genuinely community-orientated. This is not to devalue the narrower forms of work — some has been demonstrably valuable — but it is to say that partnership practice thus far is not yet equal to the challenge of the times. The need for genuine community capacity building still remains. The revitalisation of civil society — those elements of it essential to crime reduction — has barely begun. The crime and disorder partnerships undoubtedly move nearer to these ideals than the probation partnership strategy has done on its own, and the probation service has a significant part to play in making them work.

CONCLUSION: DANCING TO A NEW TUNE?

In respect of probation partnerships specifically, there seems to be no doubt that many voluntary organisations have bought into the contract culture and the new managerialism, and that the relationship with service funders has grown less strained as a result. Both sides — in many, if not all, fields of activity — accept the basic legitimacy of the contractual relationship, and sometimes, within it, relations of mutual trust and respect can be developed. Probation managers speak with relief of the growing professionalism of the voluntary sector, its acceptance of 'realities' — meaning, by and large, that it has accepted its lot as a third sector. But, as Margaret Harris (2001, p. 219) suggests, 'even if these changes are regarded as advantageous by and for individual voluntary agencies, the question of what they are doing to the voluntary sector as a whole must now be faced'. Her picture of what seems to be happening is, from a liberal democratic perspective, an alarming one, with clear evidence from a range of research studies that Government pressure to increase capacity in non-governmental organisations, and the growth of regulation over them, leads inexorably to 'standardisation, formalisation and professionalism within the voluntary sector'. However much probation services — and possibly offenders and communities — benefit from this, there is a downside in the spread of managerial forms of social control.

Although it may be legitimated by rhetoric to the contrary, this is expressly not the empowering communitarian vision that is being implemented, but something more akin to the managerialisation of civil society, the reconfiguration of voluntary and community organisations in the image of the state. The very qualities that are in theory being sought in the voluntary, community and informal sectors are being muted either by the imposition of direction and control from above, or by deliberate acquiescence and passivity in the sectors themselves, on the grounds that there is no alternative and that this is now the order of things. Local communities and ordinary citizens, whose involvement had been made to sound essential to the policy process — and to crime reduction — are only able to engage with the policy process on terms set by the statutory agencies, who fund them.

The recent transformations in the structure and administration of probation give no reason to believe that there will be a change of direction. The National Probation Service came into being in April 2001, placing central authority in a National Director for the first time and formally reducing the autonomy of the 42 — hitherto 54 — local probation areas. The mission statement of the new service, *A New Choreography*, cites 'partnership' as a core value, defining it as a 'highly collaborative approach to add value to the capacity of the NPS to achieve its stated outcomes' (Wallis 2001, p. 8). As before, the managerialist vision prevails; if anything, in order to meet tightly specified crime reduction targets by 2004, it intensifies. There is no sense in *A New Choreography* of the voluntary sector having value in its own right; it is a service provider, a third sector, nothing more. The document takes for granted that voluntary organisations will be involved in the delivery of effective practice programmes, alleviating criminogenic needs, but, beyond a token nod towards the need for flexibility at local level, its approach to targets and timescales illustrates precisely the way in which the managerial imperatives of large statutory organisations make it difficult for smaller organisations to retain integrity in their dealings with them.

The fact of centralisation may itself have implications for partnership. Local flexibility was never absolute in the old structure, but in a centralised service it may become inherently more difficult. There was arguably a political case for centralisation — it gave the Government more control over the service, it increased its accountability and it gave the service itself a strong voice at the centre — but there were no *a priori* reasons to believe that operational effectiveness would be enhanced by centralisation. The process was not evidence-led in that respect (Nellis 2000b), and a number of commentators believed it to be quite inconsistent with the emphatically local — and wholly sensible — approach to crime reduction taken in the Crime and Disorder Act 1998. Policy appeared to be pulling the probation service in incompatible directions, raising anxieties that, if the new centre stripped too much autonomy from the 42 local areas (as well it might, simply in order to establish its identity and its authority in a field where nothing like it had existed before), sensitivity towards local voluntary organisations and to the contours of local need might be jeopardised.

For now, the outcomes of centralisation must remain speculative; all that can be said are that there are no real signs — certainly not in the criminal justice field — that the autonomy of the voluntary sector is being safeguarded in the manner hoped for by the Deakin Commission. There are clear variations in the way in which different voluntary organisations, in different fields of activity, relate to the probation service, but the dominant trend appears to be towards incorporation. While this reflects the success of one aspect of Government policy — to be an efficient manager of social policies — it neglects and distorts the communitarian vision, stifling the constructive elements of civil society, rather than empowering them. The situation may be helped, if campaigning organisations such as the Howard League and the Prison Reform Trust could form strategic alliances with service-providing voluntary bodies, in order that alternative visions of the voluntary sector's role in criminal justice can be kept alive. In the meantime, two permutations are likely to occur within the existing partnership framework, and one without it, which may have implications for policy and practice in this field.

First, it seems likely that the emerging debate about the role of voluntary organisations in the prison service — especially in relation to throughcare and resettlement — will eventually overlap with the ongoing probation debate on partnership. This will be especially likely if, as anticipated, the traditional distinction between community penalties and custodial penalties is superseded by the concept of 'the seamless sentence' and 'custody plus' (short initial periods of custody, followed by longer, highly intensive periods of community supervision). A national voluntary organisation, CLINKS, is already involved in promoting prison–community links by helping other voluntary organisations to develop and manage their relationship with local prisons; sooner or later its work will impinge on probation.

Secondly, within the general debate on the place of the voluntary sector in criminal justice, the Government is likely to give particular encouragement to faith-based organisations, some of which (notably Mennonites and Quakers) have in fact been significant promoters of restorative justice, many more of which already do vast amounts of unpublicised 'social work' in Britain's poorest communities. There is an element of emulating contemporary American developments in this particular strategy, where the term 'compassionate conservativism' has become code for the supplanting of state-based welfare initiatives with religious and philanthropic charity, particularly for the hard-to-reach, unlovable, undeserving poor (e.g., habitual criminals and drug addicts), on whom state expenditure is always hard to justify with 'respectable' elements of the electorate. But it is an idea that has surfaced historically more than once, not always in a context hostile to state welfare, and New Labour could, if it wished, claim an authentic Fabian root for some aspects of it. Reflecting on the manifest limitations of state agencies to effect 'reformation of character' in offenders, Sydney and Beatrice Webb asked 80 years ago, in perfect seriousness:

> Would it be quite out of the question for the Home Office to try the experiment, for a limited term of years, of entrusting the entire administration of one of the prisons to (say) the Salvation Army, the Society of Friends, the Church of England or the Roman Catholic

Church, if any of these volunteered for so onerous, and yet so important a public service? (Webb and Webb 1922, p. 242–3)

Eighty years ago this may have constituted thinking the unthinkable. The equivalent today concerns the role of the private sector, rather than the churches. We noted earlier that private sector organisations have figured little in debates on partnership since 1990, but that there has always been the possibility — and within the service, the fear — that that may change. We must now acknowledge the undoubtedly growing influence of private sector organisations in criminal justice, noting that it has largely taken place outside the discourse of partnership. Thus, neither private prison providers nor the three companies providing electronic monitoring in England and Wales — Securicor, Premier and GSSC — are usually thought of as partner organisations in the same way that voluntary and informal bodies are thought of as partners, not least because they are embedded in globe-spanning corporations and possess a level of independence and freedom from routine public scrutiny that even powerful voluntary partners cannot begin to match. On the basis of developments that have already occurred, it is not wholly unreasonable to suggest that these organisations might assume a significance in criminal justice in the near future greater than anything that has been evolving in the more obviously recognisable sphere of 'partnership'; commercial organisations are, after all, a manifestation of civil society in their own right, and they are certainly being revitalised. The key developments so far have been as follows.

First, the principled refusal of leading childcare voluntary organisations to set up secure training centres (custody for under-14s) for the Conservative Government in the mid-1990s led instead to contracts going to the private sector. Secondly, prison privatisation was deliberately used by Government to set new standards of efficiency in prison management more generally. Thirdly, failing prisons in the state sector have recently been threatened with privatisation, unless they improve their performance, mirroring processes that have already taken place with failing schools. It is not inconceivable that local probation areas, which fail to meet their targets in 2004, might be named and shamed, as schools have been (and as police forces are going to be), and treated in the same way. The New Labour Government's promise in its second term to increase private sector involvement in public service delivery will surely create a climate in which this could happen, not least because crime control remains an area of policy on which the public perceive them to have failed.

There is no doubt that the private sector has latterly been a major innovator in criminal justice and crime prevention, largely through the development of new technology, and this may be set to continue, with potentially dramatic consequences (Mair 2001). Electronic monitoring, for example, is now well established in England and Wales and cannot be disinvented. It could be used to augment certain community penalties and to facilitate a return to a penal reductionist agenda (Lilly and Nellis 2001), and it could have a place even in a system which was predominantly orientated towards restorative and community justice. But, just as easily, it could make possible a fundamental shift in community crime control towards containment and surveillance, displacing old probation ideals once and for all, and minimising rehabilitative, restorative and reintegrative possibilities. The seeds of both scenarios are implicit in the current partnership debate — conceived as something which does involve the private sector, for better or worse — and it remains to be seen which gains ascendancy in the next few years.

23 Reflections on Work in Progress

Malcolm Lacey

A LAW ENFORCEMENT AGENCY

This book appears in the first year after the creation of the new National Probation Service on 1 April 2001. The contributions were written in the time leading up to that event and to the General Election in June 2001, when 'law and order' was one of the four main issues alongside health, education and the economy. Politicians are responding to public anger about the increase in crime, the sense that in some urban areas there is a breakdown of order, and that even in rural areas people feel vulnerable. So, even as the book goes to press, new issues are continually being raised in the papers and the Government is preparing yet another Criminal Justice Bill. The new service is being born into a fractious and turbulent world, in which its philosophy as well as its performance is bound to come under scrutiny.

The contributions reflect this. There is a real engagement with the issues, which while recognising the difficulties the service will face, conveys a sense of buoyancy and a desire to get on with the job. There is a feeling of relief that the threats of the past decade to the very existence of the service have ended; but it is more than relief, it is the optimism associated with any new beginning and that, as Raynor puts it (see Chapter 11), there is now 'the best ever prospect for the probation service' and 'a real confidence that there is really something effective that can be delivered'. But, as he also says, 'if the new National Probation Service is to make a real difference, it must stand for something, and articulate what it stands for'.

The key statement that has so far been made is by the former Minister for Prisons and Probation, Paul Boateng: 'We are a law enforcement agency. This is what we are. This is what we do.' As Hopley comments (see Chapter 18), those words were used deliberately to signify the change in culture that would be necessary if a clear priority on the aims of the protection of the public, the reduction of re-offending and the proper punishment of the offender were to be achieved. Perhaps even more emphatic, though not as high-profile, was the decision to repeal the founding duty of the 'old' probation service to 'advise, assist and befriend' those on probation.

This clarity of focus is reinforced by the fact that there is now a National Directorate charged with ensuring that this policy is adhered to throughout England and Wales. The firm grasp of policy direction, together with the various mechanisms that have been put in place to ensure that it is implemented, are generally welcomed. The National Director, in her *New Choreography* (Wallis 2001), has emphasised that proper punishment means no collusion with offenders about the harm that they have done, and that enforcement is to have the highest priority in order to establish trust with the community. This policy thrust can already be seen to be making an impact on the service. Hill, in her contribution on working in the courts (see Chapter 6), uses Boateng's statement as a statement of principle, which enables a shift from 'a historical emphasis on social work to a current requirement to enforce the law'. Thurston (in Chapter 13), in exploring the role of hostels, sees a profound shift 'from seeing probation as the apologist for offenders to recognising that probation also had a responsibility to victims and the general public. In short, the emergence of probation as a major contributor to public protection.' Hill acknowledges that many found the statement 'too stark to be comfortable, and it can clearly give only a partial view of the complexity of the task'.

The strength of the contributions is that they take the new mission as read and then go on to explore the complexity. A core part of that complexity emerges in one of Hill's own statements (see Chapter 6): 'The prosecution of breaches conveys important information to offenders and to the courts about the probation service's reliability in supervising offenders effectively.' In this case, 'effectively' seems to refer to the service's success in enforcing a disciplinary process, whereas its more general use in relation to the What Works agenda refers to its rehabilitative effect. Obviously, these two senses are not necessarily in opposition, but neither do they necessarily always coincide. Breach proceedings could be taken as a sign of failure of either or both, though, it is hoped in the short run, that may not matter, if the key issue for the new service is to convey information that it is reliable, that this is where the community's trust begins. These issues are explored in depth by Raynor in Chapter 11. The service will have to clarify them through reflection on actual practice over the next few years.

The speech of the new Home Secretary, David Blunkett, to the launch conference of the new National Probation Service in July 2001, will have immeasurably strengthened optimism about the future of the service. Not only is there to be a massive increase in the size of the service to supervise many more offenders, but he has also made an explicit commitment to rehabilitation. As his speech makes clear, this does not do away with the rigour that is required of the service in law enforcement, but it does place rehabilitation at the core of the effort to reduce re-offending. That target is very ambitious, aiming at a rate of 40 per cent rather than the current one of 56 per cent. Further, the Home Secretary accepts that such a strategy needs to be accompanied by one of persuading the public that their safety is best assured through effective community supervision:

I am not going soft. I've not abandoned my roots. I represent a deeply deprived inner-city community who have had their bellyful of people apologising for those who destroy lives. Undoubtedly, people learn more about crime in prison than they will learn anywhere else in their lives. The object is not to increase the prison population, but to prevent people going into prison in the first place. *Rehabilitation is the highest possible priority for those who enter the criminal justice system.*[1]

There are several themes that emerge from the chapters in this book, which explore what rehabilitation implies in contemporary society.

---

[1] Emphasis added. The speech as reported is more emphatic than the Home Office press release, *Put the sense back into sentencing*, 5 July 2001.

FEAR AND RESPONSIBILITY

Several contributors draw attention to the some of the characteristics of modern society. Faulkner (Chapter 3) identifies neo-liberalism — the authority of the market — and consumerism and managerialism — a pragmatic, risk-averse approach, emphasising personal responsibility and social control. Both of these take 'a utilitarian and instrumental view of justice', which can lead to legal vengeance rather than the principle of fairness. Lacey (Chapter 2) draws attention to the insecurity felt by many people within a globalised economy, which can lead to de-personalising and exclusionary attitudes. Kemshall (Chapter 7) refers to 'a climate of fear' and the separation of the social causes of crime from crime management policies; and to the 'the patrolling of community and social boundaries to determine which kinds of people are deemed acceptable for inclusion and who are not'.

This climate has fostered the growth of 'responsibilisation', which Kemshall describes as the individual being made responsible for his or her risk choices, and as any failure being blameworthy, unmitigated by any structural disadvantage or misfortune. This may be viewed as echoing 'people apologising for those who destroy lives', of which the Home Secretary's constituents have had their 'bellyful'. What is at issue is more than presentation, though that will be have to be addressed, but whether rehabilitation is achievable, if the focus is kept so relentlessly on the individual's need to reform, essential though it is to recruit his or her motivation for change.

SOCIAL JUSTICE AND PARTNERSHIP

Running through many of the chapters is the impossibility of rehabili-tation unless issues of social justice and social provision are taken into account. Fullwood (Chapter 4) argues that the development of the probation service needs to be seen in a wider context, which en-compasses social policy. As he comments, there has often been an insularity in the way in which probation officers and probation managers have seen the task, though that has improved a great deal in the last decade. It is now inconceivable that a service could supervise offenders without having in place a series of agreements with health, education and accommodation providers, employers and a variety of voluntary and independent sector agencies. One very obvious example is the role envisaged by Thurston for probation hostels (see Chapter 13), of promoting positive change to prepare residents for living peacefully in society. To accomplish this, 'the strategic importance of securing appropriate move-on accommodation' has to be not just recognised, but planned. There is a similar need to agree protocols with local colleges in relation to the training and educational needs of offenders, and to develop employment prospects with local employers. NACRO has headed a 'Going Straight to Work' campaign, supported by firms such as KPMG, Tesco, Whitbread and Granada.

Probation centres also offer unique opportunities for cooperation with local health services for diagnosis and health education. The general health of offenders is amongst the lowest in the population, as well as their susceptibility to injury through accidents and assaults and the high proportion of attempted suicides. Probation can offer a gateway to the health service in reaching those the NHS finds it hardest to engage with, even though many of its health improvement targets are aimed at them. These are all mainstream provisions, to be provided without further stigma. Clearly, specific difficulties, such as alcohol related behaviour, drug taking and mental disturbance, also require joint work with a range of other services. If the probation service in future is going to be much more closely involved with providing What Works programmes in prisons and with prisoners on supervised release, then there is also scope for helping the prison service and the health service to relate to each other in a more productive way than is often the case at present.

The probation service is a pivotal agency in enabling all these organisations to work together, partly because it is small and so is released from the temptation to try to provide everything 'in-house'. If the necessary resources are to be made available to offenders, the service has to negotiate their use with its various partners. Just as Holt argues for the probation officer to take on the role of case manager (see Chapter 16), so probation management can take on a similar role at the institutional level. Just as, at the case level, the case manager provides a human link, acts as a champion, monitors the delivery of services, and combats the fragmented thinking and experience of offenders, so at the agency level, the service can undertake similar activities with the whole range of agencies within its local area. This is surely one of the purposes of the newly constituted boards.

The meaning of 'partnership' is discussed by Nellis (Chapter 22). He concentrates on the voluntary sector and worries about the way in which the probation service may simply use voluntary agencies to deliver programmes, the content and style of which will be defined by its own managers, driven to a large extent by the National Directorate rather than responsive to local concerns. The service does face a difficulty because, in relation to the statutory authorities it has to deal with, it is in a weak position. For example, as Thurston points out, the cash contribution that probation can make is tiny in comparison with that of the other accommodation and housing agencies; whereas, at least in relation to the smaller voluntary agencies, the probation service may be the major, in some cases, the only funder. Nellis is surely right in arguing that 'community capacity building' must be the logic behind both. In relation to statutory agencies, this may be expressed in bringing the needs of offenders to the attention of providers, who might otherwise tend to ignore them as less deserving. With voluntary organisations, the service may have to learn to see them 'as expressions of an independent civil society free in part to conceive and pursue purposes independent of the state. This is a vital indicator of democratic health. Voluntary organisations should be free to enter into service-providing partnership without losing their right to act as advocates of reform or as critics of the state'.

In specific terms, there are two major issues, both raised by Kemshall (Chapter 7), about which the service will have to be certain of its own practice, if joint work with other agencies is to proceed effectively. The first is the widespread use of the strange phrase 'criminogenic needs'. As Kemshall writes:

> While superficially the generation of such factors seems little more than the production of actuarially based research in to offender risks ... [it may separate] the social causes of crime from crime management policies ...

Later, she goes on to say:

> The continued language of need obscured an important transition in the service's approach and relationship to offenders. Offenders were no longer 'at risk' — they were transformed into the site of risk, a repository of 'needs' that inevitably results in criminal behaviour, if appropriate interventions are not provided ...

Kemshall, who is one of the pioneers in helping the service to identify offenders who may be a high risk to other people, worries that this 'use of criminal justice policy and risk management ... naturally weakens the service's commitment to issues of social justice'. In other words, the conflation of crime-producing factors with needs blurs the distinction between acts for which an offender can genuinely be held accountable and the circumstances over which he or she may have little control. This is well illustrated by Johnson and Rex (Chapter 12):

> As part of a general programme of estate regeneration, groups of offenders (largely from the area themselves) worked under the direction of a residents' association. Members of the association complained to probation service staff that they were being too rigorous in enforcing orders, and were not showing sufficient understanding of the problems the offenders faced — a nice demonstration of how community service brought about changed attitudes towards offenders, as well as changes in them.

It will be worthwhile for the service to reflect on this little cameo in relation to the concerns raised by Nellis and Kemshall. At the same time, the service has to manage the 'professional conundrum' identified by Thurston — 'hostels are best suited for high-risk cases, but some of these pose too much of a risk for hostels to manage'.

The second issue relates to protocols about the transmission of information. It has to be recognised that in an age of partnership and joint work, with records being passed not only between probation services, but also with the prison service and other local agencies, confidentiality can no longer be guaranteed and should not be offered. This has high costs. For example, it is generally agreed that a person who is HIV positive or who has AIDS, should have absolute control over with whom they share that information. If that person tells a probation officer, it is very hard to see how that can be recorded at all, as the probation service has no control over who may eventually see that record. More generally, offenders will become more reticent about sharing some of the intimate and painful experiences they need to talk about and come to terms with, if that information goes beyond the person they tell and a clearly defined circle of advisers or managers.

THE UNIQUE SKILL OF THE PROBATION OFFICER

This question of access to highly charged, personal communication is implicit in Chapter 10, written by Boswell. The case study she contributes brings home, very forcefully, the depth of human tragedy to which the probation officer is expected to respond. Such case studies ought to be pinned on the office wall of every Home Office civil servant, inspector, probation manager, magistrate and judge. There is a danger that this is being forgotten in the enthusiasm for the new orthodoxy of What Works, a method of working that does seem to offer dividends with many offenders. These programmes offer an accelerated course of social training, giving offenders what most of us gained through our upbringing, namely, the ability to control our impulses and gain some insight into how our behaviour affects other people. That has little relevance to those whose behaviour is beyond their control because of 'buried terror'. It is such offenders who present the greatest risk. It should never be forgotten that it is 'the unique skill of the professionally trained probation officer to identify, assess and seek to reduce the reasons for an individual's offending'. It is difficult to over-emphasise the point that Boswell is making. She relates the case study to a much bigger research sample, where it was

> very significant that many members of the sample had not been effectively helped to think through, interpret or resolve the traumatic event(s) which had occurred in their earlier lives, and that *this help, such as can be feasibly offered with probation supervision ..., could have provided a protective factor*, which might have made a difference to their later behaviour. (emphasis added)

This high expectation of the probation officer has many implications, not least for training.

One of the most telling observations in Chapter 17 by Knight is that a new and complex training provision has been put in place before the Home Office or the probation service could clearly identify the role and tasks of the qualified probation officer within the new National Service. The way in which probation training was handled by Government in the last decade of the last century, is nothing short of a public scandal. Knight's summary makes this crystal clear. Although the way training is to be provided is now settled, it cannot be forgotten that the service is lacking a whole cohort of trained officers. That puts pressure on managers to recruit other staff and to find ways of justifying their use on tasks that used to be carried out by probation officers.

What is more disturbing is that the core task, as presented by Boswell and by Holt in Chapter 16 on case management, has not been recognised by the service, with the result that training courses are unclear about what their 'end product' should be. To some extent, this stems from an under-estimation of the complexity of the role, not just by the Home Office, but also by members of the service itself. One example of this is how trainees are allowed to prepare and present pre-sentence reports. If assessment is the key process, from which all other decisions flow, how is it that some assessments are done by the least experienced members of the service, even if they are under supervision? Until they have had some experience of working with offenders, and of coordinating the resources that any one case needs, how can they assess what is necessary? It is rather like a consultant diagnosing on the information given by a houseman.

This stems from a public perception that affects social work as well as probation, that dealing with these matters is no more than common sense; and perhaps also from a lack of confidence within the service about the high level of skill that needs to be, and often is, exercised. One of the consequences is that the new training, although set at degree level, has to be completed within two years and is not followed by a confirmation year. This contrasts with the decision by the Department of Health to insist on a three-year training course for social workers followed by a probationary year. Furthermore, the course will not be linked to NVQ, presumably not because they do not want social workers to be competent, but because they recognise the importance of professional judgement in the complex human situations they will encounter. This is at least as true of probation officers, and it is hard to see how the difference in both the length and the structure of training can be justified, and how, in the long run, it will not lead to damaging comparisons of skill, status and pay.

Both Boswell and Williams (Chapters 10 and 5) make the point that there is no hard and fast distinction between perpetrators and victims. In his chapter about victims, Williams remarks that greater knowledge about the victim can also assist in the preparation of court reports and in rehabilitative work with offenders. Its routine availability has done a good deal to change the occupational culture of the probation service, increasing sensitivity to victims' needs and wishes. This is a real advance, its own intrinsic justification, and perhaps makes the National Director's aim of there being fewer victims easier to achieve. In addition, if the service can seize the opening then understanding victims can lead to new initiatives with offenders, which will be better targeted and more closely tied to reparative actions. This means forging new alliances with victims' organisations, another example of the importance of partnership.

PARTNERSHIP

As we reflect on all these matters, it becomes clear that partnerships have to be entered into at all levels of the service. Two key issues are immediately raised: the first is the crucial importance of the case manager. As Knight points out (see Chapter 17), there are statements that the role of the case manager will be crucial in the evolving What Works programmes, yet the Home Office, the Inspectorate and the service itself seem unclear about what it really constitutes. Probation officers may drift towards seeing themselves as programme deliverers, because most undoubtedly come into the service 'to work with people' and are put off by the connotations of 'manager'. Whether or not this is the case, no one can have any doubts about the centrality of the role and the high level of inter-personal skills that it requires after they have read Chapter 16. It is worth quoting substantially the whole of one of Holt's paragraphs:

> Quality issues are one set of concerns that are close to the heart of working for justice, inevitably and necessarily taking into account *what offenders have made of the supervision process*. It was noted . . . that an unintended outcome of differential supervision may be fragmentation. Should this unplanned negative outcome occur, *it may compound offenders' existing fragmented thinking patterns*, leading to the possibility that *key messages* from cognitive-behavioural programmes *may be undermined or lost*. In addition, an offender may experience such fragmentation as 'pass the parcel', and *thereby as degrading*. The failure to guard against this possibility, may even lay a service open to challenge in the courts under human rights legislation. . . . (emphasis added)

Together with assessment and supplying the 'protective factor' identified by Boswell in Chapter 10, this is clearly the key role of the probation officer of the future. And, as Holt indicates, and as noted earlier in these reflections, the case manager role can only be truly effective if the management and the board play their part in connecting the service with other agencies and the community at large. If they do then the monitoring responsibilities of the case manager can truly come into play.

This brings us to the second issue: Thurston's quote from Todd (see Chapter 13), some hostels seem to 'operate in a vacuum removed from the ethnic minority communities they claim to serve', is but one aspect of the need to try to build confidence in the local community. It is the same issue that Boswell raised in Chapter 10, saying that the service needs to be brave enough to say to the community that risks cannot be eliminated. False reassurance is more damaging than frankness. The new probation service is going to have a higher profile than the 'old' one ever achieved. Could it be that part of the difficulty about public relations was that it was about presenting an image, rather than a genuine engagement with the distrust and fear of the public about specific issues? Those of us who have been the subject of campaigns against opening a hostel, will know that this is not something to be entered into lightly. But partnership cannot be achieved without, in the modern world, a much more transparent relationship with the public. One simple step, which has already been taken, is to make meetings of the boards open to the press.

HUMAN RIGHTS

Readers will have noticed frequent allusions to the Human Rights Act 1998. In part, this is a defensive reaction to ensure that the service cannot be criticised for failing to take human rights into account. But there is also an ambition to place awareness of human rights at the centre of practice as a positive ideal. This is why Scott's outline has been placed at the beginning of the book. It is making a statement about human rights being first and foremost. It is also why Williams's chapter has been placed at the start of the section on practice; probation must start with the recognition that victims' rights have been violated, and that all the subsequent work flows from that and should be concerned with the attempt to make some reparation and to prevent any further repetition.

Human rights apply also to offenders. Worrall draws our attention to the missed opportunities in relation to women offenders (see Chapter 9). She argues that it is impossible to separate criminal justice from social justice and human rights. At one point, she asks whether the probation service has anything to offer women offenders. Her answer is that it does not, until the service helps women gain access to the 'structural pre-conditions of social justice — housing, employment and health facilities' and also, crucially, values women offenders as people who have the potential to 'sustain and be sustained in reciprocal, rather than subordinate or exploitative, relationships'. Chouhan (in Chapter 8) recites the dismal evidence for the continuation of institutional racism within the service, and contrasts, tellingly, how quickly managerial and technological innovations have been put in place. As she writes: 'It is therefore not a matter of difficulty of understanding but one of leadership, and political and individual commitment.' Quite how this can be, in a service that is ostensibly recruiting people who are committed to fairness and justice, is hard to understand. Chouhan sets out in detail what has to be done.

Canton, in his thoughtful and subtle discussion of mentally disturbed offenders in Chapter 15, draws attention to their 'enormous burdens of social and psychological deprivation. These are lives of material and spiritual poverty — lonely, disenfranchised, angry ...'. They need multi-agency help through partnerships, though they are likely to face exclusion, as do women and black people. And, he argues, there is 'a need for a much more subtle qualitative evaluation of enforcement ... Sameness is not be mistaken for justice.... The circle, which the National Standards cannot square, is how to ensure that practice can be sufficiently flexible to be fair and decent, without admitting unwarrantable discrepancies'.

Hopley, from his influential role in drafting the National Standards, argues in Chapter 18 that proper, consistent enforcement is the only way to do away with the 'lottery of a hard or soft probation officer, office or area ... [and that] this is very much in line with the principles of the European Convention on Human Rights'. Unell, in Chapter 14 on drugs, makes a similar point: 'While the new Human Rights Act 1998 could thus be used to challenge the right of the state to categorise certain drugs as dangerous, it might also be used to enhance the right of the state to detain (and possibly treat) those with drug problems'. Canton expresses the same dilemma: 'The incremental effect of censure of mentally disordered offenders makes their rights even more precarious. For mentally disordered people ... rights may be compromised not merely for social defence but "in their own interests" '. Clearly, the Human Rights Act 1998 does not dissolve disputes, but it does give them a very sharp focus. There is a further irony for the new service: the more it takes on the role of law enforcement, the more, as these four writers show, it will be drawn into resolving issues of offenders' rights, simply because many of the people it works with are vulnerable to abuse.

Principles have to be worked out in practice; the devil is in the detail. Chouhan illustrates what is entailed in implementing diversity. Thurston gives an example of how this can be overcome in relation to hostel services for offenders from ethnic minorities. However, many services will face severe logistical problems. For example, many of the smaller areas will not be able to implement a What Works group every week, unless they include offenders from a very wide catchment area. If that group is composed of people who, under the accreditation scheme, ought to be in a more specialised programme, the problem is compounded. It is already almost impossible in such areas to set up groups for women offenders on a regular basis, simply because there are so few of them. If the solution is to be more individual programme delivery, it will be much harder to maintain any consistency. Further, it seems that many offenders find groups more interesting and challenging, simply because they do not let each other get away with things. Both effectiveness and fairness will rely largely on management's ability to overcome these organisational problems. The solution will vary according to local characteristics.

MANAGING THE NEW PROBATION SERVICE

Hopley, from his perspective within the Home Office (see Chapter 18), places a great value on country-wide consistency, arising from the development of a core curriculum with National Standards, so that, while offenders may be placed in a potentially more punitive position, they will benefit from being treated more fairly. Furniss (Chapter 19) marks the change in the Inspectorate from being, by default, the professional leadership of the service to ensuring that the service meets the expectations and the standards required of it. Raine draws attention in Chapter 20 to the daunting expectations laid on the service. The most challenging of these is the quest to measure and assess the impact that practice has, even though there is always the danger that, in such a politically charged climate as the service now operates, the targets and assessments may be too short-term. He points to the optimism engendered by 'the significant rebuilding of more trustful relations in the preparedness of local chiefs to work constructively with the Home Office on the formation of a new national service'. He believes that there will still be the supremacy of the management perspective in setting the agenda, and that shaping professional practice and professional discretion will continue to be curbed. Whether, in the light of the issues raised in this book about the complexity of practice, that will remain a sensible attitude, will depend to a large extent on the ability of practitioners, including managers, to establish their judgement as trustworthy and operating within the wider enforcement expectations. What would be a shame is for Raine's prediction to come true and new forms of administrative bureaucracy begin to establish themselves, rather than the establishment of more collaborative relationships with other organisations.

If this book has shown anything, it is that partnership is the way forward for the effective social control of crime. Flynn (Chapter 21) identifies the challenge: that the management arrangements may not be adequate to deliver the ambitious targets, compounded by the heavy dependence on What Works as the basis for service development. Not only is it 'a huge criminological experiment', it is also a very centralised definition of evidence-based practice. Again, professional discretion and local experience will tend to be under-valued.

The former Central Probation Council and the Association of Chief Officers of Probation fought very hard to retain a local element in the new organisational structure. The logic of their argument was that the service needs to respond to local issues and convey that it values local ties. These are still important. The foregoing paragraph highlights how difficult this is going to be. The National Director has indicated that she sees that there are 43 centres of leadership and influence, though it has to be acknowledged that the central one carries most of the shots. What emerges from the various contributors to this book is that there are real disadvantages to too centralised control and direction, and that many of the benefits of sensitivity to individual and local issues can only be gained through devolved decision-making and discretion. Local chief officers and their boards are faced with navigating these conflicting demands; how they manage it may turn out to be the core of a successful, modernised service.

A NEW PHILOSOPHY

The old probation service has been transformed. The new one has yet to articulate a clear philosophical framework that is more than the aims set out in the Act. It is fitting that at this stage we remember that Hertfordshire cobbler, Frederic Rainer, and those police court missionaries, without whom the present opportunities for helping, even while supervising, offenders in the community would not have happened.

The old probation order was *instead of* a sentence, and the offender *consented* to be under supervision and to try and change his or her behaviour. It was introduced at a time when imprisonment was the most likely outcome of a court appearance and no official help was offered. It was an elegant and self-consistent framework. At the end of the twentieth century, it had outlived its time, partly because crime had become so much more prevalent and community sanctions had become a necessity, and partly because few people, within or outside the service, believed that consent could be freely given under the implicit threat of a more severe sanction if it were withheld.

In the last two decades of the last century, various attempts were made to work out ways in which probation and community service could become alternatives to custody. There were two obstacles. First, it endorsed the view that all punishments had to be measured against prison (which the old philosophy of an order rather than a sentence sidestepped). Secondly, there were attempts to justify the alternatives in terms of how much of a prison sentence they equaled. One has only to think of the meaning of deprivation of liberty that prison entails — not choosing your own clothes, not being free to decide on your own meals, unable to chose your own companions — to recognise how absurd this was.

Now the service is in a different position. It has the opportunity to work out a new rationale of community punishment that can be justified in its own right. The following comments are little more than hints on how this might be developed, and they are prompted by the thought-provoking chapter of Rex and Johnson (see Chapter 12):

- All supervision, whether before or after custody, is disciplinary and must be consistent, rigorous and controlling.
- As punishment, it should always contain elements of reparation. The other side of the coin is that the service could not be involved in any type of punishment which is simply humiliating or retributive. This may become more easily incorporated, if courts are given the power to make a community punishment order, as the Home Secretary is putting out for consultation, which can identify which set of interventions is appropriate. The popularity of the combination order indicates that there is a general feeling that both reparation and rehabilitation should usually be included.
- All supervision should be purposeful and directed towards change and the moral development of the offender. Effectiveness will depend on individualisation and ensuring that the right intervention is guided to the right offender. This clearly implies research-led interventions. Further, it may well require some regaining of trust in professional discretion, once the new ethos of enforcement and consistency has become the professional climate within which people work.
- Partnership work will be a central justification for a community sanction. Quite apart from the resource issue, as amply demonstrated in this book, the aim of the service should be to link offenders with positive elements in their local community. We are kept honest by the ties we value and, as Aristotle observed, men become good through practice.
- The service has to be transparent in its aims and methods, open to public scrutiny and welcoming public interaction.
- Whereas prison implies the temporary loss of citizenship symbolised through the loss of the vote, probation is about teaching offenders how to become citizens and contribute to society. This suggests that the word 'reintegration' used by Rex and Johnson may be more appropriate than rehabilitation. The former implies taking one's place within the community, whereas the latter is individualistic. It implies the legitimacy and the inclusivity that Faulkner identifies as one of the major contributions that probation can make to public life in the twenty-first century.

Bibliography

ACOP (1996), *Strategic Statement on the Role of Hostels and Housing*, London: Association of Chief Officers of Probation.

ACOP (1998), *Housing Sex Offenders in Approved Hostels*, London: Association of Chief Officers of Probation.

ACOP (1999, 2000 and 2001): *Improving Enforcement*, London: Criminal Policy Research Unit, University of the South Bank (available at http://www.sbu.ac.uk/cpru).

Addison, N. and Taylor, C. (1999), 'Rights Issue', *Police Review*, 10 December, pp. 17–20.

Advisory Council on the Penal System (1970), *Non-Custodial and Semi-Custodial Penalties* (Wootton Report), London: HMSO.

Advisory Council on the Penal System (1974), *Young Adult Offenders* (Younger Report), London: HMSO.

Afzal, S. and Schuller, N. (2000). *Getting it Right: A Guide to the Human Rights Act 1998 for Community Safety Practitioners*, NACRO Crime and Social Policy Briefing, London: NACRO.

Agranoff, R. (1977), 'Services Integration' in W. Anderson, B. Frieden and M. Murphy (eds), *Managing Human Service*, Washington DC: International City Management Association.

ALBSU (1994), *Basic Skills in Prison: Assessing the Need*, London: The Basic Skills Unit.

Allen, H. (1987), *Justice Unbalanced: Gender, Psychiatry and Judicial Decisions*, Milton Keynes, Open University Press.

Allen, Lord Philip (1995), 'In Search of the Purpose of Prison' in Prison Reform Trust, *Gladstone at 100 — Essays on the Past and Future of the Prison System*, London: Prison Reform Trust.

Allen, R. (1997), *Children and Crime: taking responsibility*, London: Institute for Public Policy Research.

American Friends' Service Committee (1971), *Struggle for Justice*, New York: Hill and Wang.

Andrews, D. and Bonta, J. (1995), *The Level of Supervision Inventory-Revised*, Toronto: Multi-Health Systems Inc.

Andrews, D. and Bonta, J. (1998), *The Psychology of Criminal Conduct*, Cincinnati OH: Anderson.

Andrews, D., Bonta, J. and Hoge, R. D. (1990a), 'Classification for effective rehabilitation' *Criminal Justice and Behaviour*, 17 pp. 19–51.

Andrews, D., *et al.* (1990b), 'Does correctional treatment work? A clinically relevant and psychologically informed meta-analysis' *Criminology*, 28(3) pp. 369–404.

Ansell, J. and Wharton, F. (1992), *Risk: Analysis, Assessment and Management*, Chichester: Wiley.

Association of Chief Officers of Probation (1996), *Strategic Statement on the Role of Hostels and Housing*, London: ACOP.

Aubrey, R. and Hough, M. (1997), *Assessing Offenders' Needs: Assessment Scales for the Probation Service*, A Report for the Home Office Research and Statistics Directorate, London: Home Office.

Audit Commission (1997), *Misspent Youth*, London: Audit Commission.

Auld, Lord Justice (2001), *Review of Criminal Justice*, London: Stationary Office.

Bachrach, L. (1983), 'An overview of deinstitutionalisation' *New Directions for Mental Health Services*, 17 pp. 5–14.

Bagley, C. and King, K. (1991), *Child Sexual Abuse: The Search for Healing*, London: Routledge.

Bailey, R. and Williams, B. (2000), *Inter-agency Partnerships in Youth Justice: Implementing the Crime and Disorder Act 1998*, Sheffield: Joint Unit for Social Services Research, Sheffield University with 'Community Care'.

Bailey, V. (1987), *Delinquency and Citizenship*, Oxford: Clarendon Press.

Bale, D. (1987), 'Uses of the risk of custody scale' *Probation Journal*, 34(4) pp. 127–31.

Bale, D. (1990), *Cambridge Risk of Custody Score, Version 3*, Cambridge: Cambridgeshire Probation Service.

Bandura, A. (1997), *Self-Efficacy: The Exercise of Control*, New York: Freeman and Co.

Barclay, G., Tavares, C. and Siddique, A. (2001), International Comparisons of Criminal Justice Statistics 1999', *Home Office Statistical Bulletin*, 6/01, London: Home Office.

Barker, M. (1981), *The New Racism*, London: Junction Books.

Barker, M. (1993), *Community Service and Women Offenders*, London: Association of Chief Officers of Probation.

Barton, R. (1996), *Case Management in Community Mental Health Services*, Norwich: University of East Anglia.

Bean, P. (1974), *The Social Control of Drugs*, London: Martin Robertson.

Beauchamp, T. and McCullough, L. (1984), *Medical Ethics*, Englewood-Cliffs, NJ: Prentice-Hall.

Beccaria, C. (1764), *Dei Delitti e Delle Pene*, translated (1963) as *Of Crimes and Punishments*, Indiana: Bobbs-Merrill.

Beck, U. (1992), *Risk Society*, London: Sage.

Beetham, D. (1991), *The Legitimation of Power*, Basingstoke: Macmillan.

Bellamy, C. and Taylor, J. (1998), *Governing in the Information Age*, Buckingham: Open University Press.

Bentham, J. (1789), *Introduction to the Principles of Morals and Legislation*, reprinted 1967, Oxford: Oxford University Press (with *A Fragment on Government*).

Bernstein, P. (1996), *Against the Gods: The Remarkable Story of Risk*, New York: Wiley.

Berridge, V. (1999), *Opium and the People*, Oxford: Free Association Books.

Bhui, H (1999) 'Probation-Led Multi-Agency Working: A Practice Model' *Probation Journal*, 46(2) pp. 119–21.

Bines, H. and Watson, D. (1992), *Developing Professional Education*, Buckingham: Open University Press.

Blackburn, R. (1993), *The Psychology of Criminal Conduct: Theory, Research and Practice*, Chichester: John Wiley.

Blackburn, R. (2000) 'Classification and assessment of personality disorders in mentally disordered offenders: a psychological perspective' *Criminal Behaviour and Mental Health*, 10 pp. 8–32.

Bloch, S. and Chodoff, P. (1991), *Psychiatric Ethics* (2nd edn), Oxford: Oxford University Press.

Blomhoff, S., Seim, S. and Friis, S. (1990), 'Can prediction of violence among psychiatric hospital patients be improved?' *Hospital and Community Psychiatry*, 41 pp. 771–5.

Boeck, T. (2001), *Social exclusion and the local welfare state (TSER Project working paper)*, Leicester: Dept of Social and Community Studies, De Montfort University (unpublished).

Boswell, G. (1991), *Waiting for change: an exploration of the experiences and needs of Section 53 offenders*, London: The Prince's Trust.

Boswell, G. (1995), *Violent Victims*, London: The Prince's Trust.

Boswell, G. (1996), *Young and Dangerous: the Backgrounds and Careers of Section 53 Offenders*, Aldershot: Avebury.

Boswell, G. (1998), 'Research-minded practice with young offenders who commit grave crimes' *Probation Journal*, 45 pp. 202–07.

Boswell, G. (ed.) (2000), *Violent Children and Adolescents: Asking the Question Why*, London and Philadelphia: Whurr Publishers.

Bottoms, A. (1977), 'Reflections on the Renaissance of Dangerousness' *Howard Journal*, 16(2) pp. 70–96.

Bottoms, A. (1980), 'An Introduction to "The Coming Crisis"', in A. Bottoms and R. Preston (eds.), *The Coming Penal Crisis: A Criminological and Theological Exploration*, Edinburgh: Scottish Academic Press.

Bottoms, A. (1987), 'Limiting Prison Use in England and Wales' *Howard Journal*, 26 pp. 177–202.

Bottoms, A. (2001), 'Morality, Crime, Compliance and Public Policy', paper presented to the Leon Radzinowicz Commemoration Symposium, Cambridge: Cambridge Institute of Criminology.

Bottoms, A. and Hay, W. (1996), *Prisons and the Problem of Order*, Oxford: Clarendon Press.

Bottoms, A. and McWilliams, W. (1979), 'A non-treatment paradigm for probation practice' *British Journal of Social Work*, 9(1) pp. 159–202.

Bowers, L., Smith, P. and Binney, V. (1992), 'Cohesion and power in the families of children involved in bully/victim problems at school' *Journal of Family Therapy*, 14(4) pp. 371–87.

Bowling, B. (1998), *Violent Racism: Victimisation, Policing and Social Context*, Oxford: Clarendon Press.

Bowling, B. (2000), 'Racist Offenders: Punishment, Justice and Community Safety' *Criminal Justice Matters*, 42 pp. 30–1.

Brah, A. (1992), 'Difference, Diversity and Differentiation', in D. James and A. Rattansi (eds), *Race, Culture and Difference*, London: Sage.

Braithwaite, J. (1989), *Crime, Shame and Reintegration*, Cambridge: Cambridge University Press.

Braithwaite, J. and Pettit, P. (1990), *Not Just Deserts*, Oxford: Oxford University Press.

Braithwaite, J. and Strang, H. (eds) (2001), *Restorative Justice and Civil Society*, Cambridge: Cambridge University Press.

Bright, J. (1997), *Turning the Tide*, London: DEMOS.

Broad, B. (1991), *Punishment under Pressure: the Probation Service in the Inner City*, London: Jessica Kingsley.

Brody, S.R. (1976), *The Effectiveness of Sentencing*, London: HMSO.

Browne, D. (1990), *Black People, Mental Health and the Courts*, London: NACRO.

Brufal, T. (1994), 'Homicide Within and Beyond The Family: A Comparative Examination of the Childhood Experiences of Matricidal Men' *Special Hospitals Research Bulletin*, 3(1) pp. 8–12.

Bryans, S. (2001) 'The Managerialisation of Prisons: Efficiency without a purpose?' *Prison Service Journal*, 134 pp. 8–10.

Bryant, M., Coker, J., Estlea, B., Himmel, S. and Knapp, T. (1978), 'Sentenced to Social Work' *Probation Journal*, 25(4) pp. 110–14.

Bureau of International Labor Affairs (1996), *Forced Labor: the Prostitution of Children*, Washington: US Department of Labor.

Bureau of International Labor Affairs (1998), *By the Sweat and Toil of Children*, Washington: US Department of Labor.

Burgess, E. (1928), 'Factors making for success or failure on parole' *Journal of Criminal Law and Criminology*, 19(2) pp. 239–306.

Burgess, E. (1929), 'Is prediction feasible in social work?' *Social Forces*, 7 pp. 533–45.

Burgess, E. (1936), 'Protecting the public by parole and parole prediction' *Journal of Criminal Law and Criminology*, 27 pp. 491–502.

Burke, E. (1826), *The Works of the Right Honorable Edmund Burk*, Boston: Wells and Littly, as quoted in the Introduction to Szasz, T. (1975), *Ceremonial Chemistry*, London: Routledge and Kegan Paul.

Burnett, R. (1994), 'The Odds of Going Straight: Offenders' Own Predictions', in *Sentencing, Quality and Risk: Proceedings of the 10th Annual Conference on Research and Information in the Probation Service*, Birmingham: Midlands Probation Training Consortium.

Burney, E. and Pearson, G. (1995), 'Mentally Disordered Offenders: Finding a Focus for Diversion' *Howard Journal*, 34(4) pp. 291–313.

Cabinet Office (1999), *Modernising Goverment*, White Paper, London: Stationery Office.

Caddick, B. and Webster, A. (1998), 'Offender Literacy and the Probation Service' *Howard Journal* 37(2) pp. 137–47.

Cameron, D. (2001), from personal notes of a lecture delivered in Leicester University Medical School.

Canton, R. (1995), 'Mental Disorder, Justice and Censure', in D. Ward and M. Lacey (eds), *Probation: Working for Justice*, London: Whiting and Birch.

Canton, R. (1997), 'Doubts about Diversion', unpublished paper delivered at the British Criminological Society Conference, Belfast, July.

Carlen, P. (1990), *Alternatives to Women's Imprisonment*, Milton Keynes: Open University Press.

Carlen, P. (1998), *Sledgehammer: Women's Imprisonment at the Millennium*, Basingstoke: Macmillan.

Carlen, P. (2001), 'Death and the triumph of governance?' unpublished paper presented to the ANZSOC Conference, Melbourne, Australia.

Carson, D. (1996), 'Reducing Legal Repercussions' in H. Kemshall and J. Pritchard (eds), *Good Practice in Risk Assessment and Management, Vol. 1*, London: Jessica Kingsley.

Cavadino, M, (1997), 'A Vindication of the Rights of Psychiatric Patients' *Journal of Law and Society*, 4(2) pp. 235–51.

Cavadino, P. (1999), 'Diverting mentally disordered offenders from custody' in D. Webb and R. Harris (eds) *Mentally Disordered Offenders: Managing People Nobody Owns*, London: Routledge.

Cavadino, M. and Dignan, J. (1997), *The Penal System: An Introduction* (2nd edn), London: Sage.

Challis, D. (1993), 'Case Management: implementing community care', in J. Malin (ed.), *Implementing Community Care*, Buckingham: Open University Press.

Challis, D., Chessum, R., Chesterman, J., Luckett, R. and Traske, K. (1990), *Case Management in Social and Health Care*, Canterbury: Personal Social Services Research Unit (PSSRU), University of Kent.

Chapman, T. and Hough, M. (1998), *Evidenced Based Practice: a Guide to Effective Practice*(ed. J. Furniss), London: Home Office.

Chesney-Lind, M. (1997), *The Female Offender Girls, Women and Crime*, London: Sage.

Chouhan, K. and Jasper, L. (2000), *A Culture of Denial*, London: The 1990 Trust.

Christie, N. (1977), 'Conflicts as Property' *British Journal of Criminology*, 17(1) pp. 1–15.

Christie, N. (1982), *Limits to Pain*, Oxford: Martin Robertson.

Clarke, C. (2000), 'Courts to Consider Impact on Victims', Letters to the Editor, *The Times* 19 June.

Clear, T. and Karp, D. (1999), *The Community Justice Ideal: preventing crime and achieving justice*, Boulder, Colorado: Westview Press.

Clear, T., Flynn, S. and Shapiro, C. (1987), 'Intensive supervision in probation: a comparison of three projects', in B. McCarthy (ed.), *Intermediate Punishment*, Monsey: Criminal Justice Press.

Cohen, S. (1985), *Visions of Social Control*, Cambridge: Polity Press.

Colledge, M., Collier, P. and Brand, S. (1999), *Programmes for Offenders: Guidance for Evaluators*, London: Research, Development and Statistics Directorate, Home Office.

Commission on the Future of Multi-Ethnic Britain (2000), *The Future of Multi-Ethnic Britain*, London: Profile Books.

Commission on the Future of the Voluntary Sector (1996), *Meeting the Challenge of Change: Voluntary Action in the 21st century* (The Deakin Report), London: NCVO.

Copas, J., Ditchfield, J. and Marshall, P. (1994), *Development of a new reconviction score*, Research Bulletin 36, London: HMSO.

Copas, J., Marshall, P. and Tarling, R. (1996), *Predicting Reoffending for Discretionary Conditional Release*, Home Office Research Study 150, London: HMSO.

Cope, R. (1989), 'The Compulsory Detention of Afro-Caribbeans under the Mental Health Act' *New Community*, 15(3) pp. 343–56.

Corder, B., Ball, B., Haizlip T. *et al.* (1976), 'Adolescent Patricide: a comparison with other adolescent murder' *American Journal of Psychiatry*, 133 pp. 957–61.

Corney, R. (1995), 'Mental Health Services', in P. Owens, J. Carrier, and J. Horder (eds), *Interprofessional Issues in Community and Primary Health Care*, London: Macmillan.

Council of Europe (1999), 'Rights are Coming Home', *Council of Europe Conference*, London, 22 April.

Cox, M. and Pritchard, C. (1995), 'Troubles come not singly but in battalions; the pursuit of social justice and probation practice', in D. Ward and M. Lacey (eds), *Probation: Working for Justice*, London: Whiting and Birch.

Crawford, A. (1998), *Crime Prevention and Community Safety*, Harlow: Longman.

Crawford, A. and Enterkin, J. (1999), *Victim Contact Work and the Probation Service: a Study of Service Delivery and Impact*, Leeds: University of Leeds Centre for Criminal Justice Studies.

CRE (1995), *Race Equality Means Quality: Standards for Local Government*, London: Commission for Racial Equality.

Cross, B. (1997), 'Partnership in Practice: The Experience of Two Probation Services' *Howard Journal*, 36(1) pp. 62–79.

Crown Prosecution Service (2001), *Provision of Therapy for Child Witnesses Prior to a Criminal Trial*, London: CPS Communications Branch.

Daston, L. (1987), 'The domestication of risk: mathematical probability and insurance, 1650–1830', in L. Kruger, L. Daston, M. Heidelberger (eds), *The Probabilistic Revolution: Volume 1*, Cambridge, Mass: MIT Press.

Davies, J. (1993), *The Myth of Addiction*, Reading: Harwood Academic Publishers.

Davies, K. and Byatt, J. (1998), *Shropshire STOP Project; 'Something can be done!'*, Final Report, Shrewsbury: Shropshire Probation Service.

Dawtry, F. (1968), *Social Problems of Drug Abuse*, London: Butterworths.

Deakin, N. (2001), 'Public Policy, Social Policy and Voluntary Organisations', in M. Harris and C. Rochester (eds), *Voluntary Organisations and Social Policy in Britain: perspectives on change and choice*, Basingstoke: Palgrave.

Denney, D. (1992), *Racism and Anti-Racism in Probation*, London: Routledge.

Department of Health (1990), *The Care Programme Approach for People with a Mental Illness*, London: HMSO.

Department of Health (1991), *Implementing Community Care*, London: HMSO.

Department of Health (1998), *The National Treatment Outcome Research Study*, London: Stationery Office.

Department of Health (1999a), *Reform of the Mental Health Act 1983: Proposals for Consultation*, London: Stationery Office.

Department of Health (1999b), *Social Work Services in the High Security Hospitals* (Lewis Report), London: Department of Health.

Department of Health (2000), *Children accommodated in secure units, year ending 31 March 2000: England and Wales*, Statistical Bulletin 2000/15, London: Department of Health.

Department of Health and Social Security (1982), *Treatment and Rehabilitation: Report of the Advisory Council on the Misuse of Drugs*, London: HMSO.

Dersley, I, (2000), *Acceptable or Unacceptable? Local Probation Service Policy on Non-Compliance and Enforcement*, unpublished dissertation, University of Birmingham.

Dews, V. and Watts, J. (1994), *Review of Probation Officer Recruitment and Qualifying Training*, London: Home Office.

Dienstbier, R., Hiliman, D., Lehnhoff, J., Hiliman, J., and Valkenaar, M. (1975), 'An emotion — attribution approach to moral behaviour: interfacing cognitive and avoidance theories of moral development', *Psychological Review*, 82 pp. 299–315.

Dignan, J. (2000), *Youth Justice Pilots Evaluation: Interim Report on Reparative Work and Youth Offending Teams*, London: Home Office Research, Development and Statistics Directorate.

DiMaggio, P. and Powell, W. (1983), 'The Iron Cage Revisited: Institutional Isopmorphism and Collective Rationality in Organisational Fields' *American Sociological Review*, 48 pp. 147–60.

Dixon, L. (2000), 'Punishment and the Question of Ownership: Groupwork in the criminal justice system', *Groupwork*, 12(1) pp. 7–25.

Dobash, R.E., Dobash, R.P., Cavanagh, K. and Lewis, R. (1996), *Research Evaluation of Programmes for Violent Men*, Edinburgh: Scottish Office Central Research Unit.

Dobson, G. (1997), 'Is there a "Core" of a Probation Service' *Vista* 3(1) pp. 28–35.

Dodd, V. (2000), *The Guardian*, 5 August.

Dominelli, L. (1984), 'Differential justice: domestic labour, Community Service and female offenders' *Probation Journal*, 31(3) pp. 100–3.

Dominelli, L. (1988), *Anti-Racist Social Work*, Basingstoke: Macmillan.

Dominey, J. (forthcoming), 'Addressing victim issues in pre-sentence reports', in B. Williams (ed.), *Reparation and Victim-focused Social Work*, London: Jessica Kingsley.

Douglas, M. (1992), *Risk and Blame: Essays in Cultural Theory*, London: Routledge.

Dowden, C. and Andrews, D. (1999), 'What Works for Female Offenders: A Meta-Analytic Review' *Crime and Delinquency*, 45(4) pp. 438–52.

Downes, D. and Morgan, R. (1997), 'Dumping the "hostages to fortune"? The politics of law and order in post-war Britain', in M. Maguire, R. Morgan and R. Reiner (eds), *The Oxford Handbook of Criminology*, Oxford: Clarendon.

Downing, A. and Hatfield, B. (1999), 'The Care Programme Approach: Dimensions of Evaluation' *British Journal of Social Work*, 29 pp. 841–60.

Drakeford, M. and McCarthy, K. (2000), 'Parents, responsibility and the New Youth Justice', in B. Goldson (ed.), *The New Youth Justice*, Lyme Regis: Russell House.

Drakeford, M. and Vanstone, M. (eds) (1996), *Beyond Offending Behaviour*, Aldershot: Ashgate.

Driver, S. and Martell, L. (1997), 'New Labour's communitarianisms' *Critical Social Policy*, 52 pp. 27–46.

Dyer, C. (2001), 'The Rights Stuff', *The Guardian*, Section 2, 3 April, pp. 10–11.

Eaton, M. (1986), *Justice for Women: Family, Court and Social Control*, Milton Keynes: Open University Press.

Eaton, M. (1993), *Women after prison*, Buckingham: Open University Press.

Edwards, I. (2001), 'Victim Participation in Sentencing: the Problems of Incoherence' *Howard Journal*, 40(1) pp. 39–54.

Elias, R. (1993), *Victims Still*, London: Sage.

Elliot, N. (1997), 'The Qualification of Probation Officers: Thoughts for the Future' *Probation Journal* 44(4) pp. 205–10.

Ellis, T. (2000), 'Enforcement Policy and Practice: Evidence-Based or Rhetoric-Based, *Criminal Justice Matters*, 39 pp. 6–8.

Erez, E. (1999), 'Who's Afraid of the Big Bad Victim? Victim Impact Statements as Victim Empowerment and Enhancement of Justice' *Criminal Law Review*, July pp. 545–56.

Ericson, R. and Haggerty, K. (1997), *Policing the Risk Society*, Oxford: Oxford University Press.

Fabiano, E., La Plante, J. and Loza, A. (1996), 'Employability: from research to practice', *FORUM*, 8(1), Ottawa: Corrections Service of Canada.

Fallon, P., Bluglass, R., Edwards, B. and Daniels, G. (1999), *Report of the Committee of Inquiry into the Personality Disorder Unit, Ashworth Special Hospital*, London: Stationery Office.

Falshaw, L., Browne, K. and Hollin, C. (1996), 'Victim to offender: a review' *Aggression and Violent Behaviour*, 1 pp. 389–404.

Farrington, D. and Tarling, R. (1985), *Prediction in Criminology*, Albany NY: Albany State University Press.

Faulkner, D. (1996), *Darkness and Light: Justice, Crime and Management for Today*, London: The Howard League.

Faulkner, D., Freedland, M. and Fisher, E. (1999), *Public Services: Developing Approaches to Governance and Professionalism*, a report of a series of seminars held April–June 1999, Oxford: St Johns College.

Faulkner, D. and Gibbs, A. (eds) (1998), 'New Politics, New Probation?, in *Proceedings of the Probation Studies Unit Second Colloquium*, Oxford: University of Oxford Centre for Criminological Research.

Feeley, M. and Simon, J. (1992), 'The New Penology: notes on the emerging strategy of corrections and its implications' *Criminology*, 30(4) pp. 452–74.

Feeley, M. and Simon, J. (2000), 'Acturarial Justice: the Emerging New Criminal Law' *Punishment and Society*, 2(1) pp. 23–65.

Fennell, P. (1999), 'The Third Way in Mental Health Policy: Negative Rights, Positive Rights, and the Convention' *Journal of Law and Society*, 26(1), pp. 103–27.

Fernando, S., Ndegwa, D. and Wilson, M. (1998), *Forensic Psychiatry, Race and Culture*, London: Routledge.

Floud, J. and Young, W. (1981), *Dangerousness and Criminal Justice*, London: Heinemann and Howard League for Penal Reform.

Flynn, E. (1978), 'Classifications for risk and supervision' in J. Freeman (ed.), *Prisons Past and Future*, Cambridge: Cambridge Studies in Criminology.

Folkard, M., Smith, D.E. and Smith, D.D. (1976), *IMPACT Vol. II*, London: HMSO.

Foucault, M. (1977), *Discipline and Punishment*, London: Allen Lane.

Fox, J. (2000), *Human Rights Act 1998: Introduction Pack*, London: Home Office and Association of Chief Officers of Probation (available from National Probation Service, South Yorkshire).

Fullwood, C. (1998), *Civil Liberties and Social Control in the Community* (the Fifth Public Lecture in memory of Professor Derek McClintock, Professor of Law, University of Edinburgh), Edinburgh: SACRO.

Fullwood, C. (1999), 'Civil Liberties and Social Control in the Community' *Vista*, 5(1) pp. 4–14.

Furedi, F. (1997), *A Culture of Fear: Risk-taking and the Morality of Low Expectation*, London: Cassell.

Garland, D. (1985), *Punishment and Welfare*, London: Gower.

Garland, D. (2001), *The Culture of Control: Crime and Social Order in Contemporary Society*, Oxford: Oxford University Press.

Garland, Mr Justice (2000), *Address to the AGM of Central Probation Council*, 16 May.

Garmezy, N. (1981), 'Children under stress: Perspectives on anteced- ents and correlates of vulnerability and resistance to psychopathol- ogy', in A. Rabin, J. Arnoff, A. Barclay and R. Zucker (eds), *Further Explorations in Personality*, New York: Wiley.

Geelan, S., Griffin, N., Briscoe, J. and Sayeed Haque, M. (2000), 'A bail and probation hostel for mentally disordered defendants' *Journal of Forensic Psychiatry*, 11(1) pp. 93–104.

Gelles, R. and Straus, M. (1988), *Intimate Violence*, New York: Simon and Schuster.

Gendreau, P. (1996), 'The principles of effective intervention with offenders', in A. Harland (ed.), *Choosing Correctional Options that Work: Defining the Demand and Evaluating the Supply*, London: Sage.

Georgiou, J. (2000), *Breach And Effective Practice: An Evaluation Of Breach Policy in The Modern Probation Service,* unpublished dissertation, University of Birmingham.

Gibbs, A. (1999), 'The Forgotten Voice: Probation Service Users and Partnerships' *Howard Journal*, 38(3) pp. 283–99.

Gibbs, A. (2001), 'Partnership between the Probation Service and Voluntary Sector Organisations' *British Journal of Social Work*, 31(1) pp. 15–27.

Gibran, K. (1991), *The Prophet*, London: Pan Books.

Giddens, A. (1984), *The Constitution of Society*, Cambridge: Polity Press.

Giddens, A. (1991), *Modernity and Self-Identity*, Oxford, Polity Press, in association with Blackwell Publishers.

Giddens, A. (1998), *The Third Way: the Renewal of Social Democracy*, Cambridge: Polity Press.

Giddens, A. (2000), *The Third Way: a reply to the critics*, Cambridge: Polity Press.

Gillis, C., Robinson D., and Porporino F. (1996), 'Inmate Employment: the increasingly influential role of generic work skills', *FORUM*, 8(1), Ottawa: Corrections Service of Canada.

Gladstone, H. (1895), *Report to Parliament of the Departmental Committee on Prisons* (The Gladstone Report), London: HMSO.

Glaser, D. (1955), 'The efficacy of alternative approaches to parole prediction' *American Sociological Review*, 20 pp. 283–7.

Glaser, D. (1962), 'Prediction tables as accounting devices for judges and parole boards' *Crime and Delinquency*, 8(3) pp. 253–8.

Glaser, D. (1973), *Routinizing Evaluation*, Rockville, Maryland: National Institute of Mental Health.

Glueck, S. and Glueck, E. (1950), *Unravelling Juvenile Delinquency*, New York: Commonwealth Fund.

Goddard, C. and Stanley, J. (1994), 'Viewing the abusive parent and the abused child as captor and hostage: the application of hostage theory to the effects of child abuse' *Journal of Interpersonal Violence*, 9(2) pp. 258–69.

Goffman, E. (1968), *Asylums: Essays on the Social Situation of Mental Patients and Other Inmates*, Harmondsworth: Penguin.

Goldson, B. (2000), 'Simple Toughness meets Tough Complexity' *Criminal Justice Matters*, 41 pp. 4–5.

Gorman, K. (2001), 'Cognitive Behaviourism and the Holy Grail: The Quest for a Universal Means of Managing Offender Risk', *Probation Journal*, 48(1) pp. 3–9.

Gottfredson, S. and Gottfredson, D. (1985), 'Screening for risk among parolees: policy, practice and research', in D. Farrington and R. Tarling (eds), *Predicting Crime and Delinquency*, Albany, NY: Albany State University Press.

Gottfredson, S. and Gottfredson, D. (1986), 'Accuracy of prediction models', in A. Blumstein, J. Cohen, J. Roth, and C. Visher (eds), *Criminal Careers and 'Career Criminals'*, Washington DC: National Academy of Sciences.

Gottfredson, S. and Gottfredson, D. (1993), 'The Long-Term Predictive Utility of the Base Expectancy Score' *Howard Journal*, 32(4) pp. 276–90.

Graham, J. and Bowling, B. (1995), *Young People and Crime*, Home Office Research Study No. 145, London: Home Office.

Gray, B. (2000), 'Helping women into jobs' *Prison Service Journal*, 132 pp. 54–6.

Gray, M. (1998), *Drug Crazy: How we got into this mess and how we can get out*, New York: Random House.

Green, J. (1997), *Risk and Misfortune*, London: UCL Press.

Grounds, A. (1991), 'The mentally disordered offender in the criminal process: some research and policy questions', in K. Herbst and J. Gunn (eds), *The Mentally Disordered Offender*, Oxford: Butterworth-Heinemann.

Grounds, A. (1995), 'Risk Assessment and Management in Clinical Context', in J. Crichton (ed.) *Psychiatric Patient Violence: Risk and Relapse*, London: Duckworth.

Grubin, D. (1998), *Sex Offending against Children: Understanding the Risk*, Police Research Series Paper 99, London: Home Office.

Gunn, J. (1996), 'Let's get serious about dangerousness', *Criminal Behaviour and Mental Health*, Supplement, pp. 51–64.

Gunn, J., Maden, A. and Swinton, M. (1991), 'Treatment Needs of Prisoners with Psychiatric Disorders' *British Medical Journal*, 303 pp. 338–40.

Hacking, I. (1987), 'Was there a probabilistic revolution 1800–1930?' in L. Kruger, L. Daston and M. Heidelberger (eds), *The Probabilistic Revolution: Volume 1*, Cambridge, Mass: MIT Press, pp. 45–55.

Hacking, I. (1990), *The Taming of Chance*, Cambridge: Cambridge University Press.

Haines, K. (1990), *After-Care Services for Released Prisoners: A Review of the Literature*, Cambridge: Institute of Criminology.

Haines, K. (2000), 'Referral Orders and Youth Offender Panels: restorative approaches and the new youth justice', in B. Goldson (ed.), *The New Youth Justice*, Lyme Regis: Russell House.

Hampshire Probation Service (1992), *Targeting Matrix: a guide to decision making for practitioners and sentencers*, Winchester: Hampshire Probation Service.

Hannah-Moffat, K. (1999), 'Moral agent or actuarial subject: risk and Canadian women's imprisonment' *Theoretical Criminology*, 3(1) pp. 71–94 .

Harding, J. (1999), 'Providing Better Services for Mentally Disordered Young Offenders: Pitfalls and Prospects' *Probation Journal*, 46(2) pp. 83–8.

Harding, J. (2000), 'A Community Justice Dimension to Effective Probation Practice' *Howard Journal*, 39(2) pp. 132–49.

Harris, M. (2001), 'Voluntary Organisations in a Changing Social Policy Environment', in M. Harris and C. Rochester (eds), *Voluntary Organisations and Social Policy in Britain: perspectives on change and choice*, Basingstoke: Palgrave.

Harris, R. (1985), 'Towards Just Welfare' *British Journal of Criminology*, 25(1) pp. 31–45.

Harris R. (1992), *Crime, Criminal Justice and the Probation Service*, London: Routledge.

Harrison, S. (1993), *The Use of Schedule 1, Part II, Section (6) of the Criminal Justice Act, 1991*, MA thesis, Leicester University (unpublished).

Hasenfeld, Y. (1983), *Human Service Organisations*, Englewood-Cliffs, NJ: Prentice-Hall.

Hay, A. and Stirling, A. (1998), 'Women need women' *Probation Journal*, 45(1) pp. 36–8.

Hayden, A., Hopkinson, J., Sengendo, J. and von Rabenau, E. (1999), 'It ain't (just) What You Do, Its The Way That You Do It' *Groupwork*, 11(1), pp. 41–53.

Hayman, S. (1996), *Community Prisons for Women*, London: Prison Reform Trust.

Hebenton, B. and Thomas, T. (1996), 'Tracking Sex Offenders' *Howard Journal*, 35(2) pp. 97–112.

Hebenton, B. and Thomas, T. (1997), *Keeping Track? Observations on Sex Offender Registrations in the US*, Crime Detection and Prevention Series, Paper 83, London: Home Office.

Hedderman, C. and Gelsthorpe, L. (1997), *Understanding the Sentencing of Women*, Home Office Research Study No. 170, London: Home Office.

Hedderman, C. and Hearnden, I. (2000), 'The Missing Link: Effective Enforcement and Effective Supervision' *Probation Journal*, 47(2) pp. 126–8.

Herrenkohl, E., Herrenkohl, R. and Toedter, L. (1983), 'Perspectives on the Intergenerational Transmission of Abuse', in D. Finkelhor, R. Gelles, G. Hotaling and M. Straus (eds), *The Dark Side of Families: Current Family Violence Research*, Newbury Park: Sage.

Herrenkohl, R. and Herrenkohl, E. (1981), 'Some antecedents and developmental consequences of child maltreatment' *New Directions for Child Development*, 11 pp. 57–76.

Herzberger, S. (1983), 'Social Cognition and the Transmission of Abuse', in D. Finkelhor, R. Gelles, G. Hotaling and M. Straus (eds), *The Dark Side of Families: Current Family Violence Research*, Newbury Park: Sage.

Hester, R. (2000), *Crime and Disorder Partnerships: Voluntary and Community Sector Involvement*, Home Office Briefing Note 10/00, London: Home Office.

Himmelfarb, G. (1974), *On Liberty: John Stuart Mill*, New York: Penguin.

Hirschi, T. (1969), *Causes of Delinquency*, Berkeley: University of California Press.

HM Chief Inspector of Prisons (1999), *Report of a full announced Inspection of HM Prison Birmingham 10th–18th July 1998*, London: Stationery Office.

HM Chief Inspector of Prisons (2000), *Report on a full announced Inspection of HM YOI Portland, 24th Oct.–3rd Nov. 1999*, London: Stationery Office.

HMIP (1993), *Thematic Inspection Report on Approved Probation and Bail Hostels*, London: Home Office.

HMIP (1996a), *Probation Orders with Additional Requirements: Report of a Thematic Inspection 1995*, London: Home Office.

HMIP (1996b), *Probation Services Working in Partnership; Increasing Impact and Value for Money: Report of a Thematic Inspection*, London: Home Office.

HMIP (1997), *The Work of the Probation Service in the Crown and Magistrates Courts: Report of a Thematic Inspection*, London: Home Office.

HMIP (1998a), *Evidence-Based Practice: A Guide to Effective Practice*, London: Home Office.

HMIP (1998b), *Strategies for Effective Offender Supervision*, London: Home Office.

HMIP (1998c), *Thematic Inspection Report on Approved Probation and Bail Hostels*, London: Home Office.

HMIP (1999), *Letter from Chief Inspector of Probation to CPOs: HMIP 5/99*, London: Home Office.

HMIP (2000a), *Annual Report 1999/2000*, London: Home Office.

HMIP (2000b), *The Use of Information by Probation Services: Making National Standards Work*, London: Home Office.

HMIP (2000c), *The Use of Information by Probation Services: The Deployment of Resources*, London: Home Office.

HMIP (2000d), *The Use of Information by Probation Services: Probation Service's Contributions to Crime and Disorder Partnerships*, London: Home Office.

HMIP (2000e), *The Victim Perspective: Ensuring the Victim Matters*, London: Home Office.

HMIP (2000f), *Toward Race Equality: A Thematic Inspection*, London: Home Office.

HMIP (2000g), *Using Information and Technology to Improve Probation Service Performance*, London: Home Office.

HMIP (2001), *Notification of Serious Incidents*, London: Home Office.

Hobbes, Thomas (1651), *Leviathan*, Pt II, ch. xxviii.

Holt, P. (2000a), *Case Management: Context for Supervision: Design Implications for Effective Practice*, Community and Criminal Justice Monograph, Leicester: De Montfort University.

Holt, P. (2000b), *Take-up and Roll Out: Contexts and Issues in the Implementation of Effective Practice in the Probation Service*, Leicester: De Montfort University.

Holt, P. (forthcoming), *Report on the Implementation and Evaluation of an Original Case Management Model for Merseyside Probation Service*, Community and Criminal Justice Monograph, Leicester: De Montfort University.

Home Office (1980), *Young Offenders*, London: HMSO.

Home Office (1981), *Racial Attacks: Report of a Home Office Study*, London: Home Office.

Home Office (1988a), *Punishment, Custody and the Community*, London: HMSO.

Home Office (1988b), *Tackling Offenders: An Action Plan*, London: HMSO.

Home Office (1988c), *The Registration and Review of Serious Offenders*, Home Office Letter to Chief Probation Officers, July, London: Home Office.

Home Office (1990a), *Crime Justice and Protecting the Public*, London: HMSO.

Home Office (1990b), *The Victims Charter*, London: Home Office.

Home Office (1990c), *Punishment in Dealing with Offenders in the Community: a discussion document*, London: Home Office

Home Office (1990d), *Provision for Mentally Disordered Offenders*, Home Office Circular 66/90, London: Home Office.

Home Office (1992a), *Gender and the Criminal Justice System*, London: Home Office.

Home Office (1992b), *National Standards for the Supervision of Offenders in the Community*, London: Home Office.

Home Office (1992c), *Punishment in Dealing with Offenders in the Community: a discussion document*, London: Home Office

Home Office (1993a), *H.M. Inspectorate of Probation Annual Report 1992–3*, London: Home Office.

Home Office (1993b), *Partnership in Dealing with Offenders in the Community: submission of Partnership plans 1994–97*, Probation Circular 17/1993, London: Home Office.

Home Office (1993c), *Probation Services and the Management of Voluntary Sector Organisations*, London: Home Office.

Home Office (1993d), *Probation Statistics England and Wales 1991*, London: Home Office.

Home Office (1995a), *National Standards for the Supervision of Offenders in the Community*, London: Home Office.

Home Office (1995b), *Probation Circular 77/1995*, London: Home Office.

Home Office (1995c), *Review of Probation Officer Recruitment and Qualifying Training*, Discussion Paper, London: Home Office.

Home Office (1995d), *The Approved Probation and Bail Hostel Rules*, London: Home Office.

Home Office (1996), *Protecting the Public: The Government's Strategy on Crime*, London: Home Office.

Home Office (1997a), *Addressing the Literacy Needs of Offenders Under Probation Supervision*, Home Office Research Study 169, London: Home Office.

Home Office (1997b), *The Crime Sentences Act*, London: Home Office.

Home Office (1998a), *Guidance on Statutory Crime and Disorder Partnerships*, London: Home Office Communications Directorate.

Home Office (1998b), *Partnership and Accommodation Grants*, Probation Circular 41/1998, London: Home Office.

Home Office (1998c), *Probation Circular 35/1998*, London: Home Office.

Home Office (1998d), *Reducing Offending: an assessment of research evidence on ways of dealing with offending behaviour*, Home Office Research Study 187, London: Home Office.

Home Office (1998e), *Speaking Up for Justice: Report of the Interdepartmental Working Group on the Treatment of Vulnerable or Intimidated Witnesses in the Criminal Justice System*, London: Home Office.

Home Office (1998f), *The Crime and Disorder Act*, London: Home Office.

Home Office (1999a), *A Learning and Development Programme for Working with Mentally Disordered Offenders*, London: Home Office.

Home Office (1999b), *Developing Minority Ethnic Representation in Probation Services*, London: Home Office.

Home Office (1999c), *Digest 4: Information on the Criminal Justice System in England and Wales*, London: Home Office.

Home Office (1999d), *Probation Circular 3/1999*, London: Home Office.

Home Office (1999e), *The Correctional Policy Framework: Effective execution of the sentences of the courts so as to reduce re-offending and protect the public*, London: Home Office.

Home Office (1999f), *The Prison-Probation Review*, London: Home Office.

Home Office (1999g), *The Stephen Lawrence Inquiry: Home Secretary's Action Plan* http://www.homeoffice.gov.uk/ppd/oppu/slpages.pdf (visited 20 June 2000).

Home Office (2000a), *A Review of the Sentencing Framework*, London: Home Office.

Home Office (2000b), *Calling Time on Crime: A Thematic Inspection on Crime and Disorder* (conducted by Her Majesty's Inspectorate of Constabulary in collaboration with the Home Office, Audit Commission, Local Government Association, Ofsted and Social Services Inspectorate), London: Home Office.

Home Office (2000c), *Criminal Justice: The Way Ahead*, London: Home Office.

Home Office (2000d), *Criminal Statistics England and Wales 1999*, London: Stationery Office.

Home Office (2000e), *First Report from the Joint Prison/Probation Accreditation Panel*, London: Home Office.

Home Office (2000f), *Home Office Circular 55/2000*, London: Home Office.

Home Office (2000g), *Home Office Circular 60/2000*, London: Home Office.

Home Office (2000h), *Human Rights Act 1998: Guidance*, Probation Circular 59/2000, London: Home Office.

Home Office (2000i), *Initial Guidance to the Police and Probation Services on Sections 67 & 68 of the Criminal Justice and Court Services Act 2000*, London: Home Office.

Home Office (2000j), *Modernising the Management of the Prison Service*, an independent report by the Targeted Performance Initiative, chaired by Lord Laming, London: Home Office.

Home Office (2000k), *National Standards for the Supervision of Offenders in the Community*, London: Home Office.

Home Office (2000l), *Pre-trial therapy for vulnerable and intimidated witnesses: current good practice guidance*, Draft Consultation Paper, London: Home Office Justice and Victims Unit.

Home Office (2000m), *Race Relations (Ammendment) Act 2000. New Laws for a Multi-Racial Britain. Proposals for Implementation*, London: Home Office.

Home Office (2000n), *Statistics on Race and the Criminal Justice System*, London: Home Office.

Home Office (2000o), *The Crime and Disorder Act: Guidance for Practitioners Involved in Drug Treatment and Testing Order Pilots*, http://www.homeoffice.gov.uk/cdact/dttguid.htm

Home Office (2000p), *The Government's Strategy for Women Offenders*, London: Home Office.

Home Office (2000q), *The National Probation Service Aims: The Home Secretary's Priorities and Action Plan 2001–02 and Performance Measures for the Service 2001–04*, Probation Circular 92/2000, London: Home Office.

Home Office (2000r), *The Stephen Lawrence Inquiry: Home Secretary's Action Plan: First Annual Report on Progress* www.homeoffice.gov.uk/ppd/oppu/slpages.pdf (visited 26 June 2000).

Home Office (2000s), *What Works Strategy for the Probation Service*, Probation Circular 60/2000, London: Home Office.

Home Office (2001a), *A Review of the Victim's Charter*, London: Home Office Communications Directorate.

Home Office (2001b), *Criminal Justice: The Way Ahead* (The Auld Report), London: Stationery Office.

Home Office (2001c), *Drug Seizure and Offender Statistics, United Kingdom 1999*, London: Stationery Office.

Home Office (2001d), *Home Office Circular 24/2001*, London: Home Office.

Home Office (2001e), *Probation Statistics England and Wales 1999*, London: Home Office Research, Development and Statistics Directorate.

Home Office (2001f), *Race Equality in the Public Services*, Home Office Communications Directorate.

Home Office (2001g), *Remarks at the National Case Management Seminar*, London, 21 March.

Home Office (2001h), *Review of Sentencing* (The Halliday Review), London: Home Office.

Home Office (2001i), *Statistics on women and the criminal justice system (Section 95, Criminal Justice Act 1991)*, London: Home Office.

Home Office/Department of Health (1995), *Mentally Disordered Offenders: Inter-Agency Working*, London: Home Office and Department of Health.

Home Office/Department of Health (1999), *Managing Dangerous People with Severe Personality Disorder: Proposals for Policy Development*, London: Home Office and Department of Health.

Hood, R. (1974), *Tolerance and the Tariff*, London: NACRO.

Hood, R. (1992), *Race and Sentencing*, Oxford: Clarendon.

Horlick-Jones, T. (1998), 'Meaning and contextualisation in risk assessment' *Reliability Engineering and System Safety*, 59 pp. 79–89.

House of Commons (1998), *Tackling Drugs To Build a Better Britain: The Government's 10-year Strategy for Tackling Drug Misuse*, London: Stationery Office.

House of Commons (2001a), 'Innovations in Citizen Participation in Government' in *Sixth Report from the Select Committee on Public Administration, Session 2000–2001*, London: Stationery Office.

House of Commons (2001b), 'Making Government Work: the Emerging Issues' in *Seventh Report from the Select Committee on Public Administration, Session 2000–2001*, London: Stationery Office.

Howard, J. (1777), *State of the Prisons in England and Wales*.

Howard League (1997), *Lost Inside: the imprisonment of teenage girls*, London: The Howard League for Penal Reform.

Howard League (1999), *Do women paint fences too? Women's experience of Community Service*, London: The Howard League for Penal Reform.

Howard League (2000), *A chance to break the cycle: women and the Drug Treatment and Testing Order*, London: The Howard League for Penal Reform.

Howard, M. (1993), Speech to Conservative Party Conference, October.

Howden-Windell, J. and Clark, D. (1999), *Criminogenic Needs of Female Offenders: A Literature Review*, London: HM Prison Service.

Hoyle, C., Cape, E., Morgan, R. and Sanders, A. (1998), *Evaluation of the 'One Stop Shop' and Victim Impact Statement Pilot Projects*, London: Home Office.

Hudson, B. (1987), *Justice as Punishment*, London: Macmillan.

Hudson, B. (1998), 'Restorative Justice: the Challenge of Sexual and Racial Violence' *Journal of Law and Society*, 25(2) pp. 237–56.

Hudson, B. (2001a), 'Human Rights, Public Safety and the Probation Service: Defending Justice in the Risk Society' *Howard Journal*, 40(2) pp. 103–13.

Hudson, B. (2001b), 'Punishment, rights and difference: defending justice in the risk society', in K. Stenson and R. Sullivan (eds), *Crime, Risk and Justice: The Politics of Crime Control in Liberal Democracies*, Devon: Willan Publishing.

Hughes, B., Parker, H. and Gailagher, B. (1996), *Policing Child Sexual Abuse: The View from Police Practitioners*, London: Home Office Police Research Group.

Husband, C. (1994), *'Race' and Nation: The British Experience*, Perth, Australia: Paradigm Books.

Hutton, W. (2000), *New Life for Health*, London: Vintage.

Iganski, P. (1999), 'Why Make "Hate" a Crime?' *Critical Social Policy*, 19(3) pp. 386–95.

Intagliata, J. (1992), 'Improving the Quality of Community Care for the Chronically Mentally Disabled: The Role of Case Management', in S. Rose (ed.), *Case Management and Social Work Practice*, White Plains, NY: Longman.

James, A. and Bottomley, K (1994)), 'Probation Partnerships Revisited' *Howard Journal*, 33 pp. 158–68.

James, O. (1994), 'Violent Children', *Harpers and Queen*, May, pp. 135–7 and 188–90.

Johnson, R. (1993), *Intensive Work with Disordered Personalities 1991–1993*, unpublished report to the Reed Committee, January.

Jordan, B. (2000), *Social Work and the Third Way: Tough Love as Social Policy*, London: Sage.

JRF (1999), *National User Involvement Project*, York: Joseph Rowntree Foundation.

Justice (1998), *Victims in Criminal Justice: Report of the Justice Committee on the Role of the Victim in Criminal Justice*, London: Justice.

Justice of the Peace (1908), 'Practical Point 14: Probation of Offenders' *Justice of the Peace*, LXII (14), p. 165.

Kay, J., Gast, L., Clarke, P., Mason, G., Mayer, J., Sisodia, B. and Squires, S. (1998), *From Murmur to Murder: working with racially motivated and racist offenders*, Birmingham: Midlands Probation Training Consortium.

Kay, R. (1992), 'Developing Partnerships between the Probation Service and the Voluntary Sector', *NAPO News*, November, pp. 12–13.

Kazi, M., Holroyd, C., Kazi, S. and May, T. (2001), *The Integration of Minority Ethnic Groups in West Yorkshire Probation/Bail Hostels*, Wakefield and Huddersfield: West Yorkshire Probation Board/ University of Huddersfield.

Kelso, P. (2000), *The Guardian*, 2 November.

Kempe, C., Silverman, F., Steele, B., Droegemueller, W. and Silver, H. (1962), 'The battered-child syndrome' *Journal of the American Medical Association*, 181 pp. 17–24.

Kemshall, H. (1996), *Reviewing Risk: A review of research on the assessment and management of risk and dangerousness: implications for policy and practice in the Probation Service*, a report for the Home Office Research and Statistics Directorate, London: Home Office.

Kemshall, H. (1998a), 'Defensible Decisions for Risk: Or "it's the Doers Wot Get the Blame"' *Probation Journal*, 45(2) pp. 67–72.

Kemshall, H. (1998b), *Risk in Probation Practice*, Aldershot: Ashgate.

Kemshall, H. (1999), 'The Assessment and Management of Violent Offenders', in H. Kemshall and J. Pritchard (eds), *Good Practice in Working with Violence*, London: Jessica Kingsley.

Kemshall, H. (2000a), *Risk Assessment and Management of Known Sexual and Violent Offenders: A Review of Current Issues*, London: Home Office Police Research Unit 140.

Kemshall, H. (2000b), *Risk is Risky Business: Difficulties and Dilemmas in Researching Offender Risk*, Inaugural Lecture, November 2000, Leicester: De Montfort University.

Kemshall, H. and Holt, P. (2001), *Evaluation of the Leicester, Leicestershire and Rutland Public Protection Panel*, Leicester, De Montfort University (unpublished).

Kemshall, H. and Maguire, M. (forthcoming), 'Partnership and Public Protection: Issues in the Multi-Agency Risk Management of Dangerous Offenders' *Punishment and Society* 3(2).

Kendall, K. (1998), 'Evaluation of Programs for Female Offenders', in R. Zaplin (ed.) *Female Offenders, Critical Perspectives and Effective Interventions*, Maryland: Aspen Publishers.

Kendall, K. (2000), 'Anger management with women in coercive environments', in R. Horn and S. Warner (eds), *Positive Directions for Women in Secure Environments*, Leicester: The British Psychological Society.

Kendall, K. (2001), 'Unfair treatment' *The Howard League Magazine*, 19(1) p. 13.

Kennedy, M., Truman, C., Keyes, S. and Cameron, A. (1997), 'Supported Bail for Mentally Vulnerable Defendants' *Howard Journal*, 36(2) pp. 158–69.

Keyes, S. (1995), 'Revolving Doors: Eggs, Empathy and Erewhon' *Criminal Justice Matters*, 21 pp. 3–4.

Khan, U. (1998), 'Up and ATAM' *Health Service Journal*, 30 April, pp. 32–3.

Killias, Aebi M. and Ribeaud, D. (2000), 'Does Community Service Rehabilitate Better than Short-term Imprisonment? Results of a Controlled Experiment' *Howard Journal*, 39(1) pp. 40–57.

Kitzinger, J. (1999), 'Researching risk and the media' *Health, Risk and Society*, 1(1) pp. 55–69.

Knight, C. and Chouhan, K. (forthcoming), 'Supporting Victims of Racist Abuse and Violence', in B. Williams (ed.), *Reparation and Victim-focused Social Work*, London: Jessica Kingsley.

Knight, C. and Taylor, R. (eds) (1996), *The Empowerment of Practice Teachers in the Changing Context of Qualifying Training*, London: CCETSW.

Knight, C. and Ward, D. (2001), 'Qualifying Probation Training: Implications for Social Work Education' *Social Work Education*, 20(2) pp. 175–86.

Knight, C. and White, K. (2001), 'The Integration of theory and practice within the Diploma in Probation Studies: how is it achieved?' *Probation Journal* 48(3) pp. 203–10.

Kohut, H. (1985), *Self Psychology and the Humanities: Reflections on a new Psycholanalytic Approach* (co-editor C. B. Strozien), New York and London: W.W. Norton.

Kolb, D. (1984), *Experiential Learning: Experiences as the Source of Learning Development*, Englewood-Cliffs, NJ: Prentice-Hall.

Koons, B., Burrow, J., Morash, M. and Bynum, T. (1997), 'Expert and Offender Perceptions of Program Elements Linked to Successful Outcomes for Incarcerated Women' *Crime and Delinquency*, 43 pp. 512–32.

Labour Party (2001), *Ambitions for Britain*, London: Labour Party.

Lacey, M. (1995), 'Fairness', in D. Ward and M. Lacey (eds) *Probation: Working for Justice*, London: Whiting and Birch.

Lacey, N. (2001), 'Beset by Boundaries: the Home Office Review of Sex Offences' *Criminal Law Review* 15 pp. 15–30.

Langan, M. (2000), 'Series editor's preface', in J. Batsleer, and B. Humphries, *Welfare, Exclusion and Political Agency*, London: Routledge.

Leach, T. (1999), 'Effective Practice: some possible pitfalls' *Vista*, 5(2) pp. 141–9.

Leiss, W. and Chociolko, C. (1994), *Risk and Responsibility*, London and Montreal: McGill University Press.

Leitner, M., Shapland, J. and Wiles, P. (1994), *Drug Usage and Drug Prevention*, London: HMSO.

Leonard, P. (1997), *Postmodern Welfare*, London: Sage.

Lerner, M. (1980), *The Belief in a Just World*, New York: Plenum.

LGA (1997), *Manifesto for Community Safety and Crime Prevention*, London: Local Government Association.

Liberty (2001), *The Human Rights Act 1998: key test cases*, Liberty website: http://www.liberty-human-rights.org.uk/mpolic2n.html (accessed 10 April 2001).

Lilly, J. and Nellis, M. (2001), 'Home Detention Curfew and the Future of Electronic Monitoring' *Prison Service Journal*, 135 pp. 59–69.

Lipsey, M. (1992), 'Juvenile delinquency treatment: a meta-analytic enquiry into the variability of effects', in T. Cook *et al.*, *Meta-Analysis for Explanation: a case-book*, New York: Russell Sage.

Lipton, D., Martinson, R. and Wilks, J. (1975), *The effectiveness of correctional treatment*, New York: Praeger.

Lishman, J. (1991), *Handbook of Theory for Practice Teachers in Social Work*, London: Jessica Kingsley.

Lister, R. (1998), 'Citizenship on the margins: Citizenship, social work and social action' *European Journal of Social Work*, 1(1) pp. 5–18.

Lloyd, C., Mair, G. and Hough, M. (1995), *Explaining Reconviction Rates: A Critical Analysis*, Home Office Research Study No. 136, London: Home Office.

Lord Chancellor's Department (1998), *Review of Civil Justice* (Woolf Report), London: Lord Chancellor's Department.

Lord Chancellor's Department (forthcoming), *Review of the Magistracy* (Morgan Report), London: Lord Chancellor's Department.

Lowthian, J. (2000), 'Housing needs of women prisoners' *Prison Service Journal*, 132 pp. 59–63.

Lucas, J., Raynor, P. and Vanstone, M. (1992), *Straight Thinking on Probation One Year On* (second report of the evaluation study), Bridgend: Mid-Glamorgan Probation Service.

MacArthur (2001) http://macarthur.virginia.edu/

MacLean, D. (1993), Speech to Children's Society Conference, 25 November.

Macpherson, W. (1999), *The Stephen Lawrence Inquiry Report*, London: Stationery Office.

Maguire, M., Kemshall, H., Noaks, L., and Wincup, E. (2000), *Risk Management of Sexual and Violent Offenders: The Work of Public Protection Panels*, London: Home Office Police Research Unit 139.

Maguire, M., Raynor, P., Vanstone, M. and Kynch, J. (2000), 'Voluntary After-Care and the Probation Service: a case of diminishing responsibility' *Howard Journal*, 39 pp. 234–48.

Mair, G. (1996), 'Intensive Probation' in G. McIvor (ed.), *Working with Offenders*, London: Jessica Kingsley.

Mair, G. (1997), 'Community Penalties and the Probation Service', in M. Maguire, R. Morgan and R. Reiner (eds), *The Oxford Handbook of Criminology*, (2nd edn), Oxford: Clarendon Press.

Mair, G. (2000), 'Credible Accreditation?' *Probation Journal*, 47(4) pp. 268–71.

Mair, G. (2001), 'Technology and the Future of Community Penalties', in A. Bottoms, L. Gelsthorpe and S. Rex (eds), *Community Penalties: Change and Challenges*, Cullompton, Devon: Willan Publishing.

Maitland, J. (1997), *Guidance Manual for Voluntary Managed Hostel Committees*, London: National Association of Probation and Bail Hostels.

Mann, A. and Moran, P. (2000), 'Personality disorder as a reason for action' *Journal of Forensic Psychiatry*, 11(1) pp. 11–16.

Manning, N. (2000), 'Psychiatric diagnosis under conditions of uncertainty: personality disorder, science and professional legitimacy' *Sociology of Health and Illness*, 22(5) pp. 621–39.

Marlow, A. and Loveday, B. (2000), *Policing after Macpherson*, Lyme Regis: Russell House.

Marshall, T. and Merry, S. (1990), *Crime and Accountability*, London: HMSO.

Marshall, T.H. (1977), *Clan, Citizenship and Social Development*, London: University of Chicago Press.

Martinson, R. (1974), 'What works? Questions and answers about prison reform' *The Public Interest*, 10 pp. 22–54.

Martinson, R. (1979), 'New findings, new views: a note of caution regarding sentencing reform' *Hofstra Law Review*, 7 pp. 243–58.

Matravers, A. (2001), 'Breaking the silence', *The Guardian*, 15 February.

Mawby, R. and Walklate, S. (1994), *Critical Victimology: International Perspectives*, London: Sage.

May, C. (1999), *Explaining Reconviction Following a Community Sentence: The Role of Social Factors*, Home Office Research Study No. 192, London: Home Office.

McFarlane, M (2001), 'Criminal Justice and Court Services Act 2000: Directions, schemes and regulations' *Vista*, 6(2) pp. 143–9.

McGuire, J. (1993), 'What works: the evidence', paper to conference on *What Works: the challenge for managers*, Loughborough, October 1993.

McGuire, J. (2000), *Cognitive-Behavioural Approaches: An Introduction to Theory and Research*, London: Home Office.

McGuire, J. and Priestley, P. (1985), *Offending Behaviour*, London: Batsford.

McIvor, G. (1990), 'Community Service and Custody in Scotland' *Howard Journal*, 29 pp. 101–13.

McIvor, G. (1990), *Sanctions for Serious or Persistent Offenders*, Stirling: Social Work Research Centre.

McIvor, G. (1998), 'Pro-Social Modelling and Legitimacy: Lessons from a Study of Community Service', in S. Rex and A. Matravers (eds), *Pro-Social Modelling and Legitimacy: The Clarke Hall Day Conference*, Cambridge: Institute of Criminology, University of Cambridge.

McMurran, M. (2000), http://www.doh.gov.uk/hspscb/fore8.htm.

McWilliams, W. (1987), 'Probation, pragmatism and policy' *Howard Journal*, 26(2) pp. 241–60.

McWilliams, W. (1990), 'Probation practice and the management ideals' *Probation Journal*, 37(2) pp. 60–7.

Merrington, S. and Hine, J. (2001), in E. Stafford (ed.), *A Handbook for Evaluating Probation Work with Offenders*, London: Home Office/ HMIP/ACOP/NPRIE.

Merrington, S. and Stanley, S. (2000), 'Doubts about the What Works Initiative' *Probation Journal*, 47(4) pp. 272–5.

Miers, D. (2000), 'Taking the Law into their own Hands: Victims as Offenders', in A. Crawford, and J. Goodey (eds), *Integrating a Victim Perspective within Criminal Justice: International Debates*, Aldershot: Ashgate.

Miller, A. (1987), *For Your Own Good: Hidden Cruelty in Child-rearing and the Roots of Violence*, London: Virago.

Miller, G. (1983), 'Case Management: the Essential Services', in C. Sanborn (ed.), *Case Management in Mental Health Service*, New York: Haworth Press.

Miller, J. (1995), 'Criminal justice policy as social policy in Does Punishment Work?' in J. McGuire and B. Rowson (eds), *Proceedings of Conference organised by the Institute for the Study and Treatment of Delinquency*, held at Westminster Central Hall, London, 1–2 November.

MIND (1998), *Understanding Dual Diagnosis*, London: MIND.

Ministry of Health (1925), *Departmental Committee on Morphine and Heroin Addiction*, London: HMSO.

Ministry of Health (1961), *Drug Addiction: Report of the Interdepartmental Committee*, London: HMSO.

Ministry of Health (1965), *Drug Addiction: The Second Report of the Interdepartmental Committee*, London: HMSO.

Moore, M.H. (1993), 'Drugs, the Criminal Law and the Administration of Justice', in R. Bayer and G. Oppenheimer, *Confronting Illicit Drugs: Drug Policy in a Free Society*, Cambridge: Cambridge University Press.

Morash, M., Bynum, T. and Koons, B. (1997), *Findings from the National Study of Innovative and Promising Programs for Women Offenders*, East Lansing: Michigan State University, School of Criminal Justice.

Morgan, J. and Zedner, L. (1992), *Child Victims: Crime, Impact, and Criminal Justice*, Oxford and New York: Oxford University Press.

Morgan, R. and Russell, N. (2000), *The Judiciary in the Magistrates' Courts*, London: Home Office.

Morran, D., Andrew, M. and Macrae, R. (forthcoming), 'Keeping the Man in the Frame and the Women in the Picture: Men's Violence Programmes and Victim Focused Work', in B. Williams (ed.), *Reparation and Victim-focused Social Work*, London: Jessica Kingsley.

Moxley, D. (1989), *The Practice of Case Management*, London: Sage.

Mullen, P. (2000), 'Preventive detention for people with personality disorder is wrong', http://www.eurekalert.orq/releases/BMJ.941026112.html.

Murray, C. (1999), 'All locked up in the American dream', *The Sunday Times*, 7 February 1999, p. 7.

NACRO (1991), *A fresh start for women prisoners*, London: NACRO.

NACRO (1993), *Community Care and Mentally Disturbed Offenders*, London: NACRO Mental Health Advisory Committee, Policy Paper One, London: NACRO.

NACRO (1997), *The Three Rs for Young Offenders: Towards a New Strategy for Children who Offend*, London: NACRO.

NACRO (1998), *Rights and Risks: Mentally Disturbed Offenders and Public Protection*, A Report by NACRO's Mental Health Advisory Committee, London: NACRO.

NACRO (2000), 'Human Rights Act 1998 and the Youth Justice System', *NACRO Briefing*, London: NACRO Youth Crime Section.

Narey, M. (2001), 'Speech to Prison Service Annual Conference', *The Guardian*, 6 February, p. 3.

Neary, M. (1992), 'Some Academic Freedom' *Probation Journal*, 39 pp. 200–2.

Nellis, M. (1995), 'Probation Partnerships, Voluntary Action and Community Justice' *Social Policy and Administration*, 29(2) pp. 91–109.

Nellis, M. (1999), 'Towards "the Field of Corrections": Modernising the Probation Service in the 1990s *Social Policy and Administration*, 33(3) pp. 302–23.

Nellis, M. (2000a), 'The New Probation Training' *Criminal Justice Matters*, 39 pp. 22–23.

Nellis, M. (2000b), *Creating Community Justice in Secure Foundations: Key Issues in Crime Prevention and Community Safety*, London: Institute for Public Policy Research.

Newell, T. (2000), *Forgiving Justice: a Quaker Vision for Criminal Justice*, London: Quaker Home Service.

Neyroud, P. and Beckley, A. (2001), *Policing, Ethnics and Human Rights*, Cullompton, Devon: Willan Publishing.

NPS (2001), *Victim Contact Work: Guidance for Probation Areas*, London: National Probation Service.

Nutley, S. and Furniss, J. (2000), 'Implementing What Works with Offenders: the Effective Practice Initiative' *Public Money and Management*, 20(4) pp. 23–8.

O'Malley, P. (1996), 'Risk and Responsibility', in A. Barry, T. Osborne and N. Rose (eds), *Foucault and Political Reason: Liberalism, neo-liberalism and rationalities of government*, London: UCL Press.

O'Malley, P. (2001), 'Policing crime risks in the neo-liberal era', in K. Stenson and R. Sullivan (eds), *Crime, Risk and Justice: The Politics of Crime Control in Liberal Democracies*, Cullompton, Devon: Willan Publishing.

Oldfield, M. (1998), 'Case Management: Developing Theory and Practice' *Vista*, 4(1) pp. 21–36.

Olson, D. (1994), *The World on Paper: The Conceptual and Cognitive Implications of Writing and Reading*, Cambridge: Cambridge University Press.

Osborne, R. and Gaebler, D. (1992), *Reinventing Government*, Reading MA: Addison Wesley.

Palmer, E. and Hollin, C. (1995), *A Literature Review: The Effectiveness of Vocational and Educational Training in Reducing Recidivism*, Report to the Prison Service Agency (unpublished).

Pease, K. (1985), 'Community Service Orders', in M. Tonry and N. Morris (eds), *Crime and Justice*, Chicago: University of Chicago Press.

Pease, K., Billingham S. and Earnshaw, I. (1977), *Community Service Assessed in 1976*, London: HMSO.

Peay, J. (1993), 'A criminological perspective — the influences of fashion and theory on practice and disposal: life chances in the criminological tombola', in W. Watson and A. Grounds (eds), *The Mentally Disordered Offender in an Era of Community Care: New Directions in Provision*, Cambridge: Cambridge University Press.

Peay, J. (1995), 'Mental Disorders and Violence: the lessons of the inquiries' *Criminal Justice Matters*, 21 pp. 21–22.

Peay, J. (1997), 'Mentally Disordered Offenders', in M. Maguire, R. Morgan and R. Reiner (eds), *The Oxford Handbook of Criminology* (2nd edn), Oxford: Clarendon.

Peele, S. (1985), *The Meaning of Addiction*, Lexington, Mass.: Lexington Books.

Peelo, M., Stewart, J., Stewart, G. and Prior, A. (1992), *A Sense of Justice: Offenders as Victims of Crime*, Wakefield: Association of Chief Officers of Probation.

Petersilia, J. (1990), 'Conditions that permit intensive supervision programmes to survive' *Crime and Delinquency*, 36 pp. 126–45.

Pilgrim, D. and Rogers, A. (1999) *A Sociology of Mental Health and Illness* (2nd edn), Buckingham: Open University Press.

Pillay, C. (ed.) (2000), *Building the Future: the creation of the Diploma in Probation Studies*, London: National Association of Probation Officers.

Pincus, L. and Minahan, A. (1970), *Social Work Practice: Model and Method*, Itasca, IL: Peacock.

Pitchers, J. (1999), 'The Parole Board and the Mentally Disordered Offender', in D. Webb and R. Harris (eds), *Mentally Disordered Offenders: Managing people nobody owns*, London: Routledge.

Pitt-Aikens, T. and Thomas Ellis, A. (1990), *Loss of the Good Authority: the cause of delinquency*, Harmondsworth: Penguin.

Player, E. (1994), 'Women's prisons after Woolf', in E. Player and M. Jenkins (eds), *Prisons after Woolf*, London: Routledge.

Player, E. (2000), 'Justice for women' *Prison Service Journal*, 132 pp. 17–22.

Plotnikoff, J. and Woolfson, R. (2000), *Evaluation of Sex Offender Registers: Report for the Home Office Policing Unit*, London: Home Office.

Porter, R. (ed.) (1991), *The Faber Book of Madness*, London: Faber and Faber.

Power, H. (1999), 'The Crime and Disorder Act 1998: Sex Offenders, Privacy and the Police' *Criminal Law Review*, 3 pp. 3–16.

Pratt, J. (1995), 'Dangerousness, Risk and Technologies of Power' *Australian and New Zealand Journal of Criminology*, 28(1) pp. 3–31.

Preston-Shoot, M. (1999), 'Recreating mayhem? Developing understanding for social work with mentally disordered people', in D. Webb and R. Harris (eds), *Mentally Disordered Offenders: Managing people nobody owns*, London: Routledge.

Prins, H. (1992), 'The diversion of the mentally disordered: some problems for criminal justice, penology and health care', *Journal of Forensic Psychiatry*, 3(2) pp. 31–43.

Prins, H. (1995), *Offenders, Deviants or Patients?* (2nd edn), London: Routledge.

Prins, H. (1999), *Will they do it again? Risk assessment and management in criminal justice and psychiatry*, London: Routledge.

Prison Reform Trust (2000a), *Justice for Women: the need for reform* (The Wedderburm Report), London: Prison Reform Trust.

Prison Reform Trust (2000b), *A Hard Act to Follow? Prisons and the Human Rights Act*, London: Prison Reform Trust.

Pritchard, C., Cotton, A., Bowen, D. and Williams, R. (1998), 'A Consumer Study of Young People's Views on their Educational Social Worker: Engagement as a Measure of an Effective Relationship' *British Journal of Social Work*, 28 pp. 915–38.

QAA (2000), *Social Policy and Administration and Social Work: Subject benchmark statements*, Gloucester: Quality Assurance Agency for Higher Education.

Radzinowicz, L. (1991), 'Penal Regressions' *The Cambridge Law Journal*, 50(3) p. 444.

Raine, J. (2001a), 'Modernising Courts or Courting Modernisation?' *Criminal Justice*, 1(1) pp. 105–28.

Raine, J. (2001b), 'Modernising Justice through ICTs', *International Journal of Law and IT*, (forthcoming).

Raine, J. and Willson, M. (1993), *Managing Criminal Justice*, Hemel Hempstead: Harvester Wheatsheaf.

Raine, J. and Willson, M. (1997), 'From Performance Measurement to Performance Enhancement' *Public Money and Management*, 17(1) pp. 19–26.

Rawls, J. (1973), *A Theory of Justice*, Oxford: Oxford University Press.

Raynor, P. (1985), *Social Work, Justice and Control*, Oxford: Blackwell (2nd edn, 1993, London: Whiting and Birch).

Raynor, P. (1988), *Probation as an Alternative to Custody*, Aldershot: Avebury.

Raynor, P. (1993), 'Developing a core research and evaluation programme', paper to conference on *What works: the challenge for managers*, October 1993.

Raynor, P. (1996), 'Evaluating Probation: The Rehabilitation of Effectiveness', in T. May and A Vass (eds), *Working with Offenders*, London: Sage.

Raynor, P., Smith, D. and Vanstone, M. (1994), *Effective Probation Practice*, London: Macmillan.

Raynor, P. and Vanstone, M. (1994a), *Straight Thinking On Probation: third interim evaluation report: reconvictions within 12 months*, Bridgend: Mid-Glamorgan Probation Service.

Raynor, P. and Vanstone, M. (1994b), 'Probation practice, effectiveness and the non-treatment paradigm' *British Journal of Social Work*, 24(4) pp. 387–404.

Raynor, P. and Vanstone, M. (1997), *Straight Thinking on Probation (STOP): The Mid Glamorgan Experiment* (Probation Studies Unit Report No. 4), Oxford: University of Oxford Centre for Criminological Research.

Reddy, S. (1996), 'Claims to expert knowledge and the subversion of democracy: the triumph of risk over uncertainty' *Economy and Society*, 25(2) pp. 222–54.

Reder, P., Duncan, S. and Gray, M. (1993), *Beyond Blame: Child Abuse Tragedies Revisited*, London: Routledge.

Reed Committee (1992), *Review of Health and Social Services for Mentally Disordered Offenders and Others Requiring Similar Services*, London: HMSO.

Reeves, H. and Wright, M. (1995), 'Victims: towards a reorientation of justice' in D. Ward and M. Lacey (eds), *Probation: Working for Justice*, London: Whiting and Birch.

Reiner, R. (1989), 'Race and Criminal Justice, *New Community*, 16(1) pp. 5–21.

Renn, P. (2000), 'The link between childhood trauma and later violent offending', in G. Boswell (ed.), *Violent Children and Adolescents: asking the question why?* London and Philadelphia: Whurr Publishers.

Rex, S. (1998), 'Community Penalties in England and Wales 1967–1998' *Overcrowded Times*, 9(6) p. 1 and pp. 16–20.

Rex, S. (1998a), 'Applying Desert Principles to Community Sentences: Lessons from Two Criminal Justice Acts' *Criminal Law Review*, pp. 381–91.

Rex, S. and Crosland, P. (1999), *Project on Pro-social Modelling and Legitimacy: Findings from Community Service*, Report to Cambridgeshire Probation Service, Cambridge: Cambridge University Centre for Criminology.

Riddell, P. (1999), 'On Politics', *The Times*, 29 October.

Rivera, B. and Widom, C. (1990), 'Childhood victimization and violent offending' *Violence and Victims*, 5 pp. 19–34.

Roberts, C. (1989), *Hereford and Worcester Probation Service Young Offender Project: first evaluation report*, Oxford: Department of Social and Administrative Studies.

Roberts, J. (forthcoming), 'Women-centred: the West Mercia community-based programme for women offenders', in P. Carlen (ed.), *Women and Punishment*, Cullompton, Devon: Willan Publishing.

Roberts, M. (2001), 'Proper punishment, public confidence and community sentences' *Community Safety*, 8 pp. 13–15.

Rock, P. (1998), *After Homicide: Practical and Political Responses to Bereavement*, Oxford: Clarendon.

Rodger, J. (2000), *From a Welfare State to a Welfare Society*, London: Macmillan.

Rose, Lord Justice (1996), *Opening speech to the ACOP Conference* (unpublished).

Rose, N. (1996), 'Governing "advanced" liberal democracies', in A. Barry, T. Osborne and N. Rose (eds), *Foucault and Political Reason: Liberalism, neo-liberalism and rationalities of government*, London: UCL Press.

Rose, N. (2000), 'Government and Control' *British Journal of Criminology* 40 pp. 321–39.

Rose, S. (1992), *Case Management and Social Work Practice*, White Plains, NY: Longman.

Ross, R. and Fabiano, E. (1985), *Time to Think*, Ottawa: Institute of Social Sciences and Arts.

Ross, R., Fabiano, E. and Ewles, C. (1988), ' Reasoning and Rehabilitation', *International Journal of Offender Therapy and Comparative Criminology*, 32 pp. 29–35.

Rothman, J. (1991), 'A model of case management: toward empirically based practice' *Social Work*, 36(6) pp. 337–43.

Rowe, M.D. (1977), *An Anatomy of Risk*, Chichester: Wiley.

Rubin, A. (1992), 'Case Management', in S. Rose (ed.), *Case Management and Social Work Practice*, White Plains, NY: Longman.

Rumgay, J. (2000), *The Addicted Offender: Developments in British Policy and Practice*, Basingstoke: Palgrave.

Rumgay, J. and Cowan, S. (1998), 'Pitfalls and Prospects in Partnership: probation programmes for substance using offenders' *Howard Journal*, 37(2) pp. 124–36.

Rutherford, A. (2001), 'The probation service after the Criminal Justice and Court Services Act' *Vista*, 6(2) pp. 150–1.

Sampson, R. and Laub, J. (1993), *Crime in the Making: Pathways and Turning Points Through Life*, Cambridge, Mass.: Harvard University Press.

Samuels, A. (1996), 'The Probation Officer in the Courthouse' *The Probation Manager*, 1.

Sanderson, C. (1992), *Counselling Adult Survivors of Child Sexual Abuse*, London: Jessica Kingsley.

Sarkis, A. and Webster, R. (1995), *Working in Partnership: the Probation Service and the Voluntary Sector*, Lyme Regis: Russell House.

Sarno, C., Hearden, I. and Hedderman, C. (2001), *Working their Way out of Offending: An Evaluation of Two Probation Employment Schemes*, Home Office Research Study No. 218, London: Home Office.

Scanlon, C. (2000), 'The Network of Moral Sentiments: The Third Way and Community' *Arena*, 15 pp. 57–80.

Scheff, T. (1984), *Being Mentally Ill: A Sociological Theory* (2nd edn), New York: Aldine.

Schofield, H. (1999), 'Reflections: Probation Training: Late Modernism or Post Modernism?' *Probation Journal*, 46(4) pp. 256–8.

Scott, J. and Ward, D. (1999), 'Human Rights and the Probation Service' *Vista*, 5(2) pp. 106–18.

Scott, M. and Stradling, S. (1992), *Counselling for Post-Traumatic Stress Disorder*, London: Sage.

Scottish Executive (2000), *Scottish Strategy for Victims*, Edinburgh: Stationery Office.

Scottish Office (1998), *Towards a Just Conclusion: Vulnerable and Intimidated Witnesses in Scottish Criminal and Civil Cases*, Edinburgh: Scottish Office.

Seed, P. (1990), *Introducing Network Analysis in Social Work*, London: Jessica Kingsley.

Seivewright, N. (2000), *Community treatment of drug misuse: more than methadone*, Cambridge: Cambridge University Press.

Senior, P. (1998a), *The Diploma in Probation Studies: Regulatory Framework*, London: Home Office.

Senior, P. (1998b), *The Diploma in Probation Studies: Guidance Document on the Core Curriculum*, London: Home Office.

Senior, P. (2000), 'Fact & Fiction: another perspective on probation training' *Criminal Justice Matters*, 40 pp. 17–18.

Sennett, R. (1998), *The Corrosion of Character: The Personal Consequences of Work in the New Capitalism*, London: W.W. Norton.

Shaw, M. and Hannah-Moffat, K. (2000), 'Gender, Diversity and Risk Assessment in Canadian Corrections' *Probation Journal*, 47(3) pp. 163–72.

Shepherd, G. (1993), 'Case Management', in W. Watson and A. Grounds (eds), *The Mentally Disordered Offender in an Era of Community Care: New Directions in Provision*, Cambridge: Cambridge University Press.

Sibbitt, R. (1997), *The Perpetrators of Racial Harassment and Violence*, Home Office Research Study 176, London: Home Office.

Singleton, N., Meltzer, H. and Gatward, R. (1998), *Psychiatric Morbidity among Prisoners: Summary Report*, London: Government Statistical Service.

Sleightholm, D. (1996) 'Reviewing Probation Court Duty', *Justice of the Peace* 160(9) pp. 148–9.

Smart, C. (1976), *Women, Crime and Criminology*, London: Routledge and Kegan Paul.

Smart, C. (1990), 'Feminist approaches to criminology or postmodern woman meets atavistic man', in L. Gelsthorpe and A. Morris (eds), *Feminist Perspectives in Criminology*, Milton Keynes: Open University Press.

Smith, A. (2001), *Specific Sentence Reports: A Survey of Probation Areas* (Report prepared on behalf of ACOP Criminal Court Work Group), London: Association of Chief Officers of Probation.

Smith, D. (1993), 'Social circumstances of younger offenders under supervision' *Criminal Justice*, 11(4) pp. 7–8.

Smith, D. (1996), 'Social Work and Penal Policy', in G. McIvor (ed.), *Working with Offenders: Research Highlights in Social Work 26*, London: Jessica Kingsley.

Smith, D., Paylor, I. and Mitchell, P. (1993), 'Partnerships between the Probation Service and the Independent Sector' *Howard Journal*, 32 pp. 25–39.

Smith, D. and Stewart, J. (1997), 'Probation and Social Exclusion' *Social Policy and Administration*, 31(5) pp. 96–115.

Smith, G. (2000), *Report by the Chief Inspector of Probation to a meeting of the Central Probation Council*, 27–29 October (unpublished).

Sparks, R. (2000), 'Risk and blame in criminal justice controversies: British press coverage and official discourse on prison security (1993–1996)', in M. Brown and J. Pratt (eds), *Dangerous Offenders: Punishment and Social Order*, London: Routledge.

Spencer, J. (1998), paper presented to the *Community Justice: Issues for Education and Practice Conference*, Manchester, 2 December 1998.

Stationery Office (2000), *Race Relations (Amendment) Act*, London: Stationery Office.

Stenson, K. and Sullivan, R. (eds) (2001), *Crime, Risk and Justice: the Politics of Crime Control in Liberal Democracies*, Cullompton, Devon: Willan Publishing.

Stewart, C. (2000), 'Responding to the needs of women in prison' *Prison Service Journal*, 132 pp. 41–43.

Straw, J., Rt Hon. (1999), Speech to the Annual Constitution Unit Lecture.

Straw, J., Rt Hon. (2000a), *Address to the AGM of Central Probation Council*, 16 May 2000.

Straw, J., Rt Hon. (2000), Interview on *Radio 4*, 14 September.

Sullivan, R. (2000), 'The Schizophrenic State: Neo-Liberal Criminal Justice', in K. Stenson and R. Sullivan (eds) *Risk, Crime and Justice: the Politics of Crime Control in Liberal Democracies*, Cullompton, Devon: Willan Publishing.

Szasz, T. (1975), *Ceremonial Chemistry — The Ritual Persecution of Drugs, Addicts and Pushers*, London: Routledge and Kegan Paul.

Szasz, T. (1996), *Our Right to Drugs*, New York: Syacuse University Press.

Taylor, C. (1992), *Multiculturalism and 'The politics of recognition'*, Princeton: Princeton University Press.

Taylor, M. (2000), *Address to West Yorkshire Probation Service Annual Conference*.

Taylor, M. (2001), 'Partnership: Insiders and Outsiders', in M. Harris and C. Rochester (eds), *Voluntary Organisations and Social Policy in Britain: perspectives on change and choice*, Basingstoke: Palgrave.

Taylor, P. and Monahan, J. (1996),'Commentary: Dangerous patients or dangerous diseases?' *British Medical Journal*, 312 pp. 967–9.

The Guardian (2001) 'On Probation' (Leader article) *The Guardian*, Feb 6, p. 20.

Thatcher, M. (1978) Speech cited in *Daily Mail*, 31st October.

Thomas, C. (1988), *Developments in Probation Education and Training*, CCETSW Paper 18.1, London: CCETSW.

Thorpe, D., Smith, D., Green, C. and Paley, J. (1980), *Out of Care*, London: Allen and Unwin.

Toch, H. (2000), 'Altruistic Activity as Correctional Treatment' *International Journal of Offender Therapy and Comparative Criminology*, 44 pp. 270–8.

Todd, M. (1996), *Opening Doors*, Manchester: Greater Manchester Probation Service.

Travers, T. (2000), 'Where now for the watchdogs?' *Public Finance*, 17 November, pp. 20–22.

Trebach, A. (1982), *The Heroin Solution*, London: Yale University Press.

Trotter, C. (1993), *The Supervision of Offenders: What Works*, Melbourne: Victorian Office of Corrections.

Trotter, C. (1996), 'The Impact of Different Supervision Practices in Community Corrections: Causes for Optimism *Australian and New Zealand Journal of Criminology*, 29 pp. 29–46.

Trotter, C. (1999), *Working with Involuntary Client*, London: Sage.

Tudor, B. (forthcoming) 'Probation work with victims of crime', in B. Williams (ed.), *Reparation and Victim-focused Social Work*, London: Jessica Kingsley.

Tuklo Orenda Associates (1999), *Making a Difference*, Bridgewater: South West Probation Training Consortium.

Tyler, T. (1990), *Why People Obey the Law*, New Haven: Yale University Press.

Tyrer, P. (2000), 'Improving the assessment of personality disorders' *Criminal Behaviour and Mental Health*, 10 ss. 51–65.

Tyrer, P. and Steinberg, D. (1998), *Models for Mental Disorder: Conceptual Models in Psychiatry* (3rd edn), Chichester: Wiley.

Underdown, A. (1998), *Strategies for Effective Offender Supervision: Report of the HMIP What Works Project*, London: Home Office.

United Nations (1948), *Universal Declaration of Human Rights*, New York: United Nations General Assembly.

United Nations (1986), *Beijing Rules: United Nations Standard Minimum Rules for the Administration of Juvenile Justice*, New York: United Nations Department of Public Information.

United Nations (1990), *Guidelines for the Prevention of Juvenile Delinquency* (The Riyadh Guidelines), New York: United Nations Department of Public Information.

van Kesteren, J., Mayhew, P. and Nieuwbeerta, P. (2001), *Criminal Victimisation in 17 Industrialised Countries: Key Findings from the 2000 International Crime Victims Survey*, The Netherlands: Westenschappelijk Onderzoek en Documentatiecentrum.

Vanstone, M. (1993), 'A "missed opportunity" reassessed: the influence of the Day Training Centre experiment on the criminal justice system and probation practice' *British Journal of Social Work*, 23(3) pp. 213–29.

Vanstone, M. (2000), 'Cognitive-Behavioural Work with Offenders in the UK: A History of Influential Endeavour' *Howard Journal*, 39(2) pp. 171–83.

Von Hirsch, A. (1976), *Doing Justice*, New York: Hill and Wang.

Wadham, J. and Arkinstall, J. (2000), *The HRA and the rights of victims of crime*, Liberty website http://www.liberty-human-rights.org.uk/mhrp6n.html (accessed 10 April 2001); also available in the *New Law Journal*, 14 July 2000.

Walker, C. and Raine, J. (2001), 'The Implications for Courts of the Human Rights Act 1998', *European Human Rights Law Review* (forthcoming).

Walker, N. (1981), 'Feminist extravaganzas' *Criminal Law Review*, 379, pp. 379–86.

Wallis, E. (2001), *A New Choreography — An Integrated Strategy for the National Probation Service for England and Wales, Strategic Framework 2001–2004*, London: Home Office.

Walsh, C. (2001), 'The trend towards specialisation: West Yorkshire innovations in drugs and domestic violence courts' *Howard Journal*, 40(1) pp. 26–38.

Walton, P. and Young, J. (eds) (1998), *The New Criminology Revisited*, Basingstoke: Macmillan.

Ward, D. (1995), 'Finding the Balance', in D. Ward and M. Lacey (eds), *Probation: Working for Justice*, London: Whiting and Birch.

Ward, D. (1996), 'Probation Training: Celebration or Wake?, in S. Jackson and M. Preston-Shoot (eds), *Educating Social Workers in a Changing Policy Context*, London: Whiting and Birch.

Ward, D. and Lacey, M. (eds), (1995), *Probation: Working for Justice*, London: Whiting and Birch.

Ward, D. and Spencer, J. (1994) 'The future of probation qualifying training', *Probation Journal*, 41(2), pp. 95–8.

Warner, S. (1992), *Making Amends: Justice for Victims and Offenders*, Aldershot: Avebury.

Warner, S. (1993), 'Standing in the shadows with our backs against the sun', in C. Roberts (ed.), *Changing Information Needs and the 1991 Criminal Justice Act*, Birmingham: Probation Research and Information Exchange.

Watkins, T., Lewellen, A. and Barrett, M. (2001), *Dual Diagnosis: An Integrated Approach to Treatment*, London: Sage.

Watson, A. (1997), *Services for Mentally Disordered Offenders in the Community: An Inspection Report*, London: Social Services Inspectorate, Department of Health.

Watson, W. and Grounds, A. (eds) (1993), *The Mentally Disordered Offender in an Era of Community Care: New Directions in Provision*, Cambridge: Cambridge University Press.

Watt, N. and Travis, A. (2000), 'Anger as Hague is accused of playing the race card', *The Guardian*, 15 December, p. 1.

Webb, D. and Harris, R. (eds) (1999), *Mentally Disorder Offenders: Managing people nobody owns*, London: Routledge.

Webb, S. and Webb, B. (1922), *English Prisons under Local Government*, London: Longman, Green and Co.

West, D. and Farrington, D. (1973), *Who becomes delinquent?* London: Heinemann.

Widom, C. (1989), 'The Cycle of Violence' *Science*, 244 pp.160–6.

Wilkinson, A. (1997), 'Improving risk based communications and decision making' *Journal of Petroleum Engineers*, 949 pp. 936–43.

Williams, B. (1999), *Working with Victims of Crime: Policies, Politics and Practice*, London: Jessica Kingsley.

Williams, B. (2000), 'Victims of crime and the new youth justice', in B. Goldson (ed.), *The New Youth Justice*, Lyme Regis: Russell House.

Williams, B. (forthcoming), 'Counselling in legal settings: provision for jury members, vulnerable witnesses and victims of crime', in P. Jenkins (ed.) *Legal Issues in Counselling and Psychotherapy*, London: Sage.

Witness (1998), *The Monsters in Our Midst*, Channel 4 Television, 8 January.

Wolf, E. (1988), *Treating the Self: Elements of Clinical Self Psychology*, New York and London: Guildford Press.

Woolf, Lord Justice (1991), *Prison Disturbances April 1990*, Report of an Inquiry by Lord Justice Woolf and His Honour Judge Stephen Tumim, London: HMSO.

Worrall, A. (1995), 'Justice through inequality? The probation service and women offenders', in D. Ward and M. Lacey (eds), *Probation: Working for Justice*, London: Whiting and Birch.

Worrall, A. (1997), *Punishment in the Community: the future of criminal justice*, Harlow: Longman.

Worrall, A. (2000), 'Failure is the new success', *Prison Service Journal*, 132 pp. 52–4.

Wright, J. and Pearl, L. (2000), 'Experience and knowledge of young people regarding drug use, 1969–99' *Addiction*, 95(8) pp. 1225–36.

Wright, M. (1982), *Making Good: Prisons, Punishment and Beyond*, London: Burnett Books.

Wright, M. (1991), *Justice for Victims and Offenders*, Buckingham: Open University Press.

Wright Mills, C. (1970), *The Sociological Imagination*, Harmondsworth: Penguin.

Wyre, R. (1997), 'Marked for Life', *Community Care*, 20–26 February, pp. 26–7.

Yule, W. (1993), 'Children as Victims and Survivors', in P. Taylor (ed.), *Violence in Society*, London: Royal College of Physicians.

Zedner, L. (1997), 'Victims', in M. Maguire, R. Morgan, and R. Reiner (eds), *The Oxford Handbook of Criminology*, Oxford: Clarendon.

Zeldin, T. (1999), *Conversation: how talk can change your life*, London: The Harvill Press.

Zimring, F. and Hawkins, G. (1994), 'The growth of imprisonment in California' *British Journal of Criminology*, 34, special issue on 'Prisons in Context', pp. 83–96.

Index

Cited only authors do not appear in the index.